LIVING BENEATH THE TAPESTRY
and
WITHIN THE VEIL

God's Sanctifying Work
in the
Lives of His Suffering Saints

Karla Podlucky

To Pastor Mark,
Thank you for all
you do in serving
His body.
Karla Podlucky
Hebrews 6:19-20
Psalm 37:23-24

Unless otherwise indicated, Scripture taken from the
NEW AMERICAN STANDARD BIBLE® (NASB)
© Copyright 1960, 1962, 1963, 1968, 1971, 1972, 1973, 1975, 1977, 1995
by The Lockman Foundation
Used by permission. *www.lockman.org*

The stories in this book reflect the author's recollections of events. Some
names and identifying characteristics have been changed or omitted to
protect the privacy of those depicted. Dialogue has been re-created from
memory.

ISBN # 978-1-64871-795-6

Cover Photo, Back Cover, and Design
Susan McConville-Harrer
SMH Illustration & Design
123 S Third ST, Youngwood, PA 15697
www.smhillustration.com

Edited by Melanie Grunwald

Printed in the United States of America

Published by Lilies of the Field Publishing

To *Pioneer Presbyterian Church*

You stand as a glistening light in this dark world as you imitate the very heartbeat of the Good Shepherd, loving and caring for His own suffering sheep. Your love pulled us in, embraced us, tenderly ministered to our broken hearts, and held us up when most were shouting, "Crucify!" All glory be to God for the love you have shown toward His name in your ministry to the saints.

To *Grace Community Church* and *Grace to You*

For your faithful commitment to preach the truth one verse at a time for over half a century and for teaching the importance of knowing and standing upon sound doctrine. You have consistently pointed us to our only refuge and hope in this life. This hope we have as an anchor of the soul, a hope both sure and steadfast, and one that enters within the veil.

FOREWORD

Before God led the children of Israel into the land of promise, He led them into the wilderness with all its difficulties and sufferings. He did not send them there, He led them. He was constantly with them, teaching, correcting, and preparing them for the land that He was giving them as a people. For the most part, they did not understand what He was doing, but He was working all things together for their good. So often, we as Christians wish that our God and Father would simply take us to the new heaven and the new earth and skip all the pain, suffering, and difficulties of this world. But He knows what He is doing. He really does work all things, even the hard things, together for our good. He is finishing the good work He has begun in us. He has given His Word, and He keeps it. God often leads us, His beloved children, into suffering.

As a pastor, I often deal with church members who are questioning God and His promises as they go through the sufferings of this life. I can and do speak to them from the Word of God, pointing to His nature and promises. Karla does more. In this book, she speaks from the Word of God to people who face suffering in this life; she also speaks from experience. She has experienced suffering in this life in ways that few of us have—the loss of a daughter, the loss of all her worldly possessions, and prison—just to name a few. And yet, she did not experience these things alone. Her good Shepherd, her Lord, was and is with her all the way. In this book, she conveys the love of God in the midst of suffering with clarity from the Word, through her experiences, and from her heart. I heartily commend this book to you.

Rev. David Kenyon
Pioneer Presbyterian Church PCA
Ligonier, Pennsylvania

ACKNOWLEDGMENTS

Ultimately, all thanks for this book goes to my Lord and Savior, Jesus Christ. He is everything. I have no story to tell that does not belong to Him. May He be glorified and honored by however He sees fit to use this testimony of His faithfulness to me.

This book has been in my heart and mind for so many years that I cannot begin to thank all the people who have contributed to it in so many ways. Without ever knowing the influence they have had on my life, the Lord has used each of my 'neighbors' to mold me and shape me, making me more like Him. Without a shadow of a doubt, I can say that the trials and tribulations He has ordained for me, and the people He has surrounded me with during those hard times, have had the greatest impact on my walk with Him. These, especially, are those I wish to thank here.

Greg, Jesse, Jordan, and Jared, you are mine and I am yours. By God's divine providence He established our family. The bonds we share, through experiencing difficult times of suffering, have strengthened the cords that bind us together. I love you and Melissa, in heaven, with all my heart! Faith endures and love lasts forever. Nothing can separate us from the love of God which is in Christ Jesus our Lord.

Daddy, you have not taken your eyes off me in my seasons of suffering. You were there for me every step of the way. I am thankful for how the Lord drew us even closer together through our most difficult days. You and Mother helped me through the dark days after Melissa's death more than you know. I love you.

Aunt Sis, thank you for going above and beyond in taking me in for a year after I was released from prison. You are the best aunt ever! A big thank you to my mother-in-law, Sandy, and to Aunt Patty for faithfully loving us and meeting so many of our material needs during and after the prison trial. Kelly, thank you for your help in getting me re-acclimated upon my release from prison. I love you, my sister and friend.

Pastor Dave Kenyon of Pioneer Church, you have a heart for wounded, suffering sheep, and the Lord has gifted you to minister to them. I will always be grateful to you for coming to our side to walk with us through our prison trial. Your support was the balm of His lavish grace poured out on our weary souls. Thank you for previewing this book; I asked you because I trust you.

Tracey, thank you for your faithful friendship to Jesse and me. Your weekly letters (with Sunday bulletins enclosed) and words of encouragement kept us tied to people who cared. Beloved Rick and Dody, you have faithfully ministered Christ's love to us, selflessly acting upon all the 'one another' passages found in Scripture. So grateful to God for you both, we can only thank you by striving to live out what you have modeled for us to others. Your servant hearts overflow with kindness, compassion, and sacrificial love that is rarely seen today. Pioneer Church, you showed us our vital need for His Body through your prayers, support, and practical love.

To my Facebook friends I have never met, you became very real *friends* to me while imprisoned. Your faithful service to Christ has not gone unnoticed. Your letters of encouragement, cards, sermon transcripts, and books were bread and water for my hungry soul. The light of your many kindnesses confirmed His presence with me in a very dark place. Especially, thank you Don and Shellie.

To the Friday morning Bible study girls who met weekly for 11 years in my home, thank you for allowing me the privilege of sharing what the Lord was teaching me after Melissa's death.

To my dear sisters in California: Mrs. Webb, Pam, Liz, Karen, Kim, and Cecilie, you welcomed me into the heart of your warm fellowship when I was dealing with a lot of prison baggage. You are God's choice gift of friendship to me. From the start, you embraced me as your own and encouraged me in many ways to finish this book. Your prayers, I am certain, have carried it to completion. I love you dearly and miss our like-minded fellowship of His Spirit.

Susan of SMH Illustration & Design, I am grateful the Lord has given you the gifts He has and that I was able to turn to a beloved friend whose heart is knit together with mine in like-minded faith and love for the truth to bring this project to fruition.

I wish to acknowledge an invaluable resource tool I have been using for years. Thank you **www.blueletterbible.org** for providing help to so many in defining and better understanding Greek and Hebrew words. Much appreciation goes to the work of Larry Pierce, the creator of the Online Bible who contributes to the site.

TABLE OF CONTENTS

1
Suffering Is for Real

Suffering. It's a universal subject. It's *not* a subject many enjoy talking about or studying unless one is amidst a trial, or storm clouds are hovering overhead. Then, we want answers. Years ago, I led a Bible study on the book of James. One woman told me she didn't want to study James because one of its themes is suffering, and she did not want to think about it—as if that would somehow enable her to avoid any difficult trials in life. To be fair, for many years there was one book in the Bible of which *I* steered clear, and that was Job. Suffering, even in others, makes us uncomfortable. We fear that which we do not understand and what we cannot control.

We are a culture that is enchanted with the idea of fairy tale endings. We want to realize for ourselves, "And they all lived happily ever after." The problem is twofold: Our perspective is skewed when we want it for *this* life, and when we believe we somehow *deserve* it. Chasing that elusive fairy tale ending only leads to discontentment and disillusionment. False religion and false teachers have propagated this dangerous ideology teaching us we *can* have our best life now. Reality television stars proclaim, "I want my fairy tale ending!" But fairy tales are make-believe. Suffering, pain, heartache, disease, and death are all a very real part of life.

When we witness incredible depths of suffering in those close to us, we want to believe that if we don't think about it, the things we most dread will not happen to *us*; yet suffering is unavoidable. When times of intense suffering come, we can either try to understand God's purposes for suffering and learn how to live in these seasons so that we glorify and honor Him, or we can attempt to drown it out with whatever painkiller we choose. For the believer who lives to glorify God, there is only one right option.

The Bible is clear God's sovereign hand is over all His creation. He has a purpose for everything He does, and what He purposes for His children is only good. Romans 8:28 says *we can know* that God causes all things to work together for good to those who love God, to those who are called according to His purpose. God has a good purpose in suffering. And that purpose is found in the next verse. "For those whom He foreknew, He also predestined to become conformed to the image of His Son, so that He would be the firstborn among many brethren." It would serve us well to learn how God wants us to suffer *before* those trials come into our lives that serve to mold us and shape us into the image of His beloved Son.

How can we know that suffering is inevitably coming to each of us? Because sin entered the world, and we now live in a world that is cursed and fading away. Furthermore, we are cursed! Not only is sin in the world, but sin is in us. Christians know and understand that God has purposed to conform us into the image of His Son. That work He is doing in us began at the time of our salvation and is called sanctification. Making us into the image of Jesus Christ is the process of making us holy. God uses the suffering that inevitably comes into our lives to mature us and make us more holy. It is wise to be prepared for seasons of suffering by having our minds renewed with truth, so that we may be able to stand firmly for God's glory *when*—not *if*—trouble comes.

In all reality, believers may suffer to an even greater extent in this life as God prepares them for glory. You may look at the lives of others and know that you have not suffered to the extent that they have, but you *have* suffered and will continue to do so until glory. And none of us knows what tomorrow will bring. I have suffered. More importantly, I am learning *how* to suffer. Learning how to embrace the pain and heartache that comes our way, in a way that honors God, will result in sanctifying grace that brings God glory as few other things in this life can.

The value of walking *rightly* through our seasons of suffering is inestimable. While the true worth of suffering in the life of a Christian can only be accurately assessed by God, rightly responded to, trials are precious gifts from God to the believer as they help us grow to Christlikeness. We grow in patience, learn how to comfort others, and to trust God more fully. Humility also grows out of a right response to suffering. The world may not view one's growing in humility as a beneficial character trait, but a Christian evidencing true humility is a delight to God's heart.

Regarding the topics we would choose to study, humility is right up there with suffering, but they usually go hand in hand. Any seasoned Christian knows she is not humble. If we choose to suffer in a way that glorifies and honors God, however, we will grow in humility. If we could rightly understand the extent to which God chooses to work through broken people, we would willingly embrace the crushing blows that are meant to break us. The more I experience trials and tribulations in His school of affliction, the more I realize how little I know or understand.

It may well be that my trials are not like yours. My trials were uniquely appointed for me as were yours. The circumstances can be very different, but the Author of them is the same. That is reassuring to me because I know that in our suffering, we share a bond that unites us. As suffering Christians, the truth and life we can gain from trials are pillars that are solid and sure anchoring us to the cross of Christ.

This book is meant to encourage you by giving testimony to God's faithfulness in my life—His faithfulness to justify me and to sustain me as He continues to sanctify me, especially through suffering. Knowing that sanctifying grace, I am confident that one day I will see how He kept His promise to glorify me.

I am acquainted with fellow believing sufferers—men who have suffered more than I have, to be sure. Fellow sufferers include men like Job, Joseph, David, Paul, and of course, the Lord Jesus Christ. The only one in the group who perfectly endured unfathomable suffering is the Lord. The honor God's Word bestows on these others through their honest suffering encourages my heart to persevere and endure when I do not understand what is happening, and when I fail miserably. Knowing that Christ perfectly suffered in my stead soothes my anxious heart, calms my fears, and helps me rest in Him as a child in her Father's arms.

Suffering quickly cuts us down to size as it humbles us to our knees. Suffering—and the humility that comes with it—makes our flesh uncomfortable. Our flesh is filled with pride. It says, *Suffer? Who me? I'm too good to….* You can fill in the blank. *I'm too good to lose my job. I'm too good to be homeless. I'm too good to get addicted to drugs or alcohol. I eat too healthy to get sick.* Even some who claim to follow Christ tell us, in essence, "You are too good to be poor or sick because you are a child of God."

A response to suffering that refuses to embrace the humiliation that comes with it can lead to bitter anger and self-pity. Suffering, rightly responded to, includes humility as part of the package. At first, I balked at my humbling circumstances being good for me almost as much as if someone had said to me outright, "You're going to go to prison, and it will be good for you." *Me? Not in a thousand years. May it never be! I'm too good to go to prison!* Me going to prison was laughable. After all, I was the rule keeper. I didn't take risks, and I certainly didn't break the law! I tried with all my being to be a woman after the Lord's own heart.

So, why am I convinced that the Lord has a purpose in every trial and humbling circumstance of our lives? Because the Lord saw fit to humble me through circumstances of suffering in a way I would never have imagined. He did, in fact, send me to prison. And it *was* good for me!

I was working on ideas for two books when I was *rudely and radically* interrupted—suffering (which I knew from recent firsthand experience), and this idea of what it means to love God with all my heart, soul, strength, and mind, and to love my neighbor as myself. At the same time, I was reading a convicting little book on humility that made my spirit stop and pray, *Oh Lord, I want to be humble.* I didn't fully understand that embracing suffering from the Lord's hand leads to humility which allows us to truly love God and others.

In 2001, my heart was crushed. I knew pain that no parent wants to think about and cringes when they hear of it in another's life. While the Lord humbled me at that time, it was a different type of humbling than what would come later. I got a lesson on God's sovereignty when my daughter died suddenly. My second very long season of suffering began only five years later.

When my daughter died, people who knew my family, and even those who didn't, wholeheartedly embraced us. The Lord's presence was known by us in a real way. The humbling in this second trial was different in that many people who knew us, and even more who didn't, withdrew from us, accused us, and even attacked us with such ferocity that all we had was each other. At times, it did not even *feel* as though the Lord was with us.

During the five years before the "prison test", as I like to call it, I naively believed that I could "book learn" truths in my Christian walk without experiencing any more heartbreak than I had to date. I thought losing Melissa was surely my *one* great trial in life. But children look up to their parents or other adults and think, "I want to be just like them," never realizing the cost of what it took to get them to maturity. I wanted to be holy like Christ. I would have proclaimed loudly to anyone who would listen that I was sold out to Jesus. But strength of character is never a hand-me-down nor a hand-out. It is always forged through blood, sweat, and tears.

I was convinced that the Lord would deliver me from the trial before ever actually having to go to prison. *Surely, I didn't need to learn a lesson by having to go through this trial. Surely, I had already learned what I needed to learn. Surely, a jury of my "peers" would find me innocent, and my Lord would ride in on His white horse and save me just in time. Oh, I would give Him such praise and glory!* But as time reveals to the believer whom the Lord is sanctifying, I do not know what is best for me at all. The longer I walk with Christ, the more I realize how often my will does not lead me down the path of abundant life. Suffering, never warmly welcomed or coveted, is necessary in the life of a saint.

Suffering burdens us with many unanswered questions. It slows us down, and it gets our attention. Often, we would never stop the busy-ness of life to think about or seek answers to these questions. The questions that haunted me throughout my lengthy trial may be familiar to you, too. *My life seems like one long storm. Do I really need to go through this? Surely, the trial will end soon; won't it? Why me? Why does it seem other saints do not suffer like I do? What must they think about me? What about all Your promises? How do they apply to my trial? What are You trying to teach me, Lord? What is true faith? Can I just claim a promise and believe it will come to pass the way I see it coming to pass—the way I desire it to come to pass—the way I believe* **You should** *want it to come to pass? Why does it seem like my prayers are falling on deaf ears? Where are You, Lord? It's been too long; why aren't You delivering me?* By the end of the book, I pray you will have peace that silences **your** questions even if the waters are still raging around you.

Job became a treasured gem found right next to another favorite book that helped me through my trials—namely, the Psalms. Why do I love these books? I can see in Job and David human emotions in times of suffering to which I can relate. I also see the hope and comfort that comes from the Lord in all their trouble. I am sure neither of these men would have dreamed of the extent to which the Lord would use their suffering to glorify Himself as He draws others closer through their painful circumstances.

I once had a large Hummel doll. He sat on a wooden sled flanked by a ceramic Christmas tree and a lantern. When my youngest boys were toddlers, I had someone come in and help me clean every other week. While dusting one day, she accidentally knocked the lantern onto the floor, and it shattered into many pieces.

My husband decided he would glue the pieces back together. He did a great job, even though one could still see the lines where the lantern had cracked. A perfectionist, he was not satisfied with it. Contacting the company, he told them what had happened, and they sent him a new lantern. When he came into the room to remove the lantern from where I had placed it on my desk, I shouted, "No! Don't throw it away! I want to keep it." Puzzled, he inquired, "Why on earth would you want to keep it?" I replied, "First, you took the time to glue it back together for me; second, when I look at that lantern, I imagine how much light could come through because of all those cracks." When we are broken, like Job or David, we do not know how the Lord is shining the light of His glory through our lives. But that light will draw men to Himself.

Before being able to relate to Job as the sufferer, one may tend to side with his so-called "friends". It is our human nature that wants to believe God rewards the righteous and punishes the wicked in this life. I found out just how easy it becomes to gather a lot of "friends" like Job had in a serious time of testing. I often wonder how many times I was that *friend* to someone else who was suffering. Even if I never voiced my thoughts, they were lying there on the surface of my heart. Job never got answers to his 'why' questions. But he did get understanding of something far better.

Prison seemed like a cruel joke to me. Even now, I am loath to believe I wear the label of 'convicted felon'. Everywhere I went, the joke *was* on me as the other inmates joked about my being there. In county jail one day, a group of intimidating women called me over to their table. Hesitantly, I toddled over to them to see what they wanted. After their laughter had died down, they questioned me, "We have one question for you: What on earth did **you** possibly do to get here? Were you a bad soccer mom or something?" In an attempt at levity to match their own, I informed them I was a "hockey mom" but that I seriously wasn't sure how I ended up there. I had no idea what my case involved or how I had broken the law.

When I finally got to prison, many of the inmates laughed when they came up with a book title for my story, *Mrs. P Goes to Prison.* I lost 80 pounds in prison, and they even came up with this title, which is a little cleaned up: *How Mrs. P Lost Her Derrière: The Camp Cupcake Diet.* My going to prison seemed like a sick joke to me. To this day, it is appalling and egregious to my flesh. I still find myself thinking, *I cannot believe I went to prison.* My spirit acknowledges the following **truths**, however: *Why **not** me? Look at all those who have gone before me. When God says He is working **all** things for my good, I need to trust that He can use **anything** for my good—no matter how repugnant it is to my flesh, my pride, or my ego.*

My life seemed like a big fat joke or a nightmare from which I could not wake up. One night I did wake up abruptly from a sound sleep as an unsettling question blazed across my mind, *Lord, am I in hell?* Startled by the query that instantly led to anxious panic, I immediately began to rehearse the truth I knew about heaven and hell to assure myself that I was still on earth. And what I knew about hell made prison, as bad as it was, seem like a walk in the park.

Lessons in life are rarely easy. The Lord had ordained before the foundation of the world that prison would be one of the classrooms where I would learn many things. There, I was faced with my own depravity in a way I never would have known had I not been given the opportunity to experience what the Father knew was needed to make me more like Christ. I *know* it was a gift from Him. Still, my flesh hasn't wrapped itself around that fact as much as my mind has—a mind continually being renewed by truth. Little by little, as my sinful flesh is ripped away, it becomes clearer that life's greatest blessings—His gifts to us—are not wrapped up in bright-colored packages tied up with exquisite bows, as we would expect. Horribly hideous, dark wrappings veil treasures from pain and anguish we would never choose for ourselves. After all, the greatest gift of all time was wrapped up in a torturous, bloody cross.

Before my time in prison, I taught women's Bible studies from my home for almost 11 years. That season was born after the death of my 16-year old daughter in an automobile accident. Bible study was life to me. I lived to dig deep into the Word each week to mine the gems of Scripture and pass on what I was learning. It was a balm to my soul that nothing else could touch. I had a deep hunger for the Word for years before this time; but after Missy died, the new truths I was learning were so rich, deep, and overflowing, that I could scarcely take them all in. Several women asked me to teach Bible studies because of the way they "watched me deal with her death". Clinging to His promises with white knuckles, however, I knew I was only focused on passing the test He had given me in the pain of this excruciating loss.

On our way to Missy's funeral, I began to question my parenting skills. *If only I had done this or that—Missy would still be here.* I will never forget what my oldest son said to me as I voiced these doubts out loud. It was the slap in the face and glimmer of hope I needed to grasp and hold onto. He said, "Mom, don't look backwards. Missy is in our future now." When we woke the two younger boys to tell them their sister had passed away, without skipping a beat, my youngest son, who was eight years old at the time, questioned: "Mom, this means that the rapture is going to happen soon. It has to, right?" Hope in the fulfillment of future promises was the only healing salve that soothed our crushed souls.

While teaching Bible studies, I was also homeschooling my two youngest children and was part of a local co-op where families of homeschoolers in our town got together weekly. After grieving my daughter's death for five years, believing it was *the great trial* the Lord had called me to suffer, I was beginning to heal and feel whole again, as much as is possible after losing a part of oneself. I was in a Christian bubble, and I started to like my life just fine. I prided myself on speaking the truth firmly and *hopefully* sprinkled with love, and I even took some persecution for it. Overall, life was good. The sun was coming out from behind the storm clouds.

In the trial that was to come, I would learn that even as we look at the storm clouds through our tears, we can know the Light is still shining on us. Even when we can't see it, we can trust that it's there. We must watch for the rainbow in the darkest of storms because our God is a covenant-keeping God who is always faithful to His promises. Feelings are never the gauge of truth.

As I look back, I can see that the longer I taught Bible studies and the more knowledge I gained, the more tempted I was to take a long, hard look down my nose at those who did not fit the perfect Christian mold—as I saw it. The moralist in me was often demanding answers: *Why didn't everyone around me have the same hunger I did? Why weren't they growing as I thought they should? How could they be content to feed on false teaching when I was telling them how toxic and lethal it was for them? Why couldn't they just grow up!*

Over these years, I kept coming back to the study of the doctrine of what is known as the separation of the believer and wrestled with it. Where was the dividing line of separation? Where I tended to place that line drove most people from me and from Christ. So what did His Word have to say about it?

Desperate to find the "perfect church", we had separated ourselves from every local church finding fault with each one. In the meantime, we were working with a large West Coast church to plant a church with similar doctrine on the East Coast. The reality of that church plant was so close that our new pastor was coming for a first-time visit the very week my husband was told he was the subject of a federal investigation. Ironically, before I knew it, and as God would have it, I found out firsthand all about separation.

In prison, I was quickly slapped in the face with the ugliness of sins like selfishness, entitlement, pride, jealousy, envy, sexual immorality, and every other sort of evil. But now, instead of passing judgment on women I didn't know, the Lord gave me eyes to look inward, to see the things that only He can see in me. Those I lived with 24/7 became a mirror to me of *my* own soul, and I saw the same ugliness that identifies me with the rest of humanity. After all, I was an inmate just like everyone else around me. For almost four years I was either 'Podlucky' or 'Inmate 32738-068'. Nothing at first glance made me distinct. It is true that the ground is level at the foot of the cross, but it is also level in prison. The only way to win favor with anyone was usually to break the rules—in other words, live up to the criminal status with which I was now labeled. And that was not an option for me.

God, in His grace, gave me favor with many; even though often I felt I stood out like a sore thumb. Our similarities were in our circumstances and our identity as human beings who had been convicted of felonies. The dignity we shared came from being part of His creation, created in His image, even while being treated like human waste by most of society. There was a definite divide between those on the 'inside' and those on the 'outside'. Separated from family and friends, I steadily grew in the painful realization that I was also supernaturally separated from most everyone around me, even though we lived together 24/7 in *very* close quarters. The light always shines brightest in the darkness and the darkness knows it is there. As usual, I never seemed to fit in anywhere. Prison was an extremely lonely place for me, and I turned to the Lord for His comfort and strength. One way the Lord answered my heart's cry, teaching me to trust Him more faithfully for all things, was in supporting me with His body. Suffering teaches us to trust Him.

Over the years, the Lord had developed in me discernment to be able to spiritually separate error from truth and false teachers from those who faithfully teach sound doctrine. I was quick to boldly warn those around me of the dangers caused by listening to and believing error. Ironically, however, from a worldly perspective, I generally believed people in places of authority were good and just, and I rarely questioned professional people to faithfully lead me according to their acquired wisdom. This included accountants, attorneys, and *journalists.* Before this trial began in 2006, I did not fully realize how many people blindly believe everything reported in newspapers, or just how easily the media in general, can sway public opinion. A mob mentality can be whipped up overnight. Then again, there's really nothing new under the sun. One day people were waving palm branches at Jesus singing, "Hosanna!" The next day they were yelling, "Crucify Him!" On the homefront, I rarely questioned Greg when he asked me to do something to help him regarding his responsibilities in our family. He had his role, and I had mine; but we were a team, as all married partners should be. However, the fact that I explicitly trusted my husband was widely frowned upon by my lawyer, the prosecutors, friends, and obviously the general public as seen through the eyes of a jury of my "peers". This was eye-opening and shocking to me.

I trusted and believed a jury of my "peers" would see that my son and I were innocent when we went to trial. We stood firmly in our integrity, not even considering the offer of an 18-month probation plea deal, which would be to admit guilt (or lie—as we saw it), when we believed in our hearts that we were not guilty.

I now realize that what I had been doing my whole life was putting my trust in man as basically good, which is sin. I would never have claimed that concept as truth, but I had been living as if it were true. There is no one good but God, and He alone is worthy of complete trust. Never doubt the fact that all are sinful in the sight of God in their depravity. Ironically, the greatest lessons I learned from my prison test dealt with the depths of human depravity, not necessarily of those *inside* the prison walls (except that of my own), but of those who are part of the system supposed to fight for justice, the "good" people in the world. I began to get a glimmer of man's depravity, the desperate need of all men for true salvation, how blind humans are to this need, and how to trust Christ more considering the depths of that depravity.

How can one embrace such a cataclysmic reversal of life as one knows it? When everything you have is taken away from you, you have two choices: turn to the world, or run hard toward the arms of Christ. I knew where to run because I knew the One to whom I was running. I needed to lean wholly on Christ for *everything*. He was my refuge and my strong tower. I clung to Him like a life preserver on a tempestuous sea.

I had a good rapport with most of the guards. One guard who was particularly hard to deal with, however, spoke a very truthful statement one Christmas to all the girls who worked in the CDR (Central Dining Room). He said, "We've all broken the law, every single person in this room. The only difference between you and any of us on the outside is we did not get caught." I thought about that statement for a very long time. This was the same rude guard who made older, disabled women cry, denying them food unless they could get it themselves while going through a line with a walker—the same rude guard who, when asked his permission to tweak the menu for the day, would curtly reply: "You would have a better chance of seeing Jesus return than having me say 'yes' to that request." *Well, okay, then—now we're getting somewhere!*

In my dark prison trial, through God's grace and mercy, I saw the Lord's favor shining on me as He, alone, sustained me. My Father was with me, and I knew it. And He was teaching me to trust Him more than I had ever done before.

When I first got out of prison, I had a hard time reading, writing, or just finding my place once again in the world. I began to read what I had started to write years earlier. The truths were somehow richer and deeper than I remembered when writing them. The following is an entry in my journal:

Summer of 2015 – I am overwhelmed to see how God allowed me to experience these truths before I could write the rest of my story to date. These truths are now like a gentle breeze, refreshing to my soul as home would be to a weary soldier walking off the battlefield when the war is over. He is vulnerable, weary, dazed, heavy-hearted, somewhat bewildered, but thankful to have survived…and free. I am like one who endured the war yet cannot help but ask the question—Now, what? Where do I go from here? I trust You.

In prison, it is easy to believe that the trial might not ever end. Maybe you **are** in a prison or a war that has no end in this lifetime. At times, we are not able to see even a flicker of light at the end of the tunnel. How do we reconcile that knowledge with the promises God has given us in His Word? I *believed* that God would deliver me from the trial; I stood firmly upon His promises of deliverance. I *believed* justice would prevail. When I wrote the above excerpt I was somewhere in the middle of two scenes—a weary soldier who has survived another battle but is still eagerly watching for her Savior to bring deliverance, vindication, and victory—while, at the same time, needing to move forward until then. I didn't have answers as to *how* He was going to work out all things for my good and His glory, but I knew He was doing so. I know He is faithful, that the faith He gives us endures, and that one day there will be no more sorrow, no more pain, and no more tears. I believe His promises—I admit, however, I sometimes agonize and struggle with them while waiting their fulfillment. Another thing suffering produces is patient endurance through hope.

Christmas Eve 2016—My trial continues to unfold. For the last year, I have been at a loss for words to put on paper. With such a complex and overwhelming story, I am still processing…. It has been an incredibly hard year. I have had extreme highs and equally extreme lows. I'm not sure why that is. At times, strange as it sounds—I long for my prison. Yet, I press on only in His strength. When I am weak, He is strong.

The Gospel - The Necessary Foundation for Understanding All Life's Difficulties

This book is written specifically to Christians, those who are followers of the biblical Jesus. The gospel is every bit as much for us each day as for the lost. It is life, pure and simple. Every single day we need to be reminded of what we have been saved from, for Whom we have been saved, and the great cost of that salvation. The Lord has taught me through suffering how *everything* in the life of a Christian is about the gospel and ties to our gaining a deeper understanding of Calvary's love in some way. Therefore, it's impossible to find the answers to our questions and to embrace the circumstances God has allowed in our lives if we do not fully have our focus where it needs to be.

For the Christian, the Gospel of Jesus Christ is *the* way of life. The paradox we must embrace is that it is a continual walk to death that leads to abundant life. Every aspect of our lives needs to be laid down beside the cross and the Gospel of Jesus Christ. The cross is where we learn what it means to truly live a crucified life—to fully embrace our own cross, and to drink the cup He has called us to drink just as He drank the cup His Father called Him to drink.

Amid one's trials and tribulations, feeling as though God has abandoned you, it is possible to wonder whether you really are beloved of God. While you may never voice that concern, the thought has no doubt crossed your mind at times. I know you need assurance that God is with you in your pain, that He has heard your many cries for mercy and for help, that He is on His throne, that none of what you are going through has taken Him by surprise, and that He has you exactly where He wants you to be at this very moment.

Whether you are struggling for assurance, or you want answers that will calm your fears—giving you peace in the raging waters that threaten to overcome you—you **must** get your focus on the only One who holds the answers to every soul-searching question that begs an answer. You must widen the view of your present circumstances into the eternal. The story is gloriously so much bigger than you. When we get our focus where it needs to be, we will see that the answers are just not as important as they once were. It may sound trite, but the words of the song are true. When we get our focus on Christ and look full in His wonderful face, the things of the earth will grow strangely dim, in the light of His glory and grace.

If you are not sure you are a genuine believer in the Lord Jesus Christ, or if you know you are not a Christian but have picked up this book for some reason, I implore you to stay with me to the end. But I warn you that the true gospel is not going to give you warm fuzzies and a grand boost to your self-esteem. If you want the truth that leads to eternal life, listen to the call in these pages. God's promises are sure only for those who are truly saved. There can be no peace in suffering for you apart from Christ. This book or any other won't give much help for those who cannot embrace the truths of the gospel. My heart's desire for you is that you would know the salvation of God and the God of salvation, so that you can make sense of not only your sufferings and heartaches but your whole life. Also, apart from faith in Christ alone, know that you are headed for eternal torment in hell; and as every minute of every day passes by, your time is running out to turn to Christ and to beg His mercy upon your soul.

There is 'good news' to be found in all our sorrow. It took me years to understand how our suffering helps us understand the gospel in a deeper way. Step by step, falling here and there along the way in my walk with Him, I have been surprised to learn the more I suffer, the more He allows me to plumb the depths of what happened at Calvary. His love for me shines forth brighter than a brilliantly cut diamond sparkling in all its flawless radiance on the dark canvas of my soul, and I gain a flicker of understanding of the purpose of suffering in the lives of His own dear children.

This suffering He not only allows—He purposefully, perfectly designs each situation as unique as we are individuals. For instance, that understanding applied to my prison trial looks like this, for starters: No judge, prosecutor, or jury put me in prison. No earthly judge has the power or authority but that which is given him by God. My Lord, *the* Judge of the universe, put me in prison for His good purposes. Even further—He went with me.

As the light shines on the cross, I find my cup overflowing with love, joy, and peace. Even though I have not suffered to the extent of Job, I understand why he said to his Lord, "I have heard of You by the hearing of the ear; but now my eye sees You." I want to see

Him more clearly. How will that happen? One way is by embracing all that comes to my life as coming from His hands—those loving, nail-scarred hands engraved with my name written upon them.

Our stories are part of a much bigger story—His story. None of us stands alone suffering in a box. Suffering is universal in scope, yet it is uniquely designed for us individually by One who knows exactly what is needed for Him to mold us, shape us, and bring us to completion. On that day we will be presented to Him, having no spot or wrinkle or any such thing, holy and blameless like Christ. Finally, we will be able to accurately reflect the radiance of His glory.

Like Job, when the waves of my trials slammed against my life, questions flooded my mind. These questions revealed my heart and questioned His sovereign plan for my life. *Why would you ever want my witness and testimony for You to be so tarnished? Don't You care, Lord? I thought I had Your will for me figured out, but if You allowed this—if You caused this trial in my life—this trial that ruined all my hopes, plans, and dreams, how can I know for sure what You want me to do?* Honest questions. Not "theologically-correct" questions. I know the answers. Because I still dwell in a body of flesh, I struggle to believe them in the time of testing and trials.

I have a compulsion to share the story of how God has worked in my life. I want to shout from my rooftop what I have learned in the darkness. Maybe you will be able to identify with how the Lord has worked in my life, and He will use the story He's weaving in my life to resonate with your heart transforming it for your good and His glory. Whatever way He chooses to use it, I want to be found obedient and faithful. Maybe you have not really stopped to think about how the Lord has used affliction in your life to date. Some suffering the Lord has used in my life includes the following:

- Through the death of close relatives, the Lord used that exposure at a tender age to begin viewing life through eternal lenses.
- Rejection from both a dear friend and a boyfriend in high school.
- Life-long struggles with my weight and the social effects relating to it.

- The death of my first love as a young adult.
- Material hardship to extreme wealth and back to material hardship once again.
- Marriage conflicts.
- A miscarriage.
- The death of my beloved daughter eight days before her 17th birthday.
- The death of my father-in-law at age 63 to cancer.
- Failed relationships with family and friends.
- The loss of my husband's business of 19 years. A five-year federal investigation of my husband along with the massive media scandal that went with it.
- An all-day search of our home by more than twenty federal agents (three times federal agents stormed our home). Twice they took my husband out in handcuffs and shackles; twice I watched officers hold a large gun to my oldest son's back, and once agents swarmed our kitchen with body shields.
- Watching my middle son struggle to go off to the college of our dreams across the country while everything at home seemed to be falling apart.
- Severe back disk pain on and off for years. During the investigation, it returned and resulted in my sitting and sleeping in a chair for a month before walking into a chiropractor's office dragging my right foot and undergoing months of therapy. Years spent sleeping in a recliner were followed by years sleeping in an upright position with my back against the cement wall on my prison bunk bed.
- The death of my 69-year-old mother to a one-and-a-half-year struggle with cancer while the scandal was going on.
- Watching my father suffer the death of his wife of 50 years and trying to console him while grieving my own loss. During this time, he was forced to testify at the grand jury against my oldest son and me. Later, the government would threaten

to indict my father for perjury if my husband did not accept their plea deal.

- The indictments of my oldest son and myself on money laundering charges six months after my mother's death, being put on a home monitoring curfew, and seeing the end of my beloved Bible study.
- Watching my youngest son move to the same college as my middle son as he agonized over all the uncertainties of what was going on at home.
- Seeing my husband face-to-face one time in the last 9 years. I have not seen my oldest son since we both went to prison.
- One week after my husband was sentenced to 20 years in federal prison, we proceeded to trial. My son and I embarked on a 12-day trial (over the span of several weeks) in federal court at the end of which time we were found guilty, even though we continue to maintain our innocence.
- Watching my oldest son's hopes and dreams seem to die before him as he heard the verdict "guilty on all counts".
- Watching my two younger boys suffer embarrassment and the pain of separation of losing their father, brother and mother, not knowing where or how they were going to live with all family members incarcerated.
- Being sentenced to house arrest until our sentencing five months from the day the verdict was read.
- Watching my son be sentenced to 9 years in federal prison at age 31 unjustly accused and taken off in handcuffs directly to jail. Then, my sentence of 51 months, being handcuffed and taken directly to jail.
- Over three and a half agonizing years in prison separated from all my loved ones, trying to fight an impossible legal battle.
- Going through menopause in prison.

- Going through a five-month halfway house/home confinement process while trying to maintain a job at the only local grocery store as a cashier—still separated from all of my immediate family members.
- Living with the status of a convicted felon.

There have been many blessings that have come through these trials. The One who has meticulously designed every detail of my suffering has taught me to trust that every tear and every painful blow is for my good and His glory whether I understand it or not.

The Lord, according to His sovereign plan, has been pleased to humble me using various trials and tribulations to do so. Life, for the believer, is one big, continuous lesson taught by the Lord. Our 'classrooms' can take on many different forums. My most humbling classroom just happened to be a cubicle no bigger than a small horse stall—my 'cube-dominium'—my 'home' away from 'home'.

No longer having a 'home' to call my own, this small cubicle (one of 75 open to a space for 150 federal inmates, with absolutely no privacy), is where bonds of sin were broken; it was my sanctuary—my holy place. This very place where the law had placed visible bars to inhibit my freedom became the dwelling place where the Lord would tabernacle with me, inviting me to freely commune with Him behind the veil. Access to His presence was offered with no limitations. Times of worship and intimate fellowship there were sweet. No judge, no prison guards, no false accuser of the brethren could keep me from the Lover of my soul, this One who would never leave me nor forsake me. My soul knew it very well.

The Tapestry and the Veil

Life is But a Weaving
(The Tapestry Poem)
Quoted often by Corrie Ten Boom

My life is but a weaving
Between my God and me.
I cannot choose the colors
He weaveth steadily.
Oft' times He weaveth sorrow;
And I in foolish pride
Forget He sees the upper
And I the underside.
Not 'til the loom is silent
And the shuttles cease to fly
Will God unroll the canvas
And reveal the reason why.
The dark threads are as needful
In the weaver's skillful hand
As the threads of gold and silver
In the pattern He has planned
He knows, He loves, He cares;
Nothing this truth can dim.
He gives the very best to those
Who leave the choice to Him.[1]

This illustration of the tapestry has been widely used to teach us about God's sovereignty in our suffering. A man by the name of Grant Colfax Tullar[2] wrote a poem entitled, "The Weaver," but it came to be associated with Corrie Ten Boom. Corrie Ten Boom was a Holocaust survivor who died in 1983 at the age of 91. Her story is horrendous and gloriously victorious at the same time. Corrie is most well known for her book, *The Hiding Place*.[3] I saw the movie many years ago, and I can vouch for it as one that leaves an indelible impression on its viewers. I have thought of it often, especially while imprisoned myself. Speaking about the tapestry illustration,

Corrie told this story in a book:

> *As she spoke, she slowly unfolded the purple cloth in her hands and revealed hundreds of strings tied in knots and pulled through the cloth. It all looked so random. She showed the children how the strings didn't seem to make sense from where they sat at her feet on the floor of the living room.*
>
> *"That's the whole point," she exclaimed. She said it was because of our limited vision, our limited perspective of what God is doing in our lives, that we question Him.*
>
> *At that point Tante (aunt) Corrie slowly turned the purple tangled mess around to reveal a beautiful tapestry: a crown of gold with multicolored jewels. "This," she said, "is what God sees…from His perspective…a **masterpiece!**"*
>
> -Reflections of God's Glory, Corrie ten Boom[4]

Although hers was much more severe, bearing similar battle scars, Corrie Ten Boom would understand *my* suffering. She would understand the separation, humiliation, and loneliness I felt in my trial. She would, no doubt, know some of the same temptations I faced to fear and to lose all hope rather than to trust God. Together we share in the fellowship of *His* sufferings.

Having tried my hand at both embroidery and cross-stitch, I have concluded I lack the necessary patience to master anything resembling needlepoint. The knots frustrate me. Even the most skilled in the craft of needlepoint would agree that while the top side of the piece can be exceptionally exquisite, the underneath is rarely a work of art, looking nothing like the top. What we can see on the working side is an image, whether it be a picture or script. It has meaning and significance, ideally portraying what the artist intended. On the contrary, the underneath where we are burying our threads—knotting them when they can't be buried—appears chaotic, confusing, and convoluted.

My mother owned a professional embroidery machine. She stitched her designs (often Scripture related) onto clothing, hats, baby blankets, and other household items. In this process, there was very little time involved compared to embroidery done by hand. And there were no visibly loose strings. On the other hand, my grandmother-in-love did a lot of needlepoint. From my little experience, I know the time involved in each piece over which she labored. It was a time-consuming process, and each labor of love was valuable to her and to anyone who would appreciate the work involved. I coveted any one of her pieces knowing it would be a treasured family heirloom. So, between the two, I would rather have the strings.

My mother also made exceptionally beautiful quilts that were desired from as far away as Germany. Her small, painstakingly, and perfectly-placed hand stitches were so flawless that it was almost impossible to know whether they were quilted by hand or machine. They are precious to me. I take great care to keep them because they are beautiful, but mostly because of the one who created them.

When searching my husband's office, federal agents took one piece of framed needlepoint his grandmother had done depicting the lion and the lamb lying down together. I do not care about much else that was never returned to us, other than my daughter's piano which was being stored at his office building. I just pray they were not destroyed, but that someone appreciates them.

"The Tapestry Poem" speaks about those times of suffering in our lives when it looks to us as though God is not in control, and we can't understand the purpose for the trial we are experiencing. The disarray of strings hanging loosely, seemingly unsecured, may threaten to shake me from my foundation, but He has promised to redeem every facet of my pain. He has proven Himself faithful to me time and time again; and I am learning to walk by faith in these dark times knowing that He is redeeming every tear and fear and creating something beautiful that will glorify Him through-out eternity. He redeems the mess; *I am* that mess!

Salvation is all God's work in us. At a point in time, God saved me. He changed my heart from one who unknowingly hated Him and was marked as His enemy to a friend who seeks to love Him more each day as I get to know Him. He took me, a daughter of Satan from the kingdom of darkness, and made me His own daughter who will live forever with Him in His kingdom. Before that time, I owed Him an insurmountable debt for my sin against Him, a debt that an eternity could never cancel. That debt stood between us as a great chasm fixed, with absolutely nothing I could do to bridge the gap. The sad reality is I would never *want* to pay it in my prior state of rebellion. Before He gave me a new heart to believe, I knew nothing of spiritual things with any assured belief, nor did I care. The Bible says I was dead in my trespasses and sins. (Ephesians 2:1) A dead man can do nothing. Consequently, for my status of 'enemy of God' to change, **He** had to do something. And He did. He gave me a new heart, wiping my slate clean before Him. He made me a new creation in Christ Jesus and drew me into that relationship with Him for which I was created. **But God, being rich in mercy, because of His great love with which He loved us, even when we were dead in our transgressions, made us alive together with Christ (by grace you have been saved).** (Ephesians 2:4-5) **For by grace you have been saved through faith; and that not of yourselves, it is the gift of God; not as a result of works, so that no one may boast. For we are His workmanship, created in Christ Jesus for good works, which God prepared beforehand so that we would walk in them.** (Ephesians 2:8-10)

Believers are *His* workmanship. We are *His* product. The definition of the Greek word used for *workmanship* means a product, i.e., **fabric (literally or figuratively)**: a thing that is made, a work of art. Because He is the Master Creator, some would say a 'masterpiece'. He created us, and He caused new life to occur when we were dead in our trespasses and sins so that we were born again spiritually. He redeemed us *for* good works that God prepared beforehand *so that* we would walk in them. He is molding us and shaping us into the image of Christ. No artist intends to create a work that will be hidden but to be put on display as a reflection of himself. By design, we have been created to reflect God.

I have a chest of thread—a full spectrum of dark, vibrant, shiny metallic and softly-muted hues. It is beautiful thread I bought for a few needlepoint designs. Mixed in are threads passed down from my husband's grandmother never used for designs developed in her mind. As it sits there in the box year after year, it is, in a sense, worthless. Paints on a shelf do not hold any value until the painter uses them to transform them into a masterpiece.

Imagine that your life is like a tapestry. The Master Weaver is God. Going through trials that serve to humble us, life at any given time from my point of view looking up at the underneath side of my tapestry looks chaotic, uncontrollable, and messy. The original thought was that while we can only see the unseemly underneath side now, which appears a mess due to trials and tribulations in our lives, God is working it into a perfectly designed masterpiece.

Expanding the illustration, I would venture to use it to show that we *are* the underneath side as Christians still clothed in flesh as we journey through this life. Therefore, the underneath side is the practical or physical side the world sees, while He is making something beautiful out of this mess that is our lives. Some parts of the underneath side are more distinct than others, reflecting the design on the other side. Sanctification is a process, and because we still live in a body of flesh, life is sometimes messy. Just as growing up is sometimes painful for us physically; the same can be said for our spiritual life because there are many lessons to learn. Sanctification is taking place when we embrace or bow the knee to whatever the Lord uses to mold us and shape us into the image of His Son. We are saying, *Lord, you are God. You are sovereign over everything— even this thing I do not understand. I choose to trust You.*

Man was created to display God's glory perfectly. When the Fall and resulting curse came, so did trials, tribulations, suffering, and death. Trials and tribulations are very much a part of this life because of sin; but God redeems them for His purposes, using them to sanctify us. Just as a baby learns to walk, life for the believer is all about being taught in progressive steps how to trust Him. As we walk by His Spirit step by step, He is leading us back to full restoration of all that we were created to be.

At the Fall, man doubted God. We were born doubting Him. It is part of our nature in Adam to doubt God. Our walk of faith began the moment He gave us new hearts to believe. The Christian life is very much a walk of faith learning to trust our Lord wholeheartedly. We are sincere when we *say* we believe/trust Him. We are eager as new believers to affirm this trust in our Father out of love for what He has done for us. We say we believe a lot of things until the belief system we have is tested. Then, things start to get wobbly. We could say in our illustration that each step is a stitch.

Just like children of all ages, we are eager to please our Father in obedience, but we fail and fall—a lot! Instead of letting the Father do His work in us, we get in His way and attempt to pull our own strings as we struggle to yank the control from His hands. Wanting our own way, we fight the Weaver's hand for each stitch wrestling Him for their placement where we believe they should go. The results are more strings, gnarls, and knots, and we end up making a bigger mess of things. Each time we fall, our Father is faithful to pick us up and put us back on the right path.

While children are very much dependent upon those who take care of them, they have a natural bent towards independence. As they grow in maturity, they can see some of their failures and recognize their need for dependency once again. If wise, they admit and learn from their mistakes sooner rather than later, and growth takes place more quickly.

New believers, like teenagers, often falsely assess their maturity level early on in their walk (which is rarely attractive to others). Maturity in the Christian life is a process of learning, and it takes time. Very seldom does growth come about without some sort of suffering involved. New believers are quick to profess their devotion by telling the Lord and others of those things they intend to do for Him, even to die for Him if necessary. They are unbridled in their passion to serve. After a few trials have slapped us in the face, however, we sadly admit we are prone to wander, and we question the depth of our love for Him while agonizing over our sinful hearts.

Ironically, it's as we grow that we begin to realize our utter dependence upon God for everything. Where once we were quick to affirm, "Lord, I believe. I trust you with my whole heart," we learn to humbly admit, "Lord, I believe, help my unbelief." At times we can barely whisper, "I really do *want* to believe You, Lord."

We see this lived out for us in the life of the Apostle Peter. You will remember the discourse our Lord had with him after he had denied Him three times. Jesus questions Peter's love for Him in John 21. Once over-confident, independent Peter would not have hesitated to respond, "Of course, I love you, Lord. I love you with my whole heart!" Now, having had a glimpse of his sinful heart and human depravity, he is grieved to speak the truth. It's as if he is trying to say, "Yes, Lord, I love you; help me love you as I should, as You deserve. How could I ever deny You if I really love You?"

Have you ever wondered why God does not save us and take us home immediately? Wouldn't it be so much easier for us? I believe one reason He does not whisk us away to heaven the moment we are saved is this need for us to see our own depravity. The fact is, the longer we live here wrestling with our sinful flesh, the more we appreciate the grace and mercy poured out upon us by God in all three aspects of our salvation—our justification, sanctification, and ultimately, our glorification. We will be a trophy of His grace for all eternity, and we will *know* the lavishness of that grace. We will see the top of our tapestry and wonder in awe at its splendor. Of course, this whole tapestry idea is just an illustration, but I really want us to grasp the fact that sanctification is a process. We are going to need that knowledge in severe trials.

So we are saved and *think* we love God with all our hearts. The reality is we need to be taught to love. We need to learn to love God, and we need to learn to love others as much as we love ourselves. We hear a lot about love today in our world of "positive thinking and positive confession". Love is undeniably the grandest theme in all the world, yet the reality of true love is rare and misunderstood.

We experience daily conflicts with the people God puts in our lives. We explosively confront them head on, or we refuse to deal with them by running away from them. We experience conflicts with God because we are our number one idol. God says *this*, but we believe and then do *that*. True love serves *others*, yet we worship and serve *ourselves*; we love ourselves above all else, only serving others when it serves us first.

These are the knots—the conflicts—as we wrestle to obtain our desires, wanting what we want when we want it. Like children, we tend to want those things we *feel* will benefit us the most. But just like every good parent, our Father teaches us and trains us in righteousness, even by replacing and reshaping our desires. Most of the things we desire as children should never be given to us— even the good things—at least until we are ready to handle them.

When my husband and I lived in Oklahoma, we had a desire that was not realized. Please keep in mind as I paint this portrait the mindset of two *"mature"* 20-year-olds. Picture this: We lived in a rent-free home with a hole in the bathroom wall. You could literally see outside! The ceiling in the living room was exposed to the roof in one section. Greg fixed both of these problems the best he could. With a one-year-old baby, Greg was going to school full time, and I was working as a 'word-processor' for the ministry associated with his school. The one thing we had to do to continue not paying rent was to keep up the landlord's yard work. We were happy and content—until we got the bug for a new car.

My parents sold us a nice car for little money. It was a blessing until we had our first "problem" with it. A red, faded out, mid-sized sedan, once the clogged fuel filter was replaced at a cost of $5, there was nothing else wrong with it. We decided, however, we *needed* a shiny, black coupe sports car with gold pinstripes. Never mind it was a two-door, and we would have to get a baby car seat in and out of there day in and day out. We coveted that car and came up with a full-proof plan to get what we wanted. Greg would ask his father to co-sign a loan for us! Imagine our devastation when we found out through the dealer that Dad wouldn't sign. Didn't he understand he would not *actually* have to make payments? We were miffed for months. It wasn't long, however, before we were thanking the Lord for this door that had been slammed shut in our faces. Maturity, wisdom, and tough love knew what was best for these two *children*. Suffering helps us grow up; therefore, suffering is good for us.

In Philippians 3:7-12, Paul suffering in prison says, **But whatever things were gain to me, those things I have counted as loss for the sake of Christ. More than that, I count all things to be loss in view of the surpassing value of knowing Christ Jesus my Lord, for whom I have suffered the loss of all things, and count them but rubbish so that I may gain Christ, and may be found in Him, not having a righteousness of my own derived from the Law, but that which is through faith in Christ, the righteousness which comes from God on the basis of faith, that I may know Him and the power of His resurrection and the fellowship of His sufferings, being conformed to His death; in order that I may attain to the resurrection from the dead. Not that I have already obtained it or have already become perfect, but I press on so that I may lay hold of that for which also I was laid hold of by Christ Jesus.** There are times when I am in the Spirit and would likewise confess these things with all my heart. I would readily say I believe that to lose everything, but to have Christ, is the greatest of all treasure. I *know* that is truth. We **say** we want to know Him, and we truly long to know Him more. What we often mean is that we want to know the power of His resurrection (what we think *that* looks like). If we're honest, we wince at what the fellowship of His sufferings and being conformed to His death will look like in our lives. But resurrection follows death. We see a picture of what this looks like at every baptism. We died to ourselves and were raised to walk in newness of life. We walk in that resurrection power by the Holy Spirit as we live out and embrace the gospel. A daily walk to death is life-giving. To know the fellowship of His sufferings is to fellowship with Him—trusting Him—in the middle of our deepest, darkest trials and tribulations. Times of intense suffering can bring with them the sweetest fellowship with Christ you will ever know. Believers can learn to walk in joy and love, even in suffering.

It does not mean we will always have smiles on our faces. We are not to paint smiles on our faces and live like we believe a prosperity gospel. Painted smiles are for clowns. Sadly, too many professing Christians *do* believe a false gospel—a false gospel that deceives and does not save. The gospel is *not*: 'God loves you and has a wonderful plan for your life.' It is not: 'He wants you happy, healthy, and wealthy.' That is easy to believe. That's what I call the cotton candy gospel—it's all fluff! Tasting sweet, it goes down easy, but it has no nutritional value for your soul; instead, it will kill you in the end. Our flesh wants to believe it because we really think we deserve it; and it is just so much easier. But it will not hold you when the raging rapids threaten to overtake you in a severe trial.

The reality is God will do whatever it takes to make His children holy—to make us into the image of Christ. The more we grow in holiness, the more we learn to say with confidence, "For I consider that the sufferings of this present time are not worthy to be compared with the glory that is to be revealed to us." Everything in life is about the Gospel of Jesus Christ and **His** glory, **not ours**. The health, wealth, and prosperity gospel preachers promise you the underneath side of your tapestry looks exactly like the top right now, or at least that it can. But it is not possible because we are *not* yet glorified.

I am enough of a perfectionist to want order on the underneath side of my needlepoint project right now. I like all my ducks in a row. But my life looks more like a hunter firing off a machine gun into the air, for those ducks never stay where I want them. We want to think we have life and God figured out. But just when we think we do, the rug is pulled out from under us and we find ourselves dismayed, disillusioned, and devastated by circumstances in life. With a lot of questions, we go back to the Word to have our thinking refined regarding what we truly believe. And we are forced to live in the gospel. In physical needlepoint, the underneath is not typically seen once the piece is framed or fashioned into its intended purpose. Then, it is displayed for all to admire the work of the creator. But in the spiritual life, the Master Weaver is going to use each painful, unsightly thread for His glory.

Each person is a unique masterpiece with only the Master Weaver knowing how every design will ultimately glorify Him. All knots will be secure, and there will be no loose threads when the image is complete. Each predesigned, completed image will be a perfect masterpiece created by God to tell a different story reflecting His faithfulness in Christ Jesus. If it were my needlepoint project, I would choose designs that mean something to me or tell something about who I am. They would reflect my personality. It is the same with the Master Weaver. His work will be put on display in us throughout all eternity. We will be trophies of His grace reflecting His glory.

Another tapestry we must consider is the veil in the temple. In the Old Testament, God gave laws regarding how He was to be worshiped. The shedding of blood was required to cover sin as far back as Adam and Eve in the Garden of Eden. Later, sacrifices were offered for the sins of the Jewish people in a formal setting in the tabernacle; and after that, in the temple. Identically set up as a reflection of the heavenly, there were different sections for different functions the priests performed. The Holy Place was the room immediately before the Holy of Holies. The Holy of Holies was *the* Most Holy Place, as it was the very place where God dwelt. A veil, or curtain, separated the two areas. This curtain in the Jerusalem Temple is said to have been 60 feet high, 30 feet wide, and 4 inches thick. God had told Moses the exact specifications of the veil and its purpose in passages such as Exodus 26:31-34. Leviticus 16:2 reads—**The LORD said to Moses: "Tell your brother Aaron that he shall not enter at any time into the holy place inside the veil, before the mercy seat which is on the ark, or he will die; for I will appear in the cloud over the mercy seat".**

The veil or curtain in the temple was a visual divider between sinful man and holy God. *Veil* means separation. The veil was not only needed so that man would recognize the distinction and chasm between God and man, it was an object lesson to teach the people that God's holiness was a serious matter. Because God is holy, the divider *protected* sinful man from His presence. It was a reminder to the people that irreverence for God would never be tolerated. In fact, only the high priest, the mediator for the people, could enter the Holy of Holies once a year to make atonement for the people after intense preparation. The bells he wore were his only alarm system to let the people know that he was accomplishing God's purpose on their behalf. Should the bells stop sounding, he was dead. Because no one could ever go in after him for any reason, he would need to be pulled out by the rope he wore. The Jewish people carried on their worship practices in this manner year after year.

The New Covenant was instituted when Jesus Christ first came to earth. Fully God and fully man, He became the fulfillment of every symbol in the temple. **Therefore, brethren, since we have confidence to enter the holy place by the blood of Jesus, by a new and living way which He inaugurated for us through the veil, that is, His flesh…** (Hebrews 10:19-20) John 2:19 says Jesus' body was the temple. The torn veil represented Jesus' flesh. To the people, the veil represented separation. When we think of the word *veil* we think of concealing, hiding, or obscuring something. God ripped the veil in the temple when Jesus died. What does this all mean? I hope to tie this together for the reader by the end of the book. Please, do not miss Chapter 18!

Because of what Christ has done on our behalf, we can now have *confidence* to enter the holy place. The word for *confidence* means to be able to speak freely, to be completely open, and without concealment. In our relationships, we usually have this confidence to speak freely and openly only with those with whom we are most comfortable, those with whom we have intimate communion and trust. This is about making a way for intimate fellowship with God—the same type of relationship Adam and Eve had with God before the Fall that brought separation, enmity, and death.

Each time I entered the federal courtroom where I was accused, tried, convicted, and sentenced, I grew physically sick in my stomach from the fear of judgment I was required to face. I went hesitantly and timidly into that courtroom. I knew the prosecution had one goal in mind—to convict me and ultimately have me sentenced in judgment. However, it was bittersweet in the fact that every time I walked in there, I knew that one day I would walk freely, confidently, and with joyous anticipation into the great Courtroom of God in heaven to face the ultimate Judge over all creation. Into the earthly, the judgment was guilt assigned. Into the eternal, the judgment was guilt acquitted.

I had no relationship with my earthly judge. He did not know my heart; his only judgment of me was to be according to the law he was commanded to uphold based upon the evidence he would hear from the prosecution and the defense. The prosecution carried great weight in his courtroom. We were created for relationship with our Creator, the Judge of the Universe. In the days to come, I will enter God's Courtroom. My Defense Counselor carries all the weight in the heavenly courtroom because the evidence He offers is firsthand and irrefutable. The accuser of the brethren, the prosecutor, has already been exposed for the lying charlatan that he is, and his judgment is sure.

So the veil in the temple represented separation. It did conceal and hide something—God's presence from sinful man. It was there to teach us something gospel important about God and man. It was also there for protection.

In the Old Testament, you will remember that God called Moses to lead the children of Israel out of Egypt and into the Promised Land. Moses found favor with God, and at one point we see him asking God to show him His glory. God's glory was associated with His presence and His splendor. Seeing God's glory would assure the prophet that God's presence would go with him and with the nation of Israel. **Then Moses said, "I pray You, show me Your glory!" And He said, "I Myself will make all My goodness pass before you, and will proclaim the name of the LORD before** you; and I will be gracious to whom I will be gracious, and will show compassion on whom I will show compassion." But He said, "You cannot see My face, for no man can see Me and live!" Then the LORD said, "Behold, there is a place by Me, and you shall stand there on the rock; and it will come about, while My glory is passing by, that I will put you in the cleft of the rock and cover you with My hand until I have passed by. Then I will take My hand away and you shall see My back, but My face shall not be seen." (Exodus 33:18-23)

The word *cover* in the above passage is interesting. It can mean to weave a hedge of protection. Moses asked to see God's presence. But God told him that if He were to let Moses see Him, Moses would be struck dead. No man could see the full radiance of His glory and live. No mortal man could ever handle seeing the fullness of God's glory. But God would allow Moses to stand *on an appointed rock* to see a portion of His glory.

In Exodus 34, Moses received the Ten Commandments from God as He established His covenant with His people through the giving of the Law. **It came about when Moses was coming down from Mount Sinai (and the two tablets of the testimony were in Moses' hand as he was coming down from the mountain), that Moses did not know that the skin of his face shone because of his speaking with Him. So, when Aaron and all the sons of Israel saw Moses, behold, the skin of his face shone, and they were afraid to come near him. Then Moses called to them, and Aaron and all the rulers in the congregation returned to him; and Moses spoke to them. Afterward all the sons of Israel came near, and he commanded them to do everything that the LORD had spoken to him on Mount Sinai. When Moses had finished speaking with them, he put a veil over his face. But whenever Moses went in before the LORD to speak with Him, he would take off the veil until he came out; and whenever he came out and spoke to the sons of Israel what he had been commanded, the sons of Israel would see the face of Moses, that the skin of Moses' face shone. So, Moses would replace the veil over his face until he went in to speak with Him.** (Exodus 34:29-35)

Moses came down from the mountain reflecting God's glory. Every time he spoke with God this reflection shone in his face.

When Moses spoke to the people, they knew that he was God's appointed spokesman to them, and that what he said had the full weight and authority of God Himself. Moses was a judge in Israel. And what message did Moses give the people from God? He gave them the Law, and that Law came with the very glory of God. In 2 Corinthians 3:7-4:6, Paul explains this scene looking back at that time. (We will look at it further in the chapters to come.) For now, we just need to know that the Old Covenant of the Law was good. It reflected God's glory. But the New Covenant that Jesus instituted was better. The first was written on stone, the second was written on men's hearts. The first produced condemnation and death. The second one produces righteousness and life.

The veil in the tabernacle, and then later in the temple, served as a barrier between holy God and sinful man. Embroidered on it were cherubim. These angelic creatures were the guardians of the holiness of God. Also positioned at the entrance of Eden to prevent man from gaining access to the tree of life in Genesis 3:24, their likeness woven into the veil in the temple warned all who entered that they could go no further. Access to God was forbidden because God is holy, and man is not. We cannot approach God by ourselves. This would mean sure judgment and death for us. We've got a problem that must be dealt with. It's called sin. It is manifested in our 'self' life, or our sinful flesh. *We* are the problem that must be dealt with.

Those who refuse to come to God His way, that is through the crucified veil of Jesus' flesh, can never have access to or have intimate fellowship with God. When we come to God through Jesus Christ, we are made one with God—because of *His* sacrifice alone. We were created for this oneness, this most intimate communion and love relationship with God. It was His sacrifice that made our communion with the Father, Son, and the Spirit possible. There was nothing we could do in ourselves. When we embrace His sacrifice for us as our own, we can see His life manifested through us as we live amid our human relationships. Just as sacrifice was required to restore our relationship to the Father, we too will be living sacrificially as we come to realize the communion that we long for in our human relationships. We see this innate longing in every human being in wanting to be accepted, to be understood, and to have like-minded bonds of camaraderie.

The greatest picture of that oneness in human relationships is that which is seen in the God-ordained institution of marriage. When two Christians marry, God is supernaturally at the center of their union. In our day, it is extremely important to stand upon God's perfectly designed purpose and definition of marriage. The writer of Hebrews in Chapter 13:4 says that marriage is to be held in honor among all. God established the marriage union, and He also sanctified it, which means it is a relationship that is set apart and restricted. Consequently, when God joins one man and one woman together in marriage, no one is to separate them. Oneness in marriage is experienced in the unity and intimacy that is shared physically, spiritually, and emotionally between husband and wife. The fellowship shared between a husband and wife is to be the deepest bond of any other human relationship.

Just as we must walk through the veil of Christ's flesh in order to know intimate communion with and oneness with God, there is a similar picture of this union that takes place in the physical act of consummating the marriage covenant when two become one flesh. Because of the sacrifice involved, a covenant relationship involves a walk to the death of self. Both relationships are viewed as covenants in God's eyes. Speaking of the marriage relationship, Ephesians 5:31-32 says it is a mystery: **FOR THIS REASON, A MAN SHALL LEAVE HIS FATHER AND MOTHER AND SHALL BE JOINED TO HIS WIFE, AND THE TWO SHALL BECOME ONE FLESH. This mystery is great; but I am speaking with reference to Christ and the church.**

Hopefully, we can begin to see how God is going to use our relationships, which often involve much suffering, to sanctify us and to continue to deal practically with this problem we have— that of the crucifixion of our 'self' life. A covenantal relationship involves a walk to death—death to self—wherein two become one. Just as a covenant takes place between man and God supernaturally, marriage was established to produce a supernatural oneness between married covenant partners that involves the commitment of no longer living to please self but one's spouse.

The Old Testament shows men and God 'cutting covenant'. In the covenant ceremony, the two entering into the covenant would walk through the pieces of animals which had been cut in half, in essence testifying to God, "May God do so to me if I ever break this covenant with you and God." That was known as a conditional covenant. In Genesis 15, God made an unconditional covenant with Abraham, so He alone walked through the pieces.

Looking again at verse 20 of Hebrews 10, you will see the word *new* (as in 'a new and living way'). …**by a new and living way which He inaugurated for us through the veil, that is, His flesh.** Kenneth Wuest[5] says it is better translated 'newly slain' giving us a contrast between the old slain way and the newly slain way, or a freshly slain way. It means a freshly slaughtered way. Why is it new or fresh? It is because Jesus' blood is eternally effective in producing life. It is a living way contrasted to a way that leads to death. While the old way of the sacrificial system gave the Jews a *picture* that pointed to the way to come that would lead them to life, it actually led to death because it was based on the Law which could not save. The Father tore the veil representing the veil of Jesus' own torn flesh, the flesh of the perfect sacrifice. Jesus (the veil), walked through the veil of the Holy of Holies with His own blood—shed once and for all—placed it on the mercy seat, and instituted the New Covenant for all who would believe on Him and enter into an everlasting love relationship with Him.

The old way brought death but was a foreshadow of that which was to come. Christ's sacrifice provided a new and living way, but the work was finished. The writer of Hebrews in Hebrews 1:3 says: **When He had made purification of sins, He sat down at the right hand of the Majesty on high.** It was not a perpetual offering for sin. Jesus did not need to be offered often as is done repeatedly on the altars of some religious institutions today. Unlike the priests of the Old Covenant, who were always moving (unless the bells stopped tinkling) because their work was never finished, Jesus sat down. His work of redemption was finished. No more sacrifices for sin were ever needed again. (See Hebrews 9:13-14.)

All the religious works, all the sacrifices offered for sin, could never take away the guilt of human sin. Nothing we could ever offer God on our behalf could give us confidence to enter His holy presence. Our sin, just like the veil in the temple, separated us from this holy God. But we were created for fellowship with Him and for His purposes. This is the grand dilemma in life.

The separation between God and man is so great because the One we have offended is the epitome of greatness. The veil needed to come down so we could enter God's presence boldly a*s His children,* which makes all the difference in the world. When God tore the veil in the temple, He was making a way for us into His presence. The torn veil shows us that Christ's torn flesh opened the way for us into *the* Holy of Holies in the heavenlies where God dwells. Christ, through His sacrificial death, made atonement for our sins once for all which means that those now in Christ are made right before God. We can come to God through Christ, through the veil of His broken body, the torn flesh of His sacrifice at Calvary. This was the plan of redemptive history. No more animal sacrifices. They had served their purpose of preparing the people to recognize and understand their need for the Savior to come. The perfect sacrifice eliminates the need for any lesser sacrifices that any human being could ever offer. (See Hebrews 9:24-26.)

The veil in the temple was a beautifully woven tapestry. God's designs are never random. Whether we understand God's will or not, it always serves His purposes perfectly. It would seem, if a 2014 article in Israel Today[6] is accurate, both sides were finished. According to that article, a group of women called 'The Women of the Veil Chamber' have been trying to re-create the veil. The article states: "One of the more unique challenges is to weave the faces of the cherubim so that it is an eagle's face on one side of the veil and a bull's face on the other side." The tapestry of the veil representing Christ was perfect. There was no unfinished side. It represented God's design and purpose perfectly. And your tapestry will do the same.

When my daughter died, waves of darkness crashed over my soul that were more real to me than if I had been hit from behind and forcefully swept to the ocean's shore. Sitting one evening in a room full of people my world went dark, and I heard this evil voice in my mind scream: "Your daughter is dead!" While I don't ordinarily 'hear voices', this was real. I also had a death grip hold on one small portion of Scripture that came flooding into my mind repeatedly. At the time, I could not have told you where it was found, but it was Hebrews 12:2, 'fixing our eyes on Jesus, the author and perfecter of our faith, who for the joy set before Him endured the cross'. I kept telling my family, "We must keep our eyes fixed on Jesus."

As His child, when I find myself in the dark, when life seems out of control and I don't know where God is in all the mess that is my life, I must keep my eyes focused on Jesus. How? I must meditate on His Word. He is the Word; and it is the Word of God that sanctifies me. I must not focus on the loose strings, the knots, the chaotic, distorted picture of my life as I thought it would look if *I had designed it* and lose all hope. I can run to Jesus with unveiled face, beholding His glory through the pages of His Word knowing He is using all my circumstances to transform me into His image from glory to glory. I can know that He is causing me to grow up from one point of glory to the next, and that growth is all part of His perfect plan for my life—every step of the way to my ultimate glorification.

Non-Sensationalized Bad New ~ News You Can Trust

What damage can result when the news media, in order to sell papers, sensationalize, stretch, twist, and distort the 'news' until it is no longer recognizable as truth to the one who knows the facts—to the one who is being written about. Imagine picking up the daily newspaper and reading an article supposedly about you. There is just enough truth in it to make it believable to the general population but so much error and information omitted that only those who know you intimately would recognize the damnable lies. **That** is scandalous; it *should* be criminal! There was an episode of *Sherlock*[1] in which a villain named Moriarty tried to ruin Sherlock's reputation as a brilliant mastermind in London. It amazed me to see how easy it was to get people to turn on this hero and label him a fraud, even creating seeds of doubt in the minds of those closest to him.

For over a decade, my family, along with my husband's co-defendants, had been put on the (news)stand and publicly tried repeatedly—before, during, and after trial—by the news media. The amount of coverage our cases received was massive. While I don't know the exact root cause of this excessive reporting against us, I will simply say that there was enough evidence to give us reason to believe the slanted attacks were a vendetta against my husband.

The media is capable of whipping up a mob mentality with very little effort, indicating the sad reality that we are a people who are easily swayed—with very little discernment to be able to decide between what is true and what is false. There are always two sides to every story; but when only one side is told, it is often a doomed situation for the muzzled party. I've thought of that mob mentality in relation to what happened to Jesus many times. One day the people were waving palm branches at Him hailing Him King of Israel. Just days later, a crowd of chief priests, scribes, elders, Pharisees, Sadducees, and false witnesses were shouting vicious commands to Pilate, "Crucify Him!" I can easily imagine the headlines regarding Jesus' sham indictment, arrest, and trial in the kangaroo court in which He was convicted.

I have to wonder how many people who followed the 'juicy' story of the Podluckys' *fall from grace* bothered to read the Motion for

Ineffective Assistance of Counsel my son filed in our case. Attached were 2,000 plus pages disproving the lies against us with **actual evidence**. This evidence was readily accessible at trial and **should have been offered on our behalf to support our innocence.** It never was. Only God knows why—but He *does* know. Regarding daily news articles and issues like ours, you may not have to take a definitive stand as to what you believe. (It *is* becoming increasingly clear that you must choose your news wisely!) But we must all make choices regarding what is true and what is false every day.

From pictures to articles, 'fake' news is talked about everywhere today. It is so prevalent in our day that when having a discussion with someone about some intriguing, newsworthy topic, their first questions are: "Is that fake or real?" "Did you Snopes that?" "Where did you get that information?" My grandparents acknowledged their affirmation for purity of truth when they said, "I saw that on television." Or, "That was on the nightly news." There are the obviously ridiculous assertions of 'facts', but there are also the subtle lies meant to deceive and cause harm. A question that nagged at me from the onset of my trial was, "When did it become *so acceptable* to lie?" And, yet, I was accused and convicted of lying!

When I got out of prison, I was in need of a haircut. My hair was extremely long and, quite frankly, a mess. My hairstyling choices in prison were as follows: Cut it myself with approved kindergarten scissors, have someone cut it on the sly in the hair room with 'contraband' scissors, or go to the beauty school on the compound where inmates were learning how to cut hair. I tried the latter twice. Both times were a disaster. So I let it grow.

My sister graciously gifted me with a haircut soon after I was released. Having lost 80 pounds, and with hair down to my waist, she was concerned that nothing about my new appearance looked like 'me'. After almost four years in prison, while still on home confinement, I was quite humbled when she had one of my former hairdressers come to my aunt's home where I was living. When asked how I wanted my hair cut, I told my sister I really liked the picture on her Facebook profile. I ranted and raved how it was the best picture I had ever seen of her. With each compliment, she seemed to grow more upset. I asked, "What's the matter?" She was not at all happy to tell me that my niece had, "photoshopped just about everything in that picture!" I think she exaggerates more than her exaggerated picture. It fooled me, her very own sister.

When it comes to life or death issues, you had better be able to trust the source of your information. The Bible, God's Word, is the plumb line of truth for the Christian. Just because people today do not want to hear anything negative does not make hard truths any less true. Like burying our heads in the sand to avoid studying biblical issues like 'suffering' will not stop trials and tribulations from coming our way, there are truths that are hard to hear but vital to the salvation of our eternal souls. We **must** receive the whole Word of God as truth. As we bring the light of Scripture to shine upon all the teaching we hear, we reject error and even expose it as such. But we **must** believe and receive the hard truths that a pure and holy gospel speaks to our depraved hearts and let those truths cut us and reshape us into vessels for His use. That cutting and reshaping is painful, but necessary. Suffering will involve some sort of loss and separation but can always be used for our good and His glory. **For the word of God is living and active and sharper than any two-edged sword and piercing as far as the division of soul and spirit, of both joints and marrow, and able to judge the thoughts and intentions of the heart.** (Hebrews 4:12) The word for *division* in Hebrews 4:12 means causing a separation. Tim Challies says in his blog:

> "Discernment is *the skill of understanding and applying God's Word with the purpose of separating truth from error and right from wrong.*"
>
> "God's word is the standard we use to differentiate between what is true and what is false. The concepts of separating and distinguishing are inherent in the words of the original languages translated as discernment. Discernment implies that we are to separate things in order to understand their differences."
>
> "Like the laser level that shows with perfect clarity any deviations from what is straight, the Bible teaches what is true, leaving what is false standing out with glaring clearness. We use God's Word as a

tool to separate what is true from what is false. We use it to make the light appear lighter, leaving the dark to appear ever darker." ~ Tim Challies, Defining Discernment blog dated February 8, 2007.[2]

While I was in prison, a friend of mine facilitated a class called 'Separation and Divorce'. Not long after she began the class, she asked me if I would come tell my story. My first reaction was rather thoughtless: "I know nothing about separation or divorce, so what would I even talk about?" She asked me to think and pray about it saying it could be any type of separation. As I pondered the idea of separation, my eyes began to focus on the gospel. These truths that I already knew sparkled and glistened like newly fallen snow, beautiful and refreshing to my soul.

I spoke in her class many times sharing my story and how the separation we experience in our lives should drive us to see our need for the cross and the salvation of God. And just like it takes experiencing the pain of physical separation to truly appreciate the blessings of family and friends, we must understand the bad news of our standing with God before we can appreciate the extent of God's goodness in the good news of the gospel of Jesus Christ.

God is Owner and Creator of Everything

It seems odd to start bad news with God. But to understand the depth of our miserable state, we must first understand something about God, who alone is good. In Matthew 19:17, it was Jesus who said that God alone is good. It is *because* God alone is good that we are in a bad situation and maybe don't even realize how desperate we really are. The truth is I'm not God; I'm not even *a god*. I'm not in control of anything, including my own self. And I'm **not** good! I can't claim that I am *basically* a good person. I can't hope that some day my good will outweigh my bad. R.C. Sproul said, "There's nothing inherently dignified about dirt, and that's what we've been made from."[3] I love those truth arrows, or truth bombs, Dr. Sproul threw out. **Then the LORD God formed man of dust from the ground and breathed into his nostrils the breath of life; and man became a living being. (Genesis 2:7) In the beginning God created the heavens and the earth. (Genesis 1:1)**

In the beginning—God. You were not in the beginning, and neither was I. God was in the beginning. Those four little words should be enough to arrest us stopping us dead in our tracks. Why? Because God has always existed. Right from those first four words of the Bible we are confronted with staggering truth. God created everything. He owns everything, and He has the right to rule over everything. Yet men don't believe He exists. Men were created by God, yet men don't believe He exists. It is as ludicrous as a toddler raising his fist in rebellion to his mother and father telling them they cannot tell him what to do, and then most of the population agreeing with the toddler!

"In the beginning God" is a hill we must die on. Everything in our understanding of our great God flows out of those four words. Those four words render a conviction of man's smallness with no need for a jury. They reveal an immediate distinction between God and man. Instead of submitting his life to the God who created him, man wants to rule his own life. For that, he sins greatly. His guilt *should* be evident. Yet, for most human beings down through the ages, their 'not guilty pleas' echo loudly from the corridors of time. God has always existed. He created not only everything you *can* see but, also, everything you *cannot* see. There is little doubt that things in the universe which cannot be seen are embraced for what they are—take air and energy, for example. Like the toddler above, we soon understand that choosing not to believe in God is a moral issue.

People may think that what they believe about creation does not really matter. I don't know why Genesis 1 is the first book of the Bible, but I do know that the creation account is crucial to the foundation of our whole theology from that point forward. *'Why are we here?'* necessarily follows the question, *'How did we get here?'* Understanding why we are here will answer many questions we have regarding why we suffer and will get our focus where it needs to be in our suffering. Why does God own everything? God owns everything because He created everything. Can you think of one thing man created out of thin air? The logical conclusion is that because He created everything and owns everything, He has sole authority to rule over all His creation. **FOR THE EARTH IS THE LORD'S, AND ALL IT CONTAINS.** (1 Corinthians 10:26) **The**

earth is the LORD'S and all it contains, the world, and those who dwell in it. (Psalm 24:1-2) **The LORD has established His throne in the heavens, and His sovereignty rules over all.** (Psalm 103:19) As sole authority to rule over His creation, God can do whatever He pleases regarding it. He has the absolute right to rule over or govern what He has made. This is called the sovereignty of God. You will notice the word *reign* in the word *sovereignty.* In other words, He is Lord. He is Lord whether you or I ever acknowledge that fact here on earth. **Yours, O LORD, is the greatness and the power and the glory and the victory and the majesty, indeed everything that is in the heavens and the earth; Yours is the dominion, O LORD, and You exalt Yourself as head over all. Both riches and honor come from You, and You rule over all, and in Your hand is power and might.** (1 Chronicles 29:11-12a) **Declaring the end from the beginning, and from ancient times things which have not been done, saying, "My purpose will be established, and I will accomplish all My good pleasure."** (Isaiah 46:10)

Even when we don't understand what is happening to us or around us, God has a purpose or a plan He is fulfilling. Reigning on His throne in heaven, He is in control of all things. This is a very important truth to cling to when we come to questions regarding suffering. While appreciating who God is may give us answers to some of our questions, I will warn you they are not easy answers. The answers are usually beyond our grasp because God is infinite, and we are finite beings. Many things God brings into our lives we will not understand; but it is enough that He *does* understand and has a specific purpose for what He allows us and enables us to endure. Sometimes we will be given answers to the 'why' questions; but even if we are not, we *must* trust, and we *can* trust a good God who has created us and rules over all His creation.

Many people are raised believing they are owed something, they deserve better, they are entitled to the best of what the world can offer. Some conclude that if they are not given the best, they will take it from others. Their line of reasoning goes something like this: "I am just as good, work as hard, etc., as that person, so why can't I have what he has? I *deserve it* as much as anyone." So, when pain comes into our lives, the first question we usually land on is, "Why me?" We must keep in mind that God as Creator does not owe us anything, not even an explanation for what He does. Some say, "Well, I didn't ask to be born." God determined that you would be born for His good pleasure, whatever that pleasure might be. Once we understand what we *do* deserve, I am confident we will not want it any longer. We are going to see that what we deserve is not good.

For four years I witnessed conclusive evidence supporting the deeply rooted sin of rebellion in our human nature. I spoke to women who readily admitted to having committed the crime(s) that put them in prison. Yet, these same women, who had been given such incredibly humbling circumstances, were not humble! They were still shaking their fists at the law, and ultimately at God. They had no qualms about boasting of the fact that they could not wait to get back to a life of crime once they "hit the street". *Nobody* was going to control their lives! How utterly foolish! God does not need our permission to control our lives. He is controlling all things whether we want Him to or not, and whether we acknowledge He is or not. *The most* loving thing a sovereign God can do sometimes is to let people live their lives according to their desires until they come to the end of themselves. Many of these same women would be back in prison to do more time—or worse, die shaking their fists at God. But some will turn in repentance bowing the knee to His lordship. Either way, the Bible says all will one day acknowledge Jesus Christ is Lord. (See Romans 14:11; Philippians 2:9-11.)

God is Holy

What else do we need to know about God, especially when we are experiencing affliction? God is holy. This may be something you have always believed but have not understood or even stopped to consider at great length. *Holy* is a word we sing about in church. Yet it is not easily described or defined. No one can fully understand what the holiness of God looks like; but as we gaze at His glory revealed to us in the pages of Scripture—His revelation of Himself to us—we will grow in our understanding of God's holiness. This enhances our vision of the great divide between God and man. Seeing God more clearly simultaneously reveals a depth of depravity in us that we would never imagine otherwise. God's purpose for us is that we would be holy as He is holy. Suffering is part of Fatherly discipline so that we might share His holiness. **For they** (our earthly fathers) **disciplined us for a short time as seemed best to them, but He disciplines us for our good, so that we may share His holiness.** (Hebrews 12:10) God is majestic in holiness (Exodus 15:11), holiness befits His house (Psalm 93:5); and the way to God is the Highway of Holiness (Isaiah 35:8). His name is holy. His Scriptures are holy. Everything that represents God is holy. Therefore, we must be holy as His children. In 1 Peter 1:15-16, we see the command. **But like the Holy One who called you, be holy yourselves also in all *your* behavior; because it is written, "YOU SHALL BE HOLY, FOR I AM HOLY."** We are to be holy *like* the Holy One who called us. We are to be holy in *all* our behavior. We are to be holy, and we *shall* be holy. Why? Because He is holy.

Uh, Houston, we have a problem. And it is a big one! I know myself enough to know that I am not holy in all my behavior. I never have been, and the prospect that I will yet accomplish this in this lifetime does not look promising. **There is no one holy like the LORD, indeed there is no one besides You, nor is there any rock like our God.** (1 Samuel 2:2) *Only* God is holy. Even so—it does not change the command to us.

From that specific passage, we can see that God is distinguished or distinct in His holiness. He is set apart or separated from His creation in His holiness. The basic meaning of the words for *holy* or *holiness* is different or separate. Something that is holy is different from other things. Someone who is holy is different from other people. Holiness is who God is. He is wholly different and set apart from all else. I will tell you from my time in prison interacting with an extremely diverse group of women, most people in the world (if at all represented by these women) would say they are either 'religious', 'spiritual', or 'basically good'. Some know they are sinful yet believe they are somehow in right standing with God with absolutely no desire for holiness or righteousness. I went into the whole prison thing like a deer in the headlights. Before I got my focus, those lights were bright!

Having lived in a Christian bubble for many years prior, I was *not* prepared for any of it. As someone recently said, Mr. Rogers did **not** prepare me for that neighborhood (or 'hood', as my range was so affectionately called). Ladies said to me, "You *definitely* do not belong in 'the hood'!" *Uh…ya think*? In completely unchartered territory, I quickly found myself standing at a crossroads in a city called, 'Crisis of Faith,' where I had been led to an intersection marked, 'Compromise Street' and 'Stand Out Alley'. Naked and vulnerably exposed emotionally, I was challenged, virtually almost daily, to resharpen my understanding of the true gospel. I needed to determine whether my beliefs were solid enough to stand upon or had been built upon sinking sand.

What does it mean to be holy? Was I assaulted? No one ever touched me physically. It is un-settling, however, to be bombarded day in and day out with false thinking and a cultural worldview that is at polar odds with what you have lived with for most of your adult life—all while standing virtually alone. Sadly, this is an all-too-familiar scenario for many Christians—those in the workforce, children in public schools, and young men and women in secular universities all over America. The first year I walked around listening to women talk about how much they loved God, yet I kept saying, "But, where is the pursuit of holiness?" And, yes, I said that aloud. That was the dividing line of discernment where profession met reality.

What does it mean to be holy? I might be tempted to want to rationalize that God is calling me to something less than His standard of holiness. Humanly impossible to wholly understand or define with precision, the holiness of God is an attribute we can't grasp with our finite minds. In fact, none of the attributes of God are fully fathomable to us **because** He is distinct and separate from us. In Isaiah 55:8-9, God says of Himself: **"For My thoughts are not your thoughts, nor are your ways My ways," declares the LORD. "For as the heavens are higher than the earth, so are My ways higher than your ways and My thoughts than your thoughts."** The holiness of God encompasses all that He is. Yet, when God calls us to be holy, He is not using a different word for the holiness He demands of us than the Bible uses for Him. There is something else we must know; and we will get to that.

As I said, the word *holy* means apartness, separateness, set apartness. God is separate or set apart from what? Certainly, He is set apart from everything that is sinful or evil. The Bible says that God cannot look upon, participate in, or tolerate sin. We see this in Psalm 5:4 which says, **For You are not a God who takes**

pleasure in wickedness; no evil dwells with You. God's holiness demands that sinners be separated or cut off from Him. Because He is transcendent—meaning He exists above and is independent from His creation—He is necessarily set apart from all His creation. We understand that separation in a basic sense because God is in heaven and we are on earth. He is the Creator, we are the creation, and that will never change.

I know it is no coincidence that I was asked to speak at the class on 'Separation' or that I had been studying the doctrine of the 'Separation of the Believer' for years. This idea of separation is of vital importance for us to think about for it ties everything in life together in God's design and purpose. What a multi-faceted picture this idea of separation should bring to the forefront of our minds as Christians.

One is not imprisoned for long before realizing that everyone there wants o-u-t! Many are fighting and longing with all their hearts for laws to change, for motions to be ruled upon in their favor, or simply that they can do their time quickly. A wild, caged animal is a fitting picture. Every day I hoped and prayed that the red phone (sort of like the Bat phone) would ring for me, the person on the line saying, "Pack out, you are being released, and you must be off the premises in a few short hours." I watched for that white horse every single day of the week. Weekends were torture for two reasons: No mail and no possibility of the red phone ringing.

The red phone was centrally located in the front of each unit on the guard's desk where they conducted impromptu meetings, did mail call, or simply hung out at certain times observing and *'guarding'*. It was a major infraction to pick up the red phone to call Central. No inmate *would ever* pick up the phone unless someone was literally dying in the unit. *Even then*, one was probably in big trouble for picking it up. But someone had **better** pick it up when it was ringing. When an inmate got a call on the red phone, it was for some 'important' reason. Perhaps you were having a visit, your visitor had arrived, and you were being released to walk down the hill by yourself to a normally out-of-bounds area. A lot of times you were in trouble for something such as missing a 'call-out' (an appointment). On very rare occasions, it was **the call** for which everyone eagerly awaited. My heart would start racing, and I was about ready to hyperventilate whenever anyone yelled, "Podlucky, red phone!" Getting out of prison was on everyone's minds pretty much 24/7.

Everything about prison was intended to remind you on a continual basis that you were separated—from people in authority over you, from your family and friends, and from freedom in general. While making small talk with a female guard after visitation one afternoon, I told her the only thing that was often almost too hard to handle was being separated from family and loved ones. She said, "Well, that's all prison really is. Separation is the worst punishment there is."

A lightbulb went on in my mind. *Separation* **is** *the worst punishment*. When first indicted, the reality might hit hard about what a person will lose—the material things, the comforts, the well-known rhythm of life, and time lost that can never be recovered. That all changes quickly when one realizes what is truly important, when loneliness sets in, when one realizes she has no 'people'. The incarcerated fight like caged animals to be back with people they love—their community. They are in a place where communication with loved ones is difficult and minuscule, especially for those who are imprisoned far from family, seldom get any visitors, or have no outside money coming in for email or phone calls. We all know separation from those we love, in general, is a hard burden to bear.

Yet how many people in the world, ***those we love***, don't realize they are headed for an eternity separated, not only from their loved ones, but from a holy, loving God as well? They are headed for an eternal prison and don't even know it. Even now, they are imprisoned in many ways. God's holiness demands the separation of sinners from Himself. People who believe they are basically good, or not that bad, need to be told about the holiness of God. Christians, who will never be separated from God, need to tell a lost world of this certain separation to come. Instead, deceived themselves—and even fostering that deception—a large portion of *professing* Christianity can't even get the gospel right and need to hear the message themselves! And what if we have separated ourselves to the extent that we won't get close enough to lost sinners to give them the one message they so desperately need to hear? God help us!

Hell is the ultimate separation. Hell is a place of exclusion, rejection, isolation, and torment. That torment will be physical and mental anguish for all eternity. Talk about something we can't possibly understand. Any amount of time spent imprisoned can *feel* like an eternity. But it can't ever compare to hell. Many people believe their 'hell' is the life they are living here on earth. No matter how horrid your life is on this earth, it is not hell. God created hell, and His Word has quite a bit to say about it. Jesus spoke about hell more than He spoke about heaven. Sadly, while many people will know the pain of separation on earth through the death of loved ones, prison, or different circumstances, they will never connect that pain to the eternal torment of separation in hell.

I can't imagine going through the pain of separation in prison and risk eternal separation by living life my own way without regard to God and His will. In fact, it is hard for me to relate to this idea, because while I was separated from my loved ones in prison, my Lord never left me alone. Prison on earth ends. Hell has no end. Every inmate desperately wanted deliverance from prison; but even before entering the gate, I had His peace knowing ultimate deliverance from hell—and that is true freedom. Man can put a Christian in prison. That Christian can have every material possession taken from her and be separated from her loved ones for a long time...even a lifetime. What man can never take away from a believer is her eternal freedom and inheritance to come.

The unbeliever who thinks he will be in good company in hell because "all his friends will be there" needs to know there's no such concept of friendship in hell. There will be no love, no camaraderie, no dreams to fulfill, no purpose, no light, no family ties—the only thing the condemned can expect is the eternal torture of God's wrath upon a body resurrected for the purpose of enduring everlasting punishment. The Bible has much to say about hell, none of it describes any pleasure, enjoyment, or fellowship with anyone.

While enduring unfathomable suffering on the cross, the worst agony for Jesus was when the Father turned away from Him—separation—when the eternal, intimate fellowship between them was broken. What effectuated that separation was my sin and yours. The holiness of God is seen in the cross in that distinction between God and man. Because God is holy, He cannot have communion or fellowship with sin, even if it is *our* sin that Christ took upon Himself and bore in our place. God *must* judge sin.

God is just. This may be one of God's attributes to which you have given very little thought. As these last days become increasingly more evil, we may all focus on this attribute more personally, not simply as a mere acknowledgment. Deuteronomy 32:4-5 speaks of God's justice saying all His ways are just and that He is a God of faithfulness and without injustice. Deuteronomy 32:41 speaks of our just God who will render vengeance upon His adversaries and will repay their evil. Psalm 37:28 says that the Lord loves justice and will not forsake His godly ones. He will preserve them forever while cutting off the descendants of the wicked. Psalm 89:14 tells us righteousness and justice are the foundation of His throne, and lovingkindness and truth go before Him. God can do no evil. Conversely, He only does that which is right. Justice and righteousness are often used interchangeably in Scripture. Because God is holy, He must do what is right or what is just.

Girls in prison asked me why I was not bitter. I know there is a day coming when God will right all wrongs. In the meantime, I must focus on what His purpose and will for me is here and now. I do not want to waste my trial on bitterness and self-pity. I want my suffering to glorify God. When I begin to focus on the wrongs done to me and my family, *especially*; I *can* get bitter. I have had to wrestle through my beliefs, learning to walk in the truth set forth in Scripture regarding justice. As the Lord used my prison trial to sanctify me, it took me time to learn to walk in the peace and contentment truth provides. I can trust that God, the ultimate Judge, will judge all things perfectly in *His* time. What I can count on in the meantime is the knowledge that He is working all things for my good. Knowing we live in a sinful world full of injustice, I get outraged at that injustice. After all, I was made in His image, so I long for moral justice to prevail upon the earth.

What is more important than focusing on injustices done against me, I must focus on the offenses I have committed against a holy God. This sin is a crime against Him *personally*. When someone found guilty of committing a crime stands before a judge in this nation, he stands before someone who has authority to rule justly (he has **no** authority to rule unjustly) according to the laws of the land, but the criminal did not commit the offense against the judge *personally*. Judges in this land have guidelines they are supposed to follow as to what punishment will fit each crime committed. Earthly judges make mistakes. But when we sin just one time, break only one of God's Laws, which is a crime against the God of the universe *personally*, we all become criminals who do not have to wonder at the sentence that will be rendered. His justice demands a penalty of death and separation from Him for all eternity. God is holy, so the slightest infraction against Him demands this sentence. And it is right and just.

Because He is holy, the Bible speaks of God as being pure light and truth. If anything in God's creation is holy, it is because He has set it apart for Himself and made it holy. Simply put, God is *perfect*. Because this word, like most of our English words, has been stripped of absolute meaning, what is perfect to you today may not be perfect to me; and that is why we need to go to the original languages to understand the meanings of words in their context. In the Greek, *perfect* is **hagios** from the root **hagos** which means 'an awful thing'. I thought that was interesting because of what I think of when I meditate on this word *holy*. *Holiness* recalls Isaiah 6:1-5 to my mind. It would be helpful to take some time to read and meditate on this passage now.

I once read a line in a devotional, the essence of which I have never forgotten. The author said, "God is not as concerned with your happiness as He is your holiness," or something to that effect. What I understood that to mean is that if happiness is gained at the expense of your holiness, then whatever it is that makes you happy in that instance has got to go. The pursuit of holiness is evidence of true salvation. The difference between the goal of the natural man and the man who is born again is that the former lives for his own happiness and the latter lives for God's glory.

Isaiah was God's prophet who encountered God in a vision. In God's presence, he saw himself in the light of absolute holiness. Often, people in the presence of a professional athlete, movie star, or any famous person, may be mesmerized by the fame of that person. Spellbound, they might only be able to think of obtaining an autograph, a look, or a word (before swooning). Isaiah is in the presence of **true** greatness, and he sees *himself*? What's up with that? Seeing himself, he is undone or ruined. Isaiah, in the presence of holy God, got a deep sense of his own human depravity. Why?

Many of you ladies use a lighted make-up mirror. Let's say you put on your make-up in front of normal mirror this morning where the light wasn't all that great. You went throughout the day feeling pretty good about yourself because from the distance of the counter to the mirror, things looked better than normal. You were having a good hair day, and the color of your shirt made your complexion glow and your eyes sparkle. Later, you look in the make-up mirror only to notice things that make you go, "Yikes!" For instance, your eyes are immediately drawn to that long black hair growing out of your neck. Ladies my age, *you know exactly what I am talking about.* Younger ladies, trust me, it's a thing! And you walked around all day long like that. What happened?

Years ago, my sister and her husband were visiting us on our vacation at the beach. I had my make-up mirror with me. To see clearly, I need light and a magnified image to apply my make-up. I need my magnifying mirror to see those hairs growing out of crazy places. Fortunately (or unfortunately), it magnifies every little pore and every little flaw. One morning, I was putting on my makeup in front of my lighted make-up mirror and in front of a large picture window with the light streaming in. My sister asked if she could see it. She literally jumped back from it when she looked into it and screamed, "Ugh! Get that thing away from me!" She was undone.

The light of God's glory exposes the lack of glory in everything brought alongside it. Nothing can compare to God's glory. As with my lighted magnifying mirror, which gives an accurate reflection of my face, the more light that shines on us, the more we see our flaws, imperfections—our sin. We either live to magnify God or to magnify ourselves. When we see the glory of He who is pure Light, we can no longer live to magnify ourselves. His light is magnified in us. The more time we spend in His presence, the more we become aware of the depths of our sin. This is why when we got saved, those who used to run *with* us ran *from* us. The Light convicts. Merriam Webster says to be *convicted* is the state of being convinced of error or compelled to admit the truth. **This is the judgment, that the Light has come into the world, and men loved the darkness**

rather than the Light, for their deeds were evil. For everyone who does evil hates the Light and does not come to the Light for fear that his deeds will be exposed. (John 3:19-20) Conviction brings with it either a response of submission or rebellion.

While in prison, I took some women to Isaiah 6 to help them understand a right response to the holiness of the true God. When faced with the revelation of God's holiness, Isaiah, the awestruck prophet of God, fell in true worship before God's throne. Isaiah could have said that God's holiness was an awe(full) thing. When speaking about the judgment of God, the author of Hebrews rightly understood God's holiness when he said, "It is a terrifying thing to fall into the hands of the living God." The context is judgment in Hebrews 10:26-31.

Teaching Bible studies for years and spending time in prison, I have had numerous occasions to encounter women who appeared to embrace the truths of the gospel only to eventually turn and walk away, wanting nothing to do with true Christianity. At one point in time, they denounced false religion and its teaching and then sat under biblical teaching. They *looked and sounded like* Christians. After a period of time, it became painfully obvious that they, like Judas, never truly did believe. **They went out from us, but they were not really of us; for if they had been of us, they would have remained with us; but they went out, so that it would be shown that they all are not of us.** (1 John 2:19). The context of the passage in Hebrews 10:26-31 is regarding those who hear the truth of the gospel, appear to embrace it, but then they turn away from it rejecting it completely. The only thing anyone who turns away from Christ can ever expect is judgment. True salvation is not about what happened at one point in time years ago. True salvation continues to manifest itself in the life of a believer.

This ominous warning is also in Hebrews: **For we know Him who said, "VENGEANCE IS MINE, I WILL REPAY." And again, "THE LORD WILL JUDGE HIS PEOPLE."** (Hebrews 10:30) The word for *judge* is **krino** which means to decide, to determine, or to condemn. **Krino** is the root of English words like *critic* and *critical*. The basic meaning of **krino** is to form an opinion after separating and considering the particulars of a case. **Krino** means to evaluate and determine what is right, proper, and expedient for correction.

The reason God has a right to judge His creation is because He is holy. His wrath against sin is right and just. So many today think that God can't be a God of wrath because He is a God of love. That is because they do not understand the holiness of God. If they did, they would know that the wrath of God as judgment for sin against ultimate love is a great example of where the punishment perfectly fits the crime.

Puritan John Owens gave us an understanding of the word *terrifying* speaking of eternal damnation when he said: "People are prone not to think about this. But God's judgment exists and will be dreadful, terrible, and eternally destructive of everything that is not good. To **fall into the hands** of someone is a common expression and refers to anyone falling into and under the power of his enemies. When a person falls into the hands of his enemies, there is no law or love between him and them; and he can expect nothing but death. This is what it is to *fall into the hands of the living God*. There is nothing in the law and there is nothing in the Gospel for one to appeal to in order to stop the punishment."[4]

Prisons and the world, in general, are full of people playing 'Christian'. Because God is holy, and judgment is real, we must get serious about God's holiness. I remember listening to someone read the sermon by Jonathan Edwards entitled, *Sinners in the Hands of an Angry God*.[5] I have no doubt Mr. Edwards was trying to literally scare the hell out of his listeners.

The first time my eyes were opened wide to the holiness of God I was reading that passage of Scripture in Isaiah 6. Spiritually prostrated and weeping before the throne of grace, I thought of this holy God who had beckoned me to come into His presence and worship Him. I knew that my sin made me unworthy to stand in His presence. Identifying with Isaiah, I cried, *Lord, I too am undone!* The only acceptable response to the holiness of God is deep, reverent worship and a cry for mercy. As a Christian living in prison, it was inevitable that I would worship this holy God often amidst circumstances I did not understand. What I did understand was that I was a woman of unclean lips who was living among other women of unclean lips before the eyes of holy God.

God is separate and distinct from His creation. We often lose our breath at the beauty of His creation—a majestic mountain, the brilliant colors of a garden full of unique spring flowers, the glow of a sunset as it closes out a day of satisfying time spent with loved ones, or the birth of a child. We can see each of these things in our mind's eye and each picture brings a smile to our faces with a sigh of peaceful contentment. I have sat beside the ocean in awe of the mighty power of God as I see the waves crashing in front of me knowing that His hand has created every grain of sand on its shore. But nothing in God's creation, even man who has been created in His image, compares to holy God who is perfect in every way. The holiness of God includes all His perfection and His glory. In fact, His glory is the reflection of His holiness, along with all His other attributes. His holiness *should* make us tremble in awe and reverence causing us to bow down to His sovereign rule over all His creation.

Part of the bad news of the gospel is that God is holy, and I am not; therefore, I cannot stand in His presence on my own merit. That presents the ultimate dilemma for all of mankind. Also, God is in control of all things, and I am not—even though I often want to be, which is to attempt to usurp His place on His throne. Man is in a desperate condition. And ***that*** is news you can trust!

4
It's the Law, Ma'am, and His Law Is Just!

I grew up in a nominal or in name only "Christian" home; so in my youth, I equated being a Christian with being an American citizen. (I kid you not.) Ironically, I am beginning to understand how this wrong thinking develops in people. However, patriotism does not equal Christianity! Joining the church in sixth grade, I was part of the children's choir before that, occasionally attended Sunday School, and **always** attended church on Christmas Eve and Easter. After all, when else could we show off our cute, new outfits? Back then, my mom told me we were known as what some called "C & E Christians", as if that was a status of which we could be proud. Sadly, fun fashion and a good feeling of self-righteousness were the only things I associated with going to church on those occasions.

When my Aunt died at age 32 (I was in second grade), my paternal grandmother told me about heaven. I don't know that anyone ever told me about heaven before then, or maybe it just didn't have any meaning for me before that time. I do know our talk planted tiny truth seeds in my heart that would start to grow years later. My grandmother went to church every week and taught me hymns. Somehow, that was a comfort to me. There was something about *her* church attendance that gave me a sense of stability and roots. After church, dressed in her Sunday finest, she would prepare a large meal for her whole family while we waited for that meal and the fellowship of family around her table. On countless Sundays, we all gathered in her large home we called 'the big house' and then her small mobile home later in life. Grandma, the most holy person I knew, would never let us eat before saying 'the blessing'. Some of my best memories are of times spent with my cousins at Grandma's house. I associated heaven with Grandma; and because she was going there, surely, I would go there too. Cartoons taught me that hell was a place bad people went to live with the devil.

My sister would tell you she was the 'rebellious' one. As the rule keeper, I rarely took risks. The truth was, I did not want to get in trouble because I was too afraid of what people thought of me. My fear of 'the law' was for all the wrong reasons. I spilled my guts in confession to my parents because I could not stand the guilt a minute longer when I did something I knew was wrong. (My sister and I have had a few laughs regarding the irony of our lives.)

Imagine my surprise when I heard the gospel for the first time one day and realized that not only was I a sinner because I was born in Adam, I was one who broke God's Law daily. In prison, I struggled with this one fact repeatedly: Knowing my sinful condition, I did not believe that I broke any laws of the United States of America of which I was accused. While guilty of hellfire, I was not guilty to stand trial and do prison time. Yet, that is what happened, it was part of God's plan, and I needed to embrace it from His loving hand. I needed to come to terms with ultimate justice which is His alone and will come in His perfect time. God's justice, just like His holiness, is an awesome and terrible thing.

For years after my release, because of my 'run-in with the law', I had to work through new fears pertaining to the law—or at least uniformed men and authority figures who represent the law of our great nation. My boss asked me once if I was fearful of people in my neighborhood or those whom I would encounter on my walk to work who appeared to be somewhat hardened. Struggling to ask the question, she was surprised by my immediate answer which was, "Not a bit." Sharing with her some of my prison stories, I told her of how I came to love those whom God had put in my path—some I slept underneath for years. Prison, in some ways, toughened me up—or at least made me less naive. In many ways, I came to identify with my fellow inmates. What I did not tell her was my struggle now revolved around a fear of those who are *supposed* to protect me; I didn't think she would understand that because I didn't understand it myself. I was raised to believe Romans 13:1-7, even before I knew the passage existed. As a Christian, I especially believe and embrace these truths, today more than ever. In fact, I want to share with you an excerpt of a nine-page letter I wrote to our judge on behalf of my husband.

I fully believe that every citizen of this world is to be in subjection to the governing authorities and that there is no authority except from God, and those which exist are established by Him as ministers of God to me for my good. Therefore, I respect the ruling power and authority which has been given to you by the One who is sovereign overall. Consequently, as a servant of my God who approaches His majesty with fear and reverence, I humbly pray that you would allow me to speak to you as I would my Lord.

The first time I was in your courtroom, I was terrified and quite shaken due to the overwhelming awesomeness of its regal-like atmosphere. Afterwards, as I thought of how your courtroom was to me just a glimmer and glimpse into what the very throne room of God will be like, I broke down in tears, awestruck by the thought of the majestic courts of heaven and one day standing before the Sovereign Judge of all creation. As I have meditated on the parallels between what is to be the representation of His courtroom in heaven and what I know to be truth revealed in Holy Scripture, the difference is in how I long with complete exhilaration for that day when, knowing that I have been fully pardoned, justified, declared righteous because of Christ's work on my behalf, I will worship the majesty of the One who will right all wrongs done to His children in this lifetime and render perfect judgment that will stand unchallenged for all eternity. The Judge over all judges is a perfectly just God, but He is merciful and gracious and looks with compassion on those who repent of their sin before Him and turn to Him believing that He is who He says He is and who trust Him fully for their eternal life.

God Himself is judge over all, for the world is His and all it contains. He is coming to judge the earth, and He will judge the world with righteousness for He alone can judge the thoughts and intentions of every heart. I know that those who contend with the Lord will be shattered and that one day He will right all wrongs. I believe that He will execute judgment upon all and convict all the ungodly of all their ungodly deeds which they have done in an ungodly way. I believe that the sentence rendered on that day will be for all who refused to repent before Him eternal hell. This is the God I fear. This, too, is the God my husband fears and serves with complete abandon and desire to please. While we are not perfect and still sin daily in thoughts and actions, we are forgiven and strive to live lives that glorify and please Him. (In fact, the worst part of the last five years for our family is that we have brought reproach on the name of our great God.) And all who know this God also know that although He is perfectly just, He is just as perfectly rich in mercy, compassion, slow to anger, abundant in lovingkindness and truth, pouring out grace to those who could never deserve or merit it by anything they could ever do or not do.

You are to be His representative of judgment with mercy to His people on earth. As one who wholly depends on the promises of God to look with favor on those who throw themselves on His mercy and acknowledges the efficacy of the atoning sacrifice of His Son, Jesus Christ, for my redemption, I also realize that you, Judge, are an instrument in His hands to also be used for His glory and honor. I also realize that it is a grave responsibility…

At the time, I was concerned with two things—to be a good witness of the truth, and to help the judge get to know my husband. I now realize that what could have been construed as an admission of guilt for what I was accused of, was simply a Christian who knows she is a saved sinner. I was never given the chance to explain any of it. And even though our judge entered it as evidence in our case, he also demanded that no testimony be given as to our Christian beliefs or worldview. Much testimony was encouraged to shed light upon my upbringing, so long as 'religion' was not brought into that testimony. I probably should have seen the handwriting on the wall long before I did. So did this 'testimony' hurt me? Maybe to an earthly extent, it did—but never in a spiritual sense. What I know for certain is: **Everyone** must do *something* with the truth. And there are only two options. Either one will embrace the truth, proclaim it boldly, and find grounds for fellowship with those who do likewise; or he will reject the truth, finding common ground with others who also reject it. According to Scripture, those who reject the truth will persecute those who believe.

In His chambers before our hearing, our judge said, "This case will not be about religion. Religion is **not** relevant." I agree religion, *as most men know it*, is **not** relevant. But relationship with the living God, which is life to me, is the only thing that truly matters. Interestingly, the longstanding right of being sworn in as a witness with one's hand on the Bible testifying to: "Tell the truth, the whole truth, and nothing but the truth, *so help you God*," is no longer relevant either! Now, one just swears to tell the truth. You, apparently, are your own standard of truth! This explains a lot.

A timid and somewhat fearful person, I have always liked to think of myself as cautious and aware of potential dangers around me. Nevertheless, over the last thirteen years, I have been dealing with it as sin. **For God has not given us a spirit of timidity, but**

of power and love and discipline. (1 Timothy 1:7) Another way of saying this is that God has not given us a spirit of fear, but of power, love, and a *sound mind*. My mind is sound as much as it stands upon the foundation of truth found in Scripture. Satan loves to shoot fiery arrows at me to try and mess with my sound mind. Not long after I was released from prison, I began having flashbacks. Maybe your prison is your past, and you have flashbacks too. I have learned to plant my feet firmly upon the Rock and force myself to look at these enemy missiles through the lens of truth, which is the only way to kill a flashback, or any tormenting thought, when he attacks.

A couple of years after I was released from prison, my boss and I were sitting and chatting at work when, out of the corner of my eye, I saw uniforms walking towards us just as I heard loudly broadcasted, "We have a search warrant." For a moment, I sat paralyzed— unable to move or speak, fearful that my heart would literally burst from my chest. I was not breaking the law. The thought that I had never even crossed my mind. As it turned out, the security guards were just playing a silly joke on us. At the time, I was living with my two youngest sons. When I came home and told the boys what had happened, my middle son said, "You do not have to be afraid of the law if you did not break the law!" I shouted back, "That's what I thought when I was indicted!" He could not argue with that, but he *is* right. I do not need to fear man at all. I need to fear God alone.

The first three years I lived in California, I was employed by a local Christian university as a clerk in their mail room. One day, a faculty member came into the mail room to pick up some packages. After he left, my boss and I realized he had forgotten one. So close to Christmas, I grabbed the package and took off just as he was driving down the street. Between me and the street was a large open piece of ground with beautiful grass. Before my feet left the pavement, I stopped abruptly without stepping on the grass. Why? At times, we were not allowed to walk on certain areas of grass in prison, and I had to filter that through my sound mind. The sound of keys rattling was somewhat unsettling for me for quite some time. (It is good if you do not understand that reference.)

Searching my heart, I realized: I still love the law, and I have a reverent fear of authority. Authority can be misused for evil which can cause us to wrongly fear man. Even though authority can be misused for evil against me, God still sustains me and is in control because He is the ultimate authority and promises to right all wrongs in His time. Standing on that truth brings peace to my heart in this situation. Though wicked men and fools do not fear Him now, one day they will all bow the knee to His authority as Lord.

It is the *circumstances* I associate with the police that cause my heart to be anxious. Police came to our home tasked with bearing the heart-wrenching news of Melissa's death (they were wonderful, the circumstances were crushing), and police stormed our home three times during our indictments. Twice, officers held a large gun to my son's back as they held him against the wall until they did a quick search of the home. *Coincidentally(?)*, on the first occasion, we had a meeting scheduled with a trust attorney in Pittsburgh for that very morning. My two younger sons were sitting at the kitchen table eating breakfast and getting ready to do a couple of homeschool assignments before we left. Suddenly, my middle son came running back to the bedroom in a state of panic, "Dad, there are like 100 police cars coming up the driveway!" There *were* a lot. So police presence can be a bit unsettling for me until I rehearse what I know to be true through my mind's truth grid.

When I first came to California, we lived in very close proximity to the house next door. On several occasions I would suddenly become aware of flashing lights and sirens extremely close by as the police arrested one of our neighbors. Other times, helicopters flew overhead with searchlights scanning our yard and nearby streets. One morning I was getting ready to walk out my front door when I heard what sounded like gunshots and someone breaking down doors. Apparently, someone forgot to clue me in that there was a popular television show being filmed right outside my front door. My thoughts? *Toto, we are not in Ligonier anymore.*

While incarcerated, I heard girls talking about the officers in disrespectful ways. That didn't shock me. It's what they said that gave me pause. They would say things like, "Why should I respect him? He doesn't respect me." *Seriously? You would sound incredibly foolish saying, 'I don't respect you for this,' when that same guard is putting handcuffs on you!* It is the *position* of authority we must respect, regardless if the person is worthy of respect. Quite frankly, none of us are worthy of the respect we *think* we deserve.

I'm sure there have been presidents or government officials whose policies you have liked and supported—some you have agonized over all the while they were in office. Nonetheless, the President of the United States is to be respected because of the authority of his office—even if you believe he is the worst president in the history of our country—because God established the principles of authority. Romans 13 says that God ordains all authority. In John 19:11, Jesus speaking to Pilate, boldly stated: **"You would have no authority over Me, unless it had been given you from above; for this reason, he who delivered Me to you has the greater sin."**

He puts leaders and rulers in place for His purposes. Therefore, to submit to those in authority, unless they are proposing what is against the *ultimate* authority, is to submit to God. We must trust that God is ruling over all His creation for good. The ever-growing lack of respect for the greatest position of authority in our country today reveals the fact that we are in real trouble as a nation. That lack of respect has gotten progressively worse in my lifetime.

We are to have a *right* fear of the law—a reverence for the authority for which the law stands. When I start to allow that unfounded fear of the law to overtake me, I have learned to direct it where it rightly belongs. There is a law that is even greater than the law of our land, and that is God's Law. We must fear the One who alone has the authority to enforce this Law.

Jesus told His disciples, **"Do not be afraid of those who kill the body and after that have no more that they can do. But I will warn you whom to fear; fear the One who, after He has killed, has authority to cast into hell; yes, I tell you, fear Him!"** (Luke 12:4-5) **The conclusion, when all has been heard, is: Fear God and keep His commandments, because this applies to every person. For God will bring every act to judgment, everything which is hidden, whether it is good or evil.** (Ecclesiastes 12:13-14) The Bible tells us that the fear of the Lord is the beginning of wisdom. With the fear of God in our hearts, we no longer need to fear man in any position of authority.

Can you stand before Almighty God and tell Him you have kept His Law perfectly? Even as a young, unbeliever I would have known I had not kept the commandments if they had been broken down for me as Jesus did in His Sermon on the Mount in Matthew,

Chapters 5-7. I couldn't even keep my parents' rules without at least *wanting* to rebel. What does the Bible say about those who do not keep His Law? The Bible calls sin *lawlessness*. Those who practice lawlessness will be thrown into the Lake of Fire where there will be never-ending torment. We should do everything we can to find out how we may escape the horrors of hell before it is too late.

The Lord sustained me in prison. He brought me through that test of faith and very dark night of my soul. What seemed like an eternity separated from those I love was less than four short years. My oldest son has been imprisoned for eight years, now, and my husband for nine. Even when it might not seem to them that God cares, He is with them and is sustaining them. Who will sustain the souls condemned to hell for all eternity? They will *not* be sustained. God will never abandon—He will never leave nor forsake—His own children. This same God is Lord, the Judge of all the universe; He has all authority to cast into eternal hell those who practiced lawlessness—those who broke His Law with no regard.

Since experiencing the prison test in my life, I have observed reactions in numerous professing Christians before and after that have, quite frankly, shocked me. Truth be told, it may have been my reaction at one time too. While I would expect a similar response from non-believers, Christians should be different. Let me pose a question that I would ask you to answer honestly in your heart. Think of any recent high-profile legal case in the news. What was your immediate gut-level reaction to hearing the details of someone being investigated or having been indicted? Did you believe the news just because it was being reported as news? Did you have a 'Crucify' mentality? Were you secretly relishing in the *details* of someone else's fall from grace? Were your first thoughts, "I thank God I'm not like…"? Did you widen the circle of this report? Or did you stop to pray for this one, for justice to be had, saddened by the reminder and reality of man's bondage to sin in the world?

It would seem that very few people respond with an attitude of grace by giving the accused the benefit of the doubt in assuming they are innocent until being **proved** guilty. Most will probably disagree with me—at least until they experience or know someone who may experience a similar situation, but I would venture to say that we have a very big problem in our country involving our judicial process (although that's nothing new under the sun). **Nor can they prove to you the charges of which they now accuse me.** (Acts 24:13) **After Paul arrived, the Jews who had come down from Jerusalem stood around him, bringing many and serious charges against him which they could not prove…** (Acts 25:7) We can read the ultimate account of Jesus in the Bible—after the fact. We can easily see that all these men in Scripture were falsely accused and tried in kangaroo courts with sham proceedings…when we know **all** the facts. It is easy for us to now see their innocence. What did their newspapers say? How did the people in their day react? Much the same as our own. It is human nature to be quick to point the finger at the guilt of others. Somehow shifting the focus off our own sin, it makes us feel better about ourselves.

Here is the irony of the case involving my son and me. The general public was quick to believe the newspaper just because it was supposedly a reputable newspaper reporting the stories. A civil judge argued, *as a source reference*, newspaper articles that claimed something other than what my husband's defense counselor was offering as facts. However, a jury was *not* supposed to believe it was logical for **us** to give that same kind of trust to my husband in his role of head over our family based upon our biblical beliefs and our history with him. Even further, we were *not* supposed *to trust* several lawyers (supposed officers of the court) who facilitated the actions that led to our indictments years after my husband was indicted. We **were supposed to believe** the newspaper allegations and the 'fact' that countless professionals including businessmen, tax accountants, major accounting firms, lawyers, bankers, and investment bankers were also allegedly 'duped by my husband'. A lot of confusing loose threads, to be sure! Jumping ahead just 14 years later, it all makes more sense with the hidden agenda and obvious push by the mainstream media to get people to believe a false narrative continually being shoved down our throats.

Shift your attention to a **fictional** scene in heaven. Satan, that accuser of the brethren, has presented you, dear Christian, before the throne of God as a lawbreaker. His minions are behind him cheering him on and adding to the charges as they begin to stack up. The Judge, having already made up his mind, pretends to be interested in the trial while trying desperately to stay awake.

Defense Counsel puts you on the stand to stand alone, never coming to your rescue or defense, even though He is armed with all the truth He needs to stop the mouths of your accusers. The jury only ever hears one side of the story. The powers that be have seen to that. When the trial is over, the Judge, as a formality, rules with the masses and chooses to convict based upon circumstantial evidence, and you are sentenced to hell. You say, "That's absurd." It certainly is!

What you may also think is absurd (but is not), is that many whom you have judged quickly here on earth were given trials and tribulations—by a greater Judge than any earthly judge—that caused suffering as part of a greater plan—a perfect plan *meant* to break them, to turn them towards the One who would one day cause them to be able to stand in the day of judgment. Many who served time in prisons on earth will be able to stand on that day because of the salvation that came to them in their own prison trial. I will rejoice with them knowing that even though our circumstances may not have been exactly the same, I have shared in the fellowship of their sufferings as their sister in Christ. How many of their accusers will *not* be able to stand but only to wonder in awe?

Judgment in God's Court for the believer will **never** look like the above scenario. Like Job, the believer may endure many trials and tribulations all for God's good purposes here and now, never understanding why; but when judgment day comes, he will never stand alone. The unbeliever, however, will have no defense in that day. There will be judges, kings, and multitudes of VIPs this world has known and loved unable to stand as well.

A day of judgment is coming. That is *not* fiction. Who will have confidence to be able to stand in that day of judgment? **Whoever confesses that Jesus is the Son of God, God abides in him, and he in God. We have come to know and have believed the love which God has for us. God is love, and the one who abides in love abides in God, and God abides in him. By this, love is perfected with us, so that we may have confidence in the day of judgment; because as He is, so also are we in this world. There is no fear in love; but perfect love casts out fear, because fear involves punishment, and the one who fears is not perfected in love.** (1 John 4:15-18)

One may say, "I believe in God and I have always loved Him, so surely I will be okay." But what *exactly* do you believe? We say we believe in a lot of things. A popular slogan today simply says, 'Believe'. *Believe* what? Similarly, we say we *love* our home, our dog, or our morning coffee. But what does it mean to *love* God? What is your definition of love, and why does your definition matter?

American citizens who love their country obey the laws of this land. Marriage vows once used the phrase, 'love and obey'. Children who love their parents want to obey them. When correcting my children, as a young mother, I often thought: *If you love me, you will obey me.* Love and obedience go together. Why is that so hard for us to understand when it comes to loving God? After marking the words *love* and *obey* in John 14 and 15, I had a woman say to me after Bible study one morning, "Wow, I never realized that the Christian life had so much to do with obedience." Jesus tells us our love for Him is manifested in our obedience to Him.

Within God's Law is a call to obey governmental authorities. We should obey our governmental authorities so long as they do not call us to sin, even if they are wicked rulers, because God is the ultimate Judge. I will have another day in Court—the Court of heaven—when all wrongs will be made right by the One who knows all and sees all. He knows what is in the hearts of all men. I know I will be vindicated before all men, even before those who did not or would not see the truth regarding the charges brought against me in an earthly court of law.

Matthew 5:48 calls us to be holy as God is holy. Jesus has been telling His disciples in the Sermon on the Mount what holiness looks like. If you want to understand the heart of the gospel, read and meditate on Matthew 5-7. These truths are impossible to realize in our own strength. (Incidentally, we *do* act on what we believe. Our belief system *does* dictate our actions. So if we believe God's Word is true and right because it is God's Word, then we will have a heart towards obedience out of love for Him.) Jesus begins by elaborating on 'blessings' we would not ordinarily associate with joy such as the blessings of those who mourn and are persecuted. Speaking to those who were raised to know the Law as revealed in the Old Testament, He rocks their worlds by bringing the Law, as they had understood it, to its logical conclusion of absolute moral perfection. Sins such as adultery and murder become heart issues for every one of us to deal with. Jesus says lusting after another or getting angry at another bears the same guilt as those desires enacted upon and getting carried out to their ultimate fulfillment.

Now we are made painfully aware that it is not only our *actions* that condemn us but our *attitudes* and *thoughts*. These heart issues are those our world casually justifies and jokes about. Our world has come to emulate and even exalt these attitudes. And if we are honest, sometimes we do too. Our flesh wants to rationalize them away as no big deal because no one can see them. Once we understand that these internal sins offend a holy God as much as the outward ones, the 'big ten' become an insurmountable obstacle that we would rather not think about. These are hard truths that Jesus calls us to obey.

God Requires Perfect Obedience to His Law

God's people have always been called to holiness. **Then the Lord spoke to Moses, saying: "Speak to all the congregation of the sons of Israel and say to them, 'You shall be holy, for I the Lord your God am holy.'"** (Leviticus 19:1-2) **Thus, you are to be holy to Me, for I the LORD am holy; and I have set you apart from the peoples to be Mine.** (Leviticus 20:26) Some would be quick to point out that this is from the Old Testament. They would say that because we are under grace, God does not expect perfect righteousness from us today. But in 1 Peter 1:14-16, we find this command reiterated to us: **As obedient children, do not be conformed to the former lusts which were yours in your ignorance, but like the Holy One who called you, be holy yourselves also in all your behavior; because it is written, "YOU SHALL BE HOLY, FOR I AM HOLY."**

Leviticus 20:26 uses the phrase, *set you apart*, which means to divide, separate, or make a distinction. This is the same Hebrew word used in Genesis 1:4 when God separated the light from the darkness. God's people are to be as different from others as day is to night. It is the same word used in Isaiah 59:2: **But your iniquities have made a separation between you and your God, and your sins have hidden His face from you so that He does not hear.**

Remember the purpose of the veil in the Temple? In Exodus 26:33 it was said to be a partition between the holy place and the holy of holies. *Set you apart, separation,* and *partition* are all the same Hebrew word. Notice in the Leviticus passage that it is God who has done the setting apart. What does He set His people apart from in this Isaiah 59:2 passage? The peoples. He is referring to those pagan nations around them who did not know Him as their God.

Part of believing in God is believing that He has set me apart for Himself in salvation. He has separated me from my old way of life. He has caused this change in me, and I am no longer my own. In prison, I was separated, even though it would have *appeared* I was anything *but* separated. I had to separate myself at times by not choosing to participate in things that were not holy. But I did not fit in there, and people around me knew it. Where the light shines, the darkness must flee because the light has no fellowship with darkness. In the darkness of my surroundings, the Lord was never more real to me. Jesus said in the Sermon on the Mount that the pure in heart are blessed because they will see God. They will see God with the eyes of faith in this life, but they will literally see Him in heaven for all eternity.

To believers suffering fierce persecution, Peter puts forth the call for holiness in 1 Peter 1:14-16. During times of intense suffering, we must keep our minds set on pursuing holiness. Tough times often burden us with greater temptation to succumb to sin. It would be in those times when we are most distracted by difficult circumstances that we are tempted to take our focus off God. Peter knew this firsthand. When he kept his focus on Christ, he could walk on the water by faith. When his focus shifted to the storm raging around him, he started to sink. Suffering in trials can lead to great waves of doubt and lack of trust in the promises of God to deliver His best for us. So the absolute, hardest time for us to pursue holiness is when we are deeply entrenched in suffering. This is also when we realize we are most dependent upon Him to do a work of sanctification in our lives that at any other time we might be tempted to believe we could accomplish on our own.

Could it be that the best opportunities to glorify God present themselves in these seasons of greatest weakness? During hardship, the flesh is tempted to look back longingly at the way things were before we were saved. And let's face it; unlike what is being preached in so many churches today, the call to live for Christ is not a call to a life of ease, comfort, and pleasure. It's a call to embrace all that God ordains for our lives (including suffering), just as our Lord embraced His suffering on our behalf. But make no mistake about it, the world is watching us closely when we suffer because even though we are separated, we are human. Those who don't know God are watching to see if He makes a difference in our pain. As an opportunity to greatly glorify our Lord, we must view suffering as a gift of grace to embrace from His loving hand. That truth takes the eyes of faith to be able to understand. We are not victims in those circumstances but objects of His great favor and grace. In a world flooded with a victim mentality, we must fervently cling to the cross of Christ, especially during troubled times. And we can know that while we are clinging, He is holding us with His forever grip.

For those who think we take the Bible far too seriously when we get down to the issue of sin, the question becomes: Are we to take God's Word literally when it says that everyone who is angry with his brother shall be guilty before God of the sin of murder? People go to anger management classes because they believe they have a disease, or they have been victimized in life and just need to learn twelve steps to control their anger. People no longer believe that killing a baby in the womb is murder, so how can anger be extended to the sin of murder? Further, not only are we not to commit adultery, which is a cultural norm today, but a man who even *looks* at a woman with lust is already guilty of adultery. While no one would dare ask Jesus those questions, specifically, the question that might come to mind is phrased like this: *He must mean something else, right?*

It is in this context, Jesus says, "Therefore, you are to be perfect, as your heavenly Father is perfect." There might be those who believe it to mean that we can live anyway we want today, because God will make us perfect when we get to heaven. While we *will* be fully glorified when we get to heaven, all by His grace, have no doubts about it—He begins that work at the time of our salvation. If there is no evidence to prove that work has begun, we must question whether our salvation is real. Perhaps, some think, Jesus was speaking to a different age. But taking Jesus at His Word, we are pierced through our hearts knowing that we have been called to that which is humanly impossible.

Man's human flesh won't allow this dilemma to stop him. We are human; therefore, we can and we must find answers. After all, we have been (wrongly) taught since we were young that we can do anything we set our minds to. We've been conditioned to believe that doing what is good always bestows upon us acceptance and rewards. In fact, we demand a trophy just for suiting up for the game! We want to be a part of the team, and surely most of the team can't be doing things wrong. Thinking positively, we pull ourselves up by our bootstraps and set about attempting to *just do our best* with the intention of pushing this outdated standard of Jesus far from our thoughts. Our 'logic' tells us that surely He would not command us to do something that is impossible; and if we just do our best, everything will work out. We reason or rationalize that it *must* mean something different, and we *cannot possibly* be called to interpret Scriptures like these literally. Right? Wrong!

Sadly, so many people, including professing Christians, wrongly believe that we must only be *good enough* to go to heaven, or to enter the Kingdom of God. The problem with that thinking is this: How good is 'good enough'? By whose standards is one measured 'good enough'? If I get to determine what is good and what is evil, then I can rationalize that what I am doing is not as bad as what others around me are doing. This makes me feel pretty good about myself. But that person can rationalize what he is doing is not as bad as the next person, and so on. If we are honest with ourselves, we all tend to shrug off our 'little' sins as no big deal. Realistically, however, the standard for making the judgment between good and evil naturally lies with God, because it is His kingdom. And God's standard is that we be perfect or holy.

In James 2:10, James elaborates on Jesus' teaching about the moral Law and takes it a step further by saying that whoever keeps the whole Law and yet stumbles in one point has become guilty of all. In other words, if I sin just one time, I am guilty of breaking God's Law. If one breaks the law one time, that one is a lawbreaker. You can try to tell yourself you are a good person in every other way, but in that one sin you have become a lawbreaker.

Romans 1 tells us we were born understanding there was a Creator because we can see His creation. God gave us a conscience so that we can know morally what is right from wrong. So there is no excuse when we sin against God by treating Him as anything other than God, the Sovereign ruler over each of our lives. We sin when we break God's Law *because* it is God's Law.

Now putting your life up against God's Law, are you guilty or innocent? Have you had any wrong thoughts today? Have you treated God as God all day, thanking Him for every aspect of the day He has given you? We have all broken God's Law; therefore, we are all guilty before Him. Romans 6:23 says the wages of sin is death. The sentence for breaking God's Law is death. *Death* is eternal death, separated from God, experiencing the punishment of His wrath forever. Everyone dies, and they do not die the moment they sin. The verdict is in. We are all guilty as charged!

I remember an illustration John MacArthur used once on this passage in James 2:10. He said that we should think about God's Law as a chain made up of individual links. The chain requires perfect love for God and our neighbor. When we break one link in the chain, the whole chain is broken. He said we are sinners not because we commit sins but because we have a sin nature. So we commit sins because we are sinners.

When I was a little girl, my grandmother bought each of her granddaughters a charm bracelet and a new charm each year for Christmas. I can hang any charm I like on any link of my bracelet. But if there is one link broken in my bracelet, it will not matter what charms I hang on that bracelet, because I can't wear it. It is **useless** for the purpose for which it was created. In a manner of speaking, it was created to adorn or glorify my arm.

We are all guilty and have broken God's Law. But we are called to be holy as God is holy. As part of their new nature in Christ, Christians commit themselves to the pursuit of holiness. Obviously, we did not become holy, practically speaking, when we were saved. We have a desire to be holy as He is holy, but we still sin. In fact, the longer we pursue the holiness of God, the more we see the gravity of our sin.

One of the theme songs for the prison drug program was a popular "gospel" song with lyrics repeatedly referencing the power of Jesus' name to break every chain. Though the song was several minutes long, there were only three phrases in its entirety. Working in the chapel where the drug program met, I heard that song ad nauseam. It almost drove me insane with its use of repetition and the fact that it was being sung by a lot of professing believers and outright unbelievers alike. In unison they sang their hearts out to this false belief that man has the power in himself through claiming the name of 'Jesus' to break the chains of his sin. "But, Karla," some said, "It names the name of Jesus, how could it be bad?" First, no person in himself has the power to break the chains of his sin. (Unbelievers only have the power to break the chain of God's Law, as referenced above.) Secondly, the name of Jesus is not a magical incantation to be used to get Him to do the things we want Him to do. The chains and shackles of sin **can** be broken, but not by sheer willpower, determination, and strength from within ourselves. In fact, the chain of perfect fellowship between the Creator and His creation needs fixed, and we can do nothing to fix it. Better stated, it not only needs fixed but *replaced*. If we clearly understood our desperate need, we would not be *'rising up'*, but falling on our faces before a holy God begging Him for mercy to chain us to Himself!

My prison experience lent itself to a richness in my under-standing of man's true standing before holy God that I didn't have prior to my incarceration. In Ephesians 3:1, Paul said he was the prisoner of Jesus Christ. The word *prisoner* is one in bonds or one who is captive. In some of the prisons I was held, there were barbed wire walls to keep me in so that I could not escape. When I got to the camp where I would serve the bulk of my sentence, there were no walls—the law kept me there. One could literally walk out the gate and off the compound at any time. One inmate I served time with did just that and was caught within two weeks. We all knew she was wrong, but we all felt her pain. Any inmate who escapes incurs an automatic five years added to her sentence. In retrospect, she had very little time left to serve. To understand why anyone would risk doing that is to know the emotional pain of bondage and separation. To believe that any prison is 'like a country club' or could realistically be called 'Camp Cupcake' is pure ignorance.

In orientation, a unit manager told us, "We now own you!" My spirit rose up in rebellion. I'm sure my flesh was involved as well, or it would not have rubbed me the wrong way as much as it did. Of course, I could not shout out what I would have liked. *No one owns me but my Lord and Savior, Jesus Christ.* But in some sense, she was right. We *were* subject to their complete authority and rule over us in the context of doing time there; for whoever controls your freedom does, indeed, own you. Because our perspective is radically different, however, I like to think of it as the BOP being given stewardship over one of His children!

Working in the chapel, I found myself involved in interesting conversations with women who professed to follow Christ—women who should have understood what it means to be His bondservant. One such conversation that vividly stands out in my mind started out glorious, but went south fast at the mention of one word. From all appearances, this other woman was a believer. Our talk was invigorating, until I brought up this subject of being able to relate to what it means to be a prisoner of Jesus Christ. "Amen, sister," was her very loud, initial response. The conversation came to an abrupt end, however, when I referred to myself as His bondslave. As she stormed away, she spoke in sharp staccato, "I…am…nobody's… slave!"

While the judge (the law), the guards, the warden, and the Federal Bureau of Prisons maybe believed they controlled me, my life was under the sovereign control of God who gave me grace to submit my will to His and embrace the prison test from His hand. If anyone controlled me in prison, it was only because God allowed them to do so. And I was free in Christ to submit to them. Chained to Christ in His suffering took on new meaning each time I was shackled or handcuffed. Hearing what the Law demands of us can feel like we are being shackled and bound. The truth is the Law, if we let it do what it is intended to do, will lead us to freedom and eternal life.

5
Cursed!

People 'curse' people with their words every day. There was a day when a curse word was taboo. The audible gasps could easily be heard in response to words that were just not acceptable to most. There was a lack of tolerance for that which was definitively not right, and it was a better society because of it. Those days stand in stark opposition to what is accepted today.

In the small rural area where I grew up, all the kids knew where the 'witch' lived in town. I lived down over the hill, a little more than a stone's throw away from her house. In a different age, children as young as ten years old could walk to and from town day or night without any known threats of harm. It was a rite of passage and utmost privilege to be trusted enough to have that freedom to walk to the penny candy store or the local ice cream parlor for a frozen treat. My friends and I enjoyed making memories as we grew up together. However, I vividly remember scurrying past the 'witch's house' so as not to have a curse put on me.

Another thing we liked to do was to ride our bikes to the old weeping willow tree near 'the bridge'. We would sit there by the creek (pronounced 'crick') and talk for hours on hot summer days. It was a place of peaceful reflection. In order to get there, however, we had to pass several homes with multiple rebarbative deterrents. Eagerly standing on guard by these homes were ferocious dogs that seemed to run in packs. These conspiratorial dogs had a built-in radar to be able to sense when there would be kids on bicycles passing by. Possessing a misconception that this public road was somehow their territory to defend, they would aggressively appear out of nowhere with flashing eyes, bared teeth, growling, barking, and nipping at our legs. The chase would continue well beyond *their* properties.

Not to be outsmarted, as well as to save us from having a bite taken out of our legs, we learned to build up enough speed that we could lift our legs up onto the handlebars. In this position, we could coast far enough that the dogs would lose interest and give up their scheme to take us down. However, just as soon as the barking of the dogs faded from earshot, and right before our beloved weeping willow tree bridge, there stood a house with 'hex' signs hanging all over it. The lady who lived there painted and sold them. Legend was that anyone who bought a 'hex' sign was trying to put a curse on someone else. I grew up very cognizant of staying clear of anything having to do with curses (or crazy dogs). Come to think of it, a lot of houses displayed these 'hex' signs back then. Maybe even ours!

I can conclude from these fond memories: My parents' fear of what might happen to us as we walked into town was not greater than the desire to see us grow by letting us go. Our fear of passing the witch's house was not greater than wanting to exercise that freedom to go every opportunity we would get. The peace and rest offered by the trickling waters of the babbling brook, the gentle swaying of the weeping willow tree branches, along with the fellowship of friends, was worth paying the price of any obstacles of fear we might encounter along the way.

As a child, along with hearing about a 'curse' came a feeling of foreboding and a fear of the unknown. Remember the episode involving the tiki idol the Brady boys found on their family vacation to Hawaii? It was thought to have brought all kinds of curses upon them while in their possession. (Can you still hear that 'tiki idol' music?) I believe Vincent Price was added to the cast of that episode to give an extra flare of the eerie nature of curses.[1]

Superstitions aside, what is a curse? Who is cursed? One might venture to say that being falsely accused, convicted of a crime, and sent to prison was someone who had been cursed. Maybe if I had been outside of Christ I would have spent my time wondering and searching my memory for anyone who had put a curse on me or my family. The word *curse* is found many times in Scripture, more often in the Old Testament than the new. One Bible dictionary said that we are not to understand a curse pronounced against a person as a mere wish that something disastrous will happen to them. The curse itself was considered to possess inherent within it the power of carrying out the desired effect.[2] Curses were to doom someone or to imprecate evil upon them (from where we get *imprecatory* psalms).

People couldn't get enough of the titillating, front-page stories of Greg's case—as evidenced by the massive amount of newspaper coverage given it. Hungry to devour the juicy tidbits, they accepted as truth every morsel because, "Surely the newspapers could not be wrong." It appeared the prosecution was feeding the newspapers because news stories hit the stands before legal documents were ever filed. These same filings then regurgitated what was in the articles. When it came time for trial, the words then changed to, "Surely the government cannot be wrong." What's wrong with that picture?

What one must understand about judicial *due process of law* in our country is that a search of the premises of someone under investigation is made early on. In that search, most documentation is removed from the home. Thus, by the time it is received back from the government (if ever), the investigated has been indicted and is well on his or her way to either having already accepted a plea deal or in preparation for trial with little documentation or time with which to prove his innocence.

Years later, after we were already in prison, when my son was finally able to gather all the documented proof for our case, wanting to sit down and talk with a writer of a competing newspaper to explain the truth of our story and to give him that documented evidence, the response was: "Podluckys are old news." That is a very telling statement. After we went through the whole appeal process (which was farcical), our judge sat on our 2255 (claim of ineffective assistance of counsel) for three years without ruling upon it. We are in the process of appealing the 2255 which also appears to be coming to dead ends without any real explanation by the courts.

We certainly appeared to be a cursed family. But what if the average person picking up a daily newspaper, eager to feed on the supposed sins and fall of others, was equally cursed but did not know it? If he were to understand his own state, would the fall of others be so interesting then? What if the accusers and those who help propagate the 'news' were the cursed as well?

What exactly does Scripture have to say about curses? Are they real? Who is cursed? Cursed by whom? What does it mean to be cursed? *Cursed* is to be despised, devoted to destruction, consigned to harm or damnation.

God has called all mankind to keep His Law perfectly. We should realize that no one can possibly keep that Law perfectly. No one can be right with God by trying to keep the Law that he will never be able to keep perfectly. This is one place when trying your best will never be good enough. **For as many as are of the works of the**

Law are under a curse; for it is written, "CURSED IS EVERYONE WHO DOES NOT ABIDE BY ALL THINGS WRITTEN IN THE BOOK OF THE LAW, TO PERFORM THEM." (Galatians 3:10)

Cursed is who? Cursed is everyone. *Everyone* is despised, devoted to destruction, consigned to harm or damnation. Who is *everyone*? Cursed is everyone who does not abide by all things written in the book of the Law. Very simply stated, anyone who cannot keep God's Law perfectly is cursed. We are all cursed. You may not have gone to prison, but you too have offended holy God by breaking His Law. You are a criminal—not a federal convict, but a universal convict. You have been held in bondage under the Law and have been judged by the Law.

One prison job I had was serving on the salad bar crew in the dining hall. One day while waiting for the first crowd of girls to come down the hill for dinner, my co-worker was in a conversation with one of the guards. He had made a derogatory remark about 'inmates', and she angrily fired back, "You know, not everyone who is in here is guilty of what they were accused." He said in his southern drawl, "S-u-r-e." She pointed to me and said, "Well, I know for a fact Podlucky is innocent." Incidentally, she was one of my husband's co-defendants, and we became friends. He said with a wink, "Oh, r-i-g-h-t. Podlucky, have you ever run a stop sign?" I replied simply, "Have you?" The conversation ended abruptly. We have all broken *the* Law, God's Law. Cursed is everyone who has broken God's Law. The Law is not cursed, for the Law is good and right. The intent of the Law is to help us see where we fall short of God's will.

Who has cursed you? Is it Satan? Galatians 3:10 is Paul quoting Deuteronomy 27:26. Looking at Deuteronomy 27:1, Moses, as God's spokesman, is addressing the children of Israel saying, **"Keep all the commandments which I command you today."** In Chapters 27 and 28 he lays out the cursing and blessing associated with the covenant God is making with His people.

Whose Law is it we are commanded to keep? It's God's Law. Do you think Satan wants us to keep God's Law? He may try to deceive us into believing we **can** keep the Law. Satan uses two extremes to tempt us concerning God's Law. He tries to convince us that we can be right with God by striving to keep His Law; this may result in legalism. Or he may try to convince us that we do not need to keep the Law at all—that we are okay just the way we are. This leads to antinomianism (Greek **anti**, "against"; **nomos**, "law). These are both distortions of the Law. In any event, he has been around since the beginning tempting God's children to turn from obedience to sin.

In Genesis, we see that God gave Adam and Eve one law, if you will. He forbade them to eat from just one tree in the garden. Imagine a perfect world, what beauty and splendor there must have been, such abundance, a paradise like none of us have ever known. Fellowship with God was the acme of human fulfillment. God gave Adam this one command in Genesis 2:16-17: **From any tree of the garden you may eat freely; but from the tree of the knowledge of good and evil you shall not eat, for in the day that you eat from it you will surely die.**

You leave your children for the first time by themselves. They are old enough. You tell them all they *are* permitted to do, placing only one restriction on them. You have already guessed what I'm about to say next. What is the one thing they want to do? You have given them such freedom and grace! Yet, all they can think of is that one thing they know they are not allowed to do. We start to get an idea of how our flesh responds to the Law. So why do you leave them alone in the first place? Why do you let them walk into town? Why do you let them ride their bikes past the dogs? Because you have told them repeatedly what is right and what is wrong. You have *trained* them, and it is now time for all they have been taught to be put to the test. Will they obey, trusting you know best, or not? Their test, *whether they fail or whether they pass,* is all part of their growth process.

In the Garden of Eden, the serpent came along and convinced Eve that God was trying to put chains and shackles on them for that one thing they were not allowed to do. Keep in mind at that point, she was not imprisoned. But her flesh was like a caged animal reacting to imaginary chains and shackles. The flesh cries, "I must be free to do what I want to do. I must be free to do what I believe is right for me." Satan tried to get her to believe that God was holding back good from them by putting that subtle doubt in her mind to question the authority of God's Word. At that moment, she made a choice to believe the lie of the serpent as truth and to reject the truth of God. Choosing to do things her way, she invited her husband to do the same. The imaginary chains and shackles Adam and Eve feared when they were tempted to sin became real only after they sinned. When the Lord God confronted them with their sin, they began to play the blame game. And what followed immediately after? God said to the serpent: **"Because you have done this, cursed are you..."** (Genesis 3:14)

Everything now was under the curse. What was involved in the curse for Adam and Eve? Adam and Eve lost the righteousness they once knew. They now experienced separation from God they did not know prior to the Fall. Instead of walking with God in perfect fellowship, they hid from Him in fear and shame when they heard His voice. Immediately, there was spiritual death. Physically, there was going to be consequences of sin that had entered the world— hardship in life, no more paradise. From that day forward, they would experience pain and suffering as a normal part of life; and, eventually, physical death would come for them and all creation.

How do we know sin entered man from that point? Not much later we see the same sinful pattern in Cain and Abel, the children born to Adam and Eve. We see the evidence of sin in the need for animal sacrifice in worship, in Cain's rebellion in failing to worship God rightly, and also when he murdered his brother. We see death come to all, as God had promised. Sin had entered man. Sin would be in all of Adam's seed from the first to the last.

It came about in time that both Cain and Abel brought offerings to God. Cain, a tiller of the ground, brought from the fruit of the ground. Abel, a keeper of flocks, brought of the firstlings of his flock and their fat portions. It is not laid out for us in Scripture whether God previously laid down specific laws regarding how He should be worshiped. We do know that when Adam and Eve sinned, they first *tried to cover themselves* with fig leaves. Later, after having had their sin exposed, God made coverings of animal skins to cover them by sacrificing those animals. It should have been Adam and Eve who died, but God substituted the blood of animals in their place. This was a shadow of what was to come when God would provide the ultimate sacrificial substitute to redeem sinners.

Abel's offering was accepted by God, and the Lord was pleased. But with Cain's offering, God was not pleased. I believe these two brothers knew what was required in bringing an offering to God in worship. Abel worshiped God as required; Cain decided to do things his own way. That would lay down a premise in Scripture of true worship versus false worship, which has been the issue of all *religion* from that day to the present. Maybe Cain reasoned that working hard made him a good person which also made him acceptable and pleasing to God. Therefore, he chose to worship God by offering the fruit of his labor. Whatever Cain's motives were, worship is always an obedience issue because it reveals the heart. **Abel, on his part also brought of the firstlings of his flock and of their fat portions. And the Lord had regard for Abel and for his offering; but for Cain and for his offering He had no regard. So, Cain became very angry and his countenance fell.** (Genesis 4:4-5)

When confronted by God to repent of his false worship, Cain's attitude was anger. Cain's song is, "I did it my way, and I believe that should be good enough." Cain, like all false worshipers, chose to worship God his own way. What should have been Cain's reaction to God's grace in pointing out his error? Repentance. If God says something is not right in our actions, we must change. Cain did not treat God as God when he chose not to believe Him. If he had believed God, it would have shown in his obedience to Him. **By faith Abel offered to God a better sacrifice than Cain, through which he obtained the testimony that he was righteous, God testifying about his gifts, and through faith, though he is dead, he still speaks.** (Hebrews 11:4) Abel's offering to God was by faith, and his sacrifice was better than Cain's offering. From this Scripture we begin to see the problem appears to focus on *how* the offerings are given. There is a glaring unspoken distinction here between Cain and Abel. It is that Abel's offering was offered *by faith* which gave testimony to the fact that Abel was righteous. Faith is believing or trusting God. Faith obeys.

The principle we see here is that the one who does things the way God requires will be accepted; the one who does not obey will not be accepted. One will be accepted by God if he worships Him the *right* way—which is the way He says it is. Abel believed God. Cain's testimony is that his unrighteous actions proved he was of the evil one and did not believe God. Further, he killed his brother after refusing to repent. For a split second, it may have gone against your flesh when you read: *You will be accepted if you do things God's way, the right way.* Why would any believer have a negative reaction to that statement? Because our flesh wants to be accepted for who we are, just as we are. It is our spirit in tune with the heart of God that wants to do things **His way**. The flesh thinks: *I should not have to change who I am or the way I do things to be accepted by anyone—not even God.* Isn't that exactly what may have been going through Cain's mind at the time of his offering? This thinking comes from having a wrong view of ourselves—a high view—and thus, a low view of God. We err when we think God is just like us. **"These things you have done and I kept silence; you thought that I was just like you..."** (Psalm 50:21)

Many have been wrongly taught that it is we who "accept" Jesus. We would do better to be concerned whether God accepts *us*. Cain wasn't concerned about God accepting his sacrifice. He wasn't concerned about God at all, or he would have been obedient to Him. He didn't believe the Father knows best, but he listened to his own folly fed by the lies of his father, the devil. Cain created his own idea of god in his mind, and he worshiped that god (ultimately himself) how he wanted to worship. **For this is the message which you have heard from the beginning, that we should love one another; not as Cain, who was of the evil one and slew his brother. And for what reason did he slay him? Because his deeds were evil, and his brother's were righteous.** (1 John 3:11-12) In the Genesis text, catch the significance of what is going on, and do not miss God's grace in the next verses. **Then the LORD said to Cain, "Why are you angry? And why has your countenance fallen? If you do well, will not your countenance be lifted up? And if you do not do well, sin is crouching at the door; and its desire is for you, but you must master it."** (Genesis 4:6-7) I wonder at why the next sentence was added in the text. **Cain told Abel his brother.** (Genesis 4:8)

He may have wanted a little pity from a comrade who would agree with his 'side of the story'—his (wrong) belief that God was being too harsh and judgmental towards him in not accepting his offering. Cain's pride or ego was hurt, and he wanted it stroked! He may have reasoned his offering was an act of worship in "his own way". Sin loves company, especially if that support can be garnered from the light that stands separated and obedient. The father of lies knew he already had hooked Cain—maybe he could use him to get Abel to doubt God too. Scripture confirms Abel's witness. Abel stood firm in faith.

What grace the Lord extended to Cain when He gave him the opportunity to repent. He doesn't just kill him on the spot for his willful disobedience. When God corrects and disciplines, He always gives that reproof or correction with an offer of hope, which is pure grace. Because Cain went out and killed his brother, he clearly did not repent, thus revealing his rebellious, sin-infected heart. Cain was cursed, and his earthly judgment was found in Genesis 4:12 in a two-part sentencing: **When you cultivate the ground, it will no longer yield its strength to you; you will be a vagrant and a wanderer on the earth.**

Cain's judgment is seen not only in banishing him from God's presence, but in sending him away from a godly society. A vagabond or a fugitive all his life, he was now separated, set apart, and exiled to a prison of his own making. When we willfully choose to disobey, to do things our way instead of God's way—if we do not repent, turning from our wicked ways to obey God's ways—sin unchecked will lead to greater sin, greater bondage, and ultimately death.

Ladies, suppose your husband asks you what you want to do on Friday night for your anniversary. You tell him you want to go to dinner and walk along the beach afterwards. Friday night comes, and he takes you to an amusement park, which he knows you hate, but he loves. He has completely disregarded your request. Did he honor you? You told him what you wanted from him, but he dismissed it doing what he wanted instead.

Cain did not honor God as God, or he would have done *what* God wanted him to do *the way* He wanted him to do it. Cain did not believe God, because to believe is to obey. He did not love God, or he would have honored His Word. Cain told his brother about his conversation with God. Whatever the conversation was after that, Abel's siding with God was conviction that Cain could not handle. Cain's anger escalated to murder, and he killed his own brother.

The arrogant, often rude guard everyone loved to hate at the prison surprised everyone when he said everyone has broken the law, but not everyone gets caught. He is certainly right. To be found guilty of a crime in our country, there is an element of intent. One must know what he or she is doing is illegal in order to be rightly convicted of a crime. The intent to knowingly break the law involves our will. Had anyone…anyone at all…any lawyer who was involved or any government official…come to Jesse or I and said, "If you do this or that thing (*which your attorneys advised and even facilitated for you*), you will be breaking the law," we would never have gone against their advice. No, we were expected to believe the newspaper articles and the government accusations even before my husband and Jesse's father of 30-plus years was tried. While one might be able to stay on the right side of the law in our nation by being as obedient as possible, it is not the same in God's kingdom. Why? Because everyone is caught immediately, even if they don't know it, and even if punishment does not come instantaneously.

No one can be justified by keeping God's Law. Abel was not justified or right with God because he offered a right sacrifice. Both Cain and Abel knew how God wanted them to worship Him, and God gave Cain *ample opportunity to correct his error.* Abel obeyed—believing God, and acted in faith; Cain disobeyed—not believing God, and acted without faith. To disobey God is to believe that He doesn't get to make the rules because He is not Lord over all His creation. It is the created rebelling against his Creator. 'I'll do things *my way*' was worshiping the creation—*himself.* This was the evidence that his heart was not right. God alone deserves man's worship. It is rightfully due Him. When we do things our own way we are saying to God, "Get off Your throne, I am taking over my own life." To rightly understand God, one **must** worship Him.

Speaking about the Judaism of His day, Jesus quoted Isaiah 29:13 in Matthew 15:8-9. This same statement can be said of many denominations that 'profess' the name of Christ but have no true knowledge of Him—whose congregants have no relationship with Him. **"THIS PEOPLE HONORS ME WITH THEIR LIPS, BUT THEIR HEART IS FAR AWAY FROM ME. BUT IN VAIN DO THEY WORSHIP ME, TEACHING AS DOCTRINES THE PRECEPTS OF MEN."** (Matthew 15:8-9) In the text in Isaiah, God said men were drawing near to Him with their words (honoring Him with lip service), but had removed their hearts far from Him. Going through the motions of the religion they had been taught, their reverence for Him consisted of tradition learned by rote. *Tradition* is just another word for commandments made by men.

They had been taught these traditions by strict discipline. *By rote* means to goad with a rod or some form of incentive. It is used of striking or beating with a rod, especially beasts of burden. Have you ever been part of a church worship service like this? It is so scripted that you do not even have to think. Every part of the service has been memorized—what to say, when to say it, when to stand, and when to sit or kneel. This is nothing but worthless ritualism.

You and your husband are out on a date celebrating your 25th wedding anniversary. To the casual eye, he appears to be excited to be here with you tonight. He looks deeply into your eyes as though he is about to tell you of your great worth to him. Subtly, reaching into his pocket, he pulls out a script and begins to read. If that wasn't bad enough, the script clearly was not written by him. He pulled this speech off the internet many years ago. In fact, he hardly even looks at the pages because he has been quoting the same lines for more anniversaries than you care to remember. *You* have every sickening line of his speech memorized. A friend happens to walk by and says it's good to see you both. Your husband says, "We are celebrating our 25th wedding anniversary. Let me tell you about my wonderful wife." The friend listens uncomfortably as your husband starts to read all over again. Would you be offended? Would you question your relationship? Does he even know who you are? What if your husband says all the right things, but there is no passion; his words are devoid of all emotion. He tells you he loves you every single day—the same exact way—day in and day out. You know what he is going to say before he opens his mouth. There is no practical manifestation of his love for you other than things done routinely. If those scenarios were happening to us, we would question the sincerity of our husbands' love for us. Yet those two scenarios are exactly how multitudes of people sitting in churches treat God, the very Lover of their souls. Why is it so easy to see the problem when the situation is reversed towards how we expect to be loved?

You run into one of your husband's high school friends he has kept in touch with on a weekly basis over the years. You were all members of the same graduating class. You and your husband got married right out of high school, and you are hitting the 25-year milestone together. This friend asks what you have been doing since high school. A bit dismayed by the question, you proceed to tell him about your life with Bob. Shocked, this friend asks, "Wait, Bob so and so is your husband? Wow! I didn't even know you were married to him. He has never mentioned you to me."

In John 4:23, Jesus said true worshipers worship the Father in spirit and in truth. It's not enough to be passionate about worship. It's not enough to be diligent to habitually go to church and walk through the motions of traditions learned from birth. God must be worshiped in spirit and in truth. The heart of our worship which is passionate and zealous is based upon the fact that we know Him. We know Him from reading what He has revealed about Himself in His Word and then experientially as He works in and through our lives those same truths. It's having a relationship with God. And we love to tell people about Him and talk about Him often.

What was the difference in the offerings of Cain and Abel? Why did God accept one and not the other? Abel worshiped God from the heart and Cain did not. Abel believed God. Cain could sing his song, "I did it my way," all the way to hell. His heart attitude in worship was not right; or when given the opportunity to repent, he would have quickly responded in obedience. Even though no one is justified by the works of the Law, neither can one be justified by working his way to God his own way. There are not many ways to God. There is one way to God, and it is the way He says it is. Christians do not want to say, "I did it my way." We want to say, "I did it *His* way. I did it the way that pleased my Father."

In the book of Galatians, the Apostle Paul was trying to correct a wrong view of the true and saving gospel. His words were as foundationally true for the churches of Galatia as they are for us today. The people in Galatia had truly believed the gospel of faith alone by grace alone that Paul had preached to them. Then, men called Judaizers came in trying to persuade the people to believe a gospel that was distorted and, in fact, not the true gospel at all. They wanted the Galatians to add "the requirements, ceremonies, and standards of the Old Covenant as necessary prerequisites to salvation" (as John MacArthur says in the MacArthur study Bible, Galatians 1:6 note).[3] They were now being taught that faith **plus works** would save them and give them right standing with God. In response to this teaching, Paul says that anyone who teaches a gospel of works is to be accursed or cursed. The word for *accursed* is **anathema** (devoting someone to destruction in eternal hell). It has always been interesting to me that the Roman Catholic Church proclaims anathemas on anyone who ***does not*** believe in a faith plus works gospel (Council of Trent on Justification XXIV).[4] But Paul says anyone who believes the way to God is through faith plus works is cursed. Are we to believe God or the dogmas of man?

All religions in the world, except that of biblical Christianity, are based on a system of works righteousness. Religions that say, "If you do this or that you can *work* your way to eternal salvation or help *keep* your salvation," are works-based religions. Scripture ***clearly*** shows us this is false. No man can work his way to heaven by contributing anything to salvation. People in churches everywhere wrongly believe that because they have done all that their church requires, they have done enough to be right with God and go to heaven when they die. But **they** can never do anything that will make them right with God. He has made a way to *accept us*. We will continue to look at that way in the upcoming chapters. In summary, all men are called to keep God's Law perfectly, but it is not by keeping the Law by which we are saved.

Multitudes professing to follow Christ sit in churches week after week going through the motions of traditions learned by rote worshiping a false god of man-made religion, and their hearts are far from the true and living God of Scripture. Having never bothered to study His Word, they don't know Him. Many believe the lie that they can't understand God's Word unless a priest interprets it for them. When confronted by the truth, they will not believe but will continue to do things their own way, unless the Lord opens their eyes to understand the truth. Not only is their worship rejected by God, they have been deceived into believing it is ***enough*** and that they are on a broad road marked, "This Way to Heaven," with multitudes who walk with them. In reality, that road leads to hell. Every true believer has lived under the same delusion and status before God, until at some point in his life, God saved him.

Fact: The masses have never believed the Bible or believed in the God of the Bible. Even while giving lip service to the claim that they do believe the Bible, they do not know Scripture or the One who wrote it. They do not know *Him*. Born in sin, rebels at heart, we want to be our own god, calling our own shots, living for ourselves and our glory alone. We **want** the world to revolve around us. That's the nature of sin. We are born spiritually dead and blind. Hopelessly held in bondage to this sinful nature—and left alone to our sinful selves—we are imprisoned in a world where we are not even aware of the bars or boundaries that hold us captive. Deceived by sin, Satan, the world, and even our own hearts, we believe we are free to live our own lives any way we choose. But what does Scripture have to say about our sinful condition? How can we be held accountable to God and His Law when we don't know what He wants? Wouldn't it be better to stay ignorant? Couldn't we claim ignorance on judgment day? Romans 1:18-32 says **there will be no excuse because we *do* know**. There is no excuse. All stand condemned and convicted. All are cursed. Standing in the courtroom listening to a jury's decision, condemned and convicted by men, is a sick, devastating feeling. That is one thing. It is quite another to stand condemned and convicted by Almighty God. It would be helpful to stop and read all of Romans 1 now.

The one who lays down the law has the authority to enforce that law. God's Law is the ultimate Law because He is the ultimate authority. He sets forth principles of submission under authority heads within governments, families, churches, and between masters and slaves (the workplace in our day). Everyone submits to someone.

God's Law reveals to us the fact that we are not good. We are *not* basically 'good people' who have good hearts. We do not love like we ought to love. In fact, by God's standard of love, we do not really love anyone with a godly love. We do not have the capacity in ourselves to truly love. But our condition is far worse than that. **We are born cursed. We are all under the curse of God.** How do we know? First, because that is what God says. Second, because we will all die.

This curse does not involve having some swear words thrown at us. When someone is angry with us and says, 'Go to hell', there is no authority behind his words. No human being can send us to hell. But when God curses us, 'Go to hell' is literal, final, eternal, and just. Hell is not figurative. It's a real place created for a specific purpose. Hell is not jail, prison, time-out, your miserable life, or any temporary punishment you have ever known. There is no hope and no light at the end of hell's tunnel. It is a final judgment with no reversal. Nobody can pray you out, buy your way out, or light enough candles for you. This is what we ALL deserve. This is the curse we are ALL under. It's an eternal life sentence.

Hell is described as the following: fiery (Matthew 5:22), an unquenchable fire (Mark 9:43), a place where the physical body of the damned will be thrown (Matthew 5:29), the furnace of fire where there will be weeping and gnashing of teeth (Matthew 13:41-42), where the smoke of their torment rises forever and ever (Revelation 14:11); it is a place of destruction—but not annihilation. It is a place of constant, continual loss or ruin (Philippians 1:28, Matthew 7:13), separation from God's presence (2 Thessalonians 1:8-9), outer darkness (Matthew 8:12, 25:30), a lake of burning sulfur (Revelation 19:20), and eternal suffering (Matthew 25:46). Don Stewart, on the website Blue Letter Bible, says this of hell: "The Bible gives several descriptions of hell, or the place of final judgment. These are a sobering reminder of what awaits those who do not believe. Suffering in hell will be in intense anguish. People in hell will be isolated from everything else. They will realize they have been permanently cut off from God and everything good."[5]

People today fight for their 'rights' more than ever before. We have been taught to believe we deserve better. But the truth is, the only thing we all deserve is to go to hell and experience everlasting torment. (It dawned on me in prison that everyone around me was fighting like caged animals to get out of prison, yet most people imprisoned in sin are comfortable there.)

When we were younger, my sister and I enjoyed watching horror shows on television with my mother. Some, from the Pittsburgh area, may remember 'Chilly Billy' Cardille.[6] He was a broadcasting personality for *Studio Wrestling*. We watched the late-night Saturday program, *Chiller Theatre*, which Chilly Billy hosted. We watched *Dark Shadows*[7] with Barnabas Collins, the 175-year old vampire, and *The Twilight Zone*[8]. I believe these types of programs under genres like sci-fi, horror, thriller, and the like, were the beginning of programs that started to numb us to realities of hell and evil by conditioning us to view things which are frightening as make-believe. I remember only one episode of *The Twilight Zone* which haunted me for years. It was an episode called, "Little Girl Lost."[9] The Internet says the episode was originally aired in 1962. It was about a six-year-old girl who fell out of bed through a wall vent into another dimension. She was alive and in the dark. She could hear people talking, but she couldn't get to them. She was crying for her parents to save her, but they couldn't see her. *And that voice...*

While I do not believe there is anything inherently evil in watching these types of television shows or movies, I do believe it has numbed some to the point they can no longer make certain distinctions between what is real and what is fantasy or fiction. I wonder today if most people do not care to know the difference—for everyone's reality is supposedly interpreted by themselves anyways.

You have heard that heaven is for real. Hell is for real, too. As the girls were known to say in prison—*for real, for real.* Can I ask you why the need to stress the fact that something is 'real'? Is it because lying is so acceptable or because people have lost touch with reality? Hell is for real, and it is worse than anything we could possibly imagine. I don't know this because I have been there and back any more than I believe people know heaven is real because they say they have gone there and have come back. I know heaven is real and hell is real because the Bible tells me about both places.

Suffering on earth is hard, sometimes it's more than we think we can bear. Some people have suffered things incomprehensible to others. Hell is worse than anything anyone on earth has ever experienced. Jesus said there is nothing on earth we need to fear as much as the One who can destroy both soul and body in hell. Did you catch that? The only thing worse than facing hell is facing the One who created it for His purposes. That One is holy God.

Salvation is not of works; it is of God alone. We would have to keep the Law perfectly if God were to save us based upon our works. We can't begin to attain this holy standard as sinful beings fallen under the curse of sin. We have nothing good in us with which to please God. We are spiritually dead and need to be born again in order to have our eyes opened to the light of the Gospel. But we have no more to do with our spiritual birth than we did with our physical one. We have all failed to honor God as God. Because He is God, that is the gravest sin of all. When we look at God's Law, putting it up against the standard of our lives, it is easy to see that we are all guilty as charged. There are none who are innocent. Most people will never step foot inside a prison, but they are enslaved and imprisoned just as much as the one who is physically incarcerated. Those incarcerated have committed crimes against the government or against other human beings. Every human being alive carries more guilt than anyone imprisoned for his or her crimes. The universal crime committed by all is against Him, and it is personal. The sentence passed down is, 'cursed by God'. **If You, LORD, should mark iniquities, O Lord, who could stand?** (Psalm 130:3) **In Your sight no man living is righteous.** (Psalm 143:2)

We must be made right with God if we do not want our sinful condition to separate us from Him for all eternity. **But your iniquities have made a separation between you and your God, and your sins have hidden His face from you so that He does not hear.** (Isaiah 59:2) As we saw earlier, this word for *separation* is the same word used in Genesis 1:4 when God separated the light from the darkness. Light and darkness cannot ever come together. It can never be light and dark at the same time. As soon as there is light, there is no more darkness in a space.

Imagine standing in *the* Court of Law before *the* Judge of all judges. You have just been read the Law that is required of you to stay out of jail. You get that sinking pit in your stomach as you begin to realize that you are guilty. The prosecution shows you the evidence that will be used against you. Immediately, you know there is no need for a trial. This Court is perfectly just, and the Judge has infinite wisdom. He knows all and sees all. In fact, He is looking into your heart at this very moment. If you plead 'not guilty' what will be your defense? Can you dare be so bold as to stand before this holy Judge and tell Him that you know you **are** guilty, but if He just grants you mercy, you will try harder and promise to keep the Law in the future? What would be the point?

On that day, there will be no questions like this. Right now, you need to ask the hard questions: Where do you stand? You either stand under the Law, condemned in your sin, or you stand in righteousness, free from the Law. The Judge of the universe knows exactly where you stand. You should too; and you can.

To know the curse of God is to know true cursing. Unfortunately, we do not know the crushing weight of this curse until our eyes are opened to see God for who He is and see ourselves as we truly are. Without remediation, this curse will lead to separation that lasts for eternity.

6
Legal Training

Today is the second day into the new year. I am reminded of so many people making resolutions. Did you ever wonder why people need to keep making the same resolutions year after year? Why can't we do what we set our minds to do? I, too, have things upon which I would like to see myself stay more diligently focused. They are all good things. No one I know ever sets a resolution to gain 100 pounds or anger as many people as possible.

So far, we have seen the Law appear to be a harsh taskmaster. It commands we do things we are unable to do. It seems to us oppressive and burdensome heaping on us a weight we cannot carry. We are crushed beneath its heavy load each time we attempt to pick it up and carry it for any distance. God says His Law is for our good, and we believe Him; yet we cannot seem to keep His commands as we should. How can I understand the purpose of the Law?

In sharing the Gospel of Christ with others, one topic that seems to come up often is this idea of the Law. When a friend witnesses the radical changes in a new believer, he may assume that the believer is simply not *allowed* to do the things he once did. He concludes that Christianity is all about a list of do's and don'ts. He may think: "If I get saved, I will not be able to do what I want. Because I do not want to give up my desires, I do not want anything to do with Christianity." But Christianity is about freedom. Even though the Bible talks about God's Law often, the confusion comes in not understanding why the Law was given. God is good and God is love; so why did He give us His Law at all? Why do believers and unbelievers alike instinctively focus their energies on doing better? What exactly does the Bible mean when it talks about the Law?

God's Law reveals to us His standard of absolute righteousness in order that we might be convicted of our guilt before Him. Once we have seen our utter sinfulness before a holy God, we should then be able to see our need for the gospel. We should see that we need saved. The Law was given to shine the spotlight on our hearts exposing our sin. The problem in the way many Christians witness is in not understanding their need to use the Law before ever speaking about the good news of the gospel.

Some people go to church week after week and check off all the religious boxes of *duties* they believe God wants from them. Without understanding God's Law, we would **all** justify ourselves in our sin believing that we are not that bad. But we are born spiritually blind. This means that not only can we not see God's truth; we can't see ourselves as we really are in God's sight. This was the case of the rich young ruler whom Jesus encountered one day: **As He was setting out on a journey, a man ran up to Him and knelt before Him, and asked Him, "Good Teacher, what shall I do to inherit eternal life?" And Jesus said to him, "Why do you call Me good? No one is good except God alone. You know the commandments, 'DO NOT MURDER, DO NOT COMMIT ADULTERY, DO NOT STEAL, DO NOT BEAR FALSE WITNESS, Do not defraud, HONOR YOUR FATHER AND MOTHER.'" And he said to Him, "Teacher, I have kept all these things from my youth up." Looking at him, Jesus felt a love for him and said to him, "One thing you lack: go and sell all you possess and give to the poor, and you will have treasure in heaven; and come, follow Me." But at these words he was saddened, and he went away grieving, for he was one who owned much property.** (Mark 10:17-22)

This man would appear to be what some call a 'seeker'. You will notice that Jesus did not alter His message to be 'seeker-friendly'. I believe the answer to the question this young man posed was important to him in that he needed to make sure he had checked off all the right religious boxes ensuring his eternal salvation. Though he believed he had kept all these Laws from his childhood, his heart was deceived. He was spiritually blind, but Jesus could see his heart. This confident ruler couldn't see that attempting to keep the Law to gain salvation was a foundation upon which he could never stand. Maybe he could check off some boxes in his mind, but morally he had no concept of the depths of righteousness to which the Law was calling him. He stared into the face of perfect love, of perfect obedience, of God Himself, and told Jesus that he had been able to achieve the same perfection on his own.

Jesus cuts to the quick, immediately. He begins by letting the man know that He is not *just* a good teacher; He's God. Proceeding to use the Law to convict the man's heart, with one sharp thrust through the heart with the Sword of the Spirit, Jesus cuts into the root of this man's sin. It's interesting that this story is known as the story of the rich, young ruler when, the reality is, he is spiritually bankrupt and does not really believe that God is ruler over all. He could not give up his earthly treasure for real treasure in heaven.

This young ruler viewed the commandments as a list of do's and don'ts to be dutifully checked off a list. He did not understand obedience from the heart, or selling all he possessed and giving it to the poor would be the easiest thing of all to obey. Some read this and believe Jesus is asking the man to sell his possessions in order to gain eternal life and they, too, have missed the point. **And Jesus, looking around, said to His disciples, "How hard it will be for those who are wealthy to enter the kingdom of God!" The disciples were amazed at His words. But Jesus answered again and said to them, "Children, how hard it is to enter the kingdom of God! It is easier for a camel to go through the eye of a needle than for a rich man to enter the kingdom of God." They were even more astonished and said to Him, "Then who can be saved?" Looking at them, Jesus said, "With people it is impossible, but not with God; for all things are possible with God."** (Mark 10:23-27) I laughed out loud the other night as I thought about this passage while I was trying to **thread** a needle. I can't even see to get the thread through the eye of the needle any longer. But the Spirit of God has opened my eyes to see the truth of the gospel!

Some people look at this passage and condemn all who are wealthy. Some get stuck on the camel going through the eye of the needle, looking for some spiritual symbolism there. Jesus is saying that those who do not know their poverty of spirit, who believe they are self-sufficient in themselves, secure in their monetary wealth and self-righteousness, will find it difficult to enter the kingdom of God. What did He mean by the camel? A camel can't go through the narrow eye of a needle. There are many other theories, but this makes as good a point as any other. No one, not even the wealthy, have an advantage in God's kingdom. In fact, the rich may have a disadvantage. In this life, material needs of the poor cause them to cry out to God for help. The rich usually have too much stuff. John MacArthur likened the small gate and narrow road of salvation to a turnstile. You must go through it alone, and you must leave all your baggage behind. The wealthy may appear to have power and control in this life; but even if the wealthy can use their money to get men to do what they want, they cannot buy salvation. Salvation is as impossible for man as threading a camel through the eye of a needle. The disciples got it. Their reply was the only one that could be given. "Then, who can be saved?" It is **impossible** for man to save himself. But with God all things are possible.

When first indicted, Jesse and I believed that if we stood on our integrity, maintaining our innocence, a jury of our peers would see the truth, and we would be vindicated. *Why, we couldn't lose with the truth and the Lord on our side fighting the battle for us!* And yet, not only did we lose our trial, we lost our appeal; and we are still fighting a legal battle. The truth has not changed. I know God has not changed. But I have. It took a long time for me to come to a place of unshakeable peace and submission in this trial—peace and submission as a heart response to **His outcome** in this trial. I still want justice to prevail. We are fighting for justice and truth, but the outcome has always belonged to the Lord. I know beyond a shadow of a doubt whatever happens—even though life looks a lot different than it used to—it is all for my good and His glory. While trying to fight our legal case against all the weight of the United States Government, I don't know when it dawned on me, but I finally came to the realization that unless God vindicated, rescued, delivered, redeemed, or saved, there was nothing we or any man could do to help us. I would have made that statement boldly when we were first indicted, but it took some time for me to believe or accept the truth wholeheartedly. One by one every false pillar of hope I had set up was crushed to pieces. His peace came in resting in His sovereignty. We will continue to do all we are able to do in the fight, but the outcome belongs to the Lord.

I can know that as a Christian, all those things I mentioned—vindication, rescue, deliverance, redemption, and salvation—are as past tense as my glorification. They are an eternal 'done deal'. I can see their fulfillment with the eyes of faith. All His promises to me have been fulfilled—in eternity past—with ongoing results in the present and an even fuller fulfillment in the future. On the cross, Jesus said, "It is finished!" We can rest in those three words.

We know we need to understand the Law and use the Law for its intended purpose. What exactly does the Bible mean when it talks about the Law? First, the Law was given to Moses to give to God's chosen people. In the Bible we see the ceremonial law, the judicial law, and the moral law. The ceremonial laws were the laws for the nation of Israel pertaining to ceremonies, sacrifices, feasts, festivals, dietary restrictions, and clothing restrictions, etc. Christians are not under the ceremonial law. The judicial laws were given specifically to the culture and place of the Israelites. It included all the moral law except the Ten Commandments. The moral law is based upon God's holy nature. The moral law is the right way for all human beings to live. Those who adhere to the moral law of God obey for their own welfare and those around them. All of God's moral law is summed up in the Ten Commandments. Those Ten Commandments can be said to fall into two categories governing man's relationships—first with God—and then with man.

So, why do we make resolutions to do better? Why do believers and unbelievers instinctively know to focus their energies on doing better? Because God has written the moral law on our hearts. Even before the Law was given to Moses, God had written it on all hearts to some degree in the form of a conscience (Romans 2:14-15). We all know what a conscience is. When a child instinctively knows he has done something of which his parents will not approve, his guilt is written all over his face. His face says, "I did it!" Our consciences have been given to us by God as an internal warning system that we will either choose to adhere to or ignore. If we ignore it enough, it will stop working altogether. And that is why there are people in the world who can do awful things without any sense of regret or remorse.

Every person was created with a certain moral compass to be able to distinguish between right and wrong. But there is also something inside us that wants to run wild in rebellion against that which is right. Instinctively, we want what we think is best for ourselves. For some, it is seen in the urge to overeat, for others it is some other type of temptation that entices their flesh which is why we try to put some boundaries and restraints in place. We know that we need the law, even if we do not always appreciate it. Often, a rebellious child who has had no boundaries set for him will see how far he can go before someone will care enough to reign him in through some sort of discipline.

The Law is good. A world with no law would be a world of total chaos where we would not want to live. Law enforcement is designed to bring peace and freedom for those who are law-abiding citizens. It's only those who have no heart to obey the law who need penalties inflicted upon them to bring them into submission to authority, or to protect themselves and those who are obedient. At least that is the intent or purpose of the law by design. However, when those who stand to administer the laws in a nation are corrupt, there is no reasonable or logical explanation for that law, and everyone soon does what is right in his or her own eyes.

Galatians 3:19 says the Law was 'added' because of transgressions. The moral law was written on the heart of man. God gave all men a conscience, but then the Law *was added* because of sin. Through man's conscience within and the witness of a creation that demands the existence of a Creator, Romans 1 says man knows God, but he sinfully does not honor Him *as God*. He knows God, yet he continues to suppress that truth in unrighteousness. So God locked him in a prison cell with his back up against the wall with nowhere to go. Put under the Law, he is a caged animal in bondage to his sin with full disclosure of how he has offended holy God. He is without excuse. In Galatians 3, Paul explains the need for the Law. **Why the Law then? It was added because of transgressions, having been ordained through angels by the agency of a mediator, until the seed would come to whom the promise had been made. Now a mediator is not for one party only; whereas God is only one. Is the Law then contrary to the promises of God? May it never be! For if a law had been given which was able to impart life, then righteousness would indeed have been based on law. But the Scripture has shut up everyone under sin, so that the promise by faith in Jesus Christ might be given to those who believe. But before faith came, we were kept in custody under the law, being shut up to the faith which was later to be revealed. Therefore, the Law has become our tutor to lead us to Christ, so that we may be justified by faith. But now that faith has come, we are no longer under a tutor.** (Galatians 3:19-25)

If that one locked up in his sin and put under the Law is ever to be free, will it be the Law that releases him? The offense wasn't committed against the Law but against God, the Author of the Law.

The Law brings an indictment against this locked up criminal that his crimes have offended holy God. The fact that the Law reflects or shows us the holiness of God makes it good and right. But it can't save anyone. It has no power to change the heart with a desire to honor God (as God deserves to be honored) or to help a person keep the Law perfectly if he was to get out of his prison.

Adam and Eve sinned causing all mankind to then be born into sin from that time forward. Man was continually bent on evil, and God sent a great flood to destroy the whole earth. You remember the story of Noah and the ark. Noah had three sons: Shem, Ham, and Japheth. Through Shem's line, God called out from among all the nations a people who would be His chosen people. They were to be a uniquely *separated* people. God called a man from that line of people by the name of Abraham who became the patriarch of the Jewish nation. God promised Abraham that in him all the families of the earth would be blessed because through him would come the chosen Seed, the Messiah. All the promises of God (including salvation or redemption), would be fulfilled in and through the Seed who is Jesus Christ, the Son of God. Abraham believed in the Lord (Genesis 15), and God reckoned it to him as righteousness. Abraham believed in the promised Seed to come and was saved *because* he believed God. **Even so Abraham BELIEVED GOD, AND IT WAS RECKONED TO HIM AS RIGHTEOUSNESS. Therefore, be sure that it is those who are of faith who are sons of Abraham. The Scripture, foreseeing that God would justify the Gentiles by faith, preached the gospel beforehand to Abraham, saying, "ALL THE NATIONS WILL BE BLESSED IN YOU." So then, those who are of faith are blessed with Abraham, the believer.** (Galatians 3:6-9)

When Abraham was too old to bear a son, God ratified the covenant with him, and Abraham believed God. God justified (declared righteous or declared not guilty), Abraham, the believer, by faith. God saved Abraham *by grace* through faith, *not* by keeping the Law. As a matter of fact, God saved Abraham reckoning his belief to him as righteousness in the Old Testament long before Christ was born—and even *long before the Law through Moses was given.* To be exact, God saved Abraham 430 years before the Law was given. In Galatians 3:17, Paul tells us that the Law did not invalidate the covenant God made with Abraham, nullifying the promise. The covenant God made with Abraham was unconditional.

Abraham bore Isaac who bore Jacob. The Messiah came from the tribe of Judah, one of Jacob's twelve sons. All the other promises made to Abraham and the Jewish nation will come to pass in the fulfillment of time. God does not ever break His covenant promises. God could save Abraham based on his belief in the Messiah to come because God is the one who made the promise, and it was a done deal. It was a promise to be fulfilled in the future, but it had past tense ramifications for the present. In other words, God does not live 'in time'. He lives in eternity, and His promises are all fulfilled immediately when He makes them. We see their fulfillment here with the eyes of faith but in eternity with full sight.

Abraham, the father of the Jews, is also the father of Christians because the Seed who was to come was Christ. He would one day institute the New Covenant predicted in the Old Testament in places like Ezekiel 11:19, 36:26, and Jeremiah 31:31-34. Under the Old Covenant and the New Covenant, all believers have always been saved the same way—by faith alone in Christ alone. Some believed and were saved by looking forward in faith to the coming of Christ as Messiah based on the promises given to Abraham (and even in the promises of the Seed who was to come predicted as early as Genesis 3:15). Others, like us, look back to the finished work of Christ on the cross.

The Law was given to be our tutor to lead us to Christ. The transliteration of *tutor* is **paidagogos**. There is an idea of child discipline in this word. The tutor was a disciplinarian, a guardian, and a guide of boys. Among the Greeks and the Romans, the name was applied to trustworthy slaves who were charged with the duty of supervising the life and morals of boys belonging to the better class. The boys couldn't step out of the house without their guardian before arriving at the age of manhood (according to Larry Pierce, creator of the Online Bible). The **paidogogos** had the responsibility of bringing a child to adulthood, so he did whatever it took to curb the tendencies of that child and protect him from foolish ways. *But his job was temporary.* When the child reached late adolescence, the **paidogogos** was finished. As children, we did not always love the forms of discipline our parents employed with us. Maybe we thought we didn't even love our parents at the time discipline was being administered. When we grew up, we learned to appreciate the discipline they had exercised upon us, especially once we had children of our own. It was the same relationship a child had with their **paidogogos** back in Paul's day.

The law was laid down on me early in life. For example, my parents taught me when I was old enough to explore not to put anything into electrical outlets. Before this time, I would never have known this was wrong. After all, grown-ups plug things in all the time. When they said, "Don't ever touch…," they were laying down the law. They were putting up boundaries that I was not to break down or ignore for my own safety and welfare. Maybe until that time I never even considered approaching an electrical outlet. Afterwards, I had two choices—either obey or rebel against my parents' authority. Once the law was laid down for me regarding electrical outlets, electrical outlets were probably all I could think about. I may have been bent on getting to the closest outlet until another type of law was brought down upon my backside. Maybe electrical outlets were not a problem for me, especially if I had managed to test the waters for myself. My daughter's flesh nature got the best of her in this exact situation—only one time. Thankfully, my husband reached her before she had stuck the toy key she was playing with completely into the socket. Ideally, a child will love and trust her parents enough to be obedient to parental laws that are for her own good. That is what child training is all about. Maybe electrical outlets did not excite my flesh at all. What about mother putting out freshly baked cookies and saying I must not touch them until after dinner? Now, the law is more burdensome because even if I want to be obedient, I may want a cookie more. There is a *real* struggle going on inside of me. Why? Because I *love* cookies! Cookies tempt me in a way a light socket never could.

Mother's law is good. In her wisdom, she knows better than I do what is best for me. If I eat cookies before dinner, she knows I will spoil my appetite for the nutritional dinner she has made for me. Mother wants me to eat the healthier food first, not to fill up on cookies. If the cookies were set in front of me with no laws put down, I would be free to eat cookies until I am sick. The problem is not with Mother's Law or even with the cookies. It is the sin in me, my fleshly desire for that which I'm not allowed to have because it is not good for me. The law is good and is administered for my good.

If mother had put a plate of cookies in front of me saying, "Help yourself," then having as many cookies as I wanted would not have been sin for me. Mother, the authority over me to enforce her law, gave me permission to freely eat what I wanted. But Mother is wise and good, so she will put a limit on my indulgences knowing my flesh will not be able to have restraint when it comes to cookies. Because of sin, the law was added. When I am grown up and mother puts a plate of cookies in front of me—because she applied the law when I was young, that tutor to lead me to right behavior—I may decide to eat one or two cookies, but what I want more than cookies is my healthy dinner. I do not want to spoil my appetite for that which is better for me. I may even save the cookies for my desert without being told. No longer under the law, I am now free to do as I please because I have been trained and have learned to choose what is right and good.

I can't understand the reasoning of Mother's laws when I am young. I must have her law pressing down on me until I can trust her love for me in wanting my best and her wisdom becomes my own. When I was young, it seemed like torture. Mother's law was oppressive. **What shall we say then? Is the Law sin? May it never be! On the contrary, "I would not have come to know sin except through the Law; for I would not have known about coveting if the Law had not said, "YOU SHALL NOT COVET." But sin, taking opportunity through the commandment, produced in me coveting of every kind; for apart from the Law sin is dead.** (Romans 7:7-8) Paul is saying that the law arouses our flesh to sin. Why? Because our flesh is naturally rebellious.

Twenty-some years before my indictment, I watched a reality police show. Two different episodes have stuck out in my mind. A scraggly-looking older man had hired a woman to engage in sinful behavior with him. A police officer came upon his van and caught them in the act of breaking the law. Seeing the look on the man's face brought me to tears and sorrow. It was not so much a look of, "I got caught," but it was a defeated look of, "I cannot help myself." His countenance was pitiful. Without physical bars or barbed-wire fences, he was imprisoned in bondage to his sin all the same.

The second show featured a man dealing drugs who was caught breaking the law. When the police patrolling the area shined their light upon him, he fled to his home where they caught up with him. As he was being handcuffed and being read his rights, his wife and toddler were standing nearby crying. The little boy was screaming and shaking from fear. Picture his little arms reaching out but not understanding why Daddy will not take him into his strong arms for protection. Sin destroys everything and everyone it touches.

Do you think both men knew they were breaking the law? You could see the first man obviously knew because the guilt was written all over his face. When the police opened the van door, the man did not say, "Officer, what did I do wrong?" He started pleading for mercy. The second man knew he was breaking the law because the first thing he did was run from the police. The purpose of the law, they instinctively knew, was to reveal their sin to them whether they chose to give in to the temptation to break that law or not. The law then would keep them constrained under the judgment and sentence (consequences) of breaking that law.

Why do people break the law? The flesh that loves to sin is strong. Many years before I was sent to prison, I watched the first show and was heartbroken for the man who clearly was held captive in bondage to his sin. I also felt the same for the family of the drug dealer. But since prison, I am able to feel compassion for the man who was dealing drugs as well. I got to know and love those convicted of the same crime as this man. I learned to see the sinner, not so much the specific sins. I realized more fully just how much I share with all human beings. I, too, live in a body of flesh and know temptation to sin. I remember that bondage to sin before Christ. I also know from firsthand experience the pain of separation and loss of freedom he experienced in prison.

In both scenarios, I would never think the law is too oppressive. The judgment or sentence that might be applied to breaking specific laws may be too harsh, but most people can see that the laws which govern prostitution and drug dealing are right and good. What my eyes have really been opened to is something I have seen since I have been out of prison.

What discourages me involves Christians. I am grieved when I listen to how some Christians talk about people who have been

exposed as lawbreakers (people who have given in to their temptation to sin). There is such disgust and dismissiveness. Brothers and
sisters, this is our mission field! If we can't relate, how can we reach
the lost? We are depraved, too. We all sin and fall short of the glory
of God. Someone who reacts like this does not really believe that.
Did you ever wonder why God's Word talks often about prisoners
and visiting prisoners? All people need to be crushed by the Law.
Unbelievers do not need to be crushed by us as well. How dare
we! I realize that it is near impossible to get approved for legitimate
prison ministry in federal facilities, but you can pray for inmates
that God would use the Law to do its work in their hearts, and that
He would send workers with the true gospel message. You cannot
even pray for them with an attitude of disgust and disdain.

One day I was driving along the highway and was surprised
to see a crew of inmates doing some sort of clean-up detail. It is
hot in California, and even early in the day the sun was shining
brightly and the temperature was burning at close to 100 degrees.
There was an officer standing watch over the men who were doing
some sort of strenuous work in jumpsuits and boots. I knew in my
heart they were probably thrilled mentally to be in a different
setting, even while they were very uncomfortable physically. A spirit
of empathy and camaraderie came over me, and I struggled not to
break down emotionally. I later mentioned to a friend that I had
wanted to jump out of my car and hug every one of them. My friend
grimaced and gasped, "They are convicted criminals! They broke
the law; they deserve what they get. Why would you want to show
them compassion?" Stunned for a moment, I just stared at her. I
whispered, "Because I can relate to them." I wanted to say, "And you
should, too." This is a common reaction, and it makes me angry.
But then I recognize human nature rearing its ugly face, and I
look at my own heart. In what situations do I too quickly judge
another when I am guilty of the same or far worse in God's eyes?
Prison, in so many ways has shown me that I can never stand in
God's presence and open my mouth to speak saying, "I thank God
I am not like..."

The other day, I was talking with someone who knows me well
about the problem of convicted felons not being 'accepted' once
they are released from prison. I stated that I was blessed by the fact

that my hometown had welcomed me with open arms. My friend casually blurted out, "Well, you paid your dues." This same person has often told me how she believes in my innocence. I had to cut the conversation short before I said something I would have regretted.

There is a difference between God's Law and man's law. Having said that, it is the flesh in man that reacts to both. A simple illustration comes from my experiences with the dreaded 'D' word. Did you guess it? Dieting. God's Law says that I should walk in the Spirit in self-control, and that I should do all things to the glory of God, including eating and drinking. If I am obedient to God's Law in how I honor Him in my eating, I may be a certain healthy size. Man's law or my law may say, "I will not be happy unless I reach a certain size or number on the scale." I have just become legalistic in taking God's Law to an extreme, and my motive is not as much to honor God as to honor myself. And that is sin.

I can have compassion towards the one who breaks God's Law and the one who breaks man's law. If I break man's law, there may be consequences, and I may go to jail. Breaking God's Law is a much more serious offense with consequences far more grave. Breaking God's Law always results in consequences. All of God's Law can be reduced to this command: "Be holy as God is holy." If I am focused on obeying God's Law out of love for Him, I will not be bent on breaking man's law. I will also be more compassionate to come alongside the one who is breaking man's law to help him see the heart of God's Law more clearly, which can then lead him to Christ.

At first glance, it has appeared to us that the Law crushes and oppresses us with its staggering weight. The Bible says, the Law is perfect. Psalm 119 is all about God's Law. Using different words for God's Law like *precepts, testimonies, statutes, commandments, judgments,* (God's) *Word,* and *ordinances,* the psalmist needs 176 verses to exult and praise God's Law. Among these verses, the writer says he delights in God's Law and that God's Law is truth. And Isaiah says in 42:21: **The LORD was pleased for His righteousness' sake to make the Law great and glorious.** 1 John 5:13 says: **For this is the love of God, that we keep His commandments; and His commandments are not burdensome.** The Law is not the problem. We are. Our sin weighs us down when the Law is applied. And that is why the Law is good. It exposes the sin problem that is destroying us, closes our mouths so that we can no longer justify ourselves, and makes us accountable to God. (Romans 3:19-20)

There is no one living in our nation who is not under the law. Just by living here, regardless if whether one believes he is above the law or not, we are all under the laws of our land. The same is true of God's Law and His universe. All are under His Law, whether they choose to admit that truth or deny it.

All Are Under the Law of God. All Have Broken God's Law. All Are Guilty.

What is my relationship to the Law as a believer? In Romans 7, there is much debate about whether Paul is writing about a believer or an unbeliever. Please refresh your memory of this chapter by taking a few minutes to focus on verses 14-25, especially.

Believer or unbeliever? The longer I walk with the Lord by His Spirit but in this body of flesh, I agree with John MacArthur's view on this passage. In his commentary on Romans 1-8, he states, "It seems rather that Paul is here describing the most spiritual and mature of Christians, who, the more they honestly measure themselves against God's standards of righteousness the more they realize how much they fall short. The closer we get to God, the more we see our own sin. Thus, it is immature, fleshly, and legalistic persons who tend to live under the illusion that they are spiritual and that they measure up well by God's standards. The level of spiritual insight, brokenness, contrition, and humility that characterize the person depicted in Romans 7 are marks of a spiritual and mature believer, who before God has no trust in his own goodness and achievements." (MacArthur, John: Romans 1-8, Chicago: Moody Publishers, 1991.)

We are being made to grow up into the image of Christ, but it is a process that is much slower than we often realize. Even the most mature believer is so far from that image of perfection that unless God glorifies him, he would never get there. I believe this passage is one that talks about the battle that is raging inside every believer as she walks in this world. The key thing to understand is that sanctification is a process; we are growing up in Christ, and growing up involves discipline. Walking in this world and falling at times, it is because we are growing that we need discipline. You may not remember your own falling down as a child learning to walk, but all mothers know or remember the scene well. We would pick our children up *in order that they may continue* to learn to walk. 'Growing up' involves learning. When you look at that word *discipline*, you see the word *disciple (*a pupil or learner). We were not picking our children up in the spirit of punishment to scold them. It was training.

When our children were young, we put them in a prison cell. No, I'm just kidding. We put them in a wooden box with four walls of bars that kept them contained (or detained), so they could not get into any trouble. It was not the pen*(itentiary).* We called it a *play*pen! My kids never did much playing in the playpen. They kicked and screamed to get out. Sometimes, however, the playpen was the safest place for them to be when I had something urgent I needed to take care of and could not give them my complete attention. **Furthermore, we had earthly fathers to discipline us, and we respected them; shall we not much rather be subject to the Father of spirits, and live? For they disciplined us for a short time as seemed best to them, but He disciplines us for our good, so that we may share His holiness. All discipline for the moment seems not to be joyful, but sorrowful; yet to those who have been trained by it, afterwards it yields the peaceful fruit of righteousness.** (Hebrews 12:9-11) The word for *discipline* here in the Greek is **paideia** which is the training and education of children. We saw the same root in the word for *tutor*. *Training* is the word from which we get our word *gymnasium*. **Gymnázō** means to exercise vigorously, in any way, either the body or the mind. In the following two verses, we see this word used as *discipline* and *trained*. **But have nothing to do with worldly fables fit only for old women. On the other hand, discipline yourself for the purpose of godliness.** (1 Timothy 4:7) And Hebrews 5:14—**But solid food is for the mature, who because of practice have their senses trained to discern good and evil.**

As we are being sanctified, God is teaching us in His school. We are in training. I love that Paul uses so many analogies of athletic training to enable us to understand the process of sanctification from this vantage point. We are not necessarily in need of correction in a negative sense when we are being disciplined. The word is more dimensional than that. Athletic training helps us understand that. We see illustrations of children growing up, which we all understand. Some lessons are easier than others to learn. Sometimes we need to be disciplined in a way that is not very enjoyable. But all discipline takes work and sacrifice. Just like schooling, we will be tested periodically. This testing looks like a trial in our lives meant to prove our faith or prove that we have learned our lessons well. The same Greek word is in the following passages. **For to this end also I wrote, so that I might put you to the test, whether you are obedient in all things.** (2 Corinthians 2:9) **And not only this, but we also exult in our tribulations, knowing that tribulation brings about perseverance; and perseverance, proven character; and proven character, hope; and hope does not disappoint, because the love of God has been poured out within our hearts through the Holy Spirit who was given to us.** (Romans 5:3-5) **But you know of his proven worth, that he served with me in the furtherance of the gospel like a child serving his father.** (Philippians 2:22)

As children get older and can be trusted to play safely, they may graduate from playpens to periods of 'time-outs' only when they need to be disciplined for breaking the rules. Why is this discipline important? It teaches children to grow up and become law-abiding citizens who have respect and even love for authority, which ultimately should lead to a respect for and love for the greatest authority of all—Almighty God.

Sometimes, as God's children, we adults need to be put flat on our backs or in situations that God can use to get our attention because He needs to teach us something. We must know that He is training us in righteousness as He continues to sanctify us. Sometimes He needs to get us alone and get our attention. We may kick and scream to get out of our constrained circumstances, but we soon learn that to comply makes things a lot easier.

People in our nation might believe, as I once did, that the purpose of our prison system was built on these biblical principles of boundaries and discipline, not only to punish those who have committed crimes, but to facilitate their rehabilitation and restore them back to their communities. It might have been that way at one time. Sadly, greed and power have corrupted those good purposes. We need serious reform in our justice system. Many truthful, tell-all books could be written by former inmates regarding all the ways prison has been corrupted and become big business today.

We discipline our children because we love them and want them to grow up. When I was punished as a child for doing something wrong, I would go to my room, throw myself on my bed and cry to myself: *They just don't love me anymore!* (Yes, I was ever the drama queen.) Nothing could have been further from the truth. My parents loved me. Punishment is good. There is no love where sin is left unchecked. Loving me necessitated dealing with my sinful rebellion by imposing sanctions that would correct the bad attitudes and actions. My parents, whether they realized it or not, were out of love following a biblical principle. **"MY SON, DO NOT REGARD LIGHTLY THE DISCIPLINE OF THE LORD, NOR FAINT WHEN YOU ARE REPROVED BY HIM; FOR THOSE WHOM THE LORD LOVES HE DISCIPLINES, AND HE SCOURGES EVERY SON WHOM HE RECEIVES."** (Hebrews 12:5-6) The fact that my parents disciplined me proved their love for me and that I was truly their child, not illegitimate (Hebrews 12:7-8). All God's legitimate children share in Fatherly discipline. Every time my parents welcomed me back into their fellowship, after having served my sentence in my room, all was well because I somehow knew I was loved *because* of their discipline.

When I think of times when I was disciplined or when I had to discipline my own children, I think of all the reasons that discipline was necessary. Sometimes, there was guilt involved that needed to be punished. Sometimes, I had to remove my children from situations, not allowing them to go here or there for their own protection. Naturally, it is quite often that discipline involves pain because it involves getting our rebellious flesh and its desires under control. Other times, discipline came in the form of an object lesson or a lecture. The homeschool years were a continual form of discipline in child training.

When bad things happen to us, it is easy to forget that they are not necessarily happening because we have done something bad. There were many times in prison when I was tempted to sit in my cube and lick my wounds of self-pity and despair. *You don't love me. You must not love me, Lord.* I would question what I did to deserve prison reasoning that, as a parent myself, I always tried to make the punishment fit the crime. Then, I would think of Jesus on the cross or Paul, Peter, Job, or David. Prison is just another classroom. I would be pierced through my heart remembering that I deserve death. I deserve hell. It was my sin that put my Lord on the cross. Or I would come upon a verse like Hebrews 12 above, and I would know that all things do work together for my good because it is all part of my Father's plan. Whether I understand the reasons or not, Father knows best, and I can know that He loves me as I ponder the cross.

If we start walking down a road that leads to trouble, you can know that He will get you back where you belong. (I have this picture in my mind of home movies made of me when I was first learning to walk. These sections of footage always seemed to be in fast forward motion for some reason, which only adds to the effect of this picture in my mind. You could see me toddling off in one direction, and my mother running after me, picking me up, and turning me around 180 degrees in the opposite direction.) There are other times I have been running hard in the wrong direction, and He has let me fall; *then,* He picked me up and brought me back where I needed to be. The fact that He does not let us get away with sinful disobedience proves His love for us. Whether it is conviction brought by His Spirit when reading His Word, by listening to a sermon, by bringing a brother or sister into my life to reprove me, or even by sustaining me as He allows me to deal with the consequences of my sin or difficult trials that come through no fault of my own—His discipline assures me that I am truly His child and He is making me fit to be able to share in His holiness.

You would hope that discipline that is intended for growth would have its desired result. Did I come out of prison a changed person? Yes. Did everyone? To some extent, yes. Like so many, I could have been changed for the worse—bitter, angry, resentful, unloving, ungrateful, and unkind. If that had happened, I would have had to seriously question whether I belong to my Father.

My prison sentence did not pass quickly for me; but with a view to eternity, it was a blip on the screen of life. Regardless of whether a court of my peers believed I was innocent or guilty really does not matter. God knows. What matters is how much I grew during the prison trial. I am not the same person who walked into prison.

I am *far* from perfect; but I have grown a bit more in several areas of my life. I can look back at my life before prison and stand amazed at how much my thoughts and desires have changed. My belief system has been more clearly defined. I came to know Him more, love Him more, and trust Him more. I can promise you it was not because of the rehabilitative and restorative work accomplished by the BOP (Bureau of Prisons). The Law already did its work in my heart long ago. No longer under the Law, *my Father* is raising me. And I am grateful to know that His sanctification work in me is not finished. I know because I am still here, and I am still growing.

On the website, gracegems.org, I found an awesome quote by John Newton that applies. "Remember, the growth of a believer is not like a mushroom—but like an oak, which increases slowly indeed—but surely. Many suns, showers, and frosts pass upon it before it comes to perfection; and in winter, when it seems to be dead—it is gathering strength at the root. Be humble, watchful, and diligent in the means, and endeavor to look through all, and fix your eye upon Jesus—and all shall be well." https://www.gracegems.org/Newton/001.htm

How can you thank Him for an unjust situation in which you are tempted to view yourself as a *victim*? This is not 'thank you, Sir, may I have another' type of thinking. I do not enjoy pain any more than the next person. I rather hate it, to be truthful. But I welcome God's work in my life—however He chooses to do that work. The work He did in my heart through these uniquely de-signed circumstances made my faith and my witness stronger. It will be used by Him as He sees fit for His glory.

It turns out no matter how wicked or corrupt a government system can be, it truly is a minister of God to me for my good because God, my Judge and sovereign King, is on His throne. Every circumstance in life is nothing more than a tool in His hand skill-fully used to mold and shape me into His masterpiece. My Father loves me enough to discipline me as He trains me in righteousness. All God's children are being and will continue to be disciplined. How is He disciplining you? How is He training you to walk in righteousness today?

7
You Are Not Okay, and Neither Am I

As an unbeliever in high school, I took a psychology class. I read the book, *I'm Okay, You're Okay* by Thomas Anthony Harris.[1] Is the statement, 'I'm okay, you're okay' true? Are we really born into this world 'okay'? What does it even mean to be 'okay'?

When kids are little, they fall a lot. Before the dramatic scream that was soon to follow, my kids would look up at me with that lower lip quivering and with that little question mark hanging on their faces that said, "Should I cry? Am I okay?" If I quickly assured them, "You're okay," it would usually nip the wailing in the bud before it ever gained steam. Sometimes, however, their falls were serious enough that all I could do was scoop them up and take them to the Emergency Room to get them the help they needed.

The world defines 'okay' as being a good person, having a sense of purpose and worth, a person who believes he can do anything if he just sets his mind to it—a person with a healthy self-esteem. One blog I read defined being 'okay' as simply being functional. Satan and the world system would love to have us believe that we *are* okay, but God's Word tells us something entirely different. A point came in every believer's life when he fell and realized he was not okay. The fall was bad, and he knew it. Thankfully, the Father did not tell us we were okay. He scooped us up in His loving arms and rushed us to the Great Physician to perform a heart transplant. It was way worse than we ever could have imagined. We were **not** okay! What does the Bible say about man?

It is important to understand how great the separation is between holy God and sinful man—as much as we can understand this separation. Therefore, a disciplined study of God's character as revealed in His Word is vital to a proper theology. It is also vital to study the doctrine of man from Scripture, to have a proper anthropology. A failure to rightly view this unfathomable chasm between man and God results in all types of distortions in worship and stunts our ability to glorify Him in all we think, say, and do.

The first chapter of Genesis tells us that man was created by God in His image. Distinct from the rest of God's creation, man was made to resemble his Creator mentally, morally, and socially.

Unlike the animals, man was created mentally to be able to reason and to choose, reflecting God's intellect and freedom. Morally, man was created righteous and innocent reflecting the holiness of God. Lastly, as a reflection of God's love represented in the nature of the Trinity, we were created socially for fellowship.

While we may catch glimpses of the remnants of that original state in ourselves and in others, we must know that something went drastically wrong somewhere along the line. We do not have to guess because the Bible, God's story—'His-story'—tells us just three chapters from the beginning how man fell into his sad, spiritually dead state.

Sometime after God had blessed Adam with a helpmate named Eve, and before the first child born to the couple entered the world, Adam, as the head of his family, sinned. Created with a righteous nature, but also with the ability to freely choose, Adam made an evil decision to rebel against his Maker by disobeying God's command that forbid him from eating from just one, single tree in the Garden. God's Word to Adam was clear just like it is for us today. Through this one act of disobedience, not only did Adam lose his innocence and his intimate, unhindered fellowship with God, but spiritual and physical death became a reality for him and for all his descendants. In fact, all that belonged to Adam as the wages of his sin would be due his descendants from that point forward. Likewise, because we have all come from Adam, we bear the curse of sin. No longer having the capacity to glorify God—that thing which he was created to do—man, in his naturally corrupt state, became subject to the wrath of God.

The Westminster Shorter Catechism asks this very important question: What is the chief end of man? The answer is this—Man's chief end is to glorify God, and to enjoy him forever. That is what man was created to do. To that end, man will find his greatest fulfillment and purest joy. But since the Fall, in his fallen state, he has no capacity to do that whatsoever, for he is spiritually dead. In this spiritually dead state, he has no desire to glorify God or enjoy Him forever. His desire is that *he* be glorified and God give *him* all the enjoyment *he* wants (and feels he deserves) in this life. He would never believe that glorifying God and enjoying Him for-ever would bring him the fulfillment and joy for which he longs.

Genesis 3 outlines the Fall for us, but it also shows us the curses and the consequences of the Fall that would be laid upon all of Adam's progeny down through the ages. All suffering is ultimately the result of the consequences of sin that entered the world at the Fall. But, as we shall see, there is much good news in how God uses the believer's pain and suffering for our good and His glory. Our chief end for which we were created does not end when we find ourselves in a season or lifetime of suffering. Sometimes it is the means to the greatest opportunities we will ever have to glorify God. The way we view suffering reveals our hearts. Is it our greatest desire to glorify God and enjoy Him forever, or would *we* rather be glorified and find our enjoyment in the things of the world?

We are corrupt. We are not basically good people as most of us have been taught and would like to believe. This reality is the sad truth of Scripture as it relates to man. Just like someone with a deadly disease, we must understand the serious nature of our condition if we are to get the help we so desperately need. Romans 3:23 says that we have all sinned and have fallen short of the glory of God. That is what God says about our condition as we stand before Him. It does not matter who says you are 'okay' if God says you are not.

Romans 3:9 says the whole human race has fallen under sin's judgment. We have all been charged with the greatest criminal offense there is. Romans 3:10-18 is the indictment. An indictment is a formal, legal statement put forth by the prosecuting attorney's office setting forth the charge(s) of the criminal offense. Here is the indictment of all humanity:

> THERE IS **NONE** RIGHTEOUS, **NOT EVEN ONE**;
> THERE IS **NONE** WHO UNDERSTANDS,
> THERE IS **NONE** WHO SEEKS FOR GOD;
> **ALL** HAVE TURNED ASIDE, **TOGETHER** THEY
>   HAVE BECOME **USELESS**;
> THERE IS **NONE** WHO DOES GOOD,
> THERE IS **NOT EVEN ONE**.
> THEIR THROAT IS AN OPEN GRAVE,
> WITH THEIR TONGUES THEY KEEP
>   DECEIVING,

THE POISON OF ASPS IS UNDER THEIR LIPS;
WHOSE MOUTH IS FULL OF CURSING AND
   BITTERNESS;
THEIR FEET ARE SWIFT TO SHED BLOOD,
DESTRUCTION AND MISERY ARE IN THEIR
   PATHS,
AND THE PATH OF PEACE THEY HAVE **NOT**
   KNOWN.
THERE IS **NO** FEAR OF GOD BEFORE THEIR
   EYES.

Notice all the negatives here; the list goes on and on. Paul is quoting several different Old Testament verses. Not only are there none righteous, there are no 'seekers' who are actively looking for God before He begins to draw them to Himself. Furthermore, we can't speak words that are righteous because our throats are as an open grave, and we continually deceive with our tongues. Lastly, our feet are eager to run to sin. The obvious verdict to this indictment is guilty as charged. **Now we know that whatever the Law says, it speaks to those who are under the Law, so that every mouth may be closed, and all the world may become accountable to God.** (Romans 3:19) Maybe everyone should go through criminal proceedings to understand the weight of hearing these words. In these verses, we see the depravity of man. It does not mean that an individual is as depraved as he could be, but he will not get better. He can only get more depraved under the burden of sin. What is *depravity*? The English word means corrupted or perverted. We cannot get *'okay'* from that by any means.

The word *depraved,* used in the following verse, is interesting because of what we saw in the last chapter. **And just as they did not see fit to acknowledge God any longer, God gave them over to a depraved mind, to do those things which are not proper...** (Romans 1:28) The word *depraved* is **adokimos.** It means reprobate, not approved, not standing the test. What is the test? The test is pleasing God or glorifying Him by reflecting His holiness. All men have broken God's Law. Man, in himself, can never please God. Depraved people can do good deeds that are admirable in the sight of others. We can see dignity in man because he was created in the image of God but man can do nothing to make himself in right standing with God. How does that make sense? It makes sense because we are not comparing man to man. We are comparing man to God. God's absolute righteousness and what man thinks is good are two antithetical things. Man can never get out of his fallen state on his own.

Romans 3:10—**There are none righteous. Not even one.** *Righteous* is the word **dikaios**. It has the idea of upright, or straight. It defines that which is in accordance with high standards of rectitude (the quality of being straight). On the contrary, we are depraved, corrupted, or crooked. Noah Webster has the following definition of *rectitude:* In morality, rightness of principle or practice; uprightness of mind; exact conformity to truth, or to the rules prescribed for moral conduct, either by divine or human laws. Rectitude of mind is the disposition to act in conformity to any known standard of right, truth, or justice; rectitude of conduct is the actual conformity to such standard. Perfect rectitude belongs only to the Supreme Being. The more nearly the rectitude of men approaches to the standard of the divine law, the more exalted and dignified is their character. Want of rectitude is not only sinful, but debasing. ~ Webster, Noah. An American Dictionary of the English Language, 1828

Solomon concurs. **Indeed, there is not a righteous man on earth who continually does good and who never sins.** (Ecclesiastes 7:20) *Righteousness* is a key theme in the book of Romans, the book which has been called 'the Constitution of our Faith'. Righteousness is the one thing by which all sin is judged. Some people mistakenly believe that when their good and bad is put on the scales of divine justice, their good will outweigh their bad, and they will be 'okay' (meaning they will make it to heaven). The problem is that the good on the scale belongs to God alone. God's perfect holiness is on one side of the scale, and all your works on the other. You can't make that scale move an ounce. Every supposedly 'good' deed done by every human being ever created could not move the scale weighed down with the holy righteousness of their Creator. Why? Because no 'good' deed done by man is ever wholly righteous.

Romans 3:11—**There is none who understands; there is none who seeks for God.** Have you ever been at completely different points of view with somebody, and although you try your best to explain what you know is right, they just do not understand? Today, we may say something like, "She just does not get it!" This is that.

Understands is the word **suniemi** from sun/syn which means with, together with, intimate relation, plus **hiemi** which means to send. It literally means to send, bring, or put together—and then mentally to comprehend. To *understand* would be like having a jigsaw puzzle with no picture to work from, but as you get more and more pieces together you understand how they fit with the whole. Someone who has no understanding may have all the pieces; but even if you were to put the picture in front of him, he still would not understand that at which he is looking. It is like asking a blind person what picture you have just created in your most recent jigsaw puzzle challenge.

What about those whom some have labeled as 'seekers' today? In Philippians 2:21, Paul tells us what man naturally seeks: **"For they all seek after their own interests, not those of Christ Jesus."** Just like the crowds that followed Jesus in John 6 in order to get fed, those who use this label today usually refer to those who want *a Jesus* who can meet some need they have. They do not want the biblical Jesus who calls them to die to themselves.

When Adam sinned in the Garden of Eden, he ran from God. In absolute terror, he and Eve hid themselves from holy God. Created in innocence, they now knew good and evil. Instinctively, they knew Who was good and that they were not. *God* was the seeker. It was He who sought them out. In our natural heart, we will never desire to seek Him or have a loving thought of Him. The word for *seek* is **ekzeteo** meaning to seek out, to look for, to search diligently for anything that is lost. God is not lost; we are.

One day, I lost my keys. In the course of talking with a friend, I informed her I needed to get off the phone to search for them. She quickly offered, "I will pray to St. Anthony to help you find them!" Emphatically, I responded, "Please don't do that." I was faced with a dilemma. I had not thought to pray to the Lord to help me find them (which convicted me), but I certainly didn't want my friend to give some dead 'saint' the glory for supposedly causing me to find my keys. I said a prayer to the Lord to help me, then looked for them for a short while. Thinking I would come across them throughout my day, I forgot about the matter. Hours later my friend called. The first thing out of her mouth was, "Did you find your keys?" I replied, "No, not yet." Bewildered, she hesitated, "I don't understand; St. Anthony must be busy trying to find something more important right now." I countered, "The Lord will help me find my keys when I need them. It may be His way of keeping me off the roads safe in my home today." She said, "Oh, I never thought of that."

That may seem like a silly story, but we have all lost things. There have been times when we were under a time crunch and frantically searched for the missing item. And we kept after it until we found it because it was (what we acted like at the time) vital to our very existence. Natural man will never seek for God like his very life depends on it. Those who are called 'seekers' today dabble in and splash around in the shallow waters of religion believing God will give them all the blessings they *deserve* if they stay in the pool long enough. But they would never, ever attempt to wade into the deep end of truth to get to know the God they profess to 'seek' after. If God is truly drawing them to Himself—since He is the seeker—they will seek out those deep waters, hungry for the true God of the Bible. If not—well, staying in the shallow end for any length of time as an adult is going to get boring. They will get out of the pool, eventually.

…that there be no immoral or godless person like Esau, who sold his own birthright for a single meal. For you know that even afterwards, when he desired to inherit the blessing, he was rejected, for he found no place for repentance, though he sought for it with tears. (Hebrews 12:16-17) Most of those labeled 'seekers' today are like Esau. Esau wanted God's blessings. He just didn't want God. With a heart full of regret in giving up his birthright, he still didn't repent even though he sought for that blessing with tears.

Romans 3:12—**All have turned aside; together they have become useless; there is none who does good, there is not even one.** *Turned aside* is **ekklino** from **ek** meaning out, out from, and **klino** meaning incline, bend, turn aside or away. It means to lean in the wrong direction, to bend out of the regular line, to bend away. It means to steer clear of, to stay away from, to avoid, to turn aside or to deviate from the right way or course. In our natural state, all have turned away from God.

My fellow Pennsylvanians who have ever swerved to miss a deer that jumped out in front of them while driving can understand this illustration. It is like the unbeliever confronted with righteousness who swerves to get out of its way. You may know this situation all too well if you are well-known as someone who shares her faith a lot. (Why, before family members open Christmas gifts, they mumble under their breath, "It's probably a Bible or another book.") Someone catches your eye in the grocery store; pretending not to see you, it looks like they suddenly remember they forgot something in another aisle, and they scurry out of sight. Or you are sitting in a room full of people in a discussion that turns towards religion. They know what's coming; your whole worldview is different—strange to them. You finally get that split-second lull in the conversation, and you turn the conversation to the truth. One by one, people must use the restroom, they hear their name being called from another room, or they must get something ready for dinner. They *swerve away* from the boulder of truth that has just dropped in front of them back to their own crooked path leading to destruction. If they think it is awkward to leave, they have no idea how awkward it is to watch.

Another way this phrase is used is when calling Christians to *turn away from* false teachers and evil. **Now I urge you, brethren, keep your eye on those who cause dissensions and hindrances contrary to the teaching which you learned, and turn away from them.** (Romans 16:17) Speaking of the one who desires life, to love and see good days, Peter said: **"HE MUST TURN AWAY FROM EVIL AND DO GOOD; HE MUST SEEK PEACE AND PURSUE IT."** (1 Peter 3:11)

Romans 3:12 says unredeemed man has turned away from God's path of righteousness. Paul and Peter say that Christians are to turn away from false teachers who deceive with their error and from all evil. Even believers, because of our fallen flesh, are *prone* to wander away from this path from time to time. We are tempted to walk in the wrong direction, to bend away from the right path we are walking on. But all human beings born into sin naturally and eagerly avoid the path of righteousness.

Together they have become useless. What can one do with a piece of fruit that has completely decayed or become corrupt? Or, spoiled, soured milk? Or, putrid, foul, stinking, rotten potatoes? Whatever it is, it's useless, worthless—good for nothing but the outside trashcan. God made man to fulfill His purpose. Man fell into sin making him unfit or unprofitable to God, unable to do any works of righteousness, unable to glorify Him. *Become useless* is **achreioo** from **achreios** which means unprofitable, good for nothing or to render unserviceable, morally worthless, corrupt, or vile.

There is none who does good, there is not even one. *Good* is **chrestotes** which means useful, describing the quality of being helpful and beneficial. It has the idea of generosity of heart. It is goodness expressed in deeds. It is a trait relating to service. No one does good in the sense of doing anything of spiritual or eternal value. We need to understand that for works to be good works of a spiritual nature, they need to be done habitually, with pure motive, from a heart committed to honoring God.

Romans 3:13—**Their throat is an open grave; with their tongues they keep deceiving; the poison of asps is under their lips.** No truth comes from their mouths because no truth is in their hearts. There is nothing reliable in what they say. The depraved use and abuse their victims by deceitfully using flattery to feed their egos giving them a false sense of self-confidence.

You will remember when Jesus was getting ready to raise Lazarus from the grave, He commanded that the stone be rolled away. What did Martha say? "By now, Lord, surely it stinketh!" This is that picture. Every time the depraved man opens his mouth to speak, it stinks to God's nostrils. What comes out is foul and putrid. You have heard the expression: "It stinks to high heaven!" Stench comes from decay. The decay comes from the spiritually dead soul. Jesus used this idea when giving His diatribe to the 'super, duper religious elite' of His day: **"You brood of vipers, how can you, being evil, speak what is good? For the mouth speaks out of that which fills the heart. The good man brings out of his good treasure what is good; and the evil man brings out of his evil treasure what is evil."** (Matthew 12:34-35) Where do dirty jokes and gutter language come from? The sewer that is filled with dead and dying things. We say people "talk trash". Trash is filled with that which is decaying and rotten. Inside every fallen heart is a rotting corpse; spiritually dead, the stink from that decaying flesh comes out through what is said.

We can think of Job sitting at the garbage dump, scraping the oozing, pus-filled sores all over his body. The stench cannot be imagined. Just like that infectious pus seeping out from the inside, this is what comes out of the depraved heart. As I sat on my bunk in prison, I often sat there just listening (or trying not to). It is a sign of judgment to us when 'ladies' speak gutter talk as if it's as normal as any topic of conversation women usually talk about. (And, yes, there used to be a clear differentiation.) The reality is many women can't speak a complete sentence without some vulgarity in it. There was a day when those who chose to speak this type of language would at least have respect for women, the elderly, and children by refraining from using it in their presence. That day is gone. And it's not just the stench of vulgar words but the content as well. Nothing is taboo; everything is acceptable.

With their tongues they keep deceiving. *Deceiving* is **dolioo** from **dolos** which means to lure by baiting a hook, covering it with a small piece of food to disguise its danger. The fish bites the food to get its next meal. Instead, he becomes the meal for the fisherman. Those who deceive deal treacherously in that they betray trust, provide insecure footing or support, marked by hidden dangers, or use fraud (intentional perversion of truth in order to induce another to part with something of value or to surrender a legal right). Fraud usually implies a deliberate perversion of the truth. They deceive by using trickery and falsehood. Here you see this word used of men who deceive. With their words, they bait the hook with what appears to be something good to eat. Men bite, but only to find a hidden hook meant to catch them and put them into greater bondage.

Lies and deceit. Lies about others are eagerly devoured like candy to a child. The question never far from my mind during my prison trial was: *When did it become acceptable to lie?* Men have always lied, but today it is not frowned upon but deemed acceptable (and sometimes even encouraged and praised). Even in our judicial system meant to uphold the law, the ends (a conviction) justify any means, including lies and deceit (fraud). Our attorneys assured us this was a totally acceptable means of jurisprudence.

The poison of asps is under their lips. This is from Psalm 140:3. *Poison* is **ios** from **hiemi** which means to send. It is something sent out. One Greek meaning is an arrow, a meaning not found in the New Testament. The picture is of the venom ejected from the serpent's fangs. James says no one can tame the tongue (James 3:8). The asp was a deadly, Egyptian cobra whose poison was stored in a bag under its lips. The bite of the asp is deadly unless that part of the body bitten is quickly cut away. The metaphor, interestingly, is that we need to cut ourselves away from ungodly conversation. You have, perhaps, heard of the phrase, 'venomous words'. People love to strike at others with their poisonous fangs. Spurgeon in his comments on Psalm 140:3 says: **They have sharpened their tongues like a serpent.**

> "The rapid motion of a viper's tongue gives you the idea of its sharpening it; even thus do the malicious move their tongues at such a rate that one might suppose them to be in the very act of wearing them to a point, or rubbing them to a keen edge. It was a common notion that serpents inserted their poison by their tongues, and the poets used the idea as a poetical expression, although it is certain that the serpent wounds by his fangs and not by his tongue…. The deadliest of all venom is the slander of the unscrupulous. Our text, however, must not be confined in its reference to some few individuals, for in the inspired epistle to the Romans it is quoted as being true of us all. The old serpent has not only inoculated us with his venom, but he has caused us to be ourselves producers of the like poison: it lies under our lips, ready for us, and, alas, it is all too freely used when we grow angry, and desire to take vengeance upon any who have caused us vexation."
>
> ~ Treasury of David[2]

Romans 3:14—**Whose mouth is full of cursing and bitterness.** A mouth stuffed full—of toxic waste. *Cursing* is **ara** (only here in the New Testament) which originally meant a wish, a petition, a prayer. It is a prayer or invocation for harm or injury to come upon someone, an imprecation or invocation of evil upon another. Cursing refers to wanting the worst for someone and publicly expressing that desire in caustic, derisive language. It represents an open, public expression of emotional hostility against one's enemy.

Bitterness is **pikria** which is to cut or prick. Originally, it meant pointed or sharp. It spoke of arrows more than what is sharp or penetrating to the senses. Literally, it is a bitter, pungent taste or smell and what is 'painful' to the feelings. It was literally used to describe plants that produced inedible or poisonous fruit. No doubt, you have known bitter people who hold a long-standing, smoldering resentment in a spirit which refuses to be reconciled. Bitterness broods as it holds fast to its grudges. They fret and fume, irritable in their attitudes toward someone who has hurt them. Bitterness nurses its wrath, keeping it warm, so it can continually brood over insults and injuries it has received. Bitterness is like a ticking time-bomb ready to go off inside of someone. It is emotional hostility against an enemy that poisons the whole inner man. Eventually, that time bomb will go off releasing all the feelings kept inside in an explosion of wrath that can no longer be contained.

Romans 3:15—**Their feet are swift to shed blood.** We first saw man's sin through his words. Now, Paul turns to men's deeds and actions. Feet symbolize walking or conduct. Swift implies eagerness. Shed blood is murder. So, men are eager to murder others. There is hatred and malice born in the heart of every man. Two words that illustrate this, which are all too familiar in our day, are wars and abortion. And I think of something else that happened in our day— Auschwitz. All these come from the same wicked heart of man.

How quickly, as a child, did you loosely throw out the word *hate*? You did not get your way with the other children you were playing with and so you stormed away saying, "I hate you all!" Father and Mother punished you and you said, "I hate you!" Where did that come from in such a young child? Man loves violence and rushes to it. How much more exaggerated has this become today in entitled people who demand their rights or take matters into their own hands? I will remember the year 2020 as the year Americans were bombarded with the most blatant displays of lies, deceit and hatred within our own walls in my lifetime.

Romans 3:16—**Destruction and misery are in their paths.** *Destruction* is **suntrimma** which means to break into pieces, crush completely resulting in total devastation. Destruction, decimation, calamity, ruin, or that which is laid waste. Whatever fallen man touches he destroys.

Misery is **talaiporia** which means afflicted, wretched, miserable, or a distressed condition of suffering. It is the resulting harm that always belongs to the man acting in destruction against his fellow man leaving a trail of pain and despair to all involved. This word describes overwhelming hardship, trouble, suffering, or distress. *Misery* is an emotional condition that comes from inner or outer torment. His *path* is anywhere he goes in life—his daily walk through life.

Romans 3:17—**And the path of peace they have not known.** *Peace* is **eirene** which means to bind together (what is broken or divided). Used here, it does not mean that lack of inner peace or absence of peace with God, although that is a characteristic of the ungodly. It is describing man's natural tendency to move away from peace and toward violence, strife, and conflict with his fellow man. Facebook is such an obvious public display of this today. This conflict resulting in murder happened very soon after creation with Cain killing Abel. Man, almost from day one, has been intent on killing man. But the epitome is man bent on killing God. Could it be that man kills man because he cannot kill God?

Romans 3:18—**There is no fear of God before their eyes.** Men may fear other men, even what other men think of them. Men may fear the police. They may fear a judge. They may fear any person in authority over them. It can be a fear of being caught in sin or having sin exposed. These same people, though, have no fear of the Judge over all the universe.

Some people like to refer to God as 'the man upstairs' or worship like they are high at a night club. Any professing Christian who has no reverential fear of God is a nominal 'Christian'—a 'Christian' in name only. Reverential fear of God includes conviction of sin and repentance. No child of God sins flippantly, nonchalantly, without a care or thought of offending holy God. And he doesn't intentionally put himself in evil's path, but turns away from evil because he hates it. Any person who believes he can live any way he wants to and does not fear God is not a true believer.

Job feared God. **"There was a man in the land of Uz, whose name was Job, and that man was blameless, upright, fearing God, and turning away from evil."** (Job 1:1) *Before* is **apenanti** which means in a position that faces against an object or other position—opposite to, over against, in front of, in the presence of. In other words, the man of Romans 3:18 does not keep the fear of God in front of his eyes. He does not consider the fear of God in living out his life.

We have seen a man's throat, his tongue, his lips, his mouth, his feet, and his eyes. This represents the total depravity of man. His whole being is adversely affected by sin. Man has totally failed in the purpose for which he was created which is to glorify God and enjoy Him forever. In Psalm 148, we see that the whole creation is invoked to praise the Lord. When we were young and obeyed our fathers, we were honoring them as the authority God had placed over us. We were treating them as their position over us demanded. It was right, and it was good. Our obedience to their leadership enabled them to protect us as they saw best. When we disobeyed them, even though there was a rod associated with the consequences, it was because they loved us. Our obedience reflected the fact that we were our father's children. Did you ever get ready to walk out of the house as a teenager only to have one or both of your parents say to you: "Remember who you are." They were saying: "Remember whose child you are. Honor your parents and the family name by your actions."

In the Old Testament, Aaron was the High Priest of God when the children of Israel were wandering in the wilderness. Aaron's sons, Nadab and Abihu, were priests as well. They failed to follow the proper procedures for serving God in the tabernacle, so God killed them. For some, their flesh cringes when they hear stories like that because they have come to believe that the God of the Old Testament has somehow evolved into only a "God of love" in the New Testament, as if His character has changed in time. That thinking fails to honor God because it is a false view of who He is. How did Aaron respond? **Then Moses said to Aaron, "It is what the LORD spoke, saying, 'By those who come near Me I will be treated as holy, and before all the people I will be honored.'" So, Aaron, therefore, kept silent.** (Leviticus 10:3)

Try to picture yourself in similar circumstances. First, can you even imagine being in Moses' position? Basically, he was affirming to Aaron why it was right that God struck down his children. That would be tough to do—to have that kind of courage to speak the truth to a grieving parent. Today, we would probably say it was not the right time—ever! I believe Moses, in *love*, was reminding Aaron of God's holiness so that Aaron might not say something he might regret, which might further dishonor God. Moses feared God, loved Aaron, and was passionate about seeing God honored as God. Notice the next little word phrase. *So, therefore.* Aaron does something next because of what Moses had just reminded him. In an act of worship, *Aaron kept silent.* Could you hold your tongue, Beloved? Fear of God restrained Aaron.

As parents, sometimes we are compelled to make excuses for our kids' wrong behavior. My father-in-law jokingly called my mother-in-law Perry Mason, for she was often going to 'court' to defend one of her children. We may laugh about that because we can so often relate. But, here, Aaron kept silent. Being a parent, I have so much respect for Aaron in that response because it greatly honored God.

In Numbers 20, when the children of Israel started to complain against Moses because they wanted water, God told Moses to speak to the rock, and water would come forth. There wasn't any need to complain because God had continually provided their every need in the wilderness. (The Word is a mirror to us reflecting the glory of God. Did you have a whine-free day today?) As their leader, fully exasperated by the lack of faith in this rebellious people, Moses struck the rock, and water gushed forth. But *Moses* got punished! Why? God did not tell Moses to *strike* the rock, but to *speak* to the rock. We are quick to think: *Hardly seems fair.* We think: *What's the big deal? Don't the ends justify the means?* God punished Moses because, as their leader, he was to be an example to the people in honoring God as God. We get our feathers ruffled for Moses because we know how easily exasperated one can get when dealing with whiners. Once again, it is because we do not understand the holy God we are dealing with. Apparently, Moses was still learning hard lessons, too. **But the LORD said to Moses and Aaron, "Because you have not believed Me, to treat Me as holy in the sight of the sons of Israel, therefore you shall not bring this assembly into the land which I have given them."** (Numbers 20:12) You have not *believed* Me, to treat Me as holy. Disobedience is unbelief.

One may say, "Well, I am glad we do not serve the God of the Old Testament any longer and that we live in the age of grace." But can we say, "Ananias and Sapphira"? Sapphira. I don't think I've ever heard of a baby girl named Sapphira since then. Such a beautiful name for someone whose tragic story is recorded for us in the pages of the New Testament lest we somehow believe we serve a 'softer' God who is not as holy—who is more tolerant of sin.

Everyone in the early church was united in helping each other self-sacrificially as anyone had need. All who owned property were selling it and giving the proceeds to the church to help care for those who were poor and lacking. Isn't that a beautiful picture of trust? Not to be outdone, Ananias and Sapphira wanted to get in on the action. They wanted to help; however, they sold their property with the wrong motives. Whatever their reasons were, it was the rebellion in their hearts that caused them to lie about the proceeds from the sale. They could have given all or just a portion of the proceeds from the sale. It was theirs to do with as they pleased. They were free, as believers, to do whatever they wanted with their own resources as God led. They were **not** free, however, to sin. Instead of being upfront and honest about the price for which they sold their property, they lied and said what they were giving was the full price. They had kept back part for themselves. Understand, they had every right to do so. But they lied, and the Holy Spirit put it on Peter's heart to question them about it. Without the opportunity for excuses, Ananias was struck down instantly, dead on the spot.

When the men finished burying him, unaware of what had just transpired, Ms. Sapphira sauntered down the aisle approximately three hours later, no doubt fully expecting heartfelt accolades from the others as she made her grand entrance. She probably imagined the whisperers saying, "What a gracious woman. We are so blessed to have her in our congregation!" She must have shook her head twice, though, thinking she did not hear right when she was confronted. Having the opportunity to tell the truth, she was also questioned as to whether the money given was the full price received in the sale; and, she answered exactly as her husband. God didn't give her time to squirm or be embarrassed when caught in her lie. She immediately received the same fate as her husband. How many people sit in our churches today who give to be seen and acknowledged by men? What does man's opinion mean when God can see all? Even the intentions of man's heart are seen by Him. I can only imagine that lying would not be so acceptable in our day and age if each instance was responded to by God in like manner.

What is interesting is what this incident produced inside and outside the church. It produced a fear of holy God, and rightly so (Acts 5:11-14). Those within the church had a holy, reverent fear of the God of the church. Additionally, there were two groups of people outside the church—those who did not believe but still had a fear of the people in the church because of the God whom they served, and those who, because of their fear, believed and became part of the church.

I put a lot of Scripture on my daughter's tombstone when she died. I wanted it to be a witness to all who would see it (especially those her age). One of the Scriptures was Hebrews 4:13, which may have seemed odd to some people: **"And there is no creature hidden from His sight, but all things are open and laid bare to the eyes of Him with whom we have to do."** He sees it all. We will never get away with anything. Ever. We will all stand before God one day and give an account of our lives. Punishment and judgment, in this life, may or may not be as swift as that of Ananias and Sapphira, but it is as sure. A scripture verse I learned early in my Christian life is found in Numbers 32:23: **"…behold, you have sinned against the LORD, and be sure your sin will find you out."**

I thought about that Scripture in Hebrews one day while I was sitting in prison eleven years later. I never got the chance to convince a jury or the Court that I was not hiding anything during the time period of my alleged crime. One of the aspects of money laundering (the crime of which I was accused and convicted), that **must** be proven by the Government, is concealment. One must know he or she is money laundering as evidenced by types of concealment. There was hard evidence in our possession (as well as in the possession of our attorneys *and* the government) to easily disprove all government theories of concealment. However, only their theories of concealment, based on mere conjecture and circumstantial evidence, was offered to the jury. Our hard evidence was never presented in our defense. It was *concealed* from the jury. I never concealed anything. Why would I try to conceal something when I know *the* **Judge** who sees all and knows all? Fearing Him, I know that He alone has the authority to judge my sin, and His judgment would be far worse than that of any earthly court.

We were made to glorify God and to enjoy fellowship with Him. Through obedience to His will, His purpose in creating man is fulfilled. But, alas, we fail so often, because we have a deeply rooted, depraved, default belief that continues to tempt our flesh to view everything in this world as existing for our pleasure and our glory. It is a lie, and it is sinful to believe that way. The message of the Bible, on the contrary, is that the world does **not** revolve around us. If you are a child of God and have not yet learned this lesson to any depth, trust me; you will. If you are reading this book because you are suffering, this truth will become a bittersweet reality as you let the Master teach you in His school of suffering. It is not about us, it never has been about us, and we should not want it to be either. The problem is we can *say* we don't want or believe the world revolves around us, but the sad reality is that in our human depravity, in our flesh, we *do* want it to be about us. We must fight that notion with all our being. The evidence of that reality is in how much we want our own way every moment of every day. And this sin will need to be diligently fought against until we are glorified in Him.

Maybe you *do* believe everything in your world should be for your good and your pleasure. Maybe you think if your needs and desires are fulfilled, life is good and things are just as they should be. All is right with your world! In your mind, you're 'okay'. Maybe this concept of everything being about God in this life is foreign to you. You go to church and have always considered yourself to be somewhat religious, but you don't go to *extremes* like others you know. You believe you are a good person and that you will find yourself in heaven along with others just like you—at least that's what you have tried to tell yourself—but you're beginning to see the truth about yourself. You are beginning to doubt that what you have been led to believe your whole life is true. You must ask yourself some questions: Upon what are your beliefs based? What is your source of truth? Where did your beliefs come from? Will those beliefs support you on Judgment Day? Do you have hard evidence to back up your beliefs? Or are your beliefs based merely upon conjecture and circumstantial evidence? The truth of God's Word is the only solid foundation of evidence that will stand on Judgment Day.

If what you believe is contrary to God's Word, you are deceived, stand cursed, and are headed for judgment to ultimately experience God's wrath for all eternity in hell. What you believe about your standing before this holy God are lies. I pray that you will cry out to the one true and living God—the God of the

Bible—pleading with Him to pour out His mercy upon you, to help you understand what you read in His Word, and to bring you into a right relationship with Him. Maybe you find yourself suffering. It is quite possible that the pain you are experiencing at this very moment is the thing God is using to draw you to Himself. Then blessed be the Refiner's fire. It is only as He breaks us through pain and sorrow that we will start to want nothing but His glory. It is part of our fallen nature to love this world and live for the temporal. We don't want to think about eternity when life on earth is good. Imagine a hot air balloon which is tethered to the ground. Each cord represents an anchor of something temporal we love that keeps us bound to this earth. In our lives, God allows us to experience difficult trials. One by one each bond is cut loose freeing our hearts to live solely for the eternal.

But even for the believer who has experienced untold agonies and heartaches in this life, the remnants of that sin nature will linger until he or she is ultimately glorified. It is our daily duty to battle and crucify our flesh as it raises its ugly head of pride, and we can only do that in the strength that Christ provides. It is not about us. It is **His**-story because it has always only been about Him; and He alone deserves all glory, honor, and praise from His creation. Those who rightly understand not only who He is, but who we are in the light of His greatness, will find it their greatest privilege and joy to give Him what He alone deserves. We are not what God wants us to be. Not even close. How on earth did we get this way?

8
Give It to Me Straight ~ How Bad Is It?

"Give it to me straight." "Don't beat around the bush." Nobody wants to be lied to. We are always to speak the truth to one another in love, even if the news is bad. God is love and truth. The truth of our human condition is painful to hear, but love tells us like it is.

Adam's first act of disobedience was sin. Sin is lawlessness. It is rebellion against the righteous standard God has established. When Adam chose to rebel against God, he was no longer able to reflect God's image accurately. That which Adam had been able to clearly reflect was now tarnished. Sin had entered the world and into Adam. He passed this marred image to all his descendants after him. God is holy, and anything that mars or distorts His image or His glory is sin. Speaking of Adam, Paul tells us in Romans 5:12: **Therefore, just as through one man sin entered into the world, and death through sin, and so death spread to all men, because all sinned.** While we still bear God's image to some degree, we also bear the effects of sin morally, socially, and physically. So, just how far have we fallen in Adam, the father of our human race?

We are told in Romans 3 that none are righteous, not even one. Later in the chapter it is further stated that all have sinned and fallen short of the glory of God. The fact that we have all fallen short of our created purpose should devastate us to our very core. On the contrary, our cavalier attitudes reveal our ignorance. We're **failures** in life from the moment we are born because, in ourselves, no matter how great the world says we are, we fail to achieve the purpose for which we were created.

Most people believe that the ultimate failure in life is to be unhappy. But we are born failures, losers with a 'L'! No one wants to be a failure at anything, especially today when this generation has been repeatedly told that they can do and be anything they set their minds to. We are so busy handing out trophies for just showing up that we have not noticed we have already *lost* the game! To be a 'loser' in life is humiliating and painful. It's hard to wrap our minds around this truth. How many people welcome a precious child into the world and say, "Look, honey, a little loser." We're born lost, with no ability to fulfill the purpose for which we were created. The whole human race has failed its most basic and most reasonable purpose for existence. That this does not cause us the greatest sorrow and heartache reveals the depths of our sinful state. **All of us like sheep have gone astray, each of us has turned to his own way.** (Isaiah 53:6)

The grand dilemma stares us glaringly in the face. God is perfect in holiness. He is separate and distinct from His creation. In fact, His eyes are too pure to approve evil, and He cannot even look on wickedness, says the prophet Habakkuk (Habakkuk 1:3). God calls us to be holy because He is holy. God did not say we need to be 'holy enough'. He said we are to be holy. **He** is the definition of holy. So we are to be holy like He is holy.

Sitting at a gathering of friends and family, the obvious fact that I'm a sinner and you're a sinner may soothe our consciences as we rationalize in our minds that we are all in the same boat. After all, it feels so good to be a part of the crowd. If I feel any twinges of conviction whatsoever, I may assuage them by convincing myself that I am not as bad as half the people in that boat. Based on our camaraderie, we may even be able to create a god we are all able to worship as long as we are all comfortable with our miserable lot and as long as no one comes along and tries to rock our boat with a 'judgmental standard' that calls for righteousness. But what if one with beautiful feet *does* come along and forces us to give an accounting for where we believe our boat is headed and why we believe it to be so? The one who comes with beautiful feet, pointing us to the only One to whom we are to rightly compare ourselves, will not only rock our boat, but he will likely capsize it with a Rock of Offense! Isaiah 52:7 rightly says: **How lovely on the mountains are the feet of him who brings good news, who announces peace and brings good news of happiness, who announces salvation, and says to Zion, "Your God reigns!"** He may have beautiful feet, but what comes out of this one's mouth may sound anything *but* lovely—at first.

When God set down the Law of 'do not eat' that would govern Adam and Eve, it was for their own good. Everything God does is good and right. The Law given to Adam was for his good even if he did not fully understand why. What mattered was that Adam trust what God said. Trusting God means believing His Word *as* His Word.

"Because I said so," may have sounded really lame to me coming from my parents' mouths when I was a child. But when I became a parent, it made perfect sense. No doubt those of us who are mothers have used that old, but never worn-out response. Our commands to our children do not always demand a reason. We could simply say, "It is for your own good," and we believe that should suffice. There may come a day when my child is running out into the street after a ball oblivious to the truck barreling straight for him. When I shout, "Stop, now!" he does not need a lengthy explanation as to why I have the need to give him that order. It is vital that he learns to trust my love for him. A parent lays down the law—day in and day out—in disciplined training. One day, as the child is about to cross the street, the words of his parents come to mind as a warning *before* he is tempted to dart into the street. And he obeys that voice.

When reading of Adam's tragic decision in the Garden, some are quick to think, "Poor Adam! M-a-y-b-e God shouldn't have put that tree there." Or, "M-a-y-b-e God should have explained to Adam more fully why he wasn't to eat of that one tree." When Adam and Eve sinned, whose fault was it? Was their sin God's fault? Did the devil make them do it? Whose fault is it when I sin every single time? **Let no one say when he is tempted, "I am being tempted by God"; for God cannot be tempted by evil, and He Himself does not tempt anyone. But each one is tempted when he is carried away and enticed by his own lust. Then when lust has conceived, it gives birth to sin; and when sin is accomplished, it brings forth death.** (James 1:13-15)

When we sin, we choose to sin. The difference between a believer and an unbeliever is a Christian is free to obey God's Law in the Spirit. From the greatest person to the least, we choose our prisons that confine and bind us. Every time we sin it is because we choose to give in to the enticing temptations of our own lusts or desires. We want to please ourselves more than we want to obey and please God. In choosing sin, we do not treat God as holy. It is not the temptation that is sinful, but the being carried away by our lusts or giving in to them. Sadly, when sin is accomplished, it brings forth death. Every…single…time.

We also need to understand that we do not just sin without a moment's thought. Sin, as seen in the passage above, is a process. It starts with a thought. As we turn that thought over and over in our minds, it feeds our desires which, eventually, fuel our will to do what we lust after in our hearts. Sin's battle begins in the mind where truth and lies are waging war for our hearts. Once sin is born, it **always** brings forth death.

Romans 6:23 tells us the wages of sin is death. Our sin is grave because of the holiness of the One it offends. We have all earned eternal death because we have all sinned. Did Adam and Eve die when they sinned? There are three types of death which all involve separation. Physically, the moment they sinned, Adam and Eve were not separated from their bodies, but they would be later in time. Spiritually, their sin did separate them from God the moment they succumbed to temptation—thus, they did die spiritually. Lastly, there is eternal death, or what is known as the second death in Scripture. For the one who is spiritually dead, this last death is separation from God for all eternity.

Have you ever heard the expression that a car starts depreciating the moment you drive it off the lot? Every human being is born spiritually dead and begins dying physically the minute they are born. Because of sin, death is a reality for everyone. We are either dead spiritually and dying physically, heading towards eternal death; or we are spiritually alive, dying physically, heading toward eternal life. If we are in the latter category, we are crucifying and killing the flesh by overcoming the temptation to sin daily. People in this world living in sin who believe they are 'living it up' are really the walking dead. And they have no idea. Those who are willingly crucifying their sinful flesh are truly living eternal life that began the moment they put their faith in Jesus Christ to save them. While we still live in bodies of flesh, watching the spiritually dead "live it up" in this life is sometimes hard to deal with. So, we must keep an eternal perspective of that which is to come because Satan is quite adept at baiting the lure to woo us back to the world.

Everyone is going to live forever either in heaven or in hell. We will all receive resurrection bodies, some fitted for hell and some fitted for glory. There will be no annihilation. There is either eternal punishment or eternal life. *Eternal* means everlasting or without end. Hebrews 9:27 says it is appointed for men to die once and after this comes judgment, so judgment comes after death. Judgment is set or fixed at the time of one's death. There are no second chances—no 'do-overs'. In other words, there is no purgatory or reincarnation. To think that somebody could give some money to the church or light some candles to get me out of purgatory is ludicrous. Having once converted to Catholicism, I bought the lie. I never bought *that* lie, specifically, but the whole package in general. When I was Catholic, I wrongly believed that I could pick and choose what I wanted to believe from Catholic doctrine. Let me say emphatically with all the authority of God's Word behind this truth: This life is all the opportunity we get to glorify God and live for Him before final judgment. That is not my opinion but God's Word on the subject.

This news should cause every human being to be as shaken as if he were standing in the middle of the worst earthquake in the history of man. But it doesn't. Men hear this basic truth over and over condemning it as hellfire and brimstone preaching, and they proceed with their daily lives as if it did not even faze them. How **should** we react to the understanding that judgment is coming—the judgment of God Almighty's wrath against all sinners? **Sinners in Zion are terrified; trembling has seized the godless. "Who among us can live with the consuming fire? Who among us can live with continual burning?"** (Isaiah 33:14)

If people *do* get to some point of conviction, it is often, then, the backpedaling begins. In junior high, I got a 10-speed bike. I was flabbergasted to know that I could pedal backwards far easier and faster than pedaling forward, even though pedaling backwards did not take me anywhere. Another picture that pops into my mind is my little sister getting stuck on a mall escalator when my parents' backs were turned when she was very young. As we heard this blood-curdling scream, we turned to see her trying to get off the landing. Once she realized the stairs were taking her away from her family, she started trying to back off with all her strength. She was fighting against what the stairs were intended to do. She was curious enough to approach the stairs and to test them out, but when she could not understand them, she got scared and panicked.

Sometimes, people do begin to think about judgment to come, and they are convicted. However, when they begin to count the cost of salvation, they frantically start backpedaling in their thoughts. Pedaling as fast as they can, they try to get away from the truth while holding onto anything that would support their false belief that they can't possibly be as bad as Scripture says, and that there *must* be something they can **do** to earn heaven. They understand that if Scripture means what it says, their backs are up against a wall just as surely as the children of Israel were up against the Red Sea with the enemy driving them forward. Fear causes our human nature to default to rationalization. The flesh begins to reason that if a person can have his good outweigh his bad in this life, God will surely allow him to spend eternity in heaven. Thousands of years of tradition and prodigious belief systems can't be wrong, can they? They can, and *they are*. Scripture is clear that we can't do anything to save ourselves. So, 'good enough' will never apply to anyone's salvation. **He saved us, not on the basis of deeds which we have done in righteousness, but according to His mercy, by the washing of regeneration and renewing of the Holy Spirit.** (Titus 3:5)

I was born and raised in the town of Ligonier, Pennsylvania. The population is around 1,500 people. My ancestors settled in the area in the early 1700's. We were not wealthy, but with strong roots in the community and a relative on almost every corner, I was raised with the understanding that values are important. My roots, no matter where I am, ground me. While it's important to remember where you are from, it's even more important is to make sure you know where you are going. Wondering how I ended up in prison, I thought of Ligonier every day. I thought of my simple, happy childhood where it took a playing card, a clothespin, and a bicycle to keep kids occupied for hours. People sat on porches in the evening and talked about 'life'. Even when looking back at good memories, my thoughts always came back to who I am now in Christ and how I could live for and glorify Him in that hard place.

Ironically, there is more *focus* today on 'positivity' than there was in my day. According to some, all negativity is to be somehow banned from our lives. While I understand we are not to spend our lives in bitterness focusing on the faults of others and ourselves, and we are to believe the best about others in any given situation, the gospel is negative before it is positive. Some go so far as to say there is power in our positivity; and if we are positive enough, we can effectively control our future by speaking the life we want into existence. *Hogwash!* You are not God, and your words have no creative power to change your circumstances making life the way you want it to be. You have no power to make the universe conform to your will. You don't even control your next breath. This book, just from a quick look at the chapter titles, does not speak only positive words. I am not trying to blow smoke or trying to inflate anyone's already bloated ego. Positive, no. Life-giving, yes. Come to think about it, what's positive without negative anyways?

What are my spiritual roots? Get ready for some negative vibes! Ephesians 2:1-3 informs us of our fallen state before we were saved by God. This was written by Paul to those believers who had put their faith in Christ Jesus alone to save them. **And you *were* dead in your trespasses and sins, in which you *formerly walked* according to the course of this world, according to the prince of the power of the air, of the spirit that is now working in the sons of disobedience. Among them we too all *formerly lived* in the lusts of our flesh, indulging the desires of the flesh and of the mind, and *were* by nature children of wrath, even as the rest.** (Italics mine.) Just from a cursory observation, I can see several things from this text: I was dead. Because of my sinful state, I was born spiritually dead while physically alive. Walking like the world, I was going with the flow, trying to fit with the in-crowd. Swimming with the current world tide, I lived to fulfill my desires, and my mind was bent towards doing all for my glory, not God's. I wanted all the world had to offer no matter what the cost. The world systems are operating according to Satan's plan. This prince of the power of the air is working in unbelievers. I once belonged to my father, Satan. It brought him much delight when I lived for my myself. Just one of his many children, my brothers and sisters were also under his control; and my greatest fellowship was with them.

Living in the lusts of my flesh simply means that first and foremost, I lived to please myself—to make myself happy. I lived for my passions, impulsively indulging myself with anything that I craved or desired. Not wanting to hold back anything from myself, if it was in my reach, I was going to grab it. The desires I thought about, I pursued—those desires that made me feel good and happy without thought or care of consequences. This was the nature I was born with. I did not have to think about how to live. I lived out of this nature I was born with—a sinner living for myself because my world was all about me, myself, and I. In fact, I lived as though God did not exist! At that time separate from Christ, I was destined for God's wrath, and I deserved it; but I *thought* I deserved His love and favor. Even if my desires were not as sinful as someone else's, the key is that I was living according to my desires without giving any thought to how my Creator wanted me to live. Therefore, my desires and my fulfilling those desires were sinful. And that sinfulness was going to result in my eternal death.

In this state, I was imprisoned with bars far more permanent than anything I have come to know from a physical earthly prison, yet I was unaware of anything holding me in bondage. Even when life seemed good to me, I was still speeding towards judgment at breakneck speed that should have caused fear and trembling, the likes of which I have never known before. I knew fear when the police pulled into our driveway to inform me of Missy's death. I can only imagine the fear she knew the moment she realized she was going to crash her car. When the police pulled into our driveway to arrest my husband—later to search our home, and then again to arrest Greg, Jesse, and I—I knew real fear. Everyone who hears the word *cancer* or *terminal* are instantaneously paralyzed with fear. We all experience traumatic and terrifying events that mark our lives with fear. But nothing can be compared to the fear we *should* know while we are oblivious to the impending wrath of God Almighty!

My generation has been encouraged to change any situation with which one is not happy. In a popular show from the 70's, the father told his children, "If you don't like your situation, then do something about it." Even if I can come to some sort of understanding that I am a sinner, maybe not believing my condition is as bad as it really is, 'religion' tells me that I must *work* to change my status. I must *do something* to make myself acceptable to God. All man-made religion comes to this bottom-line conclusion.

Man-made religion is a belief system to which man has added rules, dogma, or tradition to the truth of God's Word. Man-made religion redefines God. In matters of interpretation pertaining to their belief systems, man-made religions make God's Word conform to *their* doctrines, rather than holding God's Word as the sole authority by which every thought is measured. In doing so, they are elevating their authority over God's authority. All man-made religion is based on the premise that man is not that bad; and if he does enough good works, he can gain favor with God.

According to human reasoning, if we work hard enough at being 'good', we believe God will reward us for it. We want to believe we will be rewarded with health, wealth, and happiness—in this life. Job's 'friends' believed this faulty ideology. Job was suffering greatly; therefore, his friends reasoned, Job must have sinned greatly. Taken to its logical conclusion, however, are these questions: How good is good enough? Who gets to determine which works are good and which works are evil? Who defines 'good'?

God cannot be in the presence of sin, but we think that somehow the good works we do will, in the end, outweigh the bad. The problem is in our 'human' reasoning. We know we sin, but we cannot believe we are that bad. Failing to understand that there is a great chasm between God's holiness and man's sinfulness, we want to believe that we are all traveling on different roads that all lead to God. But God's ways are not our ways. **There is a way which seems right to a man, but its end is the way of death.** (Proverbs 14:12)

When we did go to church growing up, I remember coming home feeling good about myself—somehow cleaner and purer. I felt as though I had done something to make myself better. I could not have told you what any of it had to do with anything regarding life or eternity, but I had a sense that I had done something good. Realistically, I had done nothing more than sit and listen to a man speak. Usually there were a few Scriptures read, a few songs sang, and then a nice, sometimes humorous story that I probably would not remember for long. In truth, what had I done? Something good? What a terrible lie from the pit of hell.

When I was Catholic, I loved having my senses aroused by the sights, sounds, and smells of the rich ceremonies and traditions—the elaborate architecture and decor, the bells, the incense, the candles, etc. There was a mystical, emotional high that connected me to *something*. I believed it was God. It absolutely was not.

A lot of people in the world say they follow Christ. At this point we would need to ask, "Will the real Jesus please stand up?" He is clearly seen in His Word. To follow Him alone, one must walk through a narrow gate. He said, **"Enter through the narrow gate; for the gate is wide and the way is broad that leads to destruction,**

and there are many who enter through it. For the gate is small and the way is narrow that leads to life, and there are few who find it." (Matthew 7:13-14) Where you end up always depends upon which road you take. Sometimes there are several different roads that will take us to one destination—in this life. Regarding eternal destinations, Jesus said there are only two gates leading to two roads. There is a wide gate leading to a wide road, and many are walking there. There is a narrow gate leading to a narrow road, and few are walking there. Jesus didn't say there are many gates. He clearly did not teach universalism. There are only two gates; one is right, and one is wrong.

Now imagine a man who has been driving for days to get to the bedside of a loved one who is gravely ill. Passing through my small town, we strike up a conversation. I quickly notice that he is going in the complete opposite direction of where he wants to go, and he is clueless. Do I tell him? Or do I smile and think to myself, *Well, it would not be tolerant for me to tell him my way is the only right way to get to his destination. He would think I am being too dogmatic. No. I will just keep my mouth shut and hope I brighten his day with my smile.* That is ludicrous. Jesus said the only way to heaven is through the narrow gate. We need to tell our loved ones, and those we encounter along the way in this life, that if they are not on that narrow road, they are not going where they think they are going.

Logically, if someone believes that God is *only* a God of love, then the road where we find the most people would be the road to God, for the broad road would accommodate or tolerate everyone. We would assume that a narrow road would be for people who hold to their narrow convictions, whom the world deems not loving but judgmental. Jesus, however, points to the narrow road as the one road we need to be on if our destination is heaven. Who do you believe?

We would assume those who are traveling on the broad road sincerely believe or at least hope they are headed to heaven. What would cause so many people to be walking on this wide road? It is because both roads are marked, 'This way to heaven'. In other words, there are those who preach a very different message who say, "Listen to me, follow my 'Jesus', and you will go to heaven. It is *easy* to be a Christian." There are two very different messages.

One is inclusive and allows for everyone, regardless of their beliefs, to come along for the journey. Travelers on this road can bring all their trophies and awards proving all the good they have done—all those things they believe will usher them into heaven. This way puts the focus on you and your good deeds. The other way is exclusive. In order to enter through the narrow gate, you must believe there is only one way. You will appear to the world to be narrow-minded. You must be stripped of everything you might try to offer God to let you into His Kingdom. This way puts the focus on God's holiness.

One message is easy to believe, and one is hard. One allows you to live the way you want to live and says you can have your best life now; the other calls you to deny yourself, to crucify your flesh daily, and understand that your best life is to come. One message says that God only cares about your happiness, the other message says God wants you to be holy—and you can't do anything yourself to achieve that holiness. One says salvation came by something you did. The other says you must throw yourself on the mercy of God and beg for His forgiveness, because He alone can save you. One says rest the hope of your eternal security on yourself and what you have done, the other says to put your whole weight upon Christ and what He has done.

My sister loves to tell the story of an incident when I was blatantly rebellious in breaking the law while driving. I was not saved at the time and was a new driver. We were driving on an interstate highway and had been driving for a long while when we realized we were heading in the wrong direction. Panicking more with each road marker we passed, I had no idea what to do. But I clearly did not choose the right thing. (There was no GPS back then. Lost was lost!) At the first opportunity, I did an illegal U-turn—you know those places where police usually sit? I was a basket case, but I accomplished the feat. My point is this: Maybe you have just realized you are on the wrong road. That U-turn, albeit illegal in this context, looks just like repentance. You need to make an immediate and dramatic U-turn and ask the Lord to get you on the other road. Right now. Ask Him to show you the truth.

Throughout my Christian walk, undoubtedly, it has been the Lord who has kept me on the straight and narrow path walking in the right direction. That is not to say that I have not tried to veer off the path at times to do things my way (I *know* my heart is prone to wander, and it grieves me). But God is always faithful, as a good and loving Father, to lead me and guide me back to where I need to be.

With that said, over the years, I have found a principle to help me discern whether something is of God or not, and it has rarely failed me. When 'everyone' else in 'Christianity' is doing something, my guard goes up and I am leery of following too readily. Almost always, it is a fad that turns out to be built upon sinking sand. Why is that true? It is human nature to love our flesh and to love the things that cater to it. It stands to reason that the crowds will be following hard after those things. If we are to find the narrow road, we must go against the crowds; and that is not going to be easy.

We must ask ourselves: Which gate did we go through, and which road are we on? The Bible tells us: **Test yourselves to see if you are in the faith; examine yourselves! Or do you not recognize this about yourselves, that Jesus Christ is in you—unless indeed you fail the test?** (2 Corinthians 13:5) Do you love the things that God loves? Do you love righteousness and holiness? Do you live to glorify God, or is your life all about you? Is your main goal and purpose in life to glorify you? Ask the hard questions, friend.

Years ago, a friend and I were at lunch talking about the Lord. A heavy burden on her heart, she began to tell me of her concern for her daughter's soul. After a little while, her daughter walked into the restaurant and sat down at our table. In her early 20's and single, she had been raised Catholic, believed she was a Christian, and that her mother had taken things to the extreme. Her attitude was that while it was okay for her mother if she wanted to do so, it was not necessary for her. While we shared Christ with her, she listened politely and intently to everything we had to say. Then she said something I will never forget: "I'll follow Christ harder when I get older. Right now, I just want to live my life and have fun." Sadly, there are many who think this way. They do the least they have to do (what they feel is their duty)—go to church, give a little bit here and there, be kind—and that, they *feel,* is good enough.

When Jesus said to enter through the narrow gate, He is using a tense of the verb for the word *enter* that conveys a sense of urgency. It means to do something now. Do not wait! Do not put off what you need to do today. Do not go to church, hear a sermon, read your Bible, read a book, give a nod of approval to the teaching, and then walk away without allowing the truths to sink deep into your heart and transform it. Jesus is calling us not only to hear His Word but to obey it. None of us knows if the next moment in time will be our last here on earth. We will all die on the day that was ordained for our death (Psalm 139:16). You can do nothing to postpone that day or control it in any way. Nobody who dies suddenly wakes up that morning knowing the exact moment death will occur. Do not keep going with the flow oblivious and blind to what eternity holds for you. Settle the issue today. It is because we don't know what the next moment holds for us that there is an extreme sense of urgency to know if we are true believers or only false professors. The idea of separating true believers from false professors permeates Jesus' teaching and all the teaching of the New Testament. Upon death, we will all wake up either in heaven or in hell.

What if you believe you do all the 'right' things, but have no real heart for God? You say, "I go to church, I serve in the church, I pray, I try to be kind and love everyone." Jesus, in Matthew 7:21-23, was speaking to the religious 'elite', if you will. My outward works would pale in comparison to those He was speaking to for sure. These words are some of the most convicting words in all of Scripture. Yet, His words would be considered harsh and unloving today, and few would tolerate someone who spoke like this: **"Not everyone who says to Me, 'Lord, Lord,' will enter the kingdom of heaven, but he who does the will of My Father who is in heaven will enter. Many will say to Me on that day, 'Lord, Lord, did we not prophesy in Your name, and in Your name cast out demons, and in Your name perform many miracles?' And then I will declare to them, 'I never knew you; DEPART FROM ME, YOU WHO PRACTICE LAWLESSNESS.'"** (Matthew 7:21-23)

Jesus is speaking to religious hypocrites. Sometimes hypocrites are easy to discern. However, when it comes to spiritual matters of the heart, hypocrites are not always so obvious. They are busy doing things that *appear* religious or spiritual, to be sure. Hypocrites call Jesus 'Lord', which implies that He has the authority to make a call to obedience and expect it to be carried out, but they do not do it. It is interesting to note the things they are doing are the showy things that would draw attention to themselves rather than God. Notice how Jesus puts His finger directly on the issue. He says, "I never knew you." He doesn't go into a dissertation about how works can't justify them, making them right with God. On judgment day He will only say to them, "I never knew you." How is it possible that Jesus does not know some of His own creation? Make no mistake about it, Jesus knew their hearts. Imagine if you believed your marriage was thriving, but your husband turned to you one day after 50 years and said, "I never knew you." Devastating!

I never knew you—As Spurgeon says: "There is more thunder in those four words than you ever heard in the most terrible tempest that has rolled over your heads. There is no stamp of the foot or fire-glance of the eye to accompany them; they are spoken calmly and deliberately, yet they are terrible and overwhelming: 'I never knew you.' Not passionately, or angrily, but in stern, sad, solemn tones He said, 'I never knew you.' 'But we used Your name, good Lord.' 'I know you did, but I never knew you, and you never truly knew Me.'"[1]

The word for *knew* is the word **ginosko** in the Greek. It is the knowledge someone gets from personally experiencing or being involved with another person—knowledge that implies relationship of the heart. Often, when Scripture uses this word it describes the intimate relationship between two people, even of marital intimacy. It is what happens when two hearts are joined together as one.

Jesus knew who they were and what was in their hearts. But He never knew any sense of fellowship or communion with them. It is not that they were once saved and lost their salvation. They never saved. They were going through the motions of religion, which is worse than going through the motions of anything else. They were phonies. They were not born again into God's own family but were children who still belonged to Satan's kingdom.

My attorney asked me a question while prepping me for trial. He said, "We must be careful about talking about your religion so much. Why is it so important to you?" I replied, "I have never been quiet about letting people know I am a follower of Jesus Christ. If the jury takes the newspapers and the government at face value and doesn't hear my heart, they will think I am a religious hypocrite." He strongly agreed, "There is *nothing* worse than that."

I discipled a woman in prison who became a close friend. One day we were walking and talking about the Lord. She said, "I have one question for you, though. I just don't understand why it is so important for you to win your case and clear your name. The Lord knows your heart. I mean, you have almost done your time. Who cares what other people think?" I knew it was going to be hard to explain to her what was in my heart. I responded, "You got saved in prison. You did the crime, and you have always admitted it. When you get out of prison and people see your changed life, they will be amazed, and God will be glorified. That is a praiseworthy thing! I claimed to be a Christian long before I was indicted. I've claimed my innocence all along. A jury of my 'peers' did not believe my testimony, so they convicted me. Now, I look like a religious hypocrite, and people's faith may be shaken because of what my 'testimony' looks like. That is why it bothers me." Since that time, I have come to realize that the people who know my heart believe me. Although I eagerly await the day that the Lord vindicates me, I can wait. It is enough that He knows my heart. I can rest in His will.

I heard a sermon that illustrated this Scripture in Matthew 7 a long time ago. I never forgot it. Suppose a friend, speaking of someone famous, says to you, "Do you know so and so?" You say, "Sure." You can respond positively because you do know **of** the person about which they speak. But what if you said, "Sure," and they said, "Does that person know you?" When you put it that way, you do not really *know* the person, or he would know you as well.

Spurgeon in his sermon above entitled, *The Disowned*, notes: "It does not appear that Christ himself openly disowned these people during their lifetime. He held his tongue concerning them until 'that day'. There they were, preaching, teaching a Sunday school class, distributing the bread and wine at the communion, going about among their fellow-members, actively engaged in Christian service, and everybody saying of them, 'What good people they are!' Yet the Lord Jesus Christ knew that they were not; why then, did He not, in His righteous wrath, at once expose them? He did not, for such is His gentleness that He will bear long—even with a Judas; so He let these hypocrites alone throughout their whole lives, and they died 'in the odor of sanctity', and somebody preached a funeral sermon upon them, and wrote their memoir, and it was only at the last great day that the impostor was discovered, and then, for the first time, Christ said publicly to them, 'I never knew you.'"

'DEPART FROM ME, YOU WHO PRACTICE LAWLESSNESS.'
Depart is the word **apochoreo** meaning a marker of dissociation
plus **choréo** (to go from a place, give space) means to move away
from a point, with emphasis upon *separation* and possible lack of
concern for what has left. To depart in the sense of desert or abandon.
The tense of the verb Jesus uses indicates the commanded separation is forever.

These people profess to having practiced their good works in His
name. He says they practiced lawlessness; their lifestyle was sin.
The way of their life is walking contrary to God's law. They reject
God's Law just by living for their own self-centered, flesh-driven
desires. For the believer, his or her life is one in which Christ is at
the center. Believers are to be in a state of constant awareness of
living in Christ's presence asking, "What would He have me do, say,
or think in this situation?" It is understanding that my life is not
my own and that I am living for the sole purpose of His glory.

The masses never picture themselves in this final judgment
scene with Jesus. Lawlessness may look like this: A topic comes up
and one gives his opinion. You simply state what the Bible clearly
says about it, which contradicts his opinion. He says, "Well, I don't
believe that." (This one may go to church, believe he is saved, say
he believes the Bible but does not live like he does; or he may say
he doesn't believe *everything* that is in the Bible.) One who practices
lawlessness is a law unto himself.

Religious hypocrites have one thing in common. They are trying
to save themselves. But they do not understand that the chasm is
too deep. We have fallen too far. We are born dead in Adam, and
anything less than new life in Christ will not make the slightest
difference to our eternal destiny. The reality is that man's efforts to
save himself are futile and will result in eternal death. To believe
anything outside what the Bible tells us is to deceive ourselves.

We may try to console ourselves by measuring our goodness
against all those who are in the same boat with us. Eventually, we
will find somebody who is worse off than we are, and we probably
will not have to look for very long. The obvious problem is that he,
too, will be able to find someone in the boat he believes is worse
than he is, and so on and so on, until it gets down to that last
wretched soul who has been right beside us all along. The Lord

says: **"The heart is more deceitful than all else and is desperately sick; who can understand it? I, the LORD search the heart, I test the mind, even to give to each man according to his ways, according to the results of his deeds."** (Jeremiah 17:9-10)

Today's advice is: "Just trust your heart. Be yourself." That advice assumes our hearts are good. Like Proverbs 14:12 tells us, there are things that may seem right to us but lead to death. We see here the *heart* in Scripture is associated with our minds. It's what we believe—our ideas that make up who we are. If I tell a serial killer to trust his heart, we know that is not a good thing. What I believe about how I will get to heaven needs to be examined along with every other thing I believe. If I want to get to God's heaven, I must know what God's thoughts are on the subject and follow His way to get there. Be yourself? No. God says, "Be holy."

No amount of good works can outweigh our offenses against a holy God. We can't begin to understand the depth and magnitude of sinfulness that is in each one of us. We can deceive ourselves and rationalize all we want. It doesn't matter if we believe most everyone in our lives is less holy. God doesn't grade on a curve; we must be perfect. For those who want to try to stand in their own righteousness on judgment day, know this: When your sinful heart is exposed— every thought, every deed, every word—there will be no excuses before the Judge. Only God's standard righteousness will stand. Because God knows every heart, He can give to each person exactly what he or she deserves. There will be no unjust sentences or false accusations on that day, nor will there be anyone who flew under the radar and got away with even one instance of breaking His Law. No one is 'above the law'; all are under its crushing weight.

The Almighty will judge the deeds done in this life because our works reflect what we value. We do what we want to do; we act according to our desires. Wrong desires that lead to wrong deeds confirm the fact that hearts are wicked. Those who don't stand in His presence perfectly righteous are headed for eternity apart from Him. The words, "Depart from Me…I never knew you," will echo in the minds of those who were a law unto themselves for all eternity.

That is the worst news anyone could ever get. Nothing could be more negative. But we better believe these truths if we are going to have ears to hear the good news.

9
My Way or the Highway

Perhaps you have heard the phrase, 'The heart wants what the heart wants.' What is often meant by this is that we have no control over our desires and emotions—emotions such as love. However, biblical love is not an emotion. This phrase always brings to **my** mind Veruca Salt in *Willie Wonka and the Chocolate Factory*[1] when she whines, "Daddy, I want an Oompa Loompa **n-o-w**!" In fact, what her heart wants is *the whole world. She doesn't want to share. And, if she doesn't get the things she is after, she is going to scream! She doesn't care how; she wants it NOW!*

We laugh and think, spoiled, entitled brat. We recoil at that attitude in others. But truth be told, our hearts tend towards Veruca Salt attitudes more often than we want to admit. We would never say these things out loud, yet these desires lay there bubbling up in our flesh waiting for opportunities to be put into action. Over the years, we have learned that Veruca Salt antics receive negative feedback from our peers. Consequently, we have learned to wear masks that cover up what is going on in our hearts. People around us don't always see the ugliness there, but God does.

I confess, and it is no surprise to those who know me best, that I struggled with the sin of materialism for a long time. After my sweet daughter died in 2001, I shopped a lot. I studied the Bible, taught Bible studies, homeschooled, and I shopped. I remember walking around stores for hours numb, buying things we didn't need. I reasoned that we had the money, we gave a lot of money to the work of the church, and I just liked pretty things for my home. After all, I used my home for Bible studies, and I bought a lot of clothes because I needed them for church, Bible study, and the homeschool co-op. All things I sincerely believed. All rationalization for my sin.

I didn't buy wildly expensive items, just an inordinate amount of 'stuff'. I loved spending the day with my mother shopping, even when she would give me some reproof for my shopping habits. My mother was not one to mince words. Often, she would say to me: "Karla, you need to slow down. You are buying too much stuff." This is from the same wise woman who often told me that the Christian life involved balance. Daddy agreed with her. But I wouldn't hear it. *Obviously, her logic was skewed. Who was I hurting? Couldn't she see it was helping me heal this enormous hurt in my heart?* But did it heal or hurt me in the end? You know the answer to that question. Sin always hurts me and others I love eventually.

I *was* out of control. When I wasn't homeschooling, studying, preparing Bible Studies for the Friday ladies' group, running the kids to their activities, or doing other domestic chores, chances are I was out shopping. I seized every opportunity to slip away and indulge the thrill of the hunt. I didn't shop at high-end boutiques like those on Rodeo Drive, but stores that were known to sell everything for half price or less. I loved a bargain! That was another reason for my rationalization. One might say I was a 'collector'. The problem was, I had collections of almost everything I owned!

As I wandered through the aisles, my instinct was to put every-thing that caught my eye into my basket. Why not? I could afford it, I reasoned. My 'biggest problem' was that of running out of places to keep all my treasures, which was causing me a lot of stress at that moment. Not to worry! Long story short, we were in the process of converting what was originally intended to be a sales training retreat center for our business (until another location in the newly constructed facility in Arizona was preferred) into a large house which would be used for ministry purposes. Over 25,000 square feet, half the structure was designated as personal living space, and the rest was to house missionaries who were home from the field and pastors on retreat. There was to be a conference room for training, a room with stadium seating for Bible studies, and a library for their use. We believed the Lord would have us do this. The place was so large that I was encouraged to keep 'furnishing' it long before it was finished. As it turned out, Barbie's dream house and ministry center would never become a reality. This is definitely one of those moments when you grind your teeth and say: "Ugh! What was I thinking?" Maybe Veruca should have been my middle name for she had nothing on me.

When my husband was told he was being investigated, and that he was being forced out of his own company, the thoughts going through my mind were not pretty ones. As if on a conveyor belt, they kept coming one after another: *If we can keep this, then I'll be fine.* Immediately, I would hear myself, ask the Lord to forgive me, get my focus where it needed to be, and find strength to stand firm and let go saying, *Not my will, but Yours be done, Lord.* When it appeared that one thing would slip through our hands, I would hear myself say, *That's okay. If we still have this, then I'll be fine.* Those thoughts burst into my mind, and I was appalled at them. What I had tried to deny and rationalize so often was at once as obvious and evident as when Nathan, the prophet, said to David, "You are the man!" One by one, the Lord saw fit to take practically all our material possessions away, for my good and His glory. Today, I am still downsizing and trying to get rid of things I've found I no longer need nor want, and I am content.

The last thing I was holding onto tightly was my family. *That's okay, if I have my family, I'll be okay.* I really wouldn't 'have' my family for long, though. We would all soon be separated for years. In prison, I had my Lord. And He was more than enough. There, I didn't rationalize, I finally *realized* that He is what my world revolves around because He is my eternity where even precious people to me may or may not be.

Desires can be good, or they can be bad. The Bible speaks a lot about desires. For example: **Delight yourself in the Lord; and He will give you the desires of your heart.** (Psalm 37:4) **What the wicked fears will come upon him, but the desire of the righteous will be granted.** (Proverbs 10:24) While I was shopping, I would have been the first to tell you that buying things never satisfied any deep longings of my heart like Jesus does. As He began taking things from me, I began to see how He not only meets my every need but changes the desires of my heart to align with His to focus on those eternal treasures found only in Christ.

I saw women in prison rip verses like these from their context and from a right understanding of the rest of Scripture. It looked like this: "I love the Lord, I delight in Him, and I desire to be released now. Therefore, He will release me." I saw some "claim" a promise like this and try to "speak it into existence" even going so far as to set specific times and dates when "the Lord told them" the promise would be fulfilled, only to be dismayed and disillusioned when that thing they wished for did not happen.

In prison, because there is little space for your personal things and your most prized possessions. i.e., your Bible, a piece of fruit, or your toiletries, what you have is never taken for granted. Most inmates make between $5-15 per month at their jobs. So they must rely on family and friends to help them get bare necessities which become treasured luxuries. One girl believed the Lord 'told her' the exact date upon which her 'miracle' release from prison was going to take place. She told everyone she had claimed it by faith, *so she knew* it was going to happen. Giving away everything she had, she sat waiting. When that day came and went, she had a little bit of a breakdown. Precious girl, she was possibly a new believer who had fallen into the hands of others who were deceived or false teachers. I had tried on many occasions to talk to her. She listened politely, but she wanted to believe God (like some genie in a bottle), would grant her the desires of her heart based on distorting His promises to fit her will, not His. If this was some girl's only exposure to God, she would surely be released thinking Christianity was a sham, not to mention the terrible witness it is to unbelievers.

What we can say for certain is those desires that God places in our hearts will be given by Him. In His perfect timing, His will for us will be accomplished. Did I desire a long-term prison stay separated from my beloved family? I *desired* to live in a large house surrounded by family and friends—a large house *in order to* 'do an array of different kinds of ministry'. Did I desire and pray for years for godliness, humility, and to know God in a deeper way? Yes. And were those godly desires planted in me by God? Yes. Can I trust that the circumstances God allows or brings into my life are going to be for my good and accomplish His purpose? Certainly. And He will accomplish the good work He began in me. His way, not mine. One thing I have learned is not to try to suppose I know how God will work to accomplish His good purpose in my life. Now, when I catch myself thinking, *Maybe God will do this or that*, I follow that thought with this: *And maybe He won't. But I can trust Him no matter how He chooses to work out the details of my life.*

Another thing suffering lends itself to, if responded to rightly, is contentment. Learning to live in a small space no bigger than a horse stall with very little possessions and comfort pleasures taught me to be thankful and grateful, appreciating every blessing that God gives freely, which I may have otherwise taken for granted. And our desires do change as He sanctifies our hearts. Even if our desires were good to begin with, He changes our hearts to not give those desires as much weight as previously given to them. Balance. Things are things. It's easier for me to say, 'No', to my wants than my needs. I learned that my needs are few. The focus of my heart was on my relationship with the Lord and the people with whom God had blessed my life. They became the exclusive objects of my affection in this world. The following are good Scriptures to memorize when Veruca raises her ugly head in me: **If we have food and covering, with these we shall be content.** (1 Timothy 6:8) **Two things I asked of You, do not refuse me before I die: Keep deception and lies far from me, give me neither poverty or riches; feed me with the food that is my portion, that I not be full and deny You and say, "Who is the Lord?" or that I not be in want and steal and profane the name of my God.** (Proverbs 30:7-9)

Again, Psalm 37:4 says: **Delight yourself in the LORD; and He will give you the desires of your heart.** What we tend to focus on in that passage is *getting our desires* fulfilled. But there is a precept that comes before the promise, a responsibility before the reward. Before our desires are met, there must be delight. We are to delight ourselves in the Lord. Look at your most recent prayer requests on your own behalf. Are you praying more for your material desires to be afforded you, or for heart issues? Can you say that you are truly delighting in God? If you're like me, you will admit there are times when you are delighting in Him, but still too often you feel the pull in your flesh to delight more in what pleases you. Delighting in the Lord means finding our enjoyment in Him and in doing the things that please Him. It means our greatest joy is to glorify God by living a life that is obedient to Him. We must ask ourselves if that is the *bent* of our hearts.

I found enjoyment in Him in prison. Pretty much everything else was taken away from me. I don't say that for pity. I treasured that time to focus on Him. In fact, I look back on my trials when I tend to lose my delight. Most want to forget everything about prison. But when I've lost my delight or joy, it's then I need to remember the joy He gave me amid my darkest times, because **I know** that joy was supernatural. I couldn't have made myself joyful in those times if I had tried. Looking back reminds me of God's faithfulness to me.

After Missy's death, a phrase from an old gospel song we used to sing flowed through my heart. **"Do not be grieved, for the joy of the LORD is your strength."** (Nehemiah 8:10) Paul, in prison, wrote the book of Philippians, the book about joy. In Chapter 4, he calls us to rejoice in the Lord always. He also says in Chapter 2:12-13: …**work out your salvation with fear and trembling; for it is God who is at work in you, both to will and to work for His good pleasure.**

Even when I don't *feel* delight in God, I can know that He is working in me to give me the desire and the power to do what pleases Him. I am responsible to do what He calls me to do. But I am also dependent upon Him to work in my heart enabling me to do so, and to do so joyfully. For example, maybe there are times when you have not 'felt' like going to Bible study. The best thing you can do in that situation is to go to Bible study. Why? Because God will work in your heart through your obedience. The Puritan Stephen Charnock says of this verse in Psalm 37:

> "This DELIGHT springs from the Spirit of God. Not a spark of fire on your own hearth is able to kindle this spiritual DELIGHT; it is the Holy Spirit Who breathes such a heavenly heat into our affections. The Spirit is the fire that kindles the soul, the spring that moves the watch, the wind that drives the ship. Just as prayer is the work of the Spirit in the heart, so DELIGHT in prayer owes itself to the same Author."[2]

What does this delight look like? Think of a time when you were first in love. You wanted to hear that person's voice and be with them as much as possible. It didn't matter what was previously on your calendar—all prior commitments were rearranged. It wasn't because it was your *duty* to be with this person. Wild horses could not drag you away from time spent with your new love. When you were around other people, they probably got tired of hearing about this one who had staked such a deep claim to your heart. You wanted to take him all in, to consume all his love. Maybe you remember when you were first saved, how you couldn't get enough of the Lord and His Word. Listen to the words that picture eager desire or delight in these verses: **Your words were found, and I ate them, and Your**

words became for me a joy and the delight of my heart; for I have been called by Your name, O Lord God of hosts. (Jeremiah 15:16) **As the deer pants for the water brooks, so my soul pants for You, O God. My soul thirsts for God, for the living God; when shall I come and appear before God?** (Psalm 42:1-2) **Jesus said to them, "I am the bread of life; he who comes to Me will not hunger, and he who believes in Me will never thirst."** (John 6:35)

There are many such passages that talk about hungering and thirsting for God. Are we like Mary, seated at His feet with a heart full of love, drinking in and savoring His every word, or are we like Martha, distracted by life's duties? Do we hunger and thirst for Him? Have we ever even experienced true hunger and thirst to understand that need? We do not desire Him as we should, yet we want *our* desires met. When we begin to delight in the Lord, our desires start to look trivial, and we find that He is our greatest desire! He delights in you, if you are His child. **The LORD your God is in your midst, a victorious warrior. He will exult over you with joy, He will be quiet in His love, He will rejoice over you with shouts of joy.** (Zephaniah 3:17)

Maybe you can't honestly say that you are delighting in the Lord right now. Beloved, can you at least tell the Lord that you *want* to delight in Him? That you desire to know that delight in Him? You can't make yourself delight in God. But you can pray for the love, obedience, and worship that He deserves to flow from your heart. Immerse yourself in the waters of His Word. It would please Him to give you a heart that delights in Him.

True contentment is when I'm not focused on my desires, even my good desires. True contentment comes when God's will is more important than my own desires. Contentment manifests itself in our relationships—in how we love others. Most often, when loving others, we find our own desires will have to be sacrificed on the altar of self. Contentment says: "Lord, because You are enough, because You are everything, I don't need to assert my 'rights' or my 'opinions' in this conflict. I can honor You by treating this person as more important than myself. I can love her as You love me. Who am I to be offended by this comment or action when I daily offend You?"

In prison, some women suffered daily as they learned to appreciate the blessings we often take for granted in life. Most, did not. Self-preservation, entitlement, selfishness, anger, jealousy, and envy produced continual conflict manifesting itself in audacious pride at every turn. So much drama! Have you ever heard something like this: "I no longer associate with Sue; I had to remove myself from that drama." Imagine not being able to do so but to, instead, be forced to deal with it 24/7. Maybe you are in a relationship full of drama that is not so easy to get away from. Maybe it's with your husband or another family member. The world says, "Get away from it. You are entitled to disregard that relationship for your greater good." Did you ever stop to think that God put you in that relationship to sanctify *you*? Imagine how dramatic our lives look to Almighty God. How do you *expect* Him to respond to *you*?

What is true love? A sincere look at the cross ought to leave an indelible impression on us of what God's love looks like. In the NASB, the word *love* is mentioned approximately 348 times. We can get a clearer picture of love from several passages of Scripture: **Love is patient, love is kind and is not jealous; love does not brag and is not arrogant, does not act unbecomingly; it does not seek its own, is not provoked, does not take into account a wrong suffered, does not rejoice in unrighteousness, but rejoices with the truth; bears all things, believes all things, hopes all things, endures all things. Love never fails. (1 Corinthians 13:4-8a) This is My commandment, that you love one another, just as I have loved you. Greater love has no one than this, that one lay down his life for his friends. (John 15:12-13) If you love Me, you will keep My commandments. (John 14:15) ...love edifies... (1 Corinthians 8:1)** Love is one aspect of the fruit of the Spirit. (Galatians 5:22) Real love can only be produced in us by Him. **Beloved, let us love one another, for love is from God; and everyone who loves is born of God and knows God. The one who does not love does not know God, for God is love. (1 John 4:7-8) A friend loves at all times, and a brother is born for adversity. (Proverbs 17:17) Love your enemies and pray for those who persecute you. (Matthew 5:44)**

I just do not love like that. I want to. I pray that the Lord would work in my heart to cause me to love like that. I want to honor Him with love like that. Prison (and it will be some humbling valley for you if you have the same desire), in different ways, exposed my depraved heart to my own eyes. Would I ever have had love for a federal convict before 2012? Not a love that looks anything like I am supposed to have. I may have felt sorry for her, or I may have judged her. I may have had a desire to minister to her in some way which would have served to boost *my* ego in the process. I may have served her in some way out of a sense of moral duty, as the "Christian thing to do". But why couldn't I love her the way I was supposed to love her? I could not relate. I didn't believe I had the same needs as she did. Was I wrong! I can't love even the most lovable people the way I am required to love them.

Before I got to my prison camp, I was given the gift of 'diesel therapy'. Most white-collar offenders are given the opportunity to self-surrender to prison. My judge obviously was not like 'most judges' and apparently didn't think I was in the same category as 'most convicted felons'. After my sentencing, the U.S. Marshals came in, handcuffed me, and took me directly to jail. Not to prison—to jail. (If you don't know the difference, count your blessings.) Straight to county jail with no get out of jail free card! Federal inmates who are being held in county jails are given the *privilege* of doing time the hard way. They, literally, do hard time until they can be moved to their destination. I was put in a pod with some who were there with life sentences. I got to spend a little bit of time talking about the Lord with one woman there who was a 'lifer' in for murder. Having grown to love many of these women, and was thankful the Lord put me with them for a time.

After spending about a month in county jail, shackled and handcuffed I was herded like cattle onto a 'plane' (lovingly referred to as 'Con-Air'). These planes are decrepit mobile prisons that no airline would consider using any longer. Having no idea where I was going, I ended up in Oklahoma. This was a processing facility where I would find out where I was designated to do my time. A step up from the county jail, the food was identifiable and hot; and you could drink as much water as you wanted...with ice! (I was dehydrated from county jail.)

After only one week in Oklahoma, I was awakened early one morning and ordered to get ready to leave within the hour. Handcuffed and shackled once again, we were herded onto yet another plane. I was weary but extremely eager to get to my final destination of Alderson, West Virginia. Rumors were it wasn't too bad there. That excitement soon dissipated, however, turning to fear and anxiety, when I got off the plane and found myself on a bus, alone, with four guards. Petrified, all sorts of things were going through my mind because they refused to tell me where I was going. They only laughed and ignored my questions.

Next stop of diesel therapy? Atlanta—not Alderson, West Virginia. I found myself in another facility like that of county jail. *Just when you think things are looking up.* Surrounded by barbed wire, I was 'safe and secure' with guard towers I could see out my window. Just like Him, though, the Lord turned the extreme discouragement I felt when I arrived there into a week-long time of worship and quiet time with Him that was incredibly sweet and precious to me. I knew His presence there with all my being. (In case you are confused, my diesel therapy went like this: Pennsylvania, Oklahoma, Georgia, and finally West Virginia.)

During this whole time from county jail to the first year at Alderson, I went through menopause, and my flow was like a river. A problem everywhere I went, it took humility to gutter level for me. I got my period the first week in County Jail, so I began sitting up to sleep because there just wasn't enough protection available. That's a whole issue that I will say is inhumane, but I will spare you the details. My sweet bunkie taught me prison life lessons I never needed to know before that time; and I thanked God for this unexpected friend who watched out for me from the start.

I got my period when I woke up on the morning I left from the Oklahoma facility. I knew it was going to be bad. In fact, things were going downhill rapidly—or so I thought. But the Lord had plans for me in Atlanta, and my heavy period was part of His plan to bless me.

After several hours of 'processing', I was led to my cell where I met my very sick, new bunkie. The odor of vomit smacked me in the face when I walked through the door—even before I could see the evidence thereof. The overall state of our cell was disgusting; and after being shuffled from holding cell to holding cell in different facilities all day, I had reached my ultimate lowest point since sentencing. My bunkie moaned and groaned incessantly for help. After futile attempts to help her, I climbed up on an unusually high top bunk to try and get some sleep. Guards eventually took this poor woman to medical. Several times during the night, two older ladies came to our cell and asked me to lie down. I would quickly comply, only to pop up soon thereafter in my sleep. I was awakened at 3:00 a.m. by these same two who ordered, "Podlucky, grab your stuff. We're moving you." I was praying, *Help me, Lord! I can't take much more!* Exhausted and afraid, for some reason I wanted to trust these women who *seemed* to be showing me some compassion.

Guiding me to another pod and another cell that was empty, these two women handed me a spray bottle and some towels and told me to clean it. My first thoughts were, *What sort of torture is this?* My exasperation must have been evident, because they quickly added, "This will be your new cell. Yours is the bottom bunk." (This move designated me for a bottom bunk pass for the rest of my prison time, which was an incredible blessing.) When I woke up the next morning, I started noticing things that seemed oddly out of place. Written in white paint on the cement wall above my head were the words, 'Jesus Saves'. Likewise, above the entrance to my cell was a white painted cross. The Lord allowed me to have this cell to myself for one week, and I praised, worshiped, and adored Him there. The whole time I was in Georgia I could not use the phone to call my family because my phone privileges were not set up yet. I had the Lord, and He was more than enough.

After one week, I was awakened in the very early hours of the morning and told I was being moved. (Incidentally, both times I was moved, I had spent most of the previous night not able to fall asleep. Both times I found myself in a sweet time of praise as I took the names of each girl I had met before the throne of God in prayer. It amazed me that every night this joyful spirit of praise came over me, the next morning I was moved.)

When I was in Oklahoma (the night before I left for Atlanta), one tough-looking woman started to talk to me in a way that made me uncomfortable. I didn't really know why at the time, but I was thankful she was not on the plane I *thought* was going to Alderson. When I was awakened to leave from Atlanta, I was the only one leaving from the pod where I had been moved. Obediently, I waited out in the hall until 10 or 11 women came from the original pod where I had been placed. As the Lord would have it, the woman who ran up to me, as if we were long lost friends was this tough-looking woman from Oklahoma. I'll call her "Sam". My still very sick ex-bunkie was also there.

Here is where I met the girls with whom I would go to Alderson. A few girls stand out in my mind. One remained a friend the whole way through my prison stay. We have nothing in common *but* prison, although I did talk to her about Christ often. She went into prison completely strung out on medication—in a zombie-like state, she had 18 pills in front of her as she sat on the floor of the holding cell. (She was my sick ex-bunkie.) Apparently, our first encounter had been a divine one. The Lord had planned for us to meet again, but first He graciously took care of my physical and spiritual needs.

Before leaving for Alderson, we were all crammed into a small holding cell as we awaited processing. "Sam" very boldly walked up to me and 'hit' on me in a lewd way. A younger girl told her to 'knock it off' because I was married. "Sam" said she didn't care if I didn't care. I assured her that I most certainly did care! Strangely enough, she became my friend. She watched out for me for the first several months at Alderson until we got split up in different units and job assignments. Having associations with the Hell's Angels, this was not her first rodeo. We had some great conversations. I truly cared for her, prayed for her salvation, and listened as she shared details of her very hard life with me. I think of her often with fondness and pray the Lord will pour out His mercy on her and save her. "Sam" was at Alderson for a couple of years until she reportedly got into a fight with another girl and tried to stab her in the eye with a pencil. They both got shipped off to county, and I never saw "Sam" again.

Had I published this book when I first began writing, I would never have ventured to write any of these 'types' of stories. *Why, they wouldn't be fitting. I don't want to be offensive.* But these are the circumstances in which the Lord placed me. The Christian bubble had been burst, and I was living in the real world—the world where Jesus placed me, so that I might win some. There are a lot of places I choose not to go even to witness as a Christian. Obviously, I would not have chosen prison as my mission field, unless it was on the side of the glass wall of those ministering to the inmates. But the Lord put me inside, up close and personal. It was a shock to my system, but sometimes we need a reminder of where we came from and what the Lord has saved us from so that we can relate to those who need rescued too.

Conflicts abound in tight quarters where 150 women live under one roof sharing bathrooms, showers, phones, and one television room. That is to be expected. But what about a husband and wife who can't agree on something as simple as what restaurant to go to on a Friday night? As their egos play a game of tug-of-war, they end up not speaking to each other for the rest of the weekend. You say, "Well, that's normal; we all have disagreements." It may be 'natural, but it shouldn't be normal. For believers, it should be *far less* normal than it once was if we are growing up. So why do we let these types of petty disagreements and conflicts get out of control?

Maybe you and another co-worker both have ideas of how to do something. The boss decides he likes your co-worker's idea better. So you seethe the rest of the day and throughout the week. After the anger subsides, you decide it wasn't a big deal because you didn't lose your temper or your witness in front of anyone. This passage in James 4 is eye opening. **What is the source of quarrels and conflicts among you? Is not the source your pleasures that wage war in your members? You lust and do not have so you commit murder. You are envious and cannot obtain; so, you fight and quarrel. You do not have because you do not ask. You ask and do not receive, because you ask with wrong motives, so that you may spend it on your pleasures.** (James 4:1-3)

First, there is Sermon-on-the-Mount-type language referenced here. James has already said in Chapter 1 that we are carried away in temptation by our own lusts enticing us. A major theme in the book of James is maturity in the Christian life—what it looks like, and how that maturity is developed. Often, he draws a picture of our human nature as it stands in direct opposition to that process of maturity. Some commentators believe that the context of this passage is speaking about unbelievers in the church. They have evil desires, and they cannot do anything about controlling them. I understand that, but I also think it is James showing believers what unbelievers look like so that they will recognize the remnants of their sinful nature, turn from sinful behavior, and grow up. I can tell you that I don't respond to conflicts today as I once did when I was first saved, which is as it should be. Passages like these affirm to me that I am growing up.

Another thing suffering does to help us mature is to learn to choose our battles. We learn what is truly important in life. Suffering puts things into perspective. There are things in life that should call for conflict, but the trivial matters need to be resolved quickly when it involves our egos and desires. We run into these conflicts daily with others the Lord puts in our paths.

To understand this passage in James further, we must look at what came in the verses before it. James 3:13-18: **Who among you is wise and understanding? Let him show by his good behavior his deeds in the gentleness of wisdom. But if you have bitter jealousy and selfish ambition in your heart, do not be arrogant and so lie against the truth. This wisdom is not that which comes down from above, but is earthly, natural, demonic. For where jealousy and selfish ambition exist, there is disorder and every evil thing. But the wisdom from above is first pure, then peaceable, gentle, reasonable, full of mercy and good fruits, unwavering, without hypocrisy. And the seed whose fruit is righteousness is sown in peace by those who make peace.**

Children always seem to want to grow up so quickly. They want to prove their maturity, even when their parents know they are not as mature as they would like to think. Lack of maturity is seen in their actions. With maturity comes responsibility, privilege, and greater freedom. A teenager might look mature and sound mature, but until his actions (revealing his true character) are mature, his wise parents will ease him into greater responsibility, privilege, and freedoms. James says a Christian is wise and understanding when his life reflects good deeds done in the gentleness of wisdom. Gentleness is another way of saying humility. The mature believer is not fighting for his rights but crucifying his own flesh for the sake of another. He is a peacemaker who considers others more important than himself. The wise and understanding Christian is going to be the one whose life is modeled after the sacrificial life of Christ.

Long-term relationships with other believers afford us the opportunity to really get to know one another. In a relationship like this, we can't 'fake it' for long. Our true self is going to be revealed sooner than later. Since we live in bodies of flesh, I can't put on a Christian mask with you for long until the real 'me' shows up. When it does (if it is ugly in its ungodly behavior), I pray you will sharpen me by telling me my behavior is not befitting a child of the King. I pray you will love me enough to help me grow in righteousness by holding me accountable to the image of Christ I am to be reflecting to a watching world that so desperately needs to see Him.

In the Christian life, those newly born again believe they are mature long before they realize the road is much longer to maturity than they could ever imagine. Not unlike the growth process of a typical teenager, pride often falls hard before humility-producing maturity. **Consider it all joy, my brethren, when you encounter various trials, knowing that the testing of your faith produces endurance. And let endurance have its perfect result, so that you may be perfect and complete, lacking in nothing.** (James 1:2-4) The word *perfect* is **teleios** in the Greek. It means mature. Testing, trials, and tribulations help us grow up by showing us where we are lacking. Growing up is painful, but necessary.

We are called to love our neighbor as we love ourselves; but instead, we have quarrels and conflicts. Where do these conflicts come from? Our desires to please ourselves. Like Veruca Salt, we want what we want when we want it, whether it belongs to someone else or not. And we don't want to share. If everyone agrees with us, we can love each other. So we just remove ourselves from those who don't agree with us instead of going the long haul by crucifying our flesh and letting go of our desires that serve only ourselves. It's so much easier to walk away and end the relationship, but we will miss a huge growth spurt unless we stay. Jealousy and selfish ambition are not character traits of the wisdom that comes from above but are earthly, natural, and demonic. They come from the world, our flesh, and the devil. Wisdom that comes from above is righteous and brings peace. Did you ever stop to think your compromise to eat at the restaurant of your husband's choice is an act of service in Christ's name? It's also evidence of wisdom.

If history were a play, we would see conflicts entering onto the stage in Act 1. We saw this earthly, natural, demonic jealousy and selfish ambition, and its consequences, in the story of Cain and Abel. One brother was willing to submit to God, and one was not.

God accepted and was pleased with Abel's offering. Because Cain didn't get what he wanted, the approval he desired from God for doing things his own way, he enters a conflict with God long before that conflict plays out in the murder of his brother. Sin is pictured, here, as a wild animal ready to pounce upon Cain. Sin desires to have us. Blood-thirsty, in-dwelling sin will stop at nothing less than our very lives and those around us.

Each step along Murder Boulevard can be arrested by making a 180-degree turn in the opposite direction. It all begins with a wrong thought. *I deserve better. That wasn't fair. Why does everyone like her better than me?* Once my thoughts are grounded and secure, they lead to wrong feelings. As I nurse those feelings of self-pity and anger, my feelings lead to wrong words. My wrong words lead to wrong actions which will become a habit, or like they are called in our world, an addiction or continual pattern of sin. This descent into sin is so easy for our human nature to fall into that a child can do it without trying. If allowed to live on, this progression always, *always* leads to death. Deceptive to the core, sin always promises delight but delivers death and destruction.

We already looked at that verse in 1 John 3:11-12 referring to Cain when it said: "…who was of the evil one and *slew* his brother." It is interesting that this word for *slew* means to butcher (especially an animal for food or in sacrifice) or (generally) to slaughter. Cain may have spitefully thought that if God wanted a blood sacrifice, he would give Him one!

Some conflicts are particularly trivial, and some are weightier. Conflicts and quarrels stem from wanting our own way. Wanting our own way is preferring self over others which is not love, but hatred. Hatred is as the sin of murder in God's eyes. The fruit of hatred and murder come from the same sin seed. Would you seriously murder someone over restaurant choices?

When conflicts arise, we must learn to love as Christ did, by laying down His life for His friends. I'm not talking about the error of tolerance being taught by post-modernists today. Truth is to be fought for vehemently. Some conflict is necessary when truth and error are in question. But when it comes to any number of petty differences we want to bicker about and whine over like immature children, we must learn to let go of those insignificant issues and give preference to the other person for the sake of peace and unity. To do so honors and glorifies our Father by rightly reflecting His character. To hold on to our wants and desires at the expense of peace and unity is to reflect the evil one.

The degree to which many people are easily offended has risen significantly over the past decade or so. It seems people are getting offended over everything imaginable, and it's publicly displayed on social media. Without really getting to know a so-called 'friend' on Facebook, some feel they have a right to lambaste any comment they don't like and to 'unfriend' anyone they disagree with at the click of a key. Some people love conflict, and it is evident. These reactions reveal a heart of selfishness and a lack of maturity.

When people agitate me and repulse my flesh, I often want to react in a way that makes me *feel* better. Sometimes the first thought that pops into my head is to hurt the one who has hurt me first. 'Do what is best for me, myself, and I' is today's slogan. For some, 'letting out steam' seems right because it makes them feel better, regardless of how it makes the other person feel. Because I really don't like conflict, I typically withdraw or run away. Anyone who knows me well would say that when I react in a way that is unbefitting a child of God, I am one who typically withdraws, pulls away, or avoids the conflict at any cost. But let me be clear, running away and lashing out are equally sinful responses to conflict. The end result for me, however, is the same. I run from the situation for as long as I am able, then… BOOM! I explode. Again, that is my fleshly default, but I see far less running and explosions today than I once did.

Every time I withdraw from conflict, the lie I believe is that it will result in my flesh being pacified bringing peace to my heart. I am somehow always dismayed when I find myself standing there alone, feeling rejected, bitter, angry, envious, and all sorts of other sinful feelings. The lies we tell ourselves when we try to rationalize our sin never ends the way we dreamed it would.

So how should I respond to conflict and the battles within my flesh when God calls me to obey Him, but my flesh wants so desperately to resist His call? As the battle begins, I must be able to see the wickedness that lies beneath this facade of religiosity that I sometimes wear. I must climb down from my throne where I'm tempted to exalt myself and start talking to myself instead of listening to myself. 'Self' starts chattering rationalizations when I am tempted to sin. Instead, I must immediately preach a sermon to myself from what I know to be truth. I may need to arrest this disobedience right on the spot by asking myself some convicting questions. For instance, *Karla, what is wrong with you? Have you forgotten who your Master is? Have you forgotten how merciful and patient your loving Father is with you? Why aren't you giving this person in front of you the same grace God afforded you? You should be thankful for the opportunity to serve this person. I know she shouldn't have said that to you, but you can give her grace instead of returning evil for evil.* You get the picture.

We are often so quick to be able to offer others advice on how to deal with situations in a godlike manner but are very slow to render that same advice to ourselves. If I do not at once recognize this sinful need to cater to my flesh, I will end up disobeying God by holding on to bitterness, resentment, anger, envy, and all sorts of other rancid emotions that will ironically end up hurting me overall.

The things I fell on my sword over twenty years ago, I wouldn't give a moment's thought to today. I cringe as I think of the fights I had with my husband. They were so trivial and pointless. How important is it today that we went to one restaurant over another? Or when he asked me to stay within the budget, but I thought we could afford something I wanted, so I found a way to buy it anyways? Where is that item today? What about all the friendships that have come and gone? What ended their life? All questions I continue to ask myself as I seek to grow up. The answer is usually found in my sinful 'self'.

What changed? Why aren't those things that caused me such anguish and anger important today? The Lord has been pleased to keep on sanctifying me. Through His Word, and even circumstances of suffering, He has changed my perspective on what is important in life. As He molds and shapes my heart, He is bringing my desires in line with His will. Today, I don't *feel* mature, and I don't believe I *am* mature, because I know what that looks like or Who that looks like. I know I fall far short of His perfection. But I **am** growing, and that brings peace to my heart because I know that He is causing that growth. And He won't stop working on me in the middle of the process or let my 'self' get in His way. When my suffering comes to an end, I can know that this tapestry will be perfect.

The context of Psalm 37:4 is on the security of those who trust in the Lord versus the insecurity of the wicked. So often when we are not getting the desires of our heart, we don't recognize that it is because our desires are being directly affected by how we are focusing on ourselves and on our circumstances, instead of on the Lord. Several times we are told, "Do not fret!" In other words, don't get yourself all worked up. We can keep ourselves from fretting in life when we keep our perspective on the eternal and not on the temporal. We would alleviate so many of our troubles if we could keep an eternal perspective in this life.

Living in this world, we have certain desires in our hearts (preconceived ideas that originated in our sin nature), regarding how we think things are supposed to be. We were born believing that everyone is entitled to live happily ever after. When life does not line up with that fairy tale ending, we begin to fret. When we fret, we are really giving ourselves over to doubt that God exists. We were born wanting what we want when we want it, which is always right now! When those desires are not met, we fret. But until we find our greatest delight in God, we will never experience the peace and contentment we long to know. Circumstances are not always going to line up according to our desires and dreams. In fact, they rarely do. As we learn to trust Him in these unsettling trials, we can know we are learning to walk by faith, and we are growing up!

10
What's Love Got to Do With It?

Job is believed to be the first book of the Bible written chronologically. Job, suffering intensely, asks the supreme question in 9:2, "How can a man be right with God?" We, too, need to know the answer to this question if we are to suffer righteously. Job's friends wrongly believed that all suffering was God's judgment upon specific sin in a person's life. When suffering comes our way, thoughts that often come to mind are, *Why, Lord? Don't You love me? What did I do to deserve this? Am I really Your child?* We reason that because God is in control of all things, then He can control the trials that come into our lives. That is true; and, He is. I have falsely reasoned like this: *I know my earthly father wouldn't want me to suffer this way, so why would my heavenly Father allow it or even ordain it?*

Gaining a right theology of suffering is why the book of Job is very important. Job was a righteous man; he was right with God. One of the most interesting things in Job is this window into the heavenly realms where we hear God's own testimony of Job. We can see what he could not. A right belief system regarding suffering includes the understanding that suffering is part of the believer's **calling**. Every creature since the Fall has suffered, but all do not suffer in a way that glorifies God. That which the Christian counts as loss in this world, in order that he may gain Christ, contributes to his suffering. Embracing that suffering from His hand as a love offering to Him glorifies and honors Him.

How can a man be made right with God? Some might wonder: *Maybe we can be good enough by just keeping the most important commandments.* A Pharisee asked Jesus: **"Teacher, which is the great commandment in the Law?" And He said to him, "'YOU SHALL LOVE THE LORD YOUR GOD WITH ALL YOUR HEART, AND WITH ALL YOUR SOUL, AND WITH ALL YOUR MIND.' This is the great and foremost commandment. The second is like it, 'YOU SHALL LOVE YOUR NEIGHBOR AS YOURSELF.' On these two commandments depend the whole Law and the Prophets."** (Matthew 22:36-40) Why these two commandments, specifically? These two interrelated-commandments sum up the Law and the Prophets. The first four commandments found in Exodus 20 have to do with loving God; the last six have to do with loving others. In other words, if I can keep these two commandments, I can keep the whole Law.

Jesus said the great and foremost commandment is that I am to love the Lord my God with all my heart, with all my soul, and with all my mind. I love Him with my mind by knowing and believing who He is according to what His Word says about Him, not loving a 'Jesus' who is a figment of my imagination who looks nothing like the Jesus of Scripture. Belief in a false 'Jesus' disqualifies a great percentage of those who profess Christianity. But that's not the only command. He added that the second command is like it: **"You shall love your neighbor as yourself."** (Matthew 22:37-39) These two commandments sum up all that God requires from man.

Why do these two commands go hand in hand? How do you know that you love God? Is it some mystical feeling that comes and goes? No. Love is seen in action, and the Bible has much to say about what type of love God requires of us for Him and for others. While I may be able to convince myself that I do love God as required, loving my neighbor has flesh and bones attached to it. John, in 1 John 3:10, makes it very clear that if I do not love my brother, I am not of God. One way I show my love for Him is by loving others. What makes this so very painful is the last part of the command. It does *not* say, "You shall love your neighbor." This is where the rubber meets the hard road. If we're being honest with ourselves, the absolute hardest duty we are called to carry out in this life is to love others as we love *ourselves.* But it is that kind of love for others that proves our love for God is real. Obeying God's Law comes down to one issue. Galatians 5:14 says that the whole Law is fulfilled in the statement, "You shall love your neighbor as yourself." The girls in Bible Study used to giggle uncontrollably when I would illustrate the last part of this verse by kissing the whole length of my arm and stressing, "And, we *do* love ourselves!" You are to love your neighbor as you already love yourself.

What does that mean? Everywhere we look today we are hit with philosophies that are meant to help us. Unfortunately, because they contradict the teaching of Scripture but have been brought into the church, Christians are more confused than ever; and the waters are muddied when it comes to understanding this phrase, 'love others as we love ourselves'. Positive thinking, self-esteem helps, and self-love philosophies infiltrate every aspect of our society. The problem, 'they' say, is that we don't love ourselves enough. And we can't possibly love others until we love ourselves and have a healthy self-esteem. But is that what Scripture teaches? Emphatically, no!

Someone told me that teachers are being asked not to use red pens to grade with any longer. The 'experts' say it may damage the student's self-esteem. What about the child whose favorite color just happens to be red? He or she would be thrilled to see 100% on his paper—in red! A 'D' to me would be a 'D' in any color of the rainbow. Maybe 'they' need to change that letter because it could mean 'D'ummie! 'C' could mean 'C'lose but you don't 'C'ut it! 'B' could mean 'B'etter try harder, because you still didn't make an 'A'! It's all silliness. 'D' or lower simply means you failed the test, and you need to learn this lesson before you can move on. Can you hear Johnny crying to his mom and dad? "I got a 'D'…AND…AND…SNIFF…IT WAS IN RED! Waaaaah!" Johnny's parents gasp, "Really, red? How dare she!" A failing grade is a signal to any student that growth is not taking place as it should and that changes need to occur in order to move ahead. It's a good thing to be tested. And failure can always be beneficial. Johnny's fiancée buys him a red sweater for Christmas years later. Johnny throws it down as if it is a hot potato and shrieks, "Take it back!" His fiancée is beside herself. "What's wrong?" Johnny grits his teeth, "It's red! My teacher used to mark all my grades in red pencil, and she scarred me for life. Whenever I see red, I just feel bad about myself." We are fast becoming a ridiculous society.

Self-esteem advocates would say our greatest need is to love ourselves before we can be right with the world. The problem with that is we love ourselves supremely. We are born with our worlds revolving around ourselves. If we didn't love ourselves so much, we would not have such fragile egos and self-esteem issues. We would not be so easily offended about—well, just about *everything*! We love ourselves more than anything else, which is why we live to make sure our desires and dreams are met. We are living in a narcissistic society that is self-obsessed, where our foremost idolatry of choice is *self*. We literally cannot get enough of our 'selfies'. The internet is literally blown up with people looking into their 'smart' phones, talking into these little inanimate but 'highly intelligent' gadgets, making faces of love at them, posing for them, and posting their selfies as if the world eagerly sits on pins and needles waiting for them. Our phones have become too smart for our own good.

Speaking of 'selfies', studies have recently been shown that social media is good for our self-esteem. Turns out, every time we 'like' a post or receive a 'like' for something we have shared or posted, our brains release Dopamine, a neurochemical known as the 'reward molecule' that is released after certain human actions or behaviors take place, such as exercising, or setting and achieving a goal. We hit the 'like' button or share and get a feeling of belonging which boosts our self-esteem. Our little smart phones have become our BFFs. After all, we spend more time with them than just about anyone or anything else. We are continually amazed at all they can do; we take them wherever we go, and through social media we can feel good about our relationships with very little conflict involved. Even 'Siri', or 'Alexa', or whatever her name is, won't argue with you. If you take a wrong turn with GPS, the system says, "Okay, make the next...". What would happen if she yelled at you? "What are you doing? Didn't you hear me? I *said* to take the next left turn, knucklehead!"

While there may be very little real communion or building of relationships going on in our self-consumed worlds, we feel good about ourselves, and that's really all we care about. We can feel good about ourselves based on how many 'friends' we have or how many 'likes' we received that day without all the heartache that goes with growing a strong bond of friendship and love. Filled with roller coaster emotions, the ride of my life is being determined by how I 'feel' about myself at any given moment.

We love *reality* television stars. They are normal people like us who, given the right opportunities, would also make it **big** and be acknowledged for our great worth to the world. And isn't that what many churches have done with God? They have watered down the truth offering a god who is just like you. You can come as you are and be accepted as you are. This god just wants you to be happy and be the best somebody you can be. He won't judge you or make you feel bad about yourself because He's a god of love. That's not the God of Scripture!

In prison, one of the things that made me chuckle was what I liked to call the 'glamour shot' photo shoots. Most of the young girls taking advantage of posing for these pictures are not even old enough to know what I'm talking about. Every weekend, there were long lines of girls waiting to have their pictures taken for a dollar a shot. The prison created inmate jobs for a photographer and girls to paint backdrops so that this service could be taken advantage of often. And these runway *divas* would find clothes that no one else had access to *'somewhere'* and have their make-up and hair done up to the extreme to pose for the camera. What did they do with these pictures? Some sent them home. Many girls had them in picture albums so they could look at themselves and their friends often; and some would even hang them up on their bulletin boards so they could look at themselves 24/7. Inmates are extremely resourceful. The inmate answer to having no access to smart phones with which to take 'selfies'? Glamour shots!

We are **commanded** by God (it's *not* a suggestion), to love our neighbor *as* we love ourselves. Believe it or not, 'self-esteem' advocates—the "experts"—say this is a command *to* love ourselves. And, they say, without that love first, we cannot possibly love our neighbors. There is not a single command in the Bible that calls for us to love ourselves. Why? Because we already do, and it is not a good thing! Romans 12:3 tells us that we are not to think too highly of ourselves. That *is* a command because it is part of our nature to do just that. We are to love our neighbor as we *already* love ourselves.

We can better understand this by looking at a passage in Ephesians 5. Paul gives a command to husbands regarding how they are to love their wives. **Husbands love your wives, JUST AS Christ also loved the church and gave Himself up for her...**(my emphasis). (Ephesians 5:25) How did Christ love the church? Sacrificially. He gave His life for her. **So, husbands ought also to love their own wives as their own bodies. He who loves his own wife loves himself; for no one ever hated his own flesh, but nourishes and cherishes it, just as Christ also does the church.** (Ephesians 5:28-29) Husbands are called to love their wives selflessly and wholeheartedly; we are all called to love our neighbor that way too. The problem is we are not selfless. We are selfish to the core.

People seem to me to be much more selfish today than they were when I was growing up. Now, it is even *celebrated* to be a selfish person. It is called being a 'Diva'. One definition of a *diva* is a self-important person who is temperamental and difficult to please. (Might this be a narcissist?) The question we must ask is this: Am I able to love others more than or even as I love myself? Paul says to Timothy: **But realize this, that in the last days difficult times will come. For men will be lovers of self, lovers of money, boastful, arrogant, revilers, disobedient to parents, ungrateful, unholy, unloving, irreconcilable, malicious gossips, without self-control, brutal, haters of good, treacherous, reckless, conceited, lovers of pleasure rather than lovers of God, holding to a form of godliness, although they have denied its power. Avoid such men as these.** (2 Timothy 3:1-5) The context of this passage is speaking about men inside the church masquerading as godly leaders in the last days. It is not a stretch to realize, however, that as the leaders go, so go the people who follow them. This is a perfect description of our sinful human nature. Today we can see where these things are not only not frowned upon but accepted as norm; and sadly, they are even encouraged. This should not be. We need to recognize sin as sin.

The love we are called to is a 'giving' love; it's a serving love. We are to love without any consideration of getting anything in return. But our world has redefined true love as a 'getting' love. "He doesn't meet my needs, so I don't love him anymore." People leave churches because they aren't getting their needs met there. "I want to find a new church; the pastor never visits me. Nobody knows who I am!"

The self-esteem lies that have been propagated have given us the false idea that we are so valuable to God that it is we who must 'accept' Him. These lies attempt to put round edges on the hard corners of the gospel message and make it palatable to us. The real gospel *should* be bitter in the mouth of the unbeliever and hard to swallow. But the gospel that has been spun out of humanistic, self-esteem teaching doesn't offend sensitive egos, so its praises are sung loudly by the crowds. When that same crowd hears the authentic gospel, they put their fingers in their ears and cry, "We're not listening to you. You're too negative—too judgmental. How dare you speak to us that way!"

When God opens our eyes to our true condition, He says this should be our reaction: **"Then you will remember your evil ways and your deeds that were not good, and you will loathe yourselves in your own sight for your iniquities and your abominations."**

(Ezekiel 36:31) God approves of us responding to a right image of ourselves with loathing. It's like looking into the mirror and being horrified at what we see there. Job did. **"I have heard of You by the hearing of the ear, but now my eye sees You. Therefore, I abhor myself and repent in dust and ashes."** (Job 42:5-6 NKJV) Doesn't sound like what we think of as a good self-image, does it? It is a *right* self-image. An intense trial with unfathomable suffering brought Job to this proclamation of the truth.

Worship is literally giving 'worth ship'. When we worship God, we acknowledge His worth. We worship what we value the most. We are born worshiping ourselves. But God alone deserves all our worship because He alone is supremely valuable and of infinite worth. Today there are many different value scales or self-esteem scales to measure or weigh a person's self-worth. The self-esteem teachers would have us value ourselves above everything else in life. But God's Word weighs us on His scale. There, spiritually speaking, we find we have no weight at all. **Men of low degree are only vanity, and men of rank are a lie; in the balances they go up; they are together lighter than breath.** (Psalm 62:9) Beauty companies have lied to me. I am not worth what I thought I was after all.

While at Alderson, I walked a lot. With not much else to do, I worked out approximately 2-3 hours every day. Much of that time was spent walking around and around the compound, never actually going anywhere. The value in that time, besides having lost 80 pounds, was the time to think and worship. Some of my deepest times of worship—singing, praying, and praising the Lord for His goodness, mercy, and love to me—were while serving time just walking around Alderson Prison Camp.

Suffering is a blessed gift. You would never *choose* to go through it. But the treasure you find there is priceless. I've gone through the pain of childbirth four times and have had one miscarriage. The pain of physical labor in childbirth was horrendous, yet the gift from God at the end of it was joy unspeakable. The separation of prison and losing my Missy Morgan brought deep, mental anguish that shattered my heart into a million pieces. Yet, I have seen God bring good through all my suffering. I think it is important to note, however, that I was watching for that good. I expected to see it because I believe His promises, His goodness, and His faithfulness to me. That's not to say I was not ever tempted to doubt, but my heart desperately wants to trust Him wholeheartedly with abandon because I know He loves me with pure love.

Who but God can bring such beauty from ashes? Who can fill us up with joy in the most tragic and painful circumstances? Who but the Lord can bind up our broken hearts, give us garland instead of ashes, the oil of gladness instead of mourning, and the mantle of praise instead of a spirit of fainting? Only the One who intimately knows us and understands our suffering by His own experience. Who am I that He should love me and care for me this way? I don't deserve anything but His wrath. Yet, He loves me. And His call to me for my life is a call to love. I want to be like my Father loving others this way. I really do. So, what's the problem? Why do I struggle to love? Again, there's this issue with my flesh.

The problem, simply put, is *me*. I really can't love God or others while preeminently loving myself. Pride fuels my flesh by feeding me lies to persuade me that this life is all about me. When those lies are believed, my flesh acts upon them, and sin stands in the way of me being all that God created me to be. In fact, that sin kills the Spirit's influence and work in my life causing me to suffer in this world. Real love exposes the heart and makes us vulnerable opening us up for hurt and pain. Because I love myself so much, I guard myself from pain and suffering at all costs. Our flesh can't get past the struggle of risking pain and suffering for the treasure that is on the other side of humbling itself to really love. On top of that, intimate relationships demand a lot of hard work. My flesh says it's not worth it. It convinces me that high maintenance relationships (that is all relationships that are worth anything) take too much of my busy and valuable time. Time, I spend on...well, me.

The struggle for the Christian is real. The truth is: We were born eternal beings. In our flesh we expect all good things to last forever. Because of sin, earthly relationships don't last forever because this life doesn't last forever. Sometimes the end of relationships through no fault of our own or through death, result in such heartache that we tell ourselves deep relationships are too painful to pursue. Simple good-byes are difficult because separation goes against the communion we were created for. For the believer, the only answer is to keep our focus on eternity and walk in the Spirit.

The reason social media platforms are so popular today is that we get the dopamine rush without expending ourselves of the time and energy it takes to really love others. We can have thousands of 'friends' but not really know any of them. I can 'make friends' a thousand times easier on Facebook than in real life. We like social media because we are in control of how close we get to anyone.

Here is a true story about my early experiences with Facebook. Many probably know that a big ministry was named after our town of Ligonier. I went to school with and am friends with the daughter of R.C. Sproul. One day I saw his name on Facebook and decided to 'friend request' him, thinking nothing of it. Within a rather short period of time, he accepted my friend request. Soon after, however, I got a message from his daughter telling me he only used that Facebook account for his close friends. I was aghast, and abruptly unfriended him. I messaged his daughter back and told her to let her father know that I was truly sorry. She didn't understand. I told her I didn't want to offend her father by having him think I didn't **want** to be his friend, but I also wanted to guard his privacy and not be the cause of anyone who saw R.C. as my friend to barrage him with friend requests. He was such a gracious man. I think I was probably the only person who ever 'unfriended' R.C. Sproul out of love for him and to *protect* him.

I think the verdict is still out on Facebook and social media. Some people love it, and some people hate it. Some, like me, have a love/hate relationship with it. I do think there needs to be a warning label to use it responsibly due to its addictive nature. In large part, dictated by our 'positive' culture, I think a lot of it is a facade. More and more, it is being censored to allow only what is culturally acceptable, so that's not reality. Only your true friends want to hear of your struggles and hardships. Most want positive messages and posts that bring warm fuzzies. *News flash! Real life is hard, painful, and full of conflict.*

So, we keep telling ourselves that love is too risky. We can't afford to experience the pain involved in developing deep, meaningful relationships or to invest the necessary time in them because we're too into ourselves. Our worlds that revolve around us keep us busy and distracted. The funny thing is we're not busy doing anything that has value. We are glued to our phones, watching for the 'likes', playing games, being entertained by television, sports, or any number of other frivolous things. We are distracted by ourselves and seeking after worthless things that hold no eternal value. Satan has very little to do to us outside of keeping us busy and focused on ourselves.

The world is calling us and encouraging us to love ourselves first and foremost; and that's not a problem, because we already do. We were born loving ourselves. Paul tells us in 2 Timothy 3:1-5 that in these difficult last days men will be lovers of self. They don't need to be commanded to love themselves because they do. *Lovers of self* is **philautos** which means to be too intent on one's interests, or selfish. The person who loves himself is concerned solely with his own desires, needs, and interests. Notice how this negative characteristic tops the list. Men who love themselves cannot love others altruistically.

The book of Judges says: With no king in Israel, everyone did what was right in his own eyes. (See Judges 21:25.) The theme of their day was much like ours, "If it feels right, do it!" Instead of, "If it's right, do it." Big difference! If I say to my child, "If it feels right, do it," what or who is the authority on his actions in life? Is it me, the parent? I, as a parent, can't govern my children's feelings. What if little Johnny is having feelings that he cannot go on any longer? That is dramatic, but I believe it makes a point. Now, if I say to my child, "If it's right, do it," who or what is the authority? The one who determines the difference between what is right and wrong. Unfortunately, we live in a sensual, hedonistic world where feelings dictate behavior because truth is no longer believed to be absolute but relative. We have gotten used to the phrase, "You just have to do what is right for you." Really?

The truth is this: We *shouldn't* feel good about ourselves apart from the life we have in Christ Jesus. If I am to live my life based solely upon my feelings, I will only try to make myself feel good by succumbing to the enticements of the lusts of my eyes, the lusts of my flesh, and my pride. But what did Jesus say we are to do? Deny ourselves. He didn't say we're to promote ourselves at every turn. **"If anyone wishes to come after Me, he must deny himself, and take up his cross and follow Me. For whoever wishes to save his life will lose it, but whoever loses his life for My sake and** the gospel's will save it. For what does it profit a man to gain the whole world, and forfeit his soul?"** (Mark 8:34-36)

Here is another ridiculous scenario, but I think it puts things into perspective: Suppose Jesus had decided that He would stay on earth to be an earthly king instead of going to the cross. What if He had said, "I do not want to *die* for them! I need to feel good about Myself and grab all the gusto I can—for Me. I feel like I can serve these people better by being King. We both win!" Where would you and I be then? Sadly, some take it for granted that because it was God's plan, He was *supposed* to come to earth and die to save us. It **was** God's plan from before the foundation of the world, but it wasn't so we could make a name for ourselves during our lives on earth. Our purpose is to make *His* name great on earth. We forget that He willingly laid down His life to save us—*from ourselves.* Paul uses similar words: **He died for all, so that they who live might no longer live for themselves, but for Him who died and rose again on their behalf.** (2 Corinthians 5:15)

We want to *be somebody.* We want to *exalt ourselves* and *be exalted*, and we think that happens when we put ourselves first or live for ourselves. Spiritually speaking, the opposite is true. **Have this attitude in yourselves which was also in Christ Jesus, who, although He existed in the form of God, did not regard equality with God a thing to be grasped, but emptied Himself, taking the form of a bondservant, and being made in the likeness of men. Being found in appearance as a man, He humbled Himself by becoming obedient to the point of death, even death on a cross. For this reason also, God highly exalted Him, and bestowed on Him the name which is above every name, so that at the name of Jesus EVERY KNEE WILL BOW, of those who are in heaven and on earth and under the earth, and that every tongue will confess that Jesus Christ is Lord, to the glory of God the Father.** (Philippians 2:5-11)

Jesus is God. He alone deserves to be exalted, praised, and honored supremely. He chose to die for us in our place—the place of sinners. And God exalted Him for it. One day every knee will bow acknowledging His Lordship; though for most, it will be too late because they chose to exalt, honor, and love themselves above all else here in this life.

Self-love is the sin that has the deepest root in the soul of man. It is the sin that will separate or cut us off from God and from one another. All the rest of the characteristics in the 2 Timothy passage flow out of the sin of self-love.

Lovers of money—Also translated covetous, greedy, avarice (an excessive or insatiable desire for wealth or gain). The Bible says it is not money but the *love* of money that is the root of all evil. A person who loves himself is selfish. Covetousness comes from a selfish heart. How many children are being raised exclusively by *their own* parents today? Instead, how many parents prioritize providing a 'better life' for their children while having *someone else* raise them? The use of our time is an indication of what we value. How much time do we spend with our children shaping their minds and hearts?

Workaholics are lovers of money and of self—whether they are wealthy or not. Like all sin, love of money is a heart issue. What is the motive for excessive work? Is it to become somebody? Does it stem from 'a martyr syndrome'? For instance, you find yourself bragging about how much harder you work than others; ergo, you *deserve* all you have worked so hard for. Is it because you want to make enough money to retire young, enjoy life and the people with whom God has blessed you? That is presumptuous—you may not have tomorrow…*or* anyone to enjoy tomorrow with after neglecting them for so long.

Solomon had it all in the eyes of today's world. Yet, his final words on 'having it all' were that it is all vanity. I don't think we should be content to live in poverty if we're able to make an honest living. We aren't to *choose* a life of poverty. But we would do well to have the attitude found in Proverbs 30:7-9, that passage we looked at earlier.

Just like the promoters of the self-esteem gospel which has infiltrated the church, lovers of money have found their own gospel to peddle revolving around money. It's not hard to understand why these two themes are most often intermingled within the same ministry. Those who support prosperity gospel hucksters pay to have their ears tickled so they can feel good about themselves!

For years, I believed I was saved in 1979 in the charismatic movement. My husband and I were married by a Catholic priest and a little-known charismatic preacher. That preacher promotes himself today as a 'faith healer', who has a 'worldwide outreach' ministry. Shortly after my husband and I were married, we moved to Tulsa, Oklahoma. Following all the televangelists of the '70s, we got caught up in the seed-faith, prosperity gospel. My husband went to a well-known university while I worked in the evangelistic ministry associated with it. By God's grace, He quickly exposed to us the errors and hypocrisy in this movement and this ministry and moved us back to the east coast after one year. Even though we were caught up in the movement for such a brief time, it took years to replace the error we had learned with truth. Disillusioned, we walked away from the church, our Bibles, and anything pertaining to God for many years. The only thing we held onto, ironically, was the faulty misconception that we were Christians.

Boastful—This is an empty pretender. Before you think of the big mouth who brags about everything, look at your Facebook page. Do you post pictures of your life as it looks 99% of the time, or just the highlights that make it appear as though the grass is greener on your front yard? Social media is raising a generation of young people who have learned to be discontent because their lives don't look like your best snapshots all the time.

Arrogant—To be arrogant is to show oneself above others, overtopping, pre-eminent, an excessive estimate of one's means or merits, despising others or even treating them with contempt. These have a look of haughty disdain for others who are 'beneath them'.

Revilers—Revilers are blasphemers. Speaking evil of others, they are slanderous, reproachful, railing, and abusive. The reviler speaks insults against God and others. He makes false accusations and misrepresentations in efforts to destroy another's reputation.

Disobedient to parents—This is to be stubbornly disobedient. It is the parents' greatest duty to teach their children to obey their God-given authority; for if a child refuses to obey his parents, he will never obey God's authority. Typically, those children who are rebellious towards their parents will have no problem rebelling against any other authority in their lives.

Ungrateful—Ungracious, unpleasing, unthankful, unapprecia-tive. John MacArthur says this in his commentary on 2 Timothy: "The person who elevates self above all others will feel he deserves everything good he receives and therefore feels no need of gratitude for it. Although he may not put it into words, the ungrateful person despises the very idea of grace, which denotes goodness received that is undeserved. This is a particularly noxious sin to God, whose wrath is revealed against sinners for being unthankful."[1]

Unholy—Impious, wicked. There are understood and accepted laws of society regarding what is proper and decent. The unholy break those laws without any regard to proper decency out of a need to grossly gratify their lustful hearts to get what they want.

Unloving—Without natural affection, unsociable, heartless. Without natural and instinctive family love. The idea here is that in order to satisfy their lustful gratifications, men and women will go to extremes to trample over even family to get what they want. We see that in the issue of abortion and epidemic proportions of infidelity in marriage today.

Irreconcilable—Unforgiving, implacable or not capable of being appeased, truce breakers, unwilling to be at peace with others, bitter haters, unyielding, covenant breakers. This person refuses to lay aside enmity or even to listen to terms of reconciliation. Covenants mean nothing to the irreconcilable and divorce courts prove as much.

Malicious gossips—**Diabolos** is the word for *malicious gossips.* It means prone to slander, slanderous, or accusing falsely. It is applied to a man who, by opposing the cause of God, may be said to act the part of the devil or to side with him. It is also used of men of unscrupulous speech who promote themselves out of jealousy, hatred, or anger. Malicious gossips take great joy in damaging the reputations of others and trying to destroy their lives. Satan is the father of lies and all slanderers. It is no wonder his children do the same.

There is much more to my family's story that we never got to tell regarding the 'fall' of my husband's business and the subsequent indictments than what the newspapers reported and the so-called 'facts' asserted by the government. There was a massive amount of media coverage and newspaper articles annihilating our reputations within a five-year period. In comparison, we had a few murders take place over the years in our small rural town, and relatively little in comparison was ever reported regarding them. God sees the truth, and He knows my heart. I know with absolute certainty that one day all wrongs will be made right. My reputation is only good for one purpose, and that is to be a witness for Him and His glory. If He wants me to have a good reputation, then He will redeem the lies. Philippians 2 tells me that Jesus, God in human flesh, made Himself of no reputation, taking the form of a bondservant (NKJV). That puts things into perspective for me.

The depth of newspaper coverage and the length of sentences associated with crimes of violence—including some murders—versus money crimes, was eye-opening to me. Crimes of money, in general, carry far greater sentences than those of violence. Scandals involving crimes of money sell more newspapers than those involving violence. Why is this? It's because the world values money more than life. This is what we tell our children when we prioritize a career over full-time motherhood, delegating that privilege to someone else. If the world did not value money more than life, abortion would be, hands down, the worst crime anyone could ever commit against another human being.

I was having a conversation with my bunkie one afternoon. She made no excuses for the fact that she was a 'well-respected' drug dealer where she lived. She bragged of how she slept at night with a gun under her pillow and was called to go out at all hours of the night to make deals, the proof that she "worked very hard and was very good at what she did." For programming credit, she was in the process of taking a drug class. The instructor apparently told her class that those who had been involved with drugs on the outside would do well to stay away from white-collar offenders as "they are evil because they stole from the government." I laughed out loud. I charged, "You sold drugs to children!" Indignant, she said, "We provided a service. And we did a lot of community service. Why, we had a neighborhood block party every year!" I said, "We were building a community church." Her face got red, and she sheepishly said, "Well, you may have me beat there."

Without self-control—Intemperate, powerless to control one's passions. This is one who has no discipline. It is heart-wrenching to see a person enslaved to his lusts that are destroying him.

Brutal—Savage, cruel, fierce, ruthless, unfeeling. Just like an animal who attacks its prey out of its instincts and with no conscience. Having no sympathy for others, this is the opposite of gentleness.

Haters of good—Despiser, opposed to goodness and good men. Haters of good have no love for virtue or integrity in men. They love what is evil and hate what is good. They can't tolerate being in the company of people who love good because light, goodness, and truth expose darkness, evil, and lies. The spiritual premise is found in John 3:19: **"This is the judgment, that the Light has come into the world and men loved the darkness rather than the Light, for their deeds were evil."**

Treacherous—A traitor, a betrayer; giving forward into the enemy's hands. The treacherous betrays a friend without a second thought; he betrays his friend's trust, confidence, and all promises of loyalty. This is the person, like Judas, who would deliver over a friend the control of another for his own gain. Joseph's brothers were treacherous. The treacherous have no allegiance to anyone but the highest bidder. 'Save his own back at all costs' is his motto.

Jesus told His disciples that brother would deliver up brother to death and so on in the family relationships. Prisons are filled with the treacherous. Our judicial system plays upon this evil trait by rewarding snitches and using their own conspiracy theories to get convictions at all costs. And what does that say about the men who serve the public who will use people in this way? Back in Paul's day there were informers to Rome as well. Just like our day, there were those in Rome who would pay back old scores by informing against the Christians to the Roman government.

Reckless—To fall forward, headlong, sloping, rash, reckless, self-willed, those who impulsively do foolish things. They fall headlong in their wickedness acting impetuously without considering the consequences. They are headstrong determined to do what they want, regardless of what anyone else advises.

The picture that comes to my mind is my strong-willed puppy when he spots a rabbit while I am walking him. He begins to run a hundred miles an hour in slow motion on his leash (because I can't run a hundred miles an hour), and I keep telling him, "Never going to happen, Buddy." However, his impulses drive him every single time.

Conceited—To inflate with self-conceit, high-minded, lifted up with pride, to be puffed up, or haughty. The conceited person can't be taught or told anything because he already knows everything.

Lovers of pleasure rather than lovers of God—Fond of pleasure, voluptuous, lover of pleasure rather than being pious. The word for *pleasure* is from **hedos** where we get our word *hedonism*, which is the idea that pleasure or happiness is the sole purpose in life.

Holding to a form of godliness—Maintaining a facade of religion. There have always been those who have professed Christianity without knowing true salvation, so Christian polls are not worth much. What is worth noting is that there have been far less professors in times of persecution. Regardless of what present-day polls are saying, multitudes of people throughout the ages have professed to some sort of religion being a part of their lives.

In one prison camp alone, we had those who adhered to (or dabbled in), Buddhism, Hinduism, Humanism, Islam, Judaism, and Mysticism. We had Jehovah's Witnesses, Native Americans (with a fully-functioning sweat lodge), New Age religions, Rastafarians, and Scientologists. There were Wiccans (with cauldrons and outside goddess worship ceremonies that took place in the grove right beside the sweat lodge), Seventh Day Adventists, and Roman Catholics. There were Metaphysical studies—and the list could go on. Alderson Federal Prison Camp appeared to be a very 'spiritual' place. Yet, the question on my lips almost daily was: "Where is the pursuit of holiness?"

All of these religions were free to worship. There was only one exception. True Christianity. I was not permitted to teach a Bible study, which was the prerogative of the prison; but Christians were not allowed to have open Bible studies outside at free time or in the privacy of their own cubes. In fact, memos came out saying that shots would be given to anyone who was seen praying with others. (I made copies of these and sent them home to family and friends lest anyone not believe me.) A 'shot' was a punishment that would make your life extra miserable incurring loss of privileges such as going to the commissary, being able to connect with loved ones on the phone, or even being remanded to the 'bus stop'. These punishments could even include losing good time. Depending on the severity, one could be shipped off to the local county jail. A friend of mine, who was in our Bible study *held outside* (you read that right) said she had observed this happening to one such girl for organizing a prayer circle outside on the National Day of

Prayer. Counting the cost, all those who participated in our study made the commitment to stay.

Jesus reserved his most scathing rebukes for the most religious of His day—the Scribes and the Pharisees. They would be the epitome of the picture here of those who held to a form a godliness. Matthew 23 is Jesus' lengthy diatribe against these religious elite. He said they were religious phonies, or hypocrites, because as leaders they didn't even do what they told the people to do. And the deeds they *did* were for the sole purpose of being noticed by men. They liked the attention and treatment of the 'ordinary' people. Expecting to be served instead of serving others, they lacked the humility that was required to be God's true servants.

Calling them hypocrites in verses 25 and 26, Jesus said, **"You clean the outside of the cup and the dish** (their outward appearance *looked* religious)**, but inside you are full of robbery and self-indulgence. You blind Pharisee, first clean the inside of the cup and of the dish, so that the outside of it may become clean also."** Then, in verses 27-28, **"Woe to you, scribes and Pharisees, hypocrites! For you are like whitewashed tombs which on the outside appear beautiful, but inside they are full of dead men's bones and all uncleanness. So, you, too, outwardly appear righteous to men, but inwardly you are full of hypocrisy and lawlessness."** Lastly, He says, **"You serpents, you brood of vipers, how will you escape the sentence of hell?"**

Lovers of self in these difficult last days will be holding to a form of godliness. They are *holding* (present tense), which means it is their lifestyle or their practice. They may go to church every week and be very active in the church. They wear the mask of spirituality. Lovers of self are only concerned with how they appear to others in order to make them feel good about themselves. They are concerned about the outside of their cup. They draw near to God with their lips, but their hearts are far from Him.

Some people are drawn to ritual and tradition. They love the old buildings, the architecture, the smells of incense, the pomp and circumstance of the ceremonies, the tastes and sounds of religion. A lady in Bible study once told me she could not leave her beloved religion for those very reasons. This religion is very sensual; it is a love of religion just like the world defines love today—according to feelings, emotions, senses, and what it does for them.

'Lovers of self' have a form of godliness. What does that mean? *Godliness* is living aware of God's presence having a desire to be pleasing to Him which is motivated by love for Him. It is to desire to live for His glory and is reflected in all we say, think, and do. It is living in such a way that acknowledges by our lifestyle that He is God and He deserves to be treated as such. It is love which comes from the heart—a heart that has been transformed by the power of God. The one who has a form of godliness may speak 'Christianese' and walk through all the motions of what he believes is Christianity, but he has no real relationship with or reverence for the Lord of this universe. His 'Christianity' is all an outward show.

These 'lovers of self' have no love for God; they have denied or refused the transforming power of His grace. In other words, they cannot love God—they are not able to love God—because He has not given them the power to do so by giving them a new heart and His Spirit, who alone is able to transform them for His glory. That's a bold statement, but the evidence of their being devoid of power to be made holy is manifested in their lifestyles. **They profess to know God, but by their deeds they deny Him, being detestable and disobedient and worthless for any good deed.** (Titus 1:16)

Webster's Dictionary defines *love* as a noun. It says love is a strong affection for another arising out of kinship or personal ties; attraction based on sexual desire; affection and tenderness felt by lovers; affection based on admiration, benevolence, or common interests, warm attachment, enthusiasm, or devotion. A "feeling".

Love has become such a convoluted notion or concept that no one may really be able to define this word used as a noun. Since God *commands* that I love Him and love my neighbor as myself, love is a verb. Because it is *His* command, we must get our definition of love from Him alone. And we will develop that understanding in the chapters to come.

11

What the World Needs Now Is Love, True Love

Pull up a Google search on words that describe *love*, and you will see words that give us all sorts of warm fuzzies. Many popular love songs focus on the singer getting his needs met by another. Sometimes love is sweet, but sometimes love is blue. *Sweet love* implies something that appeals to my senses. What we really need is true love and God's definition of it.

The Law of God can be summed up in the two great commandments to love God with all my heart, soul, mind, and strength, and to love my neighbor as myself. All that dishonors God is going to be disobedience to one of these two commandments. So our obedience or disobedience is manifested in and through our relationships with God and with others. We tell ourselves that we love as we are called to love. In fact, everything in our relationships is fine until somebody or God, Himself, rocks our boat—until we are offended by something we don't like. The Bible says love is not easily offended.

In 1 John 4:16, John says God is love and love is from God, so true love imitates God. One aspect of the fruit of the Spirit is love, so it is the Spirit who fills me with love for God and for others. **You shall love the LORD your God with all your heart, and with all your soul, and with all your might.** (Deuteronomy 6:5) Neither the world nor our flesh can interpret this passage correctly. It does not mean I simply have intense *feelings* for God. While *heart* does encompass the emotions and passions, in Scripture *heart* often refers to the mind, knowledge, thinking, reflection, memory, inclination, resolution, understanding, and the determination of will. To love God with all my *soul* carries the idea of loving Him with all my life. *Might* can mean properly, wholly, speedily, diligently, vehemently, or exceedingly; it has to do with the degree to which I love. To love God is to love Him supremely above all else.

This should be easily understood through a right understanding of marriage; but even understanding the institution of marriage has become distorted, and the divorce rate proves as much. We must get our beliefs from the Word of God alone.

We live in, what I call, a 'disposable' society. Everything—paper towels, contacts, diapers, and even spouses—are disposable. Sadly, that list even includes babies in the womb. I grew up in a traditional home just like my mother and my grandmothers before me. My father was the sole support of the family, and my mother was a stay-at-home mom who shouldered the main duties of raising my sister and me. I don't remember wanting for much until I got into my teenage years—when I saw what others had and how that affected whether they were popular or not. The obvious answer to me wanting more was to work. I had jobs working as a waitress, a deli clerk, and a bank teller before I got married at age 19. Back then, there were local shops to fix everything from shoes to appliances. When something broke, it was not thrown away and immediately replaced. The first option was to try and have it fixed. That concept is lost on this post-modern culture. The disposable ideology had already taken hold of my mindset as I got a little older.

I had been married for a few years when my mom's washing machine broke. She had it for a long time; so I inquired somewhat shortsightedly, "What model are you going to buy now?" Without hesitation, she informed me the local Mr. Fix-it would get it running smoothly in no time. I was doubtful. Within the hour, Mr. 'Z' had come and gone, leaving a receipt with my mom in the amount of $8.00. The washing machine ran for many years.

We live in a disposable, fast-food, 'I want it now', in-debt, world. Unfortunately, that doesn't just pertain to material possessions. When one 'falls out of love', or gets tired of one spouse, he or she feels little guilt in trading that spouse in for a new one—usually a newer, younger model. I have always wondered why advertisers in my day began using the term, 'New and improved'. Was the older version old and awful? *Hey, you might want to try us again. We used to be terrible, but now we're better.*

Ask the average person on the street what the word *covenant* means, and they would have no idea. It is not a word used today for the same reason a lack of commitment is seen in most relationships. But the word *covenant* and its themes are deeply embedded in Scripture. Covenant is the foundation of God's love.

My husband and I got married young by today's standards. Like most marriages, ours has had a lot of ups and downs. Our vows should have read something like: "I promise to ride the roller coaster of life with you..." Those who know me well know I'm not a thrill-seeker, and we both **hate** amusement parks. Often, in the early years of our marriage, when my husband and I would have a knock-down, drag-out fight, I would cry out to the Lord and beg Him to change *Greg*. It sounds so selfish and immature to me now, but so typical of fleshly thinking. A magnitude-9-type of fight occurred in the early '90s when I was driving an hour and a half each way to...umm...Bible study, so I had a lot of time to pray back and forth. As the Lord would have it, this Bible study just happened to be a topical study on biblical covenants, which was new truth to me. That morning, I left thinking I was facing some pretty intense spiritual warfare. Yep! Satan was using, of all people, my husband to keep me from this important study. (Rather, the Lord was teaching me an appropriate object lesson.) Crying aloud in prayer all the way to Pittsburgh, I pleaded, "Lord, if You *can't* (cringing now) change him, then You had better change me!" As soon as it left my lips, I thought it sounded so spiritual I decided to share it with the class later. (Cringing again!) Giving ultimatums to the Lord is never a good thing. Guess who was going to have radical heart surgery?

Often, during our fights, I would not hesitate to tell my husband that I had had enough, and I threatened to leave him. (Remember, "I hate you all!" It got easier and easier to say as the years went by.) Not surprisingly, the threats became less credible each time they were spoken. Around this same time, I studied the book of Hosea. I remember reading Chapter 11:8 and other passages like it where God says His heart is turned over within Him. He had steadfastly loved Israel with an everlasting love, and she continued to play the harlot in betrayal and rebellion. Her heart belonged to many other lovers. I was devastated to think how I continued to do the same in my ebb and flow periods of commitment to Him. I begged the Lord to keep me from being unfaithful to Him. At that moment, something happened in my heart as I pondered my marriage. I, too, was being unfaithful to the Lord when I refused to love my husband in and *through* our conflicts, when I refused to allow the Lord to use our differences to sanctify *my* heart. No matter what, I determined to never leave or forsake my husband by turning my back on him. That commitment has been greatly challenged, but the Lord has given me the grace and strength to grow as I seek to honor it.

Though legally bound, in every other sense of a biblical understanding of marriage, mine has had no shape or substance in nine years. I saw my husband for a short visit one time. We sat side by side in a room with hundreds of other people sitting in rows. My mother-in-law was on one side of Greg, and I was on the other. Guards were in the front facing us watching our every move. For four of those nine years, our only communication was in the form of letters or emails which were inspected and read. Over the last five years, it has been in short 10-minute phone calls. (As inmates, we received 300 minutes per month at a cost of $3.15 per 15 minutes.) He is too far away for me to visit on any regular basis. Even so, we are one in the eyes of the Lord, and I have no desire to spend my life with anyone else. We are bound by a covenant we made before the Lord even before we understood what that really entailed.

A covenant is a solemn and *binding* agreement, usually involving an oath. Marriage, a covenant made before God, is meant to last a lifetime. Covenant involves a walk to death; oneness results between covenant partners who hold nothing back from each other. Entering a covenantal relationship is the end of living for yourself. This level of commitment is a rare jewel to behold.

My prayer for my marriage has long been to see the Lord glorified through it so that the world would be able to see the love Christ has for His bride. I naturally assumed that would have to happen with us being together. However, the Lord's ways are different than ours. R.C. Sproul has said:

> "People are no longer familiar with the nature of covenants. Covenants establish relationships publicly and create accountability. If two people are simply living together, either partner may abandon the other without accountability. The covenant involves a promise to obey God and to be faithful—and also involves a curse: May God judge me if I break this pledge. People avoid the covenant of marriage because they want to have irresponsible relationships, but such relationships are hazardous to human life. God has created us so that we blossom as human beings when we conform to God's covenantal structures.

> When we live irresponsibly, we destroy ourselves
> and others…. Living by covenants is God's method
> to anchor our lives and provide security against the
> prevailing cultural disintegration."[1]

One would not expect the world to understand the serious consequences of entering a covenant before God, but how many *Christians* know that breaking covenant involves a curse by God?

In 1979, my family attended a festival called 'Jesus '79'. Many young Christian couples were wearing half a broken heart on a chain around their necks. It had a verse on it, and the idea I *thought* was that when they were apart, their hearts were broken. When they were together, the pieces fit together, and their hearts would be whole. I found out in my study of covenant that it later came to connote an emotional bond between people who were separated, but that was not the original meaning. It was Mizpah. *It was what-pah*?

In the verse from Genesis 31:49, Mizpah means a watchtower. The context of this passage is a covenant being made between Jacob and Laban. Laban says to Jacob, "**May the LORD watch between you and me when we are absent one from the other. If you mistreat my daughters, or if you take wives besides my daughters, although no man is with us, see, God is witness between you and me.**" Laban said to Jacob, "**Behold this heap and behold the pillar which I have set between you and me. This heap is a witness, and the pillar is a witness, that I will not pass by this heap to you for harm, and you will not pass by this heap and this pillar to me, for harm. The God of Abraham and the God of Nahor, the God of their father, judge between us.**" When they were apart, they could not see what the other one was doing. But God could see all. He was their witness. They both knew that God was watching over them, and that He would bring upon them the evil or the good, according to their actions, as they broke or kept the covenant. Somehow, I don't think the couples who wore these necklaces fully understood the seriousness of Mizpah!

Malachi 2 shows us how seriously God views covenants. The men of Israel were divorcing their wives in order that they might marry pagan women. There is a lot in these verses, but we simply want to look at the aspect of the marriage covenant. God indicts: **"This is another thing you do: you cover the altar of the LORD with tears, with weeping and with groaning, because He no longer regards the offering or accepts it with favor from your hand. Yet you say, 'For what reason?' Because the LORD has been a witness between you and the wife of your youth, against whom you have dealt treacherously, though she is your companion and your wife by covenant. But not one has done so who has a remnant of the Spirit. And, what did that one do while he was seeking a godly offspring? Take heed then to your spirit and let no one deal treacherously against the wife of your youth. For I hate divorce,"** says the LORD, the God of Israel, **"and him who covers his garment with wrong,"** says the LORD of hosts. **"So, take heed to your spirit, that you do not deal treacherously."** (Malachi 2:13-16)

Covenant is **beriyth** in the Hebrew. There is an idea of 'cutting' in this word. Men 'cut' covenant with one another. A covenant is a solemn, binding agreement between two parties involving a variety of responsibilities, benefits, and penalties depending on the specific covenant which is made. Some covenants are conditional; some are unconditional. Marriage is an unconditional covenant made between a man and a woman before God. It is a holy institution because it was established by God. Unfortunately, many view the institution of marriage only as a contract between two people. Everyone in our day knows the phrase 'contracts are made to be broken'; this mindset is evidenced by the divorce rate in our country (and the common misconception that marriage is 'nothing more than a piece of paper').

What's the difference? If I contract with you for certain services, the contract is satisfied when I honor my commitments and you honor yours. That would be a conditional covenant or contract. If you fail to provide me with the services you promised according to our contractual agreement, then I do not need to fulfill my end of the bargain. In other words, if you do this, then I'll do this. In an unconditional covenant, I promise to do my part whether you reciprocate at all. And God is the witness to or the overseer of the covenant. Covenant says, "I promise to be faithful to you no matter what." In my marriage covenant I am saying, "I promise to be faithful to love you *as God calls me to love you no matter what.*" God's covenant love towards those He has saved is not conditional. There is nothing I have got to *do* to earn or keep His love.

Originating in the mind of God, marriage was designed for man's good. It was defined by God to be between one man and one woman with Him at the center of their union, and it was to last a lifetime. There is no greater earthly picture of covenant for us to observe to help us understand God's desire for our relationship with Him than marriage as God intended it. It was Jesus who said: **"Have you not read that He who created them from the beginning MADE THEM MALE AND FEMALE, and said, 'FOR THIS REASON A MAN SHALL LEAVE HIS FATHER AND MOTHER AND BE JOINED TO HIS WIFE, AND THE TWO SHALL BECOME ONE FLESH'? So, they are no longer two, but one flesh. What therefore God has joined together, let no man separate."** (Matthew 19:4-6) Entering into a covenant, whether it be in a marriage or in a relationship with God, involves taking on a new identity with the idea of oneness. The result of covenant, then, is communion. It was interesting to me that the word *communion* is not found in Scripture, but the word **koinonia** or *fellowship* is; it means communion. It is a partnership that can be defined as fellowship, association, community, communion, joint participation, intercourse, intimacy; or to share what one has in anything.

Long ago I learned the word *fellowship* can be easily remembered by thinking of two fellows in the same ship working together for the same purpose. All the *one another's* in Scripture show us a picture of how fellowship is lived out. We are to be devoted to one another, to honor one another, live in harmony with one another, accept one another, serve one another in love, be kind and compassionate to one another, admonish one another, encourage one another, spur one another on toward love and good deeds, offer hospitality to one another, and love one another. Certainly, all those things should be taking place in our marriages. It is important to remember that two lives have become one. This is a foreign concept in most modern marriages. We see a great symbol of this when the wife takes her husband's name (just like when we become 'Christians').

Covenant love in marriage is committed, faithful, transparent, and honest love. I know him, and he knows me better than any other human being. He knows me better than I know myself and vice versa. There is a deep, abiding trust between covenant partners. Real love stands firm when the torrential storms come.

Jesus said: **"Greater love has no one than this, that one lay down his life for his friends."** (John 15:13). *Friend* is a covenant term; and the depth of its meaning is worlds apart from what we think of as friendship today. I'm sure there is no need to elaborate but only to mention that Facebook has given a whole new low-level meaning to the biblical word *friend*. A covenant friend is a friend for whom you would die.

One aspect of the covenant study I particularly loved was the call to defend my covenant partner as seen in the lives of Jonathan and David. This became very real in my marriage with the onslaught of all that my husband was being accused of during the time of his investigation. To defend means to protect the person from harm or danger. It means to keep someone safe from attack, to support someone when they are being falsely accused or criticized. It means to repel a charge or accusation, or to oppose. I love to think of it as being a human shield around the one you love. It is no coincidence that when the police came to arrest us, they surrounded the house kneeling behind full body shields. My thoughts went immediately to Psalm 5:12—of the Lord surrounding us as a shield.

Real love never leaves nor forsakes. Love believes the best, as far as it is reasonable to do so. My problem arose when the government expected me to believe their accusations as reported in the local newspaper over a 30-year marriage relationship with my husband; when, in fact, I knew what the newspaper was reporting was filled with lies. As I said, even a civil judge in one of my husband's hearings responded to a comment made by my husband's attorney with, "Well, that isn't what the newspaper said."

If I tell you I love you, and my love is covenant love, I will share my whole life with you. I will give you all of me, even if I get nothing in return. That type of love is irresistible because it is godly love. This is the same commitment we are called to in our love for God, in giving our whole life for Him. **Know therefore that the LORD your God, He is God, the faithful God, who keeps His covenant and His lovingkindness to a thousandth generation with those who love Him and keep His commandments.** (Deuteronomy 7:9) **You shall therefore love the LORD your God,**

and always keep His charge, His statutes, His ordinances, and His commandments. (Deuteronomy 11:1) **If you love Me, you will keep My commandments.** (John 14:15) **He who has My commandments and keeps them is the one who loves Me.** (John 14:21) **Jesus answered and said to him, "If anyone loves Me, he will keep My word; and My Father will love him, and We will come to him and make Our abode with him. He who does not love Me does not keep My words; and the word which you hear is not Mine, but the Father's who sent Me."** (John 14:23-24) True love for God is directly related to obedience to Him.

We once had guests in our home who had brought their three-year-old boy with them. While the adults were visiting, I pulled out several toys for the toddler to play with. He was perfectly behaved. When it was time for them to go, the little one's father said, "It's time to go, son. Please pick up the toys." The boy kept playing, ignoring the imperative. Dad quickly gave me a glance that said, "Please don't intervene." He added, "Son, you need to obey me." The toddler pleaded, "But, Daddy, I don't want to obey you." It stood out in my mind that he hadn't said he didn't want to pick up the toys. The father sternly replied, "Oh, but you *will* obey me." The boy cried a few crocodile tears, then obediently submitted to his father.

At that tender age, the little one may not have realized why it was necessary for him to obey his father; but he knew that he loved his father, and his father loved him. He may have had a little pressure applied in the past teaching him to obey, which gave him a healthy respect for his father's chosen tool for discipline, but I had witnessed the love between the two prior to this incident.

If I truly love God, I will obey Him because to love Him is to know Him, and to know Him is to trust Him. God's commandments are His perfect will for us. Because He is good, He would not ask us to do anything that is not good for us. To obey our Father is to trust He always has our best in mind. We may not understand why we need to do all that He asks us to do, we may think we know better, we may even hesitate or kick up our heels a bit at times, but we must learn to trust and believe that our Father knows best.

I really want you to hear me on this next point. Did the Father ask me to go to prison? You say, "No. You had no choice." At first, I thought the same thing. I thought it was more like I needed to make the best of a horrible situation. But did the Lord call me to go into the Federal Prison system? I believe He did. If He hadn't called me to go, I wouldn't have gone. There would have been something in His providential plan that would have stopped me from going. Part of being obedient is to accept from His hand whatever He ordains for my life. I could trust that prison was His perfect will for me. My love for God is tied to trusting Him by submitting to His will and fully obeying Him in all things.

My love for God is also tied to my love for my brother. I can't say I love God if I don't love my brother. **The one who says he is in the Light and yet hates his brother is in the darkness until now.** (1John 2:9) **By this we know that we love the children of God, when we love God and observe His commandments.** (1 John 5:2)

One of the purposes for the book of 1 John was to encourage its recipients in their true salvation. We can read it so that we might know whether we are truly saved or not. It is comprised of several different 'tests', if you will. The proof that eternal life resides in a person lies in three areas: faith in Jesus Christ, love for others, and obedience to God's commandments.

The little boy in my illustration was adopted by my friends. Their son by law and by love, he was chosen by them to be their child; and his sonship was sure. He didn't have to obey or do anything to *secure* his sonship. To be clear, one does not love others and obey God in order to obtain or merit salvation. Salvation is by grace alone through faith alone in the finished work of Jesus Christ. The **evidence** that there is true faith is there will also be love for others and a heart desiring to obey God's commands.

Those who have this love for God and others have it because of God's grace shed abroad in their hearts. True love is a gift from God. For those who are not saved, it is impossible for them to truly love God or others. This little boy loved his daddy because his daddy first loved him. Even at the tender age of three, he was being asked to do something he did not want to do so that he could be taught, through discipline, to learn to trust his loving father. He would grow up as he learned to trust and obey. One day, he will reflect his father's heart by doing even the hard things just because they are right. In the process of growing up, witnessing the love his father has for him, he learns to love others. **Train up**

a child in the way he should go; even when he is old, he will not depart from it. (Proverbs 22:6) *Train* is to make narrow, to instruct, to discipline, or to put something into one's mouth. It is a process that is consistent, often tedious, and requires a lot of patience and discipline on the part of the one who is doing the training, but there is a promise at the end of that work.

Child rearing sometimes involves painful discipline, but it is out of love for the child's good. The end goal is that the child would grow up to walk in righteousness. In 1 Peter, Peter was writing to Christians who were scattered and suffering. One of the main themes in the book is their sanctification which leads to brotherly love. **Since you have in obedience to the truth purified your souls for a sincere love of the brethren, fervently love one another from the heart, for you have been born again not of seed which is perishable but imperishable, that is, through the living and enduring word of God.** (1 Peter 1:22-23)

Christians want to be holy like our Father who has given us a new heart that longs for righteousness driving us towards obedience to His Word. We love the intimate relationship we have with our Father and with our brothers and sisters in Christ. The children love what the Father loves, and He has a special love for His children.

I love my children who are now grown adults. There is absolutely nothing I wouldn't do for their good. My husband has often said that I am like a mother bear when something or someone threatens my children. For the most part, my kids get along great. While nothing blesses my heart more than to see them loving each other and supporting each other, nothing makes my heart agonize more than when they are at odds with one another.

The greatest pain I have known in my life revolves around my children: the loss of my daughter, obviously, and how the prison test affected all three of my boys. My boys have been through a lot of trials in their lives. When Jesse and I were indicted and facing our criminal trial together, he told our pastor, "I just don't understand when the storms are going to end. It seems as though our life is one big, never-ending storm." *Rip my heart out!* Having been separated from my children, I don't take time with them for granted. The things that ordinarily might not bless a mother's heart, make my heart overflow with joy.

After I was released from prison, I was on home confinement for five months. Until that time, I had not seen my two youngest boys for four years. In prison, I could only afford to call them once a week for about 15 minutes. My youngest son called me the first night I was home and said, "Mom, I'm going to need to talk to you—a lot!" That was music to my ears. They did not have the time off from work to come for a visit at that time. We talked on the phone several times a day to catch up. But more important than the information we exchanged was our connection. We belong to one another, and nothing can separate the bond we share as family. Separation can cause a lot of doubts, discouragement, and strain on relationships. We needed those talks. We were coasts apart. Many nights I was already in bed and the phone would ring. "Hi, Mom! Anything going on? Okay. I love you. I'll talk to you tomorrow."

A year later, my boys flew home, we packed a 26-foot truck and traveled from Pennsylvania to California without stopping to sleep. While it was difficult, my cup was filled to overflowing to be in such close quarters with them, usually having one leaning on my shoulder sleeping as the other drove. At one point, my middle son, Jordan, needed to get some rest, so he relinquished the keys to my youngest. Jared had no prior training with the large truck, and his first feat was to get gas. While having some difficulty pulling into the gas station pumps, he panicked pleading, "Help me, Jordan!" Here was the picture of their life together as more than brothers through the difficult days of their young lives. They relied on each other. They helped one another. They were there for one another through thick and thin. They still are. The heartaches and struggles they have shared have forged bonds of steel between them. I remember telling my oldest son, Jesse, that he, Greg, and I have a bond that not many will ever understand. It will always provide reinforcing strength to the bonds of our love for each other. The bonds of Christian unity are stronger than any type of bonds we may have with others on this earth, for they are eternal.

We are to love the brethren unconditionally, with the familial love of God's own family. This isn't churchy love that pretends and masquerades as Christian love only on Sunday mornings. This is not superficial; it is deep and intense. This is not safe love. It is radical and risky stretching us to our limits because it exposes our hearts and humbles us. Self-emptying love makes us vulnerable and doesn't always look pretty. Intimacy can be messy and rough at times because it is the sharing of real life together. This love calls for me to be genuine—no masks, no phony flattery, and no hypocrisy, but this love sticks around and is in it for the long haul.

When Greg and I first started going to church in Ligonier, our normal routine was to walk into church, sit in the back row, then leave abruptly after the service. One young couple confronted us by saying that it appeared we did not really want to have anything to do with the people because of this routine and the fact that we didn't even take our coats off! Because I truly wanted to love but was so socially inept, I broke down at this point. All I could get out was, "I leave my coat on because I feel fat." Talk about vulnerability. I realize now there was also a fear of not being accepted and trying to guard myself from pain, which is pride. It has taken me years to understand that. After having exposed my heart, I wish I could say we came to know many of these people more intimately as family. We did get closer to this couple, but we had much to learn.

Foundationally, we are born again to love. We are born again into God's family, and we want to imitate our Father who has loved us. The Christians Peter was writing to were suffering. When we suffer, we tend to look inward even more so than normal. That is one of the reasons it is so important to love those who are suffering. It helps the sufferer get her focus off herself and onto Christ. When believers come alongside those who are suffering, those struggling are strengthened by their love and support. They know that God is with them because He has brought His body to minister to them. I came to know this personally when Missy died and throughout my prison trial. I will forever be grateful for those believers that our Lord used to strengthen us and cause us to know His hand was heavy upon us in our greatest trials.

We are *commanded* to love because it is not a natural thing to do. In fact, it is impossible to love like this in our flesh; it takes supernatural enablement from the Spirit of God. On our part, it takes humility and hearts full of submission to love like this, hearts that are sensitive to the Lord's leading. As we are learning to love, we are being sanctified. So, our sanctification is related to loving our brethren.

Believers have a strong desire for fellowship with other believers. However, we are called to love all our 'neighbors', anyone the Lord brings into our lives who has a need. My neighbors for a time included the 1,200 inmates I lived with at Alderson. If they are in my life, they are there for a reason. If they have a need I am able to meet, I am to meet it. One beautiful sunny day in Alderson, my friend and I were walking down 'Hallelujah Hill' on our way to work. A woman dressed in her visitation uniform was standing on the sidewalk sobbing. I walked up to her and hugged her. I told her it was going to be 'okay'. She said she had just come from her first visit, and it was hard watching her husband walk out the door without her. I gave her a couple more words of encouragement, and we went on our way. Once out of ear's reach, my friend was curious, "Do you *know* her?" I said, "No." Incredulously, she stated, "But you hugged her!" I responded matter-of-factly, "Well, she needed a hug."

When I had been in county jail for about a week, I started to notice that *look* of the newbies. A woman came in one evening and was obviously going through drug withdrawal. I welcomed her by quickly giving her a hug which was *really* frowned upon in county jail. I asked her if I could get her anything. She just stared at me and kept saying she was so cold. I asked her if I could make her a cup of tea. With tears in her eyes, she nodded affirmatively. When I was leaving, weeks later, she walked up to me and told me she would never forget me for the kindness I showed her on her first night there. She said I was an angel; I assured her I was not.

When one of the prosecutors on our case was diagnosed with cancer, Greg and I began praying for him. The only need we could meet, he needed prayer whether he knew it or not, whether he asked us for it or not. The Lord gave us an opportunity to come face to face with this man in a meeting. Looking him in the eyes, I shook his hand and told him we were praying for him. That's not natural. I continue to pray for the people involved in our cases as the Lord brings them to mind. I would love nothing more than to call them family one day.

We are to love *all* our neighbors. But we have a special love for those neighbors with whom we will spend eternity. We have a family love with other believers. We are part of one Body, and we belong to each other as brothers and sisters. The love believers have for one another is special. Unbelievers take notice of that type of love because it's not natural; it's supernatural. **By this all men will know that you are My disciples, if you have love for one another.** (John 13:35)

A sense of belonging is important to every human being, and we have a special love for 'our own'. It is easy to love all children, but no love can touch the love I have for my own children. They belong to me as a stewardship from the Lord. I belong to my children as their mother. This same love certainly applies to all our children, whether we give birth to them or choose them. I've given my life for my children by pouring myself into them. There is a day coming when they may have to give that same care back to me—even now, in my situation, they provide for me in so many ways.

There have been times over the last 13 years when people have questioned why I stay married considering my circumstances. They have no more idea of what happened than I do. They have heard one side of the story. No matter what my husband did or didn't do, Jesse and I got swept up in it with him; and a lot of people know that was not right. Some Christians have suggested I have biblical grounds for divorce because Greg 'deserted me'. That's absurd to me. Why did the thought of divorce never cross my mind? (It *has* crossed my mind that some probably think the fact that I *haven't* divorced Greg affirms my guilt.) First, I made a covenant with Greg and, more importantly, with the Lord. Second, and simply stated, I love my husband because he is mine. Just as I believe that the children God blessed us with are His precious gifts to us, I believe my husband is God's special gift to me. We are one flesh. Greg is my first true love because he is the only man I have ever loved with the love of God. Also, my relationship with Greg has been the single most important relationship the Lord has used in my sanctification. It is interesting to me that never once when Greg was abundantly providing for his family did anyone ever advise me to divorce him. I must ask these same advisors what the phrase 'for better or for worse' means?

That need for a sense of belonging is deeply satisfied in my knowledge that God is my Father, and I belong to Him. Those who refuse to acknowledge God as God can only live shallow, eternally meaningless lives as orphans without any hope, purpose, or family.

The person who will not love God and His people will never truly belong anywhere; eternity will be forever separation and rejection unimaginable to the human mind. When I hear Christ's Word to me saying: "I will never leave you nor forsake you," I have the desire to love my own the same way.

In Genesis 2:8, God said it was not good for Adam to be alone. Adam had a relationship with God, yet God said it was not good for Adam be alone. God created man to know fellowship with Himself and other human beings. It's not good to be a loner. This can sometimes be difficult for a person who is a quiet person and likes to be alone. I have always been one who has one or two close friendships in which I invest. I love to read and have no trouble keeping myself company. That can be good at times, but not *all* the time. It is too *easy* for me because I have always struggled on a social level.

I love to have alone time, but I also have an innate need to belong. I am a people-person, which sounds like an extreme paradox. There aren't too many people I don't get along with, and I really like people. Yet, I struggle socially, until I get to know someone. Parties or gatherings where I am forced to make small talk—forget about it! I will look for every excuse known to man to find a way to get out of those types of engagements. I really dislike lulls in conversation, and I'm not good at thinking up ice-breaking questions. On top of that, I have an extremely dry sense of humor, so many people don't get me at first. Now if you want to get into a great discussion regarding what the Lord is doing in our lives or a topic about theology, wild horses couldn't keep me away from a conversation like that one. But to get to that point where we are intimately sharing our life in the Lord, we need to get to know one another. If the dilemma of alone time versus needing to belong weren't bad enough, then there is the problem of friendships that always come with the possibility of rejection.

Here's the cycle as I see it. Small talk helps me get to know *about* another person. But if I am to get to know this person in a more intimate way, something is required of me. I must invest myself in that relationship. As I really get to know someone, I begin to see their flaws and they see mine. So not long into this 'friendship made in heaven', we experience tension. As I've said, my natural default is to pull away. I've *learned* to try to focus on two truths: The Lord put this relationship in my life for my good; if I submit to Him in it, He will use it to sanctify me. Instead of focusing on the faults of the other person, I must deliberately focus on crucifying my flesh in any instance where I find myself offended. As we allow the Lord to use this relationship to sanctify us, sharpening each other as our raw edges grind against one another—as we stay and humble ourselves, submitting to the Lord in acting out the one another's—we will find a treasure for keeps. And let's face it, we need to get over ourselves so that we can truly love. I believe our greatest desire in life is to be fully loved *despite* being fully known. It's unconditional love. We all want it. We just struggle to give it.

People get on our nerves because we love ourselves. We think we are 'better than', that we don't deserve to be treated badly, and that everyone should be just like us. *Well, I wouldn't do that, but you go ahead. Why can't they just do this or that or be this or that…?* (I say those types of things when I set myself up as the judge of how I think people should be.) But would I *really* like somebody just like me? Probably not, because I tend to think of myself first. And what kind of friend is that? No. I'm really looking for someone just like Jesus. Trouble is, that is the friend *I'm* called to be! **Do nothing from selfishness or empty conceit, but with humility of mind regard one another as more important than yourselves; do not merely look out for your own personal interests, but also for the interests of others.** (Philippians 2:3-4)

Since coming to California, God led me to a small group of godly women who study the Bible together, pray for each other, and share each other's lives. A few of them have been together for several decades. They are real. There is nothing I would hesitate to share with any of them. I love them; and I know they love me. From the first night I joined their group, I felt like I was home and had known them my whole life. The conversation was rich with years of practical wisdom, humility, honesty, and life-giving encouragement. I still suffer through situations where I must engage in small talk in agonizing social situations, but there's something encouraging about thinking of this bond I share with my sisters in Christ. And maybe I'm just learning to vulnerably humble myself by refusing to let shyness (which is really a form of pride) keep me from the treasure of godly friendships. Maybe I'm growing up a little more with each trial the Lord brings into my life. Being a 'convicted felon' has helped me in this situation, because for some reason I now feel the need to get everything out in the open and on the table with each new relationship. No one will ever accuse me of concealment again!

Some neighbors are not easy to love right from the start. These might be relationships that we don't choose, but the Lord has chosen them for us. If we understand that our neighbors have been brought into our lives by God to sanctify us, we will learn to be patient, forgiving, and loving with them. If I remember that God loves even me, despite knowing me fully, then it is easier to forget myself and love freely.

Have you ever heard this from a believer's mouth? "I love so and so, but I don't *like* her. I don't want to deal with her." If I say that, I have just given myself permission to distance myself from that person as an excuse so that I don't have to follow God's command to love her. What does it matter if I like someone or not? We aren't talking about feelings. We are commanded to love our enemies. This is just stubborn disobedience. I do realize that there are certain situations in life where we do have to separate from people for different reasons. What I'm saying is that this has become way too common and easy for us to use as an excuse to remove ourselves from a relationship God intends to use to sanctify us. The fact that it happens in the church is most troubling. **If someone says, "I love God," and hates his brother, he is a liar; for the one who does not love his brother whom he has seen, cannot love God whom he has not seen.** (1 John 4:20) Remember, *love* is a verb. So you can't say you love someone without doing them good and actively loving them as God commands.

We *can't* love our brother and sister as we are called to love—in our own strength. We can't just try harder. We can't love God as we're called to love Him, but we *can* love by His grace as we walk in His Spirit. We can learn to love as we submit to His will for us by His strength. It takes humility and sacrifice. The world will notice this kind of love, and they will want to know the God who is love. Proof that we have been born again from above is our love for the brethren.

Whether we *feel* love or not, we are called to love. In his book, *Mere Christianity*, C. S. Lewis wrote, "Do not waste your time bothering whether you 'love' your neighbor; act as if you did. As soon as we do this, we find one of the great secrets. When you are behaving as if you loved someone, you will presently come to love him. If you injure someone you dislike, you will find yourself disliking him more. If you do him a good turn, you will find yourself disliking him less."[2]

Jesus said a tree is known by its fruit. An apple tree produces apples—not holly berries. Nobody would mistake a holly berry for an apple and eat this little red fruit by mistake. **But the fruit of the Spirit is love, joy, peace, patience, kindness, goodness, faithfulness, gentleness, self-control; against such things there is no law.** (Galatians 5:22-23) We are to be known by our love. It should be obvious by our lives manifesting the fruit of the Spirit that we belong to God. **Owe nothing to anyone except to love one another; for he who loves his neighbor has fulfilled the law. For this, "YOU SHALL NOT COMMIT ADULTERY, YOU SHALL NOT MURDER, YOU SHALL NOT STEAL, YOU SHALL NOT COVET," and if there is any other commandment, it is summed up in this saying, "YOU SHALL LOVE YOUR NEIGHBOR AS YOURSELF." Love does no wrong to a neighbor; therefore, love is the fulfillment of the law.** (Romans 13:8-10)

When we go to a doctor, we would expect no less than that doctor would give us the best possible treatment he can give us. We expect that he will do everything in his power to help us *because* he took an oath to do that. His 'calling' was to become a doctor. We would be shocked and appalled by a doctor who shirked his responsibilities in treating us because he just didn't like us for some reason. We think the same about men in positions of law enforcement who are called to uphold the law. We would hope the same could be said about our justice system. God expects no less from us when it comes to loving others. We owed a debt we couldn't pay, and Christ paid it in full. What we owe now is love to God and to others. It's our calling.

Love is the fulfillment of the Law. If I'm loving my neighbor as myself, I would never harm him by being unfaithful to him, by murdering him, by stealing from him, by coveting what belongs to him, by slandering him, etc. I would only seek to serve him in love in whatever capacity the Lord gives me opportunity and ability.

I learned in prison how much I need people in my life—me, the loner, needs people—*vital* to my existence are fellow believers with whom I have true fellowship. God created us for community, and a picture of that reality is seen in the Church. I had very little true fellowship during the four-year prison period. What little I did have was like bread and water to a woman dying of thirst and starvation. I couldn't get enough, and my soul knew how desperate I was for it. I longed to have the freedom to sing a simple hymn with a congregation with which I was like-minded. The first one I had opportunity to sing was, "Great is Thy Faithfulness".

Before trials hit, wisdom dictates that we know what we believe so that our foundation is steady and sure. Surrounding ourselves with solid believers who can give wise counsel when we struggle to stand upon what we know as truth, keeps us steadfast in our commitment to honor and glorify Christ. In my prison trial, there were those who offered me ungodly advice. In every trial there will be those who try to get our focus off what we know to be right. In times of intense suffering, we must be able to discern what is wise counsel and what is not. In Job's trial, his friends, and even his wife, encouraged him to view the situation from a faulty perspective and to do what he knew was not right. Job stood firm. And we must, too.

Some brothers and sisters were quick to point me to Christ, to His truth, and to plead with me to allow God to work in my trial for good in every situation. They were quick to pray when I was tempted to lean into self-pity or bitterness and to gently exhort me to turn from every temptation and stand firm in the truth of the gospel. I would not hesitate to say that the prayers of the saints were vital to keeping my head above water every day. **"When you pass through the waters, I will be with you; And through the rivers, they will not overflow you. When you walk through the fire, you will not be scorched, nor will the flame burn you."** (Isaiah 43:2)

The Lord is with me in my trials. He made sure to have His children available to me when I needed them most. God is my refuge and my strength, a very present help in trouble. Through the eyes of faith, I witnessed His love to my family in the faithful prayers of His children, their hands reaching out to us in warm embraces, and their feet moving quickly to meet all our needs.

12
Grieving and Receiving Love

I have what I believe to be a bizarre history with 'the Church'. When Greg and I got married, I (falsely) believed that I had recently been saved through the ministry of a traveling charismatic preacher. During our short engagement, my family and I attended the small church this preacher planted in our town. Greg continued to attend the Catholic Church. There was quite the turmoil between our two families when it came time to plan our wedding. Eventually, we were married in a nearby charismatic church in a ceremony presided over by both my charismatic minister and a charismatic Catholic priest. Immediately following our wedding, we headed to New York, where my husband was enrolled in his second year of college in an even smaller town than Ligonier. We visited a small Catholic church off and on during the year we lived there. And we continued to watch the popular televangelists of the 70's. Towards the middle of that school year, Greg decided he wanted to play football at a large university in Oklahoma, and he was accepted with scholarship once he applied. Soon, thereafter, we became convinced that the Lord was calling us, instead, to a university associated with one of the televangelists we watched on television. 'On faith', we gave up the other opportunity and spent a year involved in the organizations associated with this televangelist before walking away disillusioned and disgusted. And we did walk away—from everything—for years.

We began to have marital conflicts years later, and I thought converting to Catholicism might be the answer. I became the best Catholic I could be and got heavily involved in a local church and its grade school (where both kids attended). About that time, my husband and his family bought a brewery located about an hour from where we grew up, so we moved back home. It wasn't long after we began watching another preacher on television and listening to biblically-strong Christian radio broadcasts. The Lord began drawing us to His Word; and my hunger was insatiable. I trained to be a leader of women's Bible studies with another ministry on television. My husband left the brewery to start a beverage business bottling juices, teas, and waters. Over those first ten years living in Ligonier, we were tied to two different Baptist churches, but continued to struggle with what we believed to be important doctrinal issues. So, again, we walked away from the church. Even as a longing for true fellowship enveloped our hearts, we stubbornly closed our eyes to what the Lord might be offering us in the way of any other local church body. We owned a house and a business, but we had no church. That was an ongoing problem.

To be clear: It is disobedience for a believer not to join with a local body of believers. I can see how much of my suffering ties itself to this disobedience. I can also see how God in His grace and mercy used this time of separation in my life to sanctify me. I dove into the waters of the Word to find answers to all the questions I had—mainly, "Who is the true God of Scripture?" and "What is the Gospel?" As someone who tends to be dogmatic, I needed clarity because of all the different types of teaching to which I had been exposed. The answers I gained gave me a deep love for the truth and for discernment. I wanted to honor the Lord in what I believed and shared with others. However, because we didn't believe there was a local body that believed *exactly* as we did, we were out of balance and still veering off the narrow road. It was Fatherly discipline that drove us into the arms of the church each time we were broken and downcast.

To strongly reiterate, I am *not* advocating that believers separate themselves from a local body of believers. On the contrary, Hebrews 10:24-25 tells us that we are not to forsake the assembling of believers together. **And let us consider how to stimulate one another to love and good deeds, not forsaking our own assembling together, as is the habit of some, but encouraging one another; and all the more as you see the day drawing near.**

When believers join themselves to a church body, there is protection for them there in mutual accountability based on love for the truth. Just as God uses circumstances in our lives to sanctify us, He also uses others. Because we did not have that accountability, we did not have the protection of going from one extreme to the other in doctrinal error. During these years of intense study, we exposed ourselves to good teaching—even *great* teaching—but we didn't have the relationships in the body of Christ to live out what we were learning within the structure of that accountability. We were like spiritual loose canons!

We literally swung from one end of the pendulum to the other. We went from believing false teaching to erroneously believing we finally had the exclusive corner on the truth. We, undoubtedly, looked more like Pharisees, at this point, than Jesus. Yet, the Holy Spirit persistently used solid biblical teaching to bring conviction to find a sound church.

I want to be crystal clear about another thing: I do believe there is absolute truth. I believe there is only one way to God. I believe in a hard gospel, not easy believism. I believe in what some would label 'Lordship salvation'. But I have also come to understand that there can be many people with whom I can have true fellowship who don't believe everything *exactly* as I do. Certainly, relationships are superficial at best with those who don't have a correct view of the gospel. In fact, that type of relationship cannot even be considered 'fellowship' in the true sense of the word.

In the late '90s, I was struggling spiritually. We couldn't find a church because we were looking for that elusive 'perfect' church. Certainly, we did not have a lot of options in the way of a local church in a small town. Regarding those churches we did try, we would start going, really start loving the people, then start to see errors being taught. Before we left, we were very vocal about the problems *as we saw them.* I do believe there were valid issues that needed to be addressed, but we did not always go about addressing them in love. We were often rigid and unbending. Couple that wrong attitude with also believing we were honoring God by our discernment and convictions to stand for the truth, and we were dangerous to the unity of each local body to which we joined ourselves. We believed wholeheartedly that there were few true churches left, and that God was going to start house churches like those in the early church. Eventually, we left the 'Church' to watch videos of sermons at home with our children, and I began to drift once again. By 2001, I was in a bad place. This whole time in my life grieves me today.

In the spring of 2001, my brother-in-law was getting married. My 16-year-old daughter was asked to be in his wedding. Sitting in the Catholic Church at the wedding (my husband's family has strong Catholic roots), the priest, Greg's third cousin, was speaking. I looked at Greg and said, "I don't even know if that is in the Bible or not." It had been some time since I had even opened my Bible. Remember, this is someone who had *taught* Bible studies! Later, I would look back on this incident amazed at just how quickly one can forget the truth one knows when it is ignored. It should have been more of a wake-up call; sadly, that would come soon enough.

At the reception, I very vividly remember standing in a large crowd of people and *feeling* very lonely. People were talking all around me, but I was having a conversation with the Lord. A tray of champagne glasses came by and I took one. Someone offered a toast. I couldn't tell you what was said, because what I said in my heart to the Lord as I raised my glass was: *Lord, I quit! I'm so tired of not fitting in anywhere, so I quit the Christian life.* Just like that. No balls of fire came down from heaven, no lightning rods struck me, and I had no emotional or sensational experiences. Nothing.

Five days later, my sweet daughter was killed in an automobile wreck. She was driving with three other kids in the car who were, thankfully, not hurt seriously. The Lord got my attention; He loves me too much to allow me to quit walking with Him. Because I'm prone to wander, the Lord had to get my attention, this time with His chastening rod of love. I knew it immediately.

My husband had grounded my daughter. I really can't remember the reason why. When she got home from school, I made her dinner as she continued to beg me to allow her to go to Bible study. There is a popular ecumenical youth group in our hometown, and Missy went to it often. *How can I say no to Bible study?* Reasoning that my husband was being too harsh in his punishment, I told her she could go. While getting ready to take our two youngest sons to their hockey league 45 minutes away, I remember everything about our conversation that evening. Her sweet voice when she came into the room saying, "Hi, Mommy!" will remain in my heart forever. After dinner, she went to her room and put on her television. We left. I didn't even tell her good-bye.

A friend and I had a certain walking routine. We had planned to walk at 9:15 p.m. when I got home. When we were leaving the rink, I called her and told her I didn't feel like walking that night. I *never* canceled. The boys went to bed shortly after we got home. At around 9:15 p.m., I started to get a sick feeling in my stomach because Missy wasn't home yet. She had promised me she would come home as soon as her Bible study was over. Missy didn't have a cell phone, so there was no way I could get in touch with her. At about 9:30 p.m., I called the home of the friend Missy had taken to Bible study. (Missy had not had her driver's license for very long which only added to my distress.) Her friend's father answered the phone. When I asked whether Missy was there, he could barely answer me: "I think you better call the hospital. There has been an accident." Hanging up, I immediately called my parents. I told my mom, "Please come up and sit with the boys. I need to go to the hospital. Missy was in an accident." As soon as I hung up the phone, I saw the headlights of the police cars in the driveway.

My husband was still at work at close to 10:00 p.m. The police never got to tell me what had happened because I knew Missy was dead. I called Greg, my in-laws, and my oldest son. My sister was one of the first people to walk through the door. Totally numb and in shock, I was just sitting on the couch. Rather bluntly, I said to her, "God must not be real after all." She knelt in front of me and started repeating to me things I had said to her over the years. It was as if she was slapping me in the face with each sentence. She needed me to hold onto God. As I was being tossed to and fro by every wind of inward *emotion*, Greg walked through the door, and I said, "I'm going back to church, and I'm taking the kids with me." I don't even know where the thought came from. He said, "Honey, I already called Pastor Ray," (this was the pastor from the last church we had walked away from because we were not happy about the way church was 'being done'.) We **had** walked away from this church in love. We needed the Body of Christ.

My friend and I had walked our route enough times that we knew how long it took us. Had we walked that night, there is a good possibility that we would have been in the exact proximity of the place where my daughter wrecked, witnessing the accident.

Every person has a day set by God, before the foundation of the world, as the day of their death. Psalm 139 confirms this truth in verse 16: **And in Your book were all written the days that were ordained for me, when as yet there was not one of them.** I don't believe God took Melissa home *to punish me* for my disobedience. I **do** believe that because He is sovereign over His creation, and because His providential hand is always at work, the day of her death coincided with a lesson I desperately needed to learn. And, note it well, the Father is working all things together for my good just as He worked all things together for Missy's good in her life. To pick me up and turn me around when I am walking in the wrong direction in life is the work of a loving Father. He loves me perfectly in every situation in which I find myself. Sometimes, love needs to be tough.

After Missy's death, I began teaching Bible studies again. This time things were very different. I was the hungry student sitting at the Lord's feet as I prepared lessons. Two different groups of women asked me to teach them; I was dismayed but eager to share all I was learning. I am ashamed to admit that years earlier I had all but demanded our pastor give me a chance to teach a ladies' Bible study in the church we were attending. (Sadly, you read that right.) That study ended not long after it began. Now there was an opportunity to do what I had previously longed to do dropped in my lap. Before, I had all the confidence in *myself* to teach. This time, however, I wasn't sure I could teach anyone anything at all. This time I wasn't focused on my being a teacher but on the Teacher Himself.

For 11 years after Missy's death, I poured over the Scriptures preparing lessons for those precious women the Lord brought into my path. Continuing to grow in my knowledge of Him and my love for Him, I was still somewhat rigid when it came to fruit inspection. For the most part, I was hesitant to join in any spiritual enterprise of any kind with those who didn't believe exactly as I did. I loved the women who came and went and was eager to point them to Christ. I still sincerely struggled with where to draw the line regarding any partnership for the sake of the gospel. I had learned to be more loving, patient, and kind, but I needed to excel still more, as Paul told the Thessalonians. I began to see clearly that His children were all at different stages of their growth, and that *always* had to be taken into consideration when ministering to others.

These two different groups of women had asked me to teach Bible studies because of the way they had watched me 'deal' with Missy's death. (One was an evening study, the other a morning study.) For the next several years, I heard rumors people were saying things like, "Nobody handles grief like that; she's going to fall apart one of these days." Christians *are* different, and we don't grieve as those who have no hope. But we **do** grieve!

I tried to be strong for everyone around me for three years, but I had not allowed myself time to grieve. Having stood against my husband by letting Missy go to Bible study when he had grounded her, I had not dealt with the burden of guilt I was carrying for her death. My *rationalization* was that he had grounded her too harshly, so I overruled him. That was sin. Three years later, on the anniversary of my daughter's death, all the untouched pain came bubbling to the surface and erupted, not just from my own heart, but from my husband's as well. From morning to night, among friends who tried to help, our grief exploded. But that was the point of real healing for me. The Lord used that day in my life with the people He placed around me to show me that His children need to grieve hard because they love hard. He showed me that sin has consequences, and the consequences of that sin in the lives of His children grieves His heart as well. Amidst all the heartache, a lesson that was being reinforced for me was this need to have His children in my life who know how to minister truth to me.

We *don't* grieve as those who have no hope. I believe Missy is in my future. The pain of my loss—of our separation—is immeasurable, to be sure; but the knowledge that we will be together in Christ one day fills my heart with joy until I see her again. In the meantime, I need to walk in obedience loving God and my neighbors. And that includes letting others love me.

Though a great wall of protection around my heart came down that day, no matter what I did, the type of deep, intimate, lasting relationships I longed for seemed inaccessible to me. I wanted deep fellowship with those who love the Lord as much as I did. (I will say that longing has only increased over time.) Even though I was growing in my knowledge of His Word as never before, I didn't have the accountability and structure of a church body to help me grow in my practical relationships. While I had more people in my life than ever before, the Lord would need to pull back the shroud covering my heart which kept people from reaching that place of vulnerability.

After Missy died, I felt as though I was the one who needed to be ministering to others. I **needed** to share my faith as a witness and testament to the Lord's faithfulness in my life. And that was good. Somewhere, I picked up a faulty misconception about suffering in the life of a believer. I wrongly believed that a Christian was not to show her need and weakness to others. Basically, Christians did not reveal their raw emotions of sadness, depression, or even anger. As a Christian, I was *supposed* to show the world I had joy! I was to be different because Christ made a difference in my life. I **did** have joy, and Christ **does** make a difference in my life, but there were times when I needed to share the grief that was in my heart with someone who understood what I was going through. I needed to keep it real!

About this time, I read one book that helped me understand why I agonized over doctrinal issues in different churches—and why I never seemed to fit in anywhere. When I tell you I struggled, my life was a spiritual battle for years as I fought to know the truth. I believe it ties in with why it was so difficult for me to receive love and ministry from others. John MacArthur wrote a book entitled, *The Gospel According to the Apostles.*[1] It was an eye-opener for me. The Lord used this book to begin to define for me the differences in how people believe salvation is received—is it a work of God or a work of man? Did I choose Him, or did He choose me? After I read this book, the picture became even more clear when I 'discovered' the doctrine of the sovereignty of God in election in all its glory.

As I began teaching through the book of Ephesians, Chapter 1 hit me square in the face. Ecstatic as I worked through each verse, one of the women in our Bible study was standing as I taught. When I was finished, she said, "Do it again!" I was passionate about what the Lord was teaching me, and I guess it was contagious. It just so happened that she was one of the reformed Presbyterians (a good friend of R.C. Sproul) who had continued to invite me to her church. At last I could understand why we agreed on so much, and the things we disagreed upon started fading from my view.

One day at Bible study she was taking part in the discussion about how different belief systems can separate people by necessity. Also, we talked about how our differences, if they did not affect a proper view of the gospel, should not separate us. Turning to me, she used me as an example and said, "Take Karla and me. We don't agree on everything." I knew there were some issues we did not agree upon, so this wasn't a surprise. She said, "Take Halloween, for instance." I was instantly offended. Indignantly, I exclaimed, "I *don't do Halloween!*" She said with a mischievous smile, "*Oh, but I do!*" We had a good laugh after I picked my mouth up off the floor, but it was a good lesson for me.

True fellowship—fellowship that is eternally meaningful—can only be between two believers. Two believers can be at different maturity levels and go to different churches. However, there are essential beliefs we must agree upon to have true fellowship. Things like holiday observations, worship styles, modes of baptism, how often a church partakes of the Lord's Supper, and the like, are *not* essential elements of true Christianity over which to break fellowship (even though we may have strong convictions regarding our beliefs concerning these issues). Views on eschatology and modes of baptism are important truths; there is absolute truth regarding those doctrines, and we must know what we believe and why we believe it. But the distinction that divides, the fundamental doctrine or truth that cuts deeper than a knife, is the Gospel of Jesus Christ. One **must** get the gospel right. The gospel is fundamental and foundational doctrine.

There is one gospel, and it is exclusive. Every other gospel is false. If one does not believe the Gospel of Jesus Christ as laid down in Scripture, he or she is not part of the body of Jesus Christ and can't have eternal fellowship with other true believers. No debate. Upon that sword we **must** fall! There is freedom in understanding that exclusivity.

After struggling to form a right belief system for many years—to finally know that you are on the right path, and that your doctrine is sound, is unbelievably freeing. It's like pieces of the puzzle start to all fit together. You know **where** you belong. You know **what** you believe, **why** you believe it, and in **Whom** you believe. You know **where** you are going and **what** you were created for. Even suffering begins to make sense. The fellowship of believers who understand that abundant life is found in a gospel that calls for death to self is gloriously rich and life-giving.

God has been calling people to believe the true Gospel of Jesus Christ as early as Genesis 3 soon after the Fall. Because sin brings death and eternal separation from Him, He provided a way for the fellowship He desired with man and the fellowship man was created for to be able to enjoy Him. And that way was for a sinless substitute to die in sinful man's place. The Cross wasn't Plan B; it has always been Plan A in God's eternal, infinite mind.

In the Old Testament we see types and shadows of the Gospel. In all the sacrifices and offerings there is a picture that points us to the spotless Lamb who was to come. In the book of Leviticus, the peace offering—also called a fellowship offering—is mentioned. Maybe you have heard the expression used of someone trying to make amends with another as 'offering a peace offering.' When a husband has wronged his wife, he may show up at the door with a 'peace offering' of flowers or something that she likes. This gift is meant to pacify or appease the offended party. That's **not a right description** of the peace offering of Leviticus, and it's important to understand the difference. God never asks us to appease Him with any works, because He knows we cannot do so. He simply wants us to confess our need for Him and thank Him for His provision to us. Most of the offerings were not to be eaten by the offender/worshiper. In the peace offering/fellowship offering, however, a small portion of it was to be burned on the altar, but the rest was to be eaten by the worshiper and the poor. The peace offering was given with the acknowledgment that God is the one who provides for us physically and spiritually.

The lie Eve believed was that God was holding back from her something she believed was for her good. Doubting God's love for her, she didn't understand that God doesn't take from us; He gives. Because God is the giver, there is no sacrifice we can give God that would merit His favor towards us. The only sacrifice that found favor with God was the sacrifice made at Calvary on behalf of all who would believe in Christ, a sacrifice *He* provided. **Therefore, having been justified by faith, we have peace with God through our Lord Jesus Christ, through whom also we have obtained our introduction by faith into this grace in which we stand; and we exult in hope of the glory of God.** (Romans 5:1-2) The only acceptable way for us to have fellowship with a holy and loving God, who has been egregiously offended by our sin, is through the atoning work of Christ that set down His pathway to peace. Jesus is our peace/fellowship offering.

Fellowship is often centered around a meal. That is established in Scripture. Just as the worshiper was to eat the peace offering in

Old Testament days, we have a fellowship meal that is represented in the Lord's Supper. When we take the cup and eat the bread, we are acknowledging God's provision in giving us the ultimate Sacrifice that would allow us to have restored fellowship with Him. Jesus tells His disciples that the cup and the bread represent what was provided by God for our justification and restored peace with Him. The peace offering centered around a meal which pointed to the atoning work of God in Jesus Christ. The Lord's Supper centers around the reality of what took place at the Cross. The act of receiving communion is not that which **gives** us peace with God, it is faith believing in the work Christ accomplished at the cross. It is this faith in our peace or fellowship offering that secures our peace, not only with God, but with fellow believers.

Partaking of the Lord's Supper ought to remind us of what we believed when we embraced the cross while reaffirming our commitment to all the ramifications of the cross life. We should realize our need to daily trust and believe in this God Who willingly laid down His life for us. We also should realize our need to have fellowship with like-minded believers who are being sanctified as they journey alongside us through this life filled with trials and tribulations. We come to understand the covenant commitment we now have one to another *because* of the covenant God cut with each of us through the sacrifice of His Son, our Lord Jesus Christ. As we walk in covenant relationship with God and with man, we learn to trust. *We learn to give and receive love.*

As His children, we need to learn to trust our Father because our trust in Him honors Him *as God*. The more we trust Him, the greater capacity we will have to see His glory. Sitting alone in prison, it was vital for me to know and trust that God was with me, that He *wanted* fellowship with me, and that He had not abandoned me. At times, I needed to know He was still working in and through my life, and that He had not rejected me like many others in my life had done. I came to realize, with absolute certainty, that He would never leave me nor forsake me no matter what it *appeared* to look like and no matter what my emotions or feelings were tempting me to believe. How can I know this for certain for *every* circumstance in which I find myself? I can know because **salvation didn't begin with me but with Him. He chose me.**

This is where I camp when I begin to doubt. The goal of redemption has always been communion with God that glorifies Him.

When we understand this love of our Father, we better understand why love for the brethren, especially, is non-threatening. There should be no sibling rivalry. He has no favorites. He loves us each the same. He loves us like He loves His own dear Son. How could we not be secure in that great love? But familial fellowship can only be had between children who know that same communion with the Father, that peace with God that produces peace with His children. We have been set free to love Him and others. We have also been set free to receive love with wide open arms.

The prison test allowed me to be able to clearly make the distinction between those with whom I already have true fellowship and those with whom I maybe never would. It helped me let go of that which I couldn't change along with the guilt that goes with it. In my own walk to the death of self—as I laid down my life next to Christ's—I was able to know Him more fully in the fellowship of His sufferings. Having seen His faithfulness to keep me from false teaching over the years, I witnessed the outworking of heretical views in the lives of women from various different religions. This not only kept my convictions sharpened in the truths of the Gospel, but it kept my attention focused on the *true* Gospel and every person's need to hear a clear presentation of it. Lastly, the lesson the Lord had been teaching me for years was memorialized inside prison walls as I experienced separation that gave me a clear understanding of my desperate need for intimate fellowship that can only be shared between true believers.

Many women in the federal prison system claim Jesus Christ as their **Savior**. However, it is easily observed that their lifestyles give little evidence that Jesus is **Lord** of their lives. They have a worldly love for 'a Jesus' they have created, but *he* certainly is not *the* Jesus of the Bible who created them because the biblical Jesus is both Savior and Lord. The call to salvation involves embracing Jesus as Lord of one's life. So while there were Bibles on almost every locker and large crowds at every service in the Chapel, I had little fellowship with like-minded believers. There was *some* fellowship and opportunities to share the truth of the gospel, and I will always be grateful for each of those precious women He put in my path.

During the five years my husband was being investigated, his attorney continued to tell us, "Just live your lives normally, and don't read the newspapers." *Okay. You try that!* Soon after my husband was indicted, the church we were trying to see planted in our town completely dissolved, and the ladies' Bible studies ended five years later when I got indicted. I remember an incident that took place as the onslaught of newspaper articles rolled out. My youngest sons were 15 and 13 years old (now 29 and 27). As we were walking out the door one morning heading to our homeschool co-op held at the local Presbyterian church, I said to my youngest son, "Hold your head up." He replied, "Why wouldn't I? I didn't do anything wrong." When we got to the co-op, the pastor there said no matter what happened, my family would always be welcomed with open arms at their church. This was the pastor of the same church I had continually turned away from because of what I perceived as doctrinal differences. The hatred kept pouring forth from the news media, blogs, social media, etc. But the words of love and encouragement offered by His children helped us hold on to Jesus through the storms. Oh, the love of God that soothes the open wounds of affliction meted out by the hands of the wicked.

Several women who had attended Bible studies in my home also attended this Presbyterian church. In fact, after my daughter died, several of these same women and I became very close. Still, because I didn't think we held to the *exact* same doctrine, I smiled politely, sincerely thanked this pastor for his offer, but knew in my heart it wasn't going to happen. After all, *I had standards and convictions! I was not blind to the differences in our beliefs. I had spent close to 15 years studying the differences in denominations and religions.* The differences I had with the Presbyterian church were insurmountable in my mind. But that love still nagged at me. That love would not go away. It resonated in my heart for years to come.

The day my husband was sentenced five years later, I said to my oldest son, "I'm going to church. I'd like you to come with me, but I really need the Body of Christ." (Okay, I see a pattern.) He agreed and went with me. And these people loved on us like nothing we had ever known. They came to us ministering love, encouragement, the Word, their prayers, and listening ears. They put arms, legs, and voices to work as their Head would direct them and lifted us up to the Father in prayer daily. (Our names are still in the bulletin for their prayer warriors to pound heaven's gate on our behalf over a decade later.) They went above and beyond to provide for our needs and loved us with Christ's love. With nothing left in ourselves to give, we received their love. And we love them dearly.

I never experienced love from the Body in this way before. It is a rare and precious gem to behold. Looking back, now, I can see how I viewed our family as the ones who always gave. We had material wealth and never hesitated to give to the needs of the church. We usually weren't the ones who asked anyone for anything. The Lord knew we needed to learn to receive. In our highly publicized, humiliating circumstances, we learned this invaluable lesson. And how significant is this lesson when applied to our understanding of the great salvation we have been *given?* When Melissa died, people loved us in all manner of practical ways. That is right, appropriate, and acceptable behavior when a loved one dies. In our prison test—we were the biggest social pariahs in Western Pennsylvania at the time—it was not natural for people to pour out such lavish grace and love upon us. It was supernatural. Such a gospel object lesson!

One of the reasons I am writing this book is because I want to love others the way this church loved us. What I have to offer is the story He gave me. One sweet lady from this church wrote me a card while I was in prison telling me to write my story. She died while I was in prison, and my commitment to write grew deeper roots.

We can have many relationships in life. The level of fellowship is determined by the importance of the common ground shared. For the Christian, the most important thing in our lives must be the glory of God in Jesus Christ. Our capacity to glorify God is determined by the measure of our love for God. If glorifying God is the most important thing in your life, your relationships that offer the deepest fellowship will be with those who have the same commitment and passion to glorify God. Partnering together to accomplish the same goal, you are two fellows in the same ship working together with the same purpose—rowing together towards eternal shores intent on seeking His glory alone.

A pastor friend wisely said to me a month or so before Greg's sentencing: "Karla, make sure you are not known for what you are against; be known for what you are for." This advice loosened some heavy chains I had been carrying for a long time. It freed me to love and be loved by the people in this Presbyterian church. I joined with them in worship knowing that even though we had some differences in our theology on some important points, we both had a passion to glorify Christ by proclaiming His true gospel.

This same wise counselor gave me another iron-sharpening piece of advice that sparked something in my heart. Shortly after my husband's investigation began, we had a privacy gate installed at the entrance to our property. Many curious people were coming onto our property and driving up our driveway which led to the front of our home at all hours of the night. Their lights shining in our bedroom windows was unnerving with all that was happening at the time. Some people demonstrated unbelievably rude behavior. When my husband's pastor friend came to visit, he inquired about the gate. We gave him *our* explanation, which made perfect sense to us. He saw things differently. He said as Christians we are to be open, drawing people to Christ through our lives. He said the gate might just represent the fact that we were trying to keep people out of our lives pushing them away from Christ. Ouch!

Some might say this pastor friend was being judgmental or negative. Can I tell you how much I loved that correction? I didn't get offended or angry. I thought, *I need to think about this.* I know it is love that speaks wisdom in words of reproof and correction. Oh, how we need Christ's Body.

What about our time spent with unbelievers? Maybe you live in a Christian bubble, and you like your life just fine. Where do we find the balance in our understanding regarding relationships with believers versus unbelievers? **As Jesus went on from there, He saw a man called Matthew, sitting in the tax collector's booth; and He said to him, "Follow Me!" And he got up and followed Him. Then it happened that as Jesus was reclining at the table in the house, behold, many tax collectors and sinners came and were dining with Jesus and His disciples. When the Pharisees saw this, they said to His disciples, "Why is your Teacher eating with the tax collectors and sinners?" But when Jesus heard this, He said, "It is not those who are healthy who need a physician, but those who are sick. But go and learn what this means: 'I DESIRE COMPASSION, AND NOT SACRIFICE,'**

for I did not come to call the righteous, but sinners." (Matthew 9:9-13) Jesus ate with tax collectors and sinners. Who gave Him grief for it? The Pharisees—those who were the religious elite.

Believers and unbelievers *live* in different realms, *serve* different masters, and *promote* very different kingdoms. Since Christ is my life, doesn't it stand to reason that I would never be able to have this same, eternal, intimate fellowship with someone who has complete disregard for Him? Whatever the unbeliever's focus and purpose in life, it is not to promote the Gospel of Jesus Christ and to glorify Him. My time and energy invested in this relationship may be different compared to that of a kindred spirit. But because I want all men to know the truth, and I am to love everyone as I love myself, I would want to spend time with unbelievers telling them about Christ and serving them, so that they might see Christ. My purpose for spending time with them and in developing relationships with them is different. My most eternally valuable time, however, is with my brothers and sisters in Christ.

The end goal of all our relationships, as believers, should center around Christ. Some people we evangelize, and with some people we participate in mutual edification. Someone close to me got frustrated with me once and blurted out: "Why do you always think you have to save everyone?" *Um...is that a trick question?* Seriously, I can't save anyone, but I want everyone to know Christ and His salvation. Because we have known the love of God and are able to love with His love, one of the most difficult challenges we face in this life is watching those, whom we love dearly, reject the truth of the gospel and this great love of Christ. It grieves us to know that they will face the judgment of God for their unbelief, for not treating God as God by believing in Him and trusting Him to save them. It grieves us to know that we will not be able to share that eternal fellowship with them, and that we will be separated from them forever. It also grieves our hearts to know that they are turning their backs on the one who is our greatest love.

Jesus, Himself, agonized over the thought of being separated from the Father on the cross. His torment is seen in the Garden of Gethsemane, and when He later cried out to the Father on the cross as He endured the greatest suffering of all time alone. Our Lord was a man of sorrows and acquainted with grief. He, the willing

Sacrifice, the one who knew no sin but who bore my curse—took every drop of my sin upon Himself (as repugnant as it was to His purity), and the sin of all those in history who would ever believe on Him. That, along with the even greater pain of separation from perfect and eternal fellowship with the Father, was all because of His love for His Father and for His bride. Ultimate love experienced ultimate grief and suffering. No one has ever or will ever suffer to that extent. Yet, there are those who cannot receive that perfect love.

As His children, we want to be where His children are as much as possible. It is in that company that we can share our same passions and goals. We are like-minded. When two people share a common interest, sparks fly in their conversations. They have so much to talk about. Imagine two people who will spend eternity with God and each other right now just beginning a relationship that will last forever. (For believers, eternal life begins the moment we are born again.) And we will never run out of things to talk about, because our greatest love is not only perfect but eternal. And, "Hallelujah for no small talk!" Every topic of conversation will be deep and rich with the things of God. I love the fellowship Paul describes in Philippians: **Therefore, if there is any encouragement in Christ, if there is any consolation of love, if there is any fellowship of the Spirit, if any affection and compassion, make my joy complete by being of the same mind, maintaining the same love, united in spirit, intent on one purpose.** (Philippians 2:2)

That is beautiful. But it is not natural. It is a supernatural fellowship that flows from the Spirit of God in believers towards each other. And it is not like any other relationship known to man. The love of this type of fellowship flows into the acting out of the one another's throughout the New Testament.

In Scripture, the Church of Jesus Christ, His bride, is also called His body. He is the Head, and each member is part of His body. Four times before Jesus died, He prayed that the Father would keep His disciples in unity as one body—His body. **I am no longer in the world; and yet they themselves are in the world, and I come to You. Holy Father, keep them in Your name, the name which You have given Me, that they may be one even as We are.** (John 17:11) **...that they may all be one; even as You, Father, are in Me and I in You, that they also may be in Us, so that the world** may believe that You sent Me. The glory which You have given Me I have given to them, that they may be one, just as We are one; I in them and You in Me, that they may be perfected in unity, so that the world may know that You sent Me, and loved them, even as You have loved Me. (John 17:21-23)

Christians are to have the same mindset or unity of thought because Paul says we have the mind of Christ to understand the Word of God. But a natural man does not accept the things of the Spirit of God, for they are foolishness to him; and he cannot understand them, because they are spiritually appraised. But he who is spiritual appraises all things, yet he himself is appraised by no one. For WHO HAS KNOWN THE MIND OF THE LORD, THAT HE WILL INSTRUCT HIM? But we have the mind of Christ. (1 Corinthians 2:14-16) Therefore, I urge you, brethren, by the mercies of God, to present your bodies a living and holy sacrifice, acceptable to God, which is your spiritual service of worship. And do not be conformed to this world, but be transformed by the renewing of your mind, so that you may prove what the will of God is, that which is good and acceptable and perfect. (Romans 12:1-2) Paul gives this exhortation in the context of speaking of the gifts of the Spirit which have been given to each believer and their ministry of those gifts to one another.

First, we are not to think more highly of ourselves than we ought. We cannot serve one another when we think we are better than the one we are serving. If we attempt to serve while thinking we are better than the one whom we are serving, we only serve our own egos. We must remember that it is Christ in us serving others. We are just the instruments He uses. Second, Paul describes the dynamic of Christ's body, of which we are members: **For just as we have many members in one body and all the members do not have the same function, so we, who are many, are one body in Christ, and individually members of one another.** (Romans 12:4-5) **Let love be without hypocrisy. Abhor what is evil; cling to what is good. Be devoted to one another in brotherly love; give preference to one another in honor; not lagging behind in diligence, fervent in spirit, serving the Lord; rejoicing in hope, persevering in tribulation, devoted to prayer, contributing to the needs of the saints, practicing hospitality.** (Romans 12:9-13)

This unity is other-worldly. It is this type of love and unity of which the world will sit up and take notice. It is only manifested if we walk in the Spirit, presenting our bodies a living and holy sacrifice, acceptable to God. Paul says we're not to be conformed to the world but to be transformed by the renewing of our minds.

There are those who believe only certain people have the mind of Christ, that having the mind of Christ is speaking of extra-biblical revelation. Some girls I encountered in prison erroneously believed that to have the mind of Christ was a mystical gifting that only some possessed. It is feeding our mind with His Word. Every believer has the mind of Christ to be able to comprehend biblical truth. It means we can discern spiritual truth as God revealed it. It means we understand God's redemptive plan for the world.

Unity, fellowship, and *love* are used together in many passages of Scripture. The unity and fellowship we covet is born out of true love. The Apostle John, also known as the apostle of love, carries these themes throughout his gospel and epistles. It is interesting to note that while being known as the apostle of love, John is extremely dogmatic. He is black and white. He minces no words. He tells the truth without skirting around it. He never compromises truth for love or love for truth. At all times, John stands with his feet firmly planted on both platforms. If we are to love others as God loves, we will do well to listen to what John, through the Spirit, has to say.

I have always been a person who sees things in a black or white, sort of rigid, way—dogmatic to a fault. Anyone who really knows me knows that about me. I'm certain this is why my mother always needed to remind me of having *balance* in my walk with Christ. She knew me well. When I got to Alderson, the big thing everyone was encouraged to participate in was 'programming'—these were classes that were 'supposed' to better us. (That concept, itself, is the *real* joke of this story.) The Psychology Department offered several classes, none of which interested me. Except for one. Everyone was talking about a class called, 'Eight Habits' of something or other. Even though that class didn't interest me, I had heard a lot of chatter about another 'class' that just *might* be beneficial to me. So, while we were sitting in the CDR waiting to be released one day from work, the girls began talking about what programming they might be interested in. I interjected, "Yes, well, I'm only really interested in one class. Has anyone taken the 'Fifty Shades of Gray' class?" Mouths dropped open and just hung there. When they all stopped laughing long enough to talk, they asked, "Umm, Karla, what *exactly* do you think that class pertains to?" I said, "I was thinking it was for people who need to learn to see some gray areas in their life instead of seeing everything so dogmatically."

As I said, often when I have struggled in my adult life, my mother would tell me, "We must learn to have balance in life." I hated when she would say that, because I knew it meant that she knew I was out of balance in some area of my life. But she was always right. Mothers usually know those things. My mom was my best friend, and I miss her terribly. How I now miss her way of telling me like it is. She was one of the few people in my life who loved me enough to tell me the truth, whether I liked it or not.

If we love at the expense of truth, we will have churches with shallow teaching filled with error that produces no pursuit of holiness in the hearts of its hearers. That, I've never been able to tolerate. But if we sacrifice love for truth, we will bear heartless, intolerant self-righteous hearers who try to bully others into the Kingdom. This is where I was usually out of balance. We need to live in the balance speaking the truth in love. *The struggle is real!*

John MacArthur, speaking about the Apostle John, said this: "So John has the ability to be narrow. He has the ability to be dogmatic. He has the ability to be exclusive. He has the ability to be prejudiced. He has the ability to isolate himself and draw a hard line. He has the ability to be black and white. You want to know something? That's usable if it's for the right things. Why would God choose a man like that? Why would the Lord Jesus make him an Apostle? Because this is the kind of man that can be shaped into strength. He had the potential to be hard for the truth. What the Lord had to do was make him loving." ~ Grace to You, Sermon 62-1 *John: The Apostle of Love – 1 John – April 14, 2002.*

I knew going into my prison trial that God had to teach me to temper all my convictions with more love. To do that, He would need to humble me unto the death of self—to have me walk through the darkest night of my soul, separated yet not alone, daily grieving for the love of those dearest to my heart.

13

I Do? Wait! Did I Sign Up for That?

If you are married, your spouse is your closest 'neighbor'. When we stand before God at the marriage *altar*, we make vows. There, two become one in the eyes of the Lord. We commit to love that neighbor whom we will never be able to move away from. Here is our greatest training ground in sanctification. This relationship can be the most trying and the most glorious because of its call to intimacy. It's also the relationship that can be a beacon of light shining gloriously as it reflects God's love in this dark world.

This is not to say that those who are not married can sit back and breathe a sigh of relief. Believers are all called to love their neighbors. And since we are not called to be reclusive, every one of us has neighbors. As His bride, we are to reflect to the world the love our Bridegroom has for us, and we can show them what our love for Him looks like as well.

So what does biblical love look like? In a word—Calvary. Love looks like a Person. Love looks like Jesus Christ, because God is love. The fullest revelation of His love took place at Calvary. The brightest spotlight shining on Love's stage was a crucified Savior hanging on a cross for all believers of all time. Love caused Jesus to willingly set His face like flint to go to Calvary for His beloved.

We see the practicality of love through the one another's in the New Testament. In the 'Love Chapter', 1 Corinthians 13, God gives us a practical description of love. **Love is patient, love is kind and is not jealous; love does not brag and is not arrogant, does not act unbecomingly; it does not seek its own, is not provoked, does not take into account a wrong suffered, does not rejoice in unrighteousness, but rejoices with the truth; bears all things, believes all things, hopes all things, endures all things. Love never fails.** (1 Corinthians 13:4-7) We can substitute the word *love* in every instance here with the name of Jesus. Jesus is patient. Jesus is kind, etc. It becomes very practical for us who have been given His Spirit to see if we are able to insert our own names with confidence. Karla is patient. Karla is kind. It's difficult, right? I can say, "Karla is much more patient than she used to be." "Karla is much kinder than she used to be." As we grow in sanctifying grace, we should be able to say with increasing certainty, "I am more patient than I was last year." If I can't say this, I need to do a heart check and find the problem. If growth is stymied, there is a reason.

There are several other words for *love* in the Greek language. This *love* is **agape.** Agape love makes a determination by the will to deliberately be patient, kind, etc. I choose to love you, whether you deserve it or not; even if you are at your most unlovable right now, or even if you are *always* unlovable. I choose to love you as Christ has loved me, because I didn't deserve His love either. I choose to love you consistently and forever. My love is not going to be like a roller coaster ride for you, one day up and one day down, so that you must walk on eggshells around me never knowing what to expect. You can count on my love. This sounds great in theory, until that theory is put to the test—which won't take long.

You may remember a popular commercial for a certain spaghetti sauce. An Italian father is visiting a newly married couple. With the empty jar nearby, his son is stirring the sauce. As the father begins to lecture on the proper ingredients needed to make an authentic spaghetti sauce, he starts with the garlic. With each ingredient, the son exclaims, "Pop, it's in there!" Imagine we are trying to identify an authentic Christian. Paul, in 1 Corinthians 13, gives us all the ingredients that make up true love which can only be produced by His Spirit in and through the lives of believers.

Love is patient. Love suffers long. The Greek word used here is **makrothymeo** which always refers to patience with people. So it would not refer to me having patience in my prison trial or any circumstances. It means to be of long spirit and to not lose heart. Instead of getting easily irritated, we are to show patience.

Something as trivial as the way a girl walks down the hall shuffling her feet in her flip-flops is enough to make someone explode when living in open quarters with 150 women 24/7. Instead of 'going off' on anyone who *offended* me in prison, in order to avoid conflict or other unwanted consequences, I prayed. *Lord, change my heart so this doesn't bother me. Help me love this person.* The Lord began to answer that prayer, and my prayers turned to: *Oh, Lord, who am I that this should offend me when I offend You daily?* After awhile, this prayer became a default.

Patience, this characteristic of love, is slow to anger. It means to have a long fuse. Love is not short-tempered. It's love's immediate response to strike back when wronged or offended. We need to see Christians modeling patience when the world today is so easily offended. When someone offends you or makes a mistake that causes you problems, patience will give that one time to grow and to change. Patience shows great strength of character.

When I was thinking of this description—someone offending you, but you give them time to grow and to change—I thought of how we are with children. This doesn't mean we let them get away with wrong behavior, but we don't discipline or correct them as we would if they were older and showing the same behavior. We would teach and correct based upon maturity level and ability according to their age remembering that we were once young too.

Love is kind. To be kind is to put patience into practice. Instead of exploding in anger when wronged, kindness finds ways to help the person who has offended, to meet a need he or she may have. It is being helpful. It means to be mild or tender and forgiving when wronged. When one is unkind to me, my kindness to them can defuse the situation by calming that person or soothing them in some way. Let's face it, the world just doesn't expect kindness any longer. Instead, because people expect rudeness, they often try to put others on the defensive before they have time to react. In other words, in order to protect themselves or their interests because they feel unsure or threatened, they throw the other person off guard with their own exploding anger first.

Love is not jealous. The word *jealous* can have a positive or negative meaning. Obviously, here it is negative, and means to be heated or to boil with envy, hatred, or anger. As we saw earlier, envy was the root of the very first murder. The jealous person wants things that other people have for himself. He's not happy when another has something great or has some success. When he says, "That's great," he's really hoping that person loses it or is thinking, "Why can't I have that?" In a marriage or a friendship, there may be one person or both who are jealous and don't want to share the other person in the relationship with others. A jealous person wants all that time for himself.

The Bible says God is a jealous God. If love is not jealous, then what does it mean that God is jealous since God is love? The word for *jealous* used of God is only used of God. It means not bearing any rival. When we say someone is *jealous*, we are saying that he is envious of someone who has something he doesn't have. There's nothing anyone has that God wants or needs. God is jealous when we give to another what only belongs to Him. God, alone, is worthy of our worship. When we give our worship to another, we are being unfaithful to Him or committing spiritual adultery. Similarly, a husband has a right to be jealous when his wife gives something to another man that solely belongs to him, or vice versa. Paul said he was jealous (with a godly jealousy) for the Corinthians who were dabbling in idol worship.

Love does not brag and is not arrogant. Bragging means to parade self or to put self on display. Bragging and being arrogant both have selfishness at their roots. "Jealousy is wanting what someone else has. Bragging is trying to make others jealous of what we have. Jealousy puts others down; bragging builds us up." (John MacArthur, Jr., *The MacArthur New Testament Commentary,* 1 Corinthians [Moody Press], p. 341.) Love is humble, but those who brag and who are arrogant are proud. If there was ever a person who walked the earth who had every right to boast, it was the Lord Jesus Christ. On the contrary, He was the perfect picture and model of complete humility and meekness.

As I've gotten older, I've learned to better keep my mouth shut. As thoughts pop into my mind, I don't blurt them out as I once did. Filtering my thoughts first, I think about whether what I am about to say will edify someone or cause that one to stumble. When I've ignored that wisdom, I've always regretted it. 'Love does not brag', is a good example. Sometimes we get so excited over God's blessings that we want to share them with everyone. It is right to praise the Lord for our blessings, but it's not always wise to broadcast them. Some have learned the 'art' of weaving their bragging into a conversation through a praise report. It is still bragging! The point is this: The flesh reacts and blurts without thinking. Biblical love filters its thoughts through the grid of truth before acting. Biblical love relies on the mind transformed by the Word of God to control and discipline its actions.

Love does not act unbecomingly. Love is not rude, but has good manners. Love behaves itself or doesn't act badly. Many Christians who err on the side of truth without love are downright rude when it comes to dealing with falsehood that others believe. While we are called to correct error, we should remember that a Christian should always be polite, courteous, and tactful. We are either dealing with a brother or sister in Christ when we are correcting error, or we are dealing with an unbeliever. Whatever the case may be, the light of our testimony and witness for Christ is dimmed when we do not speak the truth *in love*. It is especially important that we do not let our guard down when in the comfort of our own homes where we may be tempted to forget our manners and act inappropriately.

Love does not seek its own. Human beings are born selfish. We live in a day and age when being able to assert our rights in every situation is looked upon as an admirable quality. Why is this? We have been told over and over again that we deserve better, so we need to grab all the gusto we can. But love does *not* demand its rights. This is a source of contention in homes, in churches, in the workplace, and every place in general—it's 'looking out for number 1'. It is the idea behind 'climbing over others as we move up the corporate ladder' to advance ourselves at everyone else's expense—anyone, that is, who gets in our way.

Love is not provoked. The Greek word means to sharpen, to stimulate, or rouse to anger. Do people have to tiptoe on eggshells around you? Someone who is easily provoked has a temper that he cannot control. He is are overly sensitive, exploding at the slightest provocation. One who is easily provoked is irritable and not fun to be around because people cannot be themselves in his company. Watching every word and action so as not to offend is hard work. People who are easily provoked usually use this trait to intimidate, manipulate, and punish others so they get their way. Often, they will use the excuse that at least they get it out and it is over with. Sure. That may be good for *them*. Bombs that explode do so much damage that there is usually nothing left to deal with!

Love does not take into account a wrong suffered. This is an accounting word. The person who displays this type of love doesn't remember wrongs suffered against him. He doesn't hold onto them. He moves on past offenses. It's a beautiful aspect of forgiveness.

Our flesh loves to rehearse all the injustices done to us. I think of what people do when a wound starts to heal. If they truly want it to heal, they will deal with it and then let it alone. Holding on to a wrong suffered is much like what happens when you have a wound and cannot let it alone. It forms a scab, which is its way of healing, but you keep picking at it. That can lead to infection. If not treated, that infection can lead to worse problems.

It is awful to be on the receiving end of someone's grudge when they cannot forget how you have offended them. The offense gets bigger and grosser every time it is brought up because it continues to get more blown out of proportion each time it is remembered. I am getting to the age where I am starting to forget more than I used to. But there are some things in life we must *learn* to forget; this will benefit ourselves and others in the long run. I once had a friend who was a very bitter person. It didn't show up in our friendship for some time. As we got to know each other better, I noticed that bitterness reared its ugly head when certain people (actually, it was a lot of people) were mentioned. When I would ask her what the problem was, she could not always remember why she was so angry with them...*she just was!* There is no winner when a person tries to keep score in this manner.

Love does not rejoice in unrighteousness but rejoices with the truth. Think of a person with whom you have some difficulty getting along or loving as you are supposed to love. If this person were to fall into sin, what would be your first response? Would you be secretly glad? Would you be eager to spread the news of the fall far and wide, even under the guise of a prayer request? Or would you be grieved as God is grieved? Now, let's say that this same person has a great spiritual victory or has been given some incredible opportunity to serve the Lord in ministry. Now, what is your first response? As Christians, we are to love truth and hate unrighteousness. When truth wins, God is glorified, and He is pleased. When unrighteousness wins, Satan is delighted.

Love bears all things. The word *bear* means deck, thatch, or to cover. It means to protect or to keep by covering, to preserve, to cover over with silence, to hide, to conceal the errors and faults of others, covering to keep off something which threatens, and to bear up against. Love can bear any insult, injury, or disappointment.

Whenever my friend has been maligned by those she loves, she has been known to say, "That's okay, I have broad shoulders." I think that's a beautiful picture of this word. That expression can mean not being easily offended by criticism. Love does not need to stand on the rooftop and broadcast the problems of others. People only do that to make themselves feel better about themselves. Instead, love is the roof that protects the faults and mistakes of others. When someone says something negative about another's character, are you quick to chime in, or do you defend his or her character as much as is possible within the boundaries of truth? Love confronts error but does not unnecessarily expose faults and bring them into the public light. In other words, as far as it depends upon me, things that are negatively being said about another stop with me.

Love believes all things. This is one I have had to work through. Love believes the best or trusts. When my husband was indicted, all he could tell us was, "I can't talk about the case, but I will say there is more to the story than anyone knows." The case involving my son and me came down to one question: "Who do you believe?" Jesse and I were indicted because of actions which were the direct result of believing and trusting the counsel of my husband **and** numerous attorneys ('officers of the court'), who supposedly understood the law and were looking out for our best interests.

No matter what the newspaper articles were saying, we believed the best about the one we loved because that's what we are called to do. We could see with our own eyes blatant lies being reported every day to the public. That was a fact of which we were certain. When those who are doing the accusing are feeding the newspapers, and the newspapers are clearly reporting obvious lies, who would you believe? We deduced that we had *every* reason *not* to believe or trust those who were reporting lies.

Layers of attorneys supported and even facilitated transactions on our behalf—the very transactions that ended up putting us in prison. When one can easily see the lies that are being printed in the paper about her family, she believes in the one she loves, the one she knows would never intentionally harm her. My son and I were made to look gullible, naive, and having purposely turned blind eyes to the truth. We were mocked for being a traditional family and for holding to our Christian beliefs. Love believes the other person is innocent until proven guilty. A court of law never proved Greg was guilty to me. Yes, he took a plea deal, but I witnessed with my own eyes the manipulative tactics used in order to force him to take it. So what happens when someone is forced to take a plea deal they don't believe in? Greg had every intention of going to trial to fight his case. When the prosecution threatened to indict my father for perjury, my husband said, "That's enough! Where do I sign?" (My 71-year-old father had recently lost my mom to cancer and shortly thereafter was called to testify against my son and me to the grand jury. We had no idea why they even called him, let alone what he had said or how they could distort his testimony.) The dominoes of our case started falling after my husband, who had been joined to our case, took a plea. We didn't stand a chance. I sincerely believe our actions were legitimate and legal based upon what we were told by my husband and many attorneys, regardless of the rest of the story involved. In prison, I met several ladies who took plea deals who claimed they were innocent. It was easy for me to see they were as well. Why? Some were faced with massive prison sentences if they went to trial and lost, and they had small children at home. To take a plea meant they would spend a fraction of that time in prison or simply get probation. What would you do?

Only 2% of federal criminal defendants go to trial. Only 1% of those who go to trial win their cases by acquittal.[1] I heard of a well-known saying after I was indicted. It was that a prosecutor could get a grand jury to indict a ham sandwich; and, apparently so. Grand juries *almost always* indict. Does that mean our government rarely makes a mistake? I find *that* impossible to believe!

Love hopes all things. Love never gives up believing that the object of her affections will triumph. She is not waiting for him to fail because she stands on God's promises. Because love knows God is working all things together for good to those who love Him, she believes for the best in the lives of those she loves.

Love endures all things. Love will never leave nor forsake. Love stays through thick and thin. Love does not abandon or walk away when things get tough.

Many who have suffered major trials in life know one finds out who his true friends are when going through hard times. I was dismayed by some who were fair-weather friends. On the other hand, the Lord gave me some friends who put on their fishing boots and waded through the muck and mire of my life with me. They are still there whenever I need them; and I would not hesitate to lean on them again or offer my shoulder to them in any future trial *they* may experience. They are solid and will go the distance. As I said, in my trials I learned to lean on others. Without those who were the Lord's arms and legs, I would surely have fallen. Trials are opportunities for the sufferer and the one who comes alongside the sufferer to show faithfulness to Christ.

One of the special friends the Lord gave us was the pastor of the little church I mentioned previously. Throughout our trial, I clung to one specific Scripture he gave us before we went to prison. Taking us to Psalm 37, He camped on verses 23-24: **The steps of a man are established by the Lord, and He delights in his way. When he falls, he will not be hurled headlong, because the Lord is the One who holds his hand.** *Hurled headlong* is not describing falling into sin but encountering a severe disappointment. It will not result in final ruin, being cast out, or being thrown away. It is temporary. The Lord held my hand by using His body to gird me up so that I could lean on them hard; and like pillars of a tower, they strongly supported me. Every time they were there for me, I praised **the Lord** for **His** help. I knew He was the One meeting all my needs through these precious saints whose only purpose was to serve Him in love. In this beautiful process I learned to lean. I also gained the strength and understanding of how to support others in their distress.

Too many Christians leave churches when they find fault or have trivial disagreements. Husbands and wives leave one another because they 'fell' out of love. *Love doesn't leave easily!* It's not *easy* for love to walk away, even from a volatile relationship. Even when there are legitimate grounds to walk away from a marriage, it doesn't mean you need to assert your rights to do so. God is more pleased to be able to bring beauty from ashes to what seems like a hopeless situation resulting in His glory. Love stayed on the cross enduring the most difficult circumstances ever known to man for you and for me. And you are seriously going to walk away from a friendship, a church, a marriage because you are not feeling it any longer? I will probably always use R.C. Sproul's line as my default quote for foolish thinking, "What's wrong with you people?"[2] This question applies to the question he was asked in a Q and A panel discussion at one of Ligonier Ministries' conferences but also to much foolishness in the church. He continued, "I'm serious! I mean this is what's wrong with the Christian church today. We don't know who God is and we don't know who we are." Much petty thinking would be alleviated if we **did know our God** and **understood who we are** in the light of His magnificent holiness.

We need to repent of splashing around in the shallow, stagnant mud puddles of life where we tell ourselves we are loving as we are supposed to love. It is time to dive into the deep, flowing, refreshing rivers of pure love that cause us to depend on Christ with abandon. As we relish and delight in the love of Christ, His divine love will flow out of us to others. This is the love that people can count on. This love points to God and brings Him glory.

True love never fails. How could it? We stand in awe of a love that is completely selfless, focused on exclusively building up the object of its love. Yet, this is the way God loves Christ and those who are in Him. If you are His child, you are the object of His affection. Can we love like this? Of course, we can't. But it is the goal we fervently pursue! And we *will* love perfectly one day. As God continues to sanctify us, He is making us more and more like Jesus who is perfect love. Don't you want to be loved like this? The thought of being the recipient of this type of love is irresistible.

How do we walk in love? The only way we can walk in the love of God is to focus on His love for us as we look at Christ and walk in His Spirit. It is the Holy Spirit who produces the fruit of love in us and then through us (see Galatians 5:22). He is the vine, and we are the branches. The life of the vine flows through the branches and bears fruit. Jesus said: **"Abide in Me, and I in you. As the branch cannot bear fruit of itself unless it abides in the vine, so neither can you unless you abide in Me. I am the vine, you are the branches; he who abides in Me and I in him, he bears much fruit, for apart from Me you can do nothing."** (John 15:4-5)

I have mentioned the *one another's* in past chapters. The *one another's* we see throughout the New Testament are commands that should dictate the relationships we have with our brothers and sisters in Christ. Here are some of them:

We are to be at peace with one another.

    Mark 9:50; Romans 14:19; 1 Thessalonians 5:13b

We are to serve one another in humility.

    John 13:14; Galatians 5:13; 1 Peter 4:10

We are to love one another as Christ has loved us.

    John 13:34, 35; 15:12, 17; Romans 12:10; 13:8;

    1 Thessalonians 3:12, 4:9; 2 Thessalonians 1:3;

    1 Peter 1:22. 4:8; 1 John 3:11, 23, 4:7, 11, 12; 2 John 1:5

We are to give preference to one another in honor.

    Romans 12:10; Philippians 2:3

We are to be of the same mind toward one another with humility.

    Romans 12:16, 15:5

We are not to judge one another and not to cause a brother to stumble.

    Romans 14:13

We are to build one another up.

    Romans 14:19

We are to accept one another as Christ accepted us.

    Romans 15:7

We are to admonish one another.

    Romans 15:14

We are not to challenge one another or to envy one another.

    Galatians 5:26

We are to show tolerance for one another in love with all humility and gentleness and patience.

    Ephesians 4:2

We are to speak truth to one another for we are members of one another.

    Ephesians 4:25; Colossians 3:9

We are to be kind to one another, tender-hearted, forgiving each other just as God has forgiven us.

    Ephesians 4:32

We are to speak to one another in psalms and hymns and spiritual songs, singing and making melody in our hearts to the Lord.

    Ephesians 5:19; Colossians 3:16

We are to be subject to one another in the fear of Christ.

    Ephesians 5:21; 1 Peter 5:5

We are to bear with one another, forgiving each other, as the Lord forgave us.

Colossians 3:13

We are to encourage one another and build one another up.

1 Thessalonians 5:11; Hebrews 3:13, Hebrews 10:25

We are not to repay another with evil for evil, but always to seek after that which is good for one another and for all people.

1 Thessalonians 5:15

We are to consider how to stimulate one another to love and good deeds.

Hebrews 10:24

We are not to speak against one another.

James 4:11, 5:9

We are to confess our sins to one another and pray for one another.

James 5:16

We are to be hospitable to one another without complaint.

1 Peter 4:9

We are to have fellowship with one another.

1 John 1:7

These are commands to practically show us what love looks like as we live together with others in community. We were not made to love ourselves. We were created to love God and others, and to be loved by them. Can you imagine if our churches were filled with people focused on a disciplined effort to walk in the Spirit fulfilling the one-another commands? We need to pray for God's grace to make us 'one-another focused Christians'.

Each of us must answer the questions: Am I God-centered or self-centered? Am I a lover of God or a lover of self? Do I live for Him or for myself? If I love God, I will be focused on loving my neighbor as I love myself. I am called in Matthew 5:44 to love even my enemies. We love our enemies by returning good to them for their evil against us. If loving my friends and family is impossible, loving my enemies is absurd to the natural mind.

Love is something we *do,* not something we *feel.* Jesus said we are to be known by our love for one another, but is that what the world sees? Or do they see schisms and cliques and people trying to fight to be prominent? Do they see callous disregard for others who are going through struggles, heartaches, and unbelievable pain without so much as a card or phone call reaching out to them in their distress? Do they see people who are just too busy to be bothered with the problems of others? Lord, help us! We don't expect this love and care from the world, but from our own? We have no excuse. How is your love life? I confess, mine needs a lot of work.

Love is messy because we are a mess. Instead of trying to carry the burdens of others, we offer up a quick prayer on their behalf and go on our merry way. Then we will stand before them when we run into them and say, "I've been so busy," as if that is a scriptural excuse for failing to show the love of Christ to them when they need us the most. Or we say, "I've been praying for you," when they know that isn't something tangible that anyone can measure. (I am just as convicted and guilty as you are right now.) When I'm guilty, I will admit it. Do you want to know why I keep referring to that little church back home? Because they love—and it is evident in all their good deeds. They took us in as their own at our lowest point. They were a shield and refuge for us in our time of trouble. They take care of their own, and it left an indelible mark on my heart.

We can profess to believe the truths of the Bible all we want. But we must live what we profess or it's all a sham. The worst hypocrites of all are those who name the name of Christ but who live like the devil. If we say we have faith without actions that back up that faith, how can we know whether that faith is real? James says: **If a brother or sister is without clothing and in need of daily food, and one of you says to them, "Go in peace, be warmed and be filled," and yet you do not give them what is necessary for their body, what use is that?** (James 2:15-16) That is the same as seeing another brother or sister with a need we could meet; and instead of meeting that need, we say, "I hope you get what you need. I'm going to be praying for you," and walk away.

Right before His death, Jesus said in John 13:35 that it is by our love for one another that all men will know we are His disciples. We know this, yet we often see ourselves in the actions of the disciples when, upon the announcement of His upcoming death, they began to fight over who would be the greatest in His Kingdom to come. Is it any wonder that so few want any parts of Christ if we are so poorly reflecting His light to this dark world? We really should be able to easily see the filth of our wicked hearts when we cannot even love our own. More so than ever, what is happening inside the church today is merely a reflection of what is going on in the world. Instead of bringing so much of the world's influence into the church, the church *ought* to be influencing the world. Our example of Christian love ought to be causing the world to take notice that we are different. In large part, however, we are too busy trying to love the world by creating a false sense of unity with them at the expense of loving our own brothers and sisters—those Christ died for.

What is wrong with us, indeed? I pray we do not go down in history as the generation that could not love our own. But how could we not? The world we live in kills innocent, precious gifts of love from a good Creator and calls it 'our right'. And He has not wiped us out yet? Do we not tremble at this kind of holy love that will one day say, "Enough!" For those who lived for Him in name only, it will be a terrifying thing to fall into the hands of this holy, living God and Judge.

So we had better be sure that we do love God as we believe we do and not just the concept of God. We must be sure the God we say we love is the God of Scripture, and then we must love Him as He requires. Love in Scripture requires action. It's not a noun but a verb. In other words, we must put our hands and feet to what our mouths are professing. And if someone comes to us in love and rebukes us by telling us that our actions were not very loving in any particular instance, we should not be easily provoked to anger but thankful for the wounds of a friend who loved us enough to expose and uncover our sin which can lead us to repentance.

Since God is my authority, then His Word surely must tell me what it means to love Him. And it does. The Bible is our rule for living. Therefore, if we say we love God, we must study His Word to know how it applies to our daily lives. People who say they love God but do not have time to get to know Him through His Word are professing to love a god of their own imagination.

What does this love for God look like in our lives? God is not physically here with us, so how do we love Him in action? Jesus said, **"This is My commandment, that you love one another, just as I have loved you."** (John 15:12) How did Jesus love? He goes on to tell us. **"Greater love has no one than this, that one lay down**

his life for his friends." (John 15:13). Biblical love is sacrificial love. Another Scripture that helps us to clearly define biblical love comes also from the Apostle John: **We know that we have passed out of death into life, because we love the brethren. He who does not love abides in death. Everyone who hates his brother is a murderer; and you know that no murderer has eternal life abiding in him. We know love by this, that He laid down His life for us; and we ought to lay down our lives for the brethren. But whoever has the world's goods, and sees his brother in need and closes his heart against him, how does the love of God abide in him? Little children let us not love with word or with tongue, but in deed and truth.** (1 John 3:14-18)

I believe it is safe to say that John, the apostle whom Jesus loved, uses the word *love* or some form of the word in his writings more than any other Bible writer. We have seen that the two 'greatest commandments' both have to do with love. John ties them together in 1 John. **If someone says, "I love God," and hates his brother, he is a liar; for the one who does not love his brother whom he has seen, cannot love God whom he has not seen. And this commandment we have from Him, that the one who loves God should love his brother also.** (1 John 4:20-21)

Who specifically is my brother in this passage? *Brother* can be any fellow human being, a blood relative, or another believer. It is not specifically distinguished here. The context suggests it is referring to our Christian brother. How can we say we love God, our Father, when we hate His other children? Anyone can say they love God, but there needs to be proof of that love. The proof is this: If you love God, you will love His children the way He tells you to love them. You will practice the one another's, bear fruit of the Spirit, and you will look like Christ.

The rock-hard, stumbling-block truth is that we are called to love even our enemies. In Ephesians 5:1-5, God's beloved children are told to imitate Him by walking in love just as Christ also loved us and gave Himself up for us. Christ left us the perfect example to follow showing us how we are to love others. We see that life of perfect love lived out for us on the pages of Scripture. Ultimately, He died for us while we were His enemies (Romans 5:10). *That* is love!

We are called to love others as we love ourselves because we do love ourselves—contrary to what the world of modern 'Christian' psychology tries to tell us. If we didn't, we would have no problem loving people as we should. We do not have self-esteem issues; that is a lie from the pit of hell. We have sin issues. In fact, the reason we have issues at all in life is because we love ourselves too much. Multitudes say they love "God", and in a sense, they do because their *god* is "Me, Myself and I". Remember: summed up, there are only two commands. Love God. Love others as yourself. Not love God, love others, and love thyself. God used our love for ourselves as the measure by which we must love others knowing that in our human nature we love ourselves more than anything else. John Calvin said:

> And obviously, since men were born in such a state that they are all too much inclined to self-love—and however much they deviate from truth, they still keep self-love—there was no need of a law that would increase or rather enkindle this already excessive love. Hence it is very clear that we keep the commandments not by loving ourselves but by loving God and neighbor…
>
> Indeed, to express how profoundly we must be inclined to love our neighbors [Leviticus. 19:18], the Lord measured it by the love of ourselves because he had at hand no more violent or stronger emotion than this. *The Institutes of the Christian Religion* [Westminster Press], II: VII:54, (pp. 417-418).

What would our churches look like if we were caring for the needs of those around us as we care for our own needs, if we cared about the feelings of others as we care about our own feelings (especially those who are over-sensitive, whose feelings seem to get hurt a lot)? What would happen if we started praying for others' desires as we pray for our own? What if we started treating others exactly as we want to be treated? Then, take it outside the church and into the world. Showing Jesus to the world now becomes something that people cannot ignore. Make no mistake about it, every person on this earth would be affected by the love of Christ one way or another. There will always be those who are repulsed by the love of Christ, but there are also 'the many' Christ died for who will find His love irresistible.

A lack of love for others results in conflicts which lead to sin. The consequences of that sin will always be pain and suffering. Everywhere we look, we see that this life is full of conflicts. Conflicts at home end in the death of marriages; conflicts in the church result in church splits and the death of unity from like-mindedness and oneness that glorifies the Lord; conflicts in the world result in nations rising against nations in world wars. Unresolved conflicts end in war and, ultimately, death. Death to the relationship. Death to an opportunity for God to be glorified, etc.

On top of all that we have seen in these two commandments, John tells us in his gospel and his first epistle that we can know we love God if we keep His commandments. How are we to keep His commandments? Perfectly. It becomes obvious as we start to dig deeper into 'Love God–Love others' that this is going to inevitably involve sacrifice—the sacrifice of 'me'. Until I embrace the sacrifice that God calls me to make, my response will be, "What can I ***do?*** What can I do to work my way to heaven? How can I try harder to love others?" Because that is the typical response from man's flesh, he has developed religions throughout time with rules involving some form of sacrificial works of obedience for its adherents to follow. However, sacrifice to merit God's favor or right standing with Him is not the kind of sacrificial love the Word describes.

Sin demands a sacrifice. Egregious sin against God's holiness stood between God and man. In order for us to have fellowship with God, we required a holy sacrifice to make propitiation for the offense against His holiness. Our covenant partner, Jesus Christ, the one mediator between God and man, laid down His life as that perfect sacrifice on our behalf. We, His covenant partners, are called to lay down our lives for our neighbors in His name out of our love for Him. The sacrifice needed for us *to love properly* is nothing short of death—death to self. That sacrifice can only be made by God's grace working in the hearts of His own as He continues to sanctify them. From the beginning, man has known there must be a sacrifice—but sacrifice to what degree? Let's pull back the curtain even further to see our own hearts before Him.

14
The Bad Seed

When I was young, my mother and I watched an unforgettable movie entitled, *The Bad Seed*.[1] An eight-year-old girl was portrayed as evil incarnate in a chilling story that awakened all sorts of sickening emotions in me. What made this plot so horrifying was the fact that this evil was encapsulated or clothed in the body of what appeared to be a sweet, innocent child. Yet, this child was a murderer, a thief, and a liar. The simple fact that it has stuck with me for fifty years is telling. I couldn't believe that anyone could be born so evil. Truth be told, each one of us is born a bad seed.

In prison, I gained a greater perspective of human depravity—the doctrine in general and my own. Instead of swimming in the current of why bad things happen to good people, I was trying to stay afloat in the murky waters of, *How do Christians, who believe they are guilty sinners, honor and glorify God in a situation where they are unjustly accused of crimes they have not committed?* Experiencing for myself what godly men in Scripture experienced helped me to read their words from a different perspective. Paul: choose joy—even in prison. Joseph: What you meant for evil, God meant for good. Reading about their circumstances, it is easy to see their innocence in the sham charges made against them because we see the whole story. But while I knew in my heart that I am not good, in the same boat with all humanity, I still had not come to grips with the question: *Why **shouldn't** I go to prison? Why **not** me?*

Have you asked yourself this question: What if I found myself in circumstances that put *me* in prison? It may seem bizarre to contemplate, but maybe it shouldn't be such a strange scenario to ponder—especially today. Over the last couple decades, I have read countless books regarding the rise in persecution of Christians in our country, and my heart's cry was always: *Lord, whatever You call me to, give me the strength to do it for Your glory.* If I had been accused of, "being thrown into prison for proclaiming the exclusive truths of the gospel (in a world of intolerance)," I would not have struggled so much. In my wildest imaginations, it would never have been for (purportedly) intentionally breaking the law. No doubt, your flesh was first repulsed by my question. You probably balked as I did in my actual circumstances. Maybe your first thought was: "Well, *I* wouldn't do anything that would land me in jail!" Remarkably, I heard that hurtful protest slip from the mouths of friends and relatives many times.

Ask yourself this question: Would a prison sentence be different than any other trial in which I might find myself? Maybe. But the way we are to respond to all trials is the same. Deep inside every one of us we know we were made to be free. As a Christian, your flesh recoiled at that question of being unjustly accused and sent to prison because it is a question involving morality, your integrity, your character, and your testimony. It would also physically endanger your freedom. But doesn't your flesh recoil at these questions as well: What if I suddenly found myself alone in this world? What if I suddenly lost everything—my home, my job, my reputation, my health, etc.? What if, what if, what if? *Why* does our flesh recoil at these types of questions? Why do we find ourselves quickly turning our thoughts elsewhere when these hard life scenarios are forced to the forefront of our minds?

I knew a believer once who complained quite frequently to me about her status in life, mostly her monetary problems. She lived under a 'woe is me' umbrella. One day, crying on the phone to me, I admit, I had had enough. My daughter had recently died. I replied matter-of-factly, "So, you must think you are better than me." She said, "Excuse me?" I said, "You don't think you should have to go through any trials at all." She later told me it was like a slap across her face, but she got it. In retrospect, I could have been more patient, more kind—more loving!

I was no better than my friend. If I said it to myself and others once, I said it a thousand times: "Never would I ever have believed I would find myself in prison." Truth is, I didn't really believe I was *that kind* of person. I was raised in a good home surrounded with people who loved me. My husband and I had started out like so many other young married couples trying to go to school, raise a son, and make ends meet. Somewhere along the line, I came to the wrong conclusion that my life was now set. I took my blessings for granted. We gave a lot of money to ministries and to people who needed it. I thought we would always be the ones who gave. We would never have to learn to receive. My husband

and I would live comfortably, be involved in ministry, and enjoy our family and our friends. The Lord was blessing us *because* we were doing His will. Please read that last sentence again, because that is one of the greatest lies regarding suffering and the blessings of God. God's blessings are not based upon what we do. They are based upon His character. They are poured out because God is loving, faithful, good, full of grace and mercy. And His blessings sometimes come in the form of a prison sentence. *(Did you just hear a record scratch, or was that just me?)*

What happens when life takes a turn, when you find yourself in a situation where all your dreams are slipping through your fingers, or you find yourself in daily trials that threaten to overwhelm you like a flood? I wonder, if you are like me, if you honestly don't think you would ever find yourself in a repulsive situation living as a destitute beggar, a prisoner, or someone who has to rely on others for even basic needs (think of whatever scenario most makes your flesh cringe). How many who profess Christ have grasped the fact that they **really do** deserve hell? How many have ever grasped the true gospel? Have we *really* taken a hard look at it and understood our sad state? We are all bad seeds. This is what we need to hear. But we need to do more than just hear it, we need to believe it, repent of our sin, and live accordingly.

Man wants to hear about how good he is, and the great potential he has in the world. That's *easy* for our human nature to believe. And while it is true that man can do good things—with some men being more morally conscious than others—what he can't do is save himself, no matter how hard he tries. He can never be good enough to measure up to God's standards. He may measure up to the standards of men sometimes; but in the end, that won't mean anything at all. The greatest of all men on earth will one day find themselves in hell for all eternity if they did not humble themselves before God as destitute beggars. Our problem is the chasm between man and God is a depth we cannot fathom. The standard of righteousness required for man to be saved and to have eternal life is the very righteousness or holiness of God.

When Adam fell, he lost all ability to do what he was created for—to have fellowship with God and to glorify Him. The bliss experienced in the garden by Adam and Eve in their fellowship with God was lost forever in this life based upon the sin now in man. All men born thereafter were born in their father Adam. Because of the Fall, all are morally corrupt, in bondage to sin, and are born enemies of God.

When you ask someone whether or not they are saved, or why God should allow them into His eternal Kingdom, a typical response is, "Well, I hope I am good enough." But therein lies the fundamental problem. Man is not basically good but basically evil, like the little girl in *The Bad Seed* (See Romans 3:23; 5:12, 19). **This is an evil in all that is done under the sun, that there is one fate for all men. Furthermore, the hearts of the sons of men are full of evil and insanity is in their hearts throughout their lives. Afterwards they go to the dead.** (Ecclesiastes 9:3) **All of us like sheep have gone astray, each of us has turned to his own way.** (Isaiah 53:6) **If we say that we have no sin, we are deceiving ourselves and the truth is not in us. If we confess our sins, He is faithful and righteous to forgive us our sins and to cleanse us from all unrighteousness. If we say that we have not sinned, we make Him a liar and His word is not in us.** (1 John 1:8-10)

Some people make a career out of volunteering for everything under the sun. You can always count on them to work hard for any good cause. There are those who are involved in so many church activities, you would think they were on the church payroll. That's wonderful—unless these people believe their good works are helping to make them worthy of or fit for heaven. You will hear people say, "So and so is basically a good person deep down," but that is a lie that Scripture absolutely refutes. **For from within, out of the heart of men, proceed the evil thoughts, fornications, thefts, murders, adulteries, deeds of coveting and wickedness, as well as deceit, sensuality, envy, slander, pride and foolishness. All these evil things proceed from within and defile the man.** (Mark 7:21-23)

Noticing someone else's success in life, did you ever suddenly feel envious or even secretly wish they would fall flat on their face? Horrified, did you think: *Why did that thought just pop into my mind?* That is evidence that our sin is a heart issue. Deep down, we are **not** good people. The roots of our heart are rotten and evil. You just told that person how happy you were for them and threw your arms around them. They never knew what just came into your thoughts. You appear to them to be a wonderful friend. Shoving that thought down, you tell yourself you did not really mean it. But you are deceiving yourself if you believe that. That thought was evidence of sin in your heart that needs to be dealt with.

David is called by God a man after His own heart. David says of his foes who are God's own foes: **There is nothing reliable in what they say; their inward part is destruction itself. Their throat is an open grave; they flatter with their tongue.** (Psalm 5:9) David also knew he was a sinner *himself*. Psalm 51 shows David acknowledging and repenting of his sin before God. Further, he understands that he was *born* a sinner. Isaiah, the prophet, when seeing the holiness of God, was undone by the realization of the utter wretchedness of his heart before God. We know our flesh is wicked, too, but to what extent? **The heart is more deceitful than all else and is desperately sick; who can understand it?** (Jeremiah 17:9) Ephesians 4:17-18 says that man's sinful, unredeemed heart is hard. It is calloused. The obtrusiveness of mental discernment precludes truth from being recognized or received.

Soon after beginning guitar lessons as a child, I developed callouses on my fingers. Until callouses are formed, there is pain associated with doing something the guitarist loves to do. Callouses allow her to put pressure on the wire strings without pain. When I sin by doing something my flesh loves to do, my soft heart will know the pain of conviction quickly. But just as callouses dull the sense of touch in the end of my fingers, a hardened heart dulls the conscience so that it can't feel the painful conviction of sin.

Just a short time after the Fall God destroyed the earth by flood. **Then the LORD saw that the wickedness of man was great on the earth, and that every intent of the thoughts of his heart was only evil continually. The LORD was sorry that He had made man on the earth, and He was grieved in His heart. The LORD said, "I will blot out man whom I have created from the face of the land, from man to animals to creeping things and to birds of the sky; for I am sorry that I have made them."** (Genesis 6:5-7) God had been patiently observing His creation for a long while. What the Creator had made less than fifteen hundred years before, which was once declared good and blessed by Him, where He had dwelt among His holy creatures—was now only evil. The root of sin went down too deep; the cancer had spread too far. The very hearts that were created to worship His holiness were now only evil fountains of pollution corrupting every soul. The Lord was 'sorry' or grieved He had made man. If we could only understand this grief known by God because of sinful man, could we ever bear it? Horatius Bonar in 1875 said this:

> "How solemnly does this reiteration of God's mind fall upon our ears! How deeply does He feel the sin, the wrong, the dishonor that man had done! How profound the compassion for those very sinners whom, in His righteousness, He was thus compelled to sweep away! How awful must have been the scene presented to His view, when, after surveying it, He was constrained to say, in reference to the creatures which He had made, 'It repenteth me that I have made them'! Can any ignorance—can any madness exceed theirs who would make light of sin, who would treat it as a mere transient disease, which is in the course of ages working itself out of the system, and will soon pass away? Terrible will be thy position, O man, when God comes to say this of thee! It will be terrible enough when thou art brought to feel, 'Oh that I had never been made!' but it will be more overwhelming still when God comes and says, 'Oh that I had never created thee!'"[2]

Bonar says it is madness for man to make light of sin, to "treat it as a mere transient disease…" Sound familiar? God was sorry He made man. Man dishonored Him with the sin of idolatry. All sin is idolatry as a violation of the first commandment to love God with our whole being. Wrapped up in that love is trust. Sin is trusting something or someone to satisfy, fulfill, or bless us other than the God who made us. Our generation will not call sin 'sin' because it believes we are just not that bad. It was the same in Horatius Bonar's day. We do not love and worship God, we love and worship ourselves. Because we've been taught that we are to love ourselves *before* we can love others, we do not even believe the worship of self is sin. Rather, we believe it is right and good!

Most who call themselves Christians would be indignant if they were accused of not loving God. Yet, true believers understand they do not love God as they should. And they are grieved over that fact.

A person may come to a right conclusion that he sins, but how does he typically view that sin? Because sin has a such a negative connotation in the Bible and Christians use it so 'negatively', man must recreate this idea of 'sin' giving it a more acceptable label— one less offensive to the masses. He reasons that if everyone is guilty of sin, then sin cannot be that bad; after all, we are basically good people. If sin can be labeled a 'disease', then those infected are mere *victims* who need treatment and rehabilitation, not ruined sinners who need redemption, regeneration, and brought to repentance. Our culture is inundated with victims suffering from 'addictions' of every sort. Dictionary.com gives the definition of *addiction* as 'the state of being enslaved to a habit, practice, or something that is psychologically or physically habit-forming, such as narcotics, to such an extent that its cessation causes severe trauma.' So to be addicted to something is to be occupied or involved with something that becomes habitual or compulsive.

I ordered an Uber today. Uber is relatively new for me, and it fascinates me—which I would imagine reveals my age bracket. I got a driver who was my age, so we immediately struck up a lively conversation. She informed me that most of her customers are high school students. Remembering my day, I was astonished by that fact but gathered they just didn't want to ride the bus. (The bus was not cool in my day!) She said, "In fact, that is not true. Talking to a mother of a high schooler the other day, she told me that she was begging her kid to get his driver's license because she was sick of carting him around everywhere." I said, "That's odd! It was a 'rite of passage', an extreme privilege, in our day to be able to get a driver's license." She said, "I know, right?" The mother proceeded to tell her that the reason the kids don't want their driver's licenses today…? (There should be a drum roll here because my next sentence is utterly shocking.) They do not want driver's licenses because they can't text and drive! *Say what*? She said they even have a law in California now that you can't text…while crossing the street! The law doesn't shock me, but the need for the law certainly does. Might there be an addiction problem with cell phones and social media?

We are called to love God supremely. Anything that occupies our hearts that is habitual or compulsive other than God is sin. Whether we *call it* addiction, disease, or something else, it is idolatry—it is sin. Whatever occupies our hearts and demands our time, that becomes an obsession, that does not relate to loving God, that draws us away from Him instead of closer to Him—is sin. Sin is not a transient disease that can be cured by man.

One guard in the cafeteria said we could not offer too many choices of food because the girls were so 'institutionalized' that it would slow the line down. Herding us like cattle, this guard wanted to "get 'em in and get 'em out". After you have been told what to do and have had rigid rules put on you for so long, choices become an insurmountable hurdle to overcome for some. There was a saying that newbies pondered for a while before the lightbulb of understanding came on. "Do prison; don't let prison do you." Makes sense when you understand what it is to be institutionalized. The fear I had of running onto the grass in an earlier chapter would fall under this characterization. Being institutionalized means that a person has been locked up long enough that she has become used to it, and it is one reason many return there. They simply do not know how to handle being out in the world again. Freedom, in many ways, becomes more frightening than the walls that keep the person in bondage.

From the above definition of *addiction*, we can see that it also applies to being institutionalized. (A Christian in prison gets a new perspective on man in his bondage to sin.) In John 8:34, Jesus said everyone who commits sin is the slave of sin. We are prisoners of sin until we are freed from sin. The one here who *commits* sin has a bent toward sin or continually, habitually practices sin. He abides in or lives in sin, and his desire, first and foremost, is to feed his flesh and please himself. That is what comes naturally to him. This person is a slave to his master, his master being sin. He can't help but sin, and he can't free himself from sin.

Walking in the Spirit, the Christian, a slave to his Master, Jesus Christ, is free to practice righteousness. The unbeliever, still under his master, Satan, lives in his flesh and is **only** free to practice sin. Those who are not in Christ, but still in Adam, are in the snare of the devil and are being held captive by him to do his will. The

Christian still has a body of flesh and thus, **can** sin, but he doesn't **have** to sin. There is a battle raging, a war being fought in every Christian. Paul described this battle in Romans 7. **...but I see a different law in the members of my body, waging war against the law of my mind and making me a prisoner of the law of sin which is in my members. Wretched man that I am! Who will set me free from the body of this death?** (Romans 7:23-24)

Remember my 'diesel therapy'—flying to a new facility via Con-Air? I will never forget the feeling I had when I was finally able to get on the plane after walking up steps with shackles too tightly secured around my ankles and handcuffs on my wrists attached to a chain link belt around my waist. I sank down in my seat just in time for the marshals to yell, "Buckle your seatbelts!" *WHAT? You have **got** to be kidding me!* I couldn't do it. I was not free to obey. That was a picture to me of an unbeliever's response to the Law. Sin handcuffs and shackles us in every way as much as a prisoner who has been handed over to the U.S. Marshals Service. Every federal prisoner has known the agony and the reality of these restraints. Wanting to be free from them, that one can't do anything to free himself. Unbelievers who walk freely through this world unknowingly wear the same binding, fleshly accoutrements unaware of how they are restricting them from living the abundant and eternal life. They walk around daily in bondage to sin, their flesh, and Satan while believing what they are experiencing is ultimate freedom.

False teachers prey on the unbeliever's desire to feed his flesh. Corrupting by spewing satanic doctrines that deceive men, the Bible describes them as: **...promising them freedom while they themselves are slaves of corruption; for by what a man is overcome, by this he is enslaved.** (2 Peter 2:19) **For we also once were foolish ourselves, disobedient, deceived, enslaved to various lusts and pleasures, spending our life in malice and envy, hateful, hating one another.** (Titus 3:3) The Bible uses the phrase *bondage to sin,* or the word *enslaved,* to describe the hold sin has over us in our natural flesh. *Enslaved* is to confine, restrain, or restrict as if with bonds, or to constrain with legal authority. Where sin is master, there is no resistance.

While shackled and handcuffed, there is very little a prisoner can accomplish. Having most freedoms taken away from me—from having a guard tell us that the BOP now owned us, to having guards assert complete authority over all our basic human functions—I was in every sense of the word physically in bondage and enslaved. However, I could see a glaring difference between an unbeliever who is spiritually dead in bondage to sin and a believer who is incarcerated in unredeemed flesh but free in her spirit.

Enslaved to the BOP, I had no desire to kick against the goads or break the rules as others did. My motives for obedience to the rules and restrictions of Alderson Prison was my love for Christ. So even though the BOP believed they 'owned' me, I was free to be obedient to my real Master and to honor Him by obeying those whom He had placed in authority over me. Likewise, I was free to obey my Lord without fear of man when He called me to do things that were against prison rules (i.e., Bible studies and praying with others).

In our fallen state, we cannot do those things that are pleasing to God, nor do we even desire to please Him. **Therefore, God gave them over in the lusts of their hearts to impurity, so that their bodies would be dishonored among them. For they exchanged the truth of God for a lie and worshiped and served the creature rather than the Creator, who is blessed forever. Amen. For this reason, God gave them over to degrading passions; for their women exchanged the natural function for that which is unnatural, and in the same way also the men abandoned the natural function of the woman and burned in their desire toward one another, men with men committing indecent acts and receiving in their own persons the due penalty of their error.** (Romans 1:24-27) God gave them over to the impurity they craved in the lusts of their hearts.

God gave them over is the same word phrase found in another passage that talks about handing someone over to be thrown into prison. **Make friends quickly with your opponent at law while you are with him on the way, so that your opponent may not hand you over to the judge, and the judge to the officer, and you be thrown into prison.** (Matthew 5:25) After my sentencing, the judge told me I was being 'handed over' to the U.S. Marshals. I was being remanded to their control, and there was nothing my attorney or I could do about it. When God 'gave them over,' He was giving people over to the lusts and passions of their natural hearts which were bent on sin, and there was nothing they could do or wanted to do but follow the natural bent of their unredeemed hearts. This is the state of every human being born into sin.

Ephesians 2:1-3 says we all formerly *walked* according to the course of this world, according to the prince of the power of the air. We lived in our flesh, indulging the desires of our flesh and of our minds. Walking implies lifestyle. A spiritually dead person can only continue to walk or live in his flesh according to his natural desires. To those who did not believe in Him, Jesus said: **You are of your father the devil, and you want to do the desires of your father. He was a murderer from the beginning and does not stand in the truth because there is no truth in him. Whenever he speaks a lie, he speaks from his own nature, for he is a liar and the father of lies.** (John 8:44)

When we fail to honor God as God in our lives, we substitute the God who created us with the god of me, myself, and I. We climb up on thrones made with our own hands and declare ourselves to be sovereign over all that pertains to our worlds. We are saying, "God's Word says this, but I want to do this, so that is what I'm going to do; and I declare it right—for me." In that great lie is the reflection of the father of lies, Satan himself. **To the pure, all things are pure; but to those who are defiled and unbelieving, nothing is pure, but both their mind and their conscience are defiled. They profess to know God, but by their deeds they deny Him, being detestable and disobedient and worthless for any good deed.** (Titus 1:15-16)

If the root is good, the fruit that the tree produces will be good. Christians are to be fruit inspectors. In prison (like the world), there are multitudes who profess to know God. You would have thought I entered heaven for the most glorious fellowship of my life with so many professing Christians around me. Surrounded by Christians 24/7 for 4 years; could life get any better than that? What told me very quickly that the Bible on so many lockers, the 'church' attendance, or even the 'I love Jesus' chatter was a sham? Like the world of all 'professors', they were reading loose translations of the Bible and coming up with even looser interpretations—their own!

At times, we all give in to the temptation of the flesh. Living in bodies with remnants of unredeemed flesh, we will continue to do so until we are glorified. That remnant of unredeemed flesh in me wars with my spirit. Christians are not perfect, just forgiven and being sanctified. But true believers have the Spirit of God living within them who helps them overcome the temptation to sin. Paul said: **For I know that nothing good dwells in me, that is, in my flesh; for the willing is present in me, but the doing of the good is not.** (Romans 7:18) Non-believers, and those who only profess to know Christ, can't help themselves when their flesh is tempted to sin. **The mind set on the flesh is hostile toward God; for it does not subject itself to the law of God, for it is not even able to do so, and those who are in the flesh cannot please God.** (Romans 8:7-8)

Every sweet, precious baby born into this world is born a little sinner. When did you teach your children to scream for their bottles or to say, "Mine!" or "No!" How fast did they learn to manipulate you to get their way and wrap you around their little fingers? Their little worlds revolve around themselves 24/7. You quickly realized that the rebellion in that little bundle of joy would have to be brought into submission to your authority as the one who knows what is best for him. **Behold, I was brought forth in iniquity, and in sin my mother conceived me.** (Psalm 51:5) **The wicked are estranged from the womb; these who speak lies go astray from birth.** (Psalm 58:3) **That which is born of the flesh is flesh, and that which is born of the Spirit is spirit.** (John 3:6)

I was born to my parents who were born to my grandparents and so on, going all the way back to Adam. I was not born into this world born of Spirit, but of flesh. I was born spiritually dead. And that is why I needed to be born again spiritually. Those born only of the flesh live for this world alone. Those born of the Spirit live for the eternal kingdom to come even while living in this world. **Jesus answered and said to him, "Truly, truly, I say to you, unless one is born again, he cannot see the kingdom of God."** (John 3:3) **Jesus answered, "Truly, truly, I say to you, unless one is born of water and the Spirit he cannot enter into the kingdom of God. That which is born of the flesh is flesh, and that which is born of the Spirit is spirit."** (John 3:5-6)

Left alone, in the state I was born, I could never please God. I would never be able to enter His Kingdom to enjoy that eternal fellowship with Him for which I was created. For that, I would have to one day in time be born again of the Spirit. What was said of the Gentiles in Paul's day was also true of me: **…remember that you were at that time separate from Christ, excluded from the commonwealth of Israel, and strangers to the covenants of promise, having no hope and without God in the world. But now in Christ Jesus you who formerly were far off have been brought near by the blood of Christ.** (Ephesians 2:12-13)

For all of us have become like one who is unclean, and all our righteous deeds are like a filthy garment; and all of us wither like a leaf, and our iniquities, like the wind, take us away. (Isaiah 64:6) *Filthy garments* were literally soiled feminine hygiene products. In the Old Testament, according to Mosaic Law, a woman who was menstruating was considered unclean. During that time, she was separated from her husband because what was unclean was always separated from what was clean; they could never mix. Also, in her time of uncleanness, a woman was not permitted to participate in any public religious activity or even to enter the sanctuary. (See Leviticus 15:18-33.) Because she was separated from her husband, sexual intercourse only took place at a time in a woman's monthly cycle when she was most likely to conceive.

Speaking to the nation of Israel in the passage above, Isaiah was making a general point about that nation. Israel had developed a religion of works trusting in her own acts of righteousness to make herself right with God. Throughout the ages, man has created many different works-based religions attempting to merit salvation on his own accord.

When a woman was menstruating, the *evidence that new life had not taken place* was obvious. And she was viewed as unclean. Isaiah is telling us that righteous works or good deeds done to merit salvation from God will not produce life that makes us clean, wholly acceptable to Him. The miracle of spiritual birth, just like physical birth, is a supernatural work of God alone. Good works will never be able to bring about the new birth that is needed to make one right (clean) before God. Thus, their good works were as filthy rags in His sight.

Further, we can offer no true worship to God or have true fellowship with Him or others in that state of uncleanness. Our good works, done for the purpose of obtaining God's favor, are like filthy rags in that they are the *evidence that there is no new life,* only uncleanness. Works to merit righteousness, instead of drawing us to intimacy with God, separate us from Him.

The Bible often uses the word *wicked* to describe those who are unbelievers or those who are unrighteous. The wicked may profess to be Christians, doing works they believe will make them acceptable to God; but their lives proclaim loudly that they don't really believe that God is who He says He is. They believe in a god of their own making, one who will tolerate their sin and look the other way, who is only love and peace, a god who can be anything they want him to be just by believing it is so. To the world, the 'wicked' are often thought of as the dregs of society. The Bible has a different definition. The wicked are those with an unbelieving heart. The wicked can even attend 'Christian' churches where they can have their ears tickled with soft, easy, ultra-short sermonettes that make them feel good about themselves. The irony of life is that some of the 'dregs of society' will find themselves in God's Kingdom for all eternity while those who sat in churches doing good works in His name will find themselves eternally in hell.

The Light is truth. Those who are of the Light seek the light even though it exposes their sin for its offense against a Holy God. Light and darkness can never co-exist together because the light will always overcome the darkness, and the darkness will always flee from the light. Light shines a beam onto the exclusive path of righteousness—the only path that leads to the true and living God—and says, "Walk this way." Even if a believer begins to veer off the right path, when that light is shone onto the path of right-eousness, in gratitude, she will turn from the darkness to the light. **For everyone who does evil hates the Light and does not come to the Light for fear that his deeds will be exposed.** (John 3:20)

The wicked, in the haughtiness of his countenance, does not seek Him. All his thoughts are, "There is no God." (Psalm 10:4) All his thoughts are, "There is no God." His thoughts go something like this: "I can live any way I want to. I will do things my way." People who think that way do not really believe there is a God even if they profess to believe in Him.

You, dear one, are either a child of Light or a child of darkness. That is one area of life where there are no shades of gray. We are all born into this world as children of darkness whose father is Satan. Some have become children of Light because they have been born again from above. But we are all born into this world spiritually dead, headed for an eternity separated from the living God of the universe unless we are born again from above and given a new heart that seeks after righteousness—one that seeks after Him.

In recent years, 'Seeker-Friendly' or 'Seeker-Sensitive' churches have sprung up everywhere. The idea has been to make the gospel message more palatable to unbelievers who are supposedly 'seeking' after God. Desiring to create an appetite and hunger for the truth in these unbelievers, the goal is for them to leave with a good taste in their mouths. Once the 'seeker' believes (ingests or assimilates) the cotton candy gospel (no gospel at all) that these churches are promoting, the hope is they will get saved and hunger for truth. While that idea may apply to a diet of sugar, there is a foundational problem with this concept. No one seeks for God. **There is no one who calls on Your name, who arouses himself to take hold of You; for You have hidden Your face from us and have delivered us into the power of our iniquities.** (Isaiah 64:7) The true gospel is bitter before it is sweet. It is hard to swallow. Unbelievers, unless they are being drawn by God to hear the true gospel, will never seek truth or the God of the Bible. The only thing they seek and have an appetite for are their fleshly lusts. A watered-down 'gospel' does not save anyone.

In Romans 3:9, Paul, the prosecutor, speaking on behalf of the Court, is charging all of mankind with being under sin. All in Adam stand accused. When I was indicted, I received a long document explaining my charges. None of it made sense to me. In fact, *after* I was found guilty by a jury 'of my peers', sentenced to prison, in prison for a couple of years, and fighting my appeal, I found myself arguing with my appellate attorney one day. I was adamant that the prosecution had made a mistake regarding my counts in a motion they were filing with the Court of Appeals. My attorney said it was a shame that after all these years, I *still* didn't understand what I was charged with. Simply put, our legal system goes to great lengths to confuse the ordinary citizen in order that he would be forced to hire an attorney to fight his legal battles, usually to the end that he resigns himself to taking a plea deal.

Paul, as prosecutor with all the weight of the Court behind him, could go up against the greatest lawyers of all times. In the heavenly Court on Judgment Day, the judicial process in our country will be flipped on its head. There will be no need for a trial **or** a plea deal. This indictment is not meant to confuse, but to convict, and Romans 3:10-18 is clearly understood. All are guilty! The guilt weighs heavier with each line and is more clearly realized as our hearts are weighed on the balance of His scales. In verse 19 the verdict is read—*Guilty as charged!*

The fool has said in his heart, "There is no God." They are corrupt, they have committed abominable deeds; there is no one who does good. The LORD has looked down from heaven upon the sons of men to see if there are any who understand, who seek after God. They have all turned aside, together they have become corrupt; there is no one who does good, not even one. (Psalm 14:1-3) None seeks after God. Yet, some churches seem to claim that they are drawing seekers inside their doors in droves.

We were all born *physically* alive but *spiritually* dead in trespasses and sins. We all know that a dead man can do nothing. A spiritually dead man in his depravity will never call on God and recognize the need for salvation because he is blind to his spiritual state. God will turn from the wicked who stubbornly rebel against Him, delivering them over to their iniquities. Their fetters will never be loosed.

Man was born spiritually blind and can't see the real picture. The things that reveal his sinful condition he views as ultimate freedoms and successes. He *is* a seeker, but not a seeker of the one true and living, holy God. He seeks the gods of health, wealth, power, love, and happiness. He seeks only those things that satisfy the lusts of his flesh, deeming the satisfaction of these desires as 'the good life'. Success is defined by him as fulfilling all his dreams arising from the lusts and desires of his heart. **But a natural man does not accept the things of the Spirit of God, for they are foolishness to him; and he cannot understand them, because they are spiritually appraised.** (1 Corinthians 2:14) **And even if our gospel is veiled, it is veiled to those who are perishing, in whose case the god of this world has blinded the minds of**

the unbelieving so that they might not see the light of the gospel of glory of Christ, who is the image of God. (2 Corinthians 4:3-4)

In our world, the net worth of a person is based upon the value of his bank account and his possessions—his treasure. Pursuing ultimate worldly satisfaction by running toward self-promotion and self-fulfillment, that person is running *away* from the only real treasure to be pursued in life because it holds no value to him; on the contrary, it is foolishness to him. In turning aside from the real treasure, though successful and wealthy in *this* world, his actual net worth is zero, for it is eternally useless. **There is a way which seems right to a man, but its end is the way of death.** (Proverbs 14:12) Charles Hodge said it well:

> "Our guilt is great because our sins are exceedingly numerous. It is not merely outward acts of unkindness and dishonesty with which we are chargeable. Our habitual and characteristic state of mind is evil in the sight of God.
>
> Our pride and indifference to His will and to the welfare of others and our loving the creature more than the Creator are continuous violations of His holy law. We have never been or done what that law requires us to be and to do. We have never had delight win that fixed purpose to do the will and promote the glory of God. We are always sinners; we are at all times and under all circumstances in opposition to God.
>
> If we have never loved Him supremely, if we have never made it our purpose to do His will, if we have never made His glory the end of our actions, then our lives have been an unbroken series of transgressions. Our sins are not to be numbered by the conscious violations of duty; they are as numerous as the moments of our existence." ~ Charles Hodge[3]

I was sent to jail with Christ. Even as His child, it was a very dark place where a flicker of hope was extremely difficult to find. In those first few weeks in county jail, I struggle to remember how the

Light sustained me. Crying to my dad on the phone, I remember saying, "Daddy, I don't think I can make it." My dad was crying too, "Please, honey, don't say that. You **must** get through this. The Lord will help you." Not knowing how I would ever get through the darkness, I never felt so alone in my whole life. I *know* that despair firsthand. It was real, but I have learned through all my trials that we can never look at any situation through our feelings. I was never alone, not for a moment. My Father was with me.

Shortly after I got there, I was moved into an empty cell. For one glorious night, I was alone. The next day I got a bunkie who I knew, from the start, was going to be trouble. The first night she decided she was going to have a cigarette…in our cell. I tried to talk her out of it, even telling her I have asthma as I pleaded with her. She was determined and got caught soon after she lit up. (To realize my horror about what happened next, you need to understand my problem with heavy periods as I started through menopause. There were few sanitary pads offered to the women there. Some were put in a box in the front of the pod each morning. Within minutes, they were gone. Pads are like ducktape—1,001 uses—to female inmates. I had started saving them up for when I would need them next.)

As soon as my bunkie was caught, the whole pod went on lock-down. I was petrified. The guards came into our cell and led us out into the middle of the pod in handcuffs seating us on chairs to watch as they 'tossed' our cell—taking everything out and throwing it onto the floor in the middle of the pod. Amidst all our scattered belongings were my pads. They took them as *contraband!* While the other women watched from their cells, the guards took us both in the showers and strip-searched us. I was sobbing the whole time. Once cleared, they commanded we put all our things away. Ten minutes later, after everything had settled down, they came into our cell and repeated the whole process again. Standing in the shower, I was pleading with the guard (who I think may have felt sorry for me). I sobbed, "I didn't do anything wrong." She said, "I know you didn't." My voice quivering, I asked, "Is this what you do to people who didn't do anything wrong?" *Seemed to be my theme song.* The next morning, however, I saw God's grace in the whole situation. Several women said to me, "I'm so sorry this happened to you. I felt so bad for you." After that, I never had a problem with any of the ladies there. My bunkie got moved that morning.

This week I read an article in the newspaper regarding a woman in the same county jail. She committed suicide by hanging herself in her cell. I was told shortly after I left there was a young woman I had been incarcerated with who had tied a sheet around her neck and threw herself off the balcony to the same end—whether that is true or not, I do not know. Turns out, though, it *is true* that this same county jail statistically has a high rate of suicides. For so many without Christ, I do not know how it is not higher than it is. At one time, I would have read the article as just another statistic. And even though I never met this woman, I met her through the lives of so many others while I was there—women who were just like me sharing the same horrible circumstances. This woman had bail set at a very modest amount of money. Yet, no one bailed her out. It grieves my heart.

Prison fascinates our culture. One church asked me to speak to their women's group shortly after I was released. I was told, "Just speak about your experiences in prison. We want to hear about prison because none of us have experienced that." There is a thread that ties us all to prison life that is too close for comfort.

The Bible says we are all under the Law. It uses terms like *imprisoned, kept in custody,* and *held in bondage.* Every human being knows something about being imprisoned. Whether they *feel* as though they are enslaved and in bondage or not, it is reality that they were born that way. Every human being is incarcerated in his flesh. Even if you are a Christian, you are living in a body of flesh that still has remnants of unredeemed human fallenness or remnants of the sin nature. This flesh wars with your spirit. We have yet to realize the fullness of freedom that God intends His children to know.

An unbeliever is incarcerated in the flesh to the degree that he cannot help himself *but* sin. It does not mean he is always doing 'bad' things, but even his 'good' things are not done for the right reasons. So, prison for me? Why *not* me? It was Robert Murray McCheyne who said, "The seed of every sin known to man is in my heart."[4]

The following was written by a man who I would have liked the opportunity to get to know, for he was associated with the little church I love so dearly in my hometown of Ligonier.

> What irony that sinners consider the greatest problem they face in this world to be the problem of pain. The ultimate insult against God is that man thinks he has a problem of pain. Man, who deserves to be plunged into hell at this moment, and is indescribably fortunate that he is breathing normally, complains about unhappiness. Instead of falling on his knees in the fury, the sinner shakes his fist in heaven's face and complains against what he calls "pain". When he receives his due, he will look back on his present condition as paradisaical. What he now calls misery, he will then consider exquisite pleasure. The most severe torment anyone has ever known in this life will seem like heaven in comparison with one moment of the full fury of the divine Being.[5]

Have you ever known hopelessness? I remember sitting at the email computer in prison reading a message from my son who was imprisoned in South Dakota. My heart was ripped out as I read how he was having a hard time seeing the light at the end of the tunnel. I understood completely what he was experiencing, but his prison stories crushed me more than my own. Yet I could not do anything to physically help him or alleviate his despair. All I could do—the best I could do—was point him to the true Light who is always there and entrust him to our Father. Those who have Christ will never be without hope, even when our emotions lead us to *feel* that way. Our hope is not based upon our feelings, but upon the revelation of Jesus Christ in God's Word. I am thankful for those testimonies of men who went before me who suffered much so that I might know Him in my suffering. **...for which I suffer hardship even to imprisonment as a criminal; but the word of God is not imprisoned.** (2 Timothy 2:9) **So that I might know the One who opens blind eyes, brings out prisoners from the dungeon and those who dwell in darkness from the prison.** (Isaiah 42:7)

15
The Great Rescue

Rescue—to save or deliver, to free from confinement, danger, or evil, to save someone from a dangerous or distressing situation, to take someone (such as a prisoner) forcibly from custody, to recover something (such as a prize) by force

Save—to deliver from sin, to rescue or deliver from danger or harm

Deliver—to set free

When I was 15 years old, my family spent a week's vacation at the beach. I love everything about the ocean—the sights, the sounds, the smells. One day the waters seemed unusually calm, and I decided to go for a swim. While swimming contentedly, panic and fear suddenly overcame me. One moment I was without a care in the world, the next I was drifting out to sea at a rapid rate of speed. Frantically, I attempted to swim back to shore but found it to be an impossible feat. I was caught in what is known as a rip current. My father, mother, and sister were on the beach. Recognizing that something was not right, my father jumped up and swam out to me. All I could say when he approached was, "Daddy, help!" He told me to stay calm and to doggy paddle until he could reach me. But I *was already* panicking and getting weary fast. When he got to me, he lifted me up and threw me out of that current telling me to let the waves take me safely to shore. Daddy rescued me and saved me from drowning. He delivered me from the dark depths that threatened to separate me from him and the rest of my family.

When we got to shore, we slowly made our way to the blankets where my mother and sister were sitting. Falling to our knees completely exhausted, we were too overwhelmed to speak. Eventually, upon learning what had just happened, my mother told us that my sister was so excited watching us splash around in the water that she had been ready to come out and join us. Daddy said if she had, he would have lost one of us because he couldn't have saved us both. My dad was a strong man, but the current was intense. That same vacation, our car was hit by lightning while I was learning to drive. The Lord was watching over me to protect me even before He saved me—even while I was His enemy.

We have seen our sad, hopeless state. Maybe some have seen it for the very first time. The rip current of conviction threatens to overwhelm you as you sink into the understanding that unless you are rescued from your sinful state, you will sink to the depths of the darkness of hell in your wretched state for all eternity. We all need a Rescuer, a Savior, a Deliverer. But who can save us and set us free? **Save me, O God, For the waters have threatened my life.** (Psalm 69:1) **Incline Your ear to me, rescue me quickly; be to me a rock of strength, a stronghold to save me.** (Psalm 31:2)

Even as believers, we *have been saved*, and we *are being saved* daily. Because our flesh is so strong, we will need to wage war with it until the day we are taken home to eternal glory. We can't do it in our own strength. We also need wake up calls that get our attention reminding us of our depravity and our purpose when we begin to swim out into the comfortable, peaceful waters of life. Sometimes we need to be given a wake-up call and be yanked out of our comfort zones—to be reminded that we need our Savior for every breath we take. This makes me think of someone who also knew that sinking feeling in his gut while taking a ride in the 'gut' of another.

Jonah, God's own *prophet*, had been running in rebellion and disobedience from the Lord's will. He was not loving God with all his being, nor was he loving his neighbor as himself. Short story even shorter: This disobedient prophet finds himself sinking to the bottom of the sea after being tossed overboard from a ship on which he had hidden himself as a castaway. He had unsuccessfully explored every avenue attempting to outrun and escape the Lord's will for him. Once he was safely tucked away and peacefully sleeping in the bottom of the boat, the Lord caused a great storm to come up. The old salts on board were seaworthy sailors who were not afraid of just any old storm; however, they quickly realized this one was different. When these unbelieving sailors learned that the storm had arisen because Jonah had disobeyed the Lord, they feared God and asked the prophet what they should do in order that the sea might become calm for them. Jonah said they needed to throw him overboard. **However, the men rowed desperately to return to land, but they could not, for the sea was becoming even stormier against them. Then they called on the LORD and said, "We earnestly pray, O LORD, do not let us perish on**

account of this man's life and do not put innocent blood on us; for You, O LORD, have done as You have pleased." So, they picked up Jonah, threw him into the sea, and the sea stopped its raging. Then the men feared the LORD greatly, and they offered a sacrifice to the LORD and made vows. (Jonah 1:13-16) The sea stopped raging and the sailors learned salvation is from the Lord.

Now, the prophet finds himself sinking to new lows—that is, the bottom of the ocean. **The Lord appointed a great fish to swallow Jonah, and Jonah was in the stomach of the fish three days and three nights. Then, Jonah prayed to the Lord his God from the stomach of the fish…** (Jonah 1:17-2:1) *The Lord appointed.* No doubt, if we were Jonah, we would be tempted to view our circumstances as out of control. They *were* out of *his* control—but not out of God's control. If you will, please stop now and read Jonah 2:1-9. Look at the conclusion Jonah comes to at the end of his prayer. **Salvation is from the Lord.**

Imprisoned in his dark, damp, cell, chained and shackled with seaweed and bony bars detaining him, Jonah started praying the Psalms adapting different fragments of them to form his plea to the only one who could save him. **Then the LORD commanded the fish, and it vomited Jonah up onto the dry land.** (Jonah 2:10)

Providentially, Jonah was the last book of the Bible that the girls and I studied together before disbanding our 11-year old, weekly Bible study. I was indicted soon after we began, but we finished the book. Looking back, I'm afraid I would have been a Jonah if I had looked at a prison sentence as God's calling for my life. Another thing Jonah and I had in common was our love for the Psalms.

I lived in the Psalms after Melissa died. Familiar with this place of refuge, I ran to it daily from the onset of our prison trial. These life-giving words of wisdom and hope enabled me to stand firm, anchoring my faith on a foundation that would not be shaken. Jonah prayed the psalms asking God to rescue him, and God did just that in a way Jonah would never have considered.

Watching cartoons and reading fairy tales were a part of my memorable childhood. Many storylines shared a damsel-in-distress theme. The damsel was tied to railroad tracks by the villain—or found herself in some other distressful, life-threatening situation—and the hero, her prince charming, always came riding in on a white horse at the last moment to rescue her. I was serious when I said earlier that while imprisoned, I literally believed with undaunting hope that my Knight in shining armor would come riding in on His steed to rescue me from my plight, however He chose to do it.

After all, my God caused a great earthquake which shook the foundations of the prison detaining Paul and Silas. The doors were forcefully swung open, and their bonds were loosed freeing them to walk off the compound. He also made a whale vomit up an imprisoned prophet—I mean, **come on**! Did God create in us an inherent need to know we need rescued? I wonder. Are fairy tale themes of the prince rescuing the princess based on the grand theme of all history? *But I wasn't rescued from prison—or was I*? How *are* we to put our faith into practice as we learn to stand on His Word?

Sometimes, as God grows our faith, He puts a mountain or a storm between us and Him that blocks our view of His presence, and we start to waver and to doubt that He is there. We need to be brought to the place where we can stand firmly on what we *know* is true rather than only believing in what we see or feel. Physically imprisoned, was I seeing things from my perspective or from His?

A small child may need her mother or father in the room until she falls asleep. The nightlight clearly reveals her parents are there. Later, her parents may be in the next room, but the child can see the door to their room because of the nightlight still burning brightly. One night, however, mother says, "It is time to get rid of the nightlight." How that child suffers with fears and doubts in the darkness. She must come to trust what she knows—mother and father are still there even when she cannot see them. As time passes, she rests in the security of knowing that all things past have worked for her good even when the growth process, stretching her, has caused her great pain and anxiety. She can look back, remember, and embrace each new and even greater challenge with the strength she gained in the frightening, dark nights when she learned to trust; and she presses on in faith. I wrote that in my journal 16 days before I was put in jail. This was the lesson I was being taught. Prison was the test.

At first, prison was a terrifying reality. It was dark, daunting, discouraging, and disheartening. Looking back, however, I realize that He rescued me daily, sometimes hourly, and even moment by moment. I learned not only how to be content but to thrive in the security of knowing He was with me in this dark night of my soul. There, His presence was not in church services; it was not in great ministry opportunities (that I'm aware of). It was not even in enjoying great fellowship with the saints for the most part. Yet, His presence was overwhelming to me, all the same. He was the Friend who stuck closer to me than a brother ever could. I still waited expectantly for the red phone to ring for me. But whether it did or did not, I could say with confidence, "Salvation is from the Lord."

Interestingly, Jonah acknowledges in verse 3 of Chapter 2 that it is God who cast him into the deep. The circumstances in which Jonah found himself were never out of God's control. God was using the storms in Jonah's life to discipline him and make him more holy. Jonah acknowledged God's sovereign control over salvation, and God delivered him from his prison to walk in obedience to the truth he proclaimed—until his next test, anyways. (Some people learn the hard way.) He acknowledges in verse 9: Salvation is from the Lord. Psalm 3:8 says that salvation belongs to the Lord. Just like Jonah, we all need rescued, saved, and delivered. Today. Right now.

Believers need the Lord to save them from falling into temptations to indulge their sinful flesh daily, and unbelievers urgently need salvation from God's eternal wrath. Psalm 139 tells us that God has ordained all the days we have upon this earth. We don't know the day of our death; but it is certain, nonetheless. Hebrews 9:27 says that after death comes judgment. Regardless of what some religions teach, there are no second chances after death. Death is a sentence that is final.

Because we are not promised tomorrow, today is the day of salvation. We all know what it means to need saved from something. There are some who can look back on a specific date and time and say, "On that day I was saved." Great! But are you being saved today? True Christianity manifests itself in a person's life by a pursuit of holiness. Disciples are always learning. Growing in grace is the product of obedience to the truth being learned while sitting at the Master's feet in the School of Life.

It does not matter if you are a Jonah or a Job—discipline by God is always for our good and His glory to cause us to grow into the image of His Son. We can't possibly even recognize how mind-blowingly great that good is! It may be a gift given in the ugliest wrapping you ever saw. But unless we receive this package from His loving hands, using it for His glory, we will never come to the realization that the treasure inside is priceless.

We have looked at man's sorry, destitute state. Born into this world in sin, he walks in darkness; he is blind, condemned, judged, and without hope. He is dead, spiritually speaking, even though he lives physically. This is the hopeless state of self-centered man. It is a life that appears full but is empty; it feels satisfying but is vanity; it has a facade of success but is a complete failure. How can this be? Success, value, what constitutes real life, is only to be measured by what God, the creator of all life, says it is.

When my youngest boys were in elementary school, I was a volunteer teacher's aide. I will never forget a certain conversation I had with a little boy named Brandon. Going over vocabulary words with him, we came upon the word *worthless.* "Do you know what that word means?" He replied to my question, "Yes. My daddy says I am worthless." Stunned, it was all I could do not to hug that little boy close to my heart and cry for him. Immediately, I replied, "Oh, Brandon, that is not true! You are unique and very special! You have great value because God made you in His image, and He loves you." You would have thought I handed him a million dollars. He sat up straighter and taller and looked me in the eye from that day forward.

Brandon was not worthless *because his earthly father said* he was worthless any more than I am special because my earthly father tells me I am. You are not successful because the world says you are successful. You do not have eternal life because a religion says you have eternal life if you do any number of good works. You do not have eternal life just because you believe you are a good enough person. Even if you think you set the standards for your own life, you do not. The one who created you set the standard for true life. Only His standard truly defines life.

Another word we must learn is *Redeem/Redemption*—According to *Vine's Expository Dictionary of New Testament Words*, it can mean to buy out, especially of purchasing a slave with a view to his freedom. It is to buy up for oneself, to rescue from loss, or to pay a price to recover from the power of another, or ransom. It is used also in Ephesians 5:16 and Colossians 4:5 of redeeming the time or making the most of every opportunity, since none can be recalled.

We need to be rescued, saved, delivered, and redeemed. Logically, one cannot save himself according to the very definitions of these words. So just how does salvation occur? There is a Rescuer, a Savior, a Deliverer, a Redeemer. We need to know *how* one is saved. But is that enough? Is it enough to know *about* salvation? I want to *know* salvation and the One who accomplished it.

Psalm 35 became *my psalm* in 2006 when the walls of our life started coming down on top of us. I return to it often—not daily, as I once did for years, but often. It is a psalm that has a lot of legal words in it. I sat in the courtroom and repeated it over and over in my mind. It talks about situations when enemies overwhelmingly come against us. It is one of the imprecatory psalms. There is so much in it that spoke directly to my heart each time I meditated on its words. Praying it today affects me as powerfully as it always has. I believe God's promises therein. Why? Because it is His Word, and because He has already answered my own plea as spoken by David in verse 3. '**Say to my soul, "I am your salvation."**'

For much of my prison test/trial, I wanted to know vindication. I wanted deliverance from prison, my reputation back, and all that I had lost to be redeemed. I *said* I wanted it all to be done in God's time, for His glory, and my good. I waited as patiently as I knew how, certainly not in my own strength. I was released from prison without knowing that vindication fully. But slowly, the realization came that it **is** finished. It **is** done. My vindication **is** past tense as much as my glorification is past tense. Even though I do not see the reality of these things now—in time—nevertheless, my complete vindication is sure; and it will be fully realized in the day of *real* judgment. That vindication will come in a far better way than I could ever imagine because it's been in the mind of my Father since before the foundation of the world. To some extent, vindication has come through every person who has listened to and believed my story. Those who do not believe are not as much of a concern to me as they once were. How do I know full vindication is sure? Because He has assured my soul in every imaginable way, in trial after trial, that He is my salvation. In my salvation, all the promises in Jesus Christ are sure—part of my future eternal inheritance.

Salvation is not just a doctrine to which we give mental assent. Salvation is intensely personal. It is found in a Person who wants our relationship with Him to be intimate and pure. His name is Jesus Christ. He, alone, can rescue us from our flesh, from sin, from Satan, from hell, and from the eternal wrath of Almighty God. He is Lord of all! So we need to know *how* to get saved, and we need to know salvation or eternal life intimately. **This is eternal life, that they may know You, the only true God, and Jesus Christ whom You have sent.** (John 17:3)

Maybe you are one who has believed the true gospel. You have no doubts your salvation is genuine, not because someone told you never to doubt your profession of faith, but because the Holy Spirit has affirmed the truths of Scripture to your heart in the past and is still doing so today. If you are going to move forward in your walk, to minister to others what you know as truth, to relay what Christ has done in your life, and to glorify God, you must always remember where you came from (as seen in Ephesians 2:1-3), how you got where you are now, and where you are going.

If our position or standing before God has changed from children destined for wrath, we had to have been born again into another family. Before, Satan was our father, and we were in Adam, in sin. Now, we have been made sons of God, born into the family of God, and God is our Father. How is one born again if a dead man can't *do* anything? Two words. *But God...* **But God, being rich in mercy, because of His great love with which He loved us, even when we were dead in our transgressions, made us alive together with Christ (by grace you have been saved), and raised us up with Him, and seated us with Him in the heavenly places in Christ Jesus, so that in the ages to come He might show the surpassing riches of His grace in kindness toward us in Christ Jesus. For by grace you have been saved through faith; and that not of yourselves, it is the gift of God; not as a result of works, so that no one may boast.** (Ephesians 2:4-9)

Grace—The unmerited favor of God toward man. Of the merciful kindness by which God, exerting His holy influence upon souls, turns them to Christ, keeps, strengthens, and increases them in Christian faith, knowledge, and affection, and kindles them to the exercise of the Christian virtues (according to Larry Pierce, creator of the Online Bible, as found on blueletterbible.org).

Faith—Faith is hoped for (not seen), conviction, assurance, and confidence that is rooted in revelation that has been given by God. Faith's object is Jesus Christ. We *receive* the gift of salvation, which we do not deserve, just as we receive every gift He gives, including those wrapped in dark packages—by faith, believing He is the God He proclaims to be.

We were *by nature* children of wrath. Among them we too all formerly lived in the lusts of our flesh, indulging the desires of the flesh and of the mind, and were by nature children of wrath, even as the rest.

By nature, in Ephesians 2:3, contrasts with *by grace*, in verse 5. By nature, we were born children of wrath. By grace, He caused us to be born again as His own children. Salvation is by grace. We did not become children of wrath or develop into children of wrath. That was our nature from birth because we were born in Adam. We *all* need a Savior who will save us from our sinful nature and from the wrath of a holy God who must judge all sin. We are so sinful that an eternity of God's wrath poured out in judgment against us would never pay the debt of our great offense against His holiness.

We could never pay the price of our salvation. To obtain right standing or be justified in His sight and appease His righteous anger against us, we needed a perfect Substitute who could stand in our place to bear our penalty—as the Old Testament sacrificial system foreshadowed. God could only send God. He sent His Son to be that Substitute. Jesus, the second member of the Godhead, the Lamb of God who takes away the sin of the world, is God. The Father, Son, and Spirit were in the beginning and involved in creation. (Genesis 1:1-2, 26; John 1:1-4) God the Father sent God the Son to earth in the flesh—fully God and fully man, the perfect mediator between God and man. (John 1:14) By Him and for Him all things were created. (Colossians 1:16-17) He is the radiance of God's glory and the exact representation of His nature. He upholds all things by the word of His power. (Hebrews 1:1-3) Although distinct in His person from the Father, Jesus is eternal God. The Father sent Jesus to redeem and rescue those whom the Father had chosen from the foundation of the world to be in Christ.

Why would He do that? For love, but ultimately for His glory. Fulfilling His perfect will glorifies Him, and God must be glorified in all things. We are to be all about God's glory because He is all about His glory. If He wasn't, He wouldn't be God.

If you have ever had a Christian loved one die, you know the bittersweet longing to be with that person again, the sorrow of missing them, and the joyous splendor they are experiencing in all the glories of heaven. You would never wish that person back just to fill the hole left in your own heart at their passing. That would be the epitome of selfishness.

The epitome of *selflessness* is seen in what happened when God, in the second person of the Trinity, became man taking on a body of *flesh*. Knowing all the eternal glories of the heavenlies, Christ was sent to earth by the Father to redeem sinful man. He willingly put Himself in the humblest circumstance when He came as a baby. He came to *die* for us, but He also came to *live* the life we could not live in order that He could be our Substitute, the only one who could ever keep the Law perfectly. Everything about Christ's life and death was the supreme example and model of humility for us. Philippians tells us that we, too, are to have this same attitude of humility towards others. **Have this attitude in yourselves which was also in Christ Jesus, who, although He existed in the form of God, did not regard equality with God a thing to be grasped, but emptied Himself, taking the form of a bondservant, and being made in the likeness of men. Being found in appearance as a man, He humbled Himself by becoming obedient to the point of death, even death on a cross.** (Philippians 2:5-8)

In the Old Testament sacrificial system a lot of animals had to die to cover the sins of the people. There was so much blood no one should have missed the picture of what God was showing them. You will remember in the Genesis account that God sacrificed an animal to cover Adam and Eve who, after they had sinned, realized their nakedness before God. While these Old Testament sacrifices *covered* the sin of the people for which they were offered, they did nothing to *take away* the sin or the penalty of sin.

We looked at the Law and saw that we are to be perfect as God is perfect, holy as God is holy. In order to be justified, or right with God, we must be *made righteous* before Him. What was lost when Adam and Eve sinned must be redeemed in each of us individually. Because we were created in God's image, our perfect Sacrifice and

Substitute took on our image coming to earth in a body of flesh. He willingly obeyed the plan of redemption the Father had established before the foundation of the world. When Christ came, the old sacrificial system was replaced with the new, once-for-all sacrifice of the Lamb of God who would *take away* the sin of the world (John 1:29), the sin that the blood of sacrificial animals could only *cover.*

Adherents to works-based religions of the world are still trying to offer sacrifices to God without going through the Lamb of God who died *once for all.* One well-known priest has said, "The priest reaches up into the heavens, brings Christ down from His throne and places Him upon our altar to be offered again as the victim for the sins of man." (Grace to You - gty.org Sermon 90-318) This idea fails to understand that no further sacrifice is needed—the work of redemption is finished. And Christ was never a *victim.* Although striving to offer these good works continually and earnestly, Scripture says: **For we maintain that a man is justified by faith apart from works of the Law.** (Romans 3:28)

Holy God, in the person of Jesus Christ, came to earth, was born of a virgin, and lived the perfect life you and I were required to live in order that we may spend eternity with God. In that imputed righteousness of Christ, the believer stands as righteous or holy as the Son.

Hebrews 9:22 says: **And according to the Law, one may almost say, all things are cleansed with blood, and without shedding of blood there is no forgiveness.** Jesus (the Good Shepherd and Lamb of God) *willingly* died for His sheep. (John 10:15) In the sacrificial system, the animals were slain for the sins of the people. But the animals did not willingly lay down their lives. They did not literally take on the sins of the people, nor did they suffer the wrath of God for those sins. They were killed, and they just died.

Jesus, our perfect Substitute, bore the guilt of our sins in His body of flesh and suffered the wrath of God we *would have incurred for all eternity.* ...**and He Himself bore our sins in His body on the cross, so that we might die to sin and live to righteousness; for by His wounds you were healed.** (1 Peter 2:24)

The work of salvation is finished! We must receive that salvation as applied to ourselves individually. Our sins—past, present and future—have been atoned for. All that belongs to Christ now belongs to everyone who believes the truth of the Gospel of Jesus Christ. We will realize the full effects of all that was accomplished for us on the cross when we are glorified.

Many are wrongly taught that all the heavenly blessings legitimately belonging to the believer in Christ are to be *fully realized* temporally—not just in glory. For instance, someone sees promises in Scripture telling us that all the riches of Christ are ours, He sets the prisoner free, He heals us and delivers us from all our troubles, etc. Then, they point to these passages and say, "See, God says He will do this, so He **has** to do it." (What they are really saying is that, like a genie in a bottle, God **has** to do these things **now**, in their timing, the way they see it being done.)

The problem is this: What do you do with the poor, those in prison, the sick and those who suffer trials in this life? In this false understanding of appropriating God's promises, the only plausible explanation that can be offered is that those who find themselves in these situations *do not have enough faith*. So when someone endures suffering with perseverance and faith—knowing God *never* promised us we would **not** suffer *in this life*—she will be outcasted, accused of being negative, and mocked for a lack of faith. God *can* deliver us from circumstances now; and He will, if that serves His purposes. Salvation comes in God's sustaining power as much as in deliverance from circumstances. When Jesus saved me long before my years in prison, what happened at that moment (while it wasn't visible), was so much better than being delivered from any physical prison on earth. That deliverance was unseen, but radical.

Suppose my judge is an influential, incredibly wealthy, wise, loving, and utterly righteous man. Accused of committing horrific crimes against his son, I know I stand guilty before him. Having no defense before the law, there is no hope in my citing any good works I've done in the past. When judgment is rendered, the judge calls for the bailiff to bring in his son. The Justice quietly gets down from his bench; placing the handcuffs on his own son, he orders that I be released from the punishment and penalty that was to be mine. Instead, as they lead his son away to receive the death penalty in my place, he tells me the life of his son has now become mine and that he is adopting me into his own family with all the benefits that belonged to the son. I am free to live a life as his own child.

Radical, right? Most would say, "That's just absurd." No, **that's lavish grace.** The gospel is so much more radical than even this *because of the Judge.* God gave His own perfect life for my wretched one so that I might live freely as God's own child receiving all the blessings that belong to Christ. Why? Because He chose to set His steadfast love upon me from before the foundation of the world, a love with a width and depth so beyond human comprehension that there are no words for this simple writer to offer in explanation. What is the evidence that God, the Father, accepted the work of God, the Son, on my behalf? The resurrection! God raised Him from the dead. Christ conquered the grave!

God raised Him from the dead in His physical body. The resurrection of Jesus Christ is also the assurance that all believers will one day be resurrected as well. Paul talks about the resurrection in 1 Corinthians 15:3-8: **For I delivered to you as of first importance what I also received, that Christ died for our sins according to the Scriptures, and that He was buried, and that He was raised on the third day according to the Scriptures, and that He appeared to Cephas, then to the twelve. After that He appeared to more than five hundred brethren at one time, most of whom remain until now, but some have fallen asleep; then He appeared to James, then to all the apostles; and last of all, as to one untimely born, He appeared to me also.**

After Jesus was raised from the dead, He walked among His disciples and others for 50 days until which time He ascended into heaven where He sits at the right hand of the Father. Today, Jesus, having completed His work of redemption on the cross acts as our Mediator, High Priest, and Intercessor.

A mediator is someone who brings two parties in a conflict together. In Scripture, the word for *mediator* is defined as someone who intervenes between two, either to make or restore peace and friendship, to form a compact, or for ratifying a covenant. It is a medium of communication, an arbitrator.

In the Old Testament, Moses, the prophet, was the mediator of the Old Covenant. Later, in the temple, the High Priest was the one who offered the sacrifices for the people and for himself to God. The priests were the mediators between God and man, but they could never make a way for man to enter God's presence himself.

The separation between God and man since the Fall is a chasm man cannot comprehend. Because of His holiness, the depth of sin that separates us is like a bottomless pit as deep as God's love for us. The curtain in the temple stood as a glaring reminder to the priests and people that God was too holy to be approached by sinful man without a mediator. The Jewish people knew that they could not just waltz into the presence of holy God and have a conversation with Him.

Some religions today teach their adherents that there must still be mediator priests between God and the people. However, that idea is contrary to what Scripture teaches and grossly betrays the understanding of what Christ did on the cross. This teaching ultimately puts people in bondage to a religious system that holds their spiritual life in its hands. When I first started teaching Bible study in my home, some told me that I had no authority to interpret Scripture—that a priest was needed to that end. Jesus, as High Priest *and* Sacrifice, eliminates the need for a religious priesthood. 1 Peter 2 says the church is a royal priesthood.

Hebrews 4:13-16 talks about our great High Priest: **And there is no creature hidden from His sight, but all things are open and laid bare to the eyes of Him with whom we have to do. Therefore, since we have a great high priest who has passed through the heavens, Jesus the Son of God, let us hold fast our confession. For we do not have a high priest who cannot sympathize with our weaknesses, but One who has been tempted in all things as we are, yet without sin. Therefore, let us draw near with confidence to the throne of grace, so that we may receive mercy and find grace to help in time of need.** God sees us exactly as we are. There is no hiding from Him, as Adam and Eve found out. He sees our hearts, our thoughts, our motives—everything. That *should* scare us if we don't know the High Priest who represents us individually before God's throne.

Because we have a High Priest who represents us to God, we are urged to come boldly to the throne of grace to obtain mercy and find grace to help us in time of need. We cannot go through another human being; we do not need to light candles or pay fees to have our requests be made known to God. We have a great High Priest who has extravagantly, lavishly invested in us having offered the greatest sacrifice that could ever be made on our behalf. He offered Himself. What more can be offered?

Hebrews 5 tells us a lot about this earthly priesthood of old, and it is interesting to see how it foreshadows the ultimate great High Priest who would come. According to verses 1-4, there were certain requirements of a high priest in the Old Testament sacrificial system: **For every high priest taken from among men is appointed on behalf of men in things pertaining to God, in order to offer both gifts and sacrifices for sins; he can deal gently with the ignorant and misguided, since he himself also is beset with weakness; and because of it he is obligated to offer sacrifices for sins, as for the people, so also for himself. And no one takes the honor to himself, but receives it when he is called by God, even as Aaron was.**

First, every high priest was appointed on behalf of men. Second, as a man, he was sympathetic to the people to whom he ministered. Thirdly, his job would be to offer sacrifices on their behalf. Jesus, God incarnate and our great High Priest, became a man, and thus was able to sympathize with our weaknesses. He offered Himself on our behalf as the ultimate sacrifice. A great mediator understands both sides of the table, so to speak. I don't suffer because He suffered. He suffered because I would suffer.

I often remind myself of one truth when I am distressed. *Jesus understands. He knows exactly what I'm going through right now.* My High Priest is God! This is the ultimate reassurance bringing peace and comfort to any trial or storm in life. My High Priest, who fully knows all my pain and suffering experientially, is in control of all things. That He is faithful, good, just, kind, loving, merciful, gracious, sovereign, etc., soothes my soul and gives me hope for the future. Intimately involved in every circumstance of my life, including my trials and suffering, He understands my weaknesses. Even when I don't mean to blow it but I stumble and fall, I know He is there; not to condemn me, but to pick me up and deal gently with me as His own child. Was I the perfectly obedient, trusting child in prison? I was not. Some days I had feelings of fear, hopelessness, and despair. But I knew the One to whom I should run. And running to Him, I clung to Him like a child desperately clings to her father's leg upon the threat of being separated from him. Ultimately, those daily runs to Jesus strengthened my faith causing me to grow to trust Him more, especially for those times when I could not 'feel' His presence with me in the darkness.

Jesus is not only my High Priest, He is also my Intercessor. **Therefore, He is able also to save forever those who draw near to God through Him, since He always lives to make intercession for them.** (Hebrews 7:25) That He is sympathetic to all my weaknesses having known the greatest suffering of all time is a comforting truth, but to know that He is interceding for me in a way that no other can ever begin to do brings the peace that passes all understanding. Not only does He know what I'm going through because He has experienced the same and more, He victoriously overcame suffering and death and will help me do the same. At all times, He is praying His perfect will for me to that end.

Jesus is High Priest *forever*, never to be replaced. **The former priests, on the one hand, existed in greater numbers because they were prevented by death from continuing, but Jesus, on the other hand, because He continues forever, holds His priesthood permanently. Therefore, He is able also to save forever those who draw near to God through Him, since He always lives to make intercession for them. For it was fitting for us to have such a high priest, holy, innocent, undefiled, separated from sinners and exalted above the heavens; who does not need daily, like those high priests, to offer up sacrifices, first for His own sins and then for the sins of the people, because this He did once for all when He offered up Himself. For the Law appoints men as high priests who are weak, but the word of the oath, which came after the Law, appoints a Son, made perfect forever.** (Hebrews 7:23-28)

We will talk more about salvation in the next chapter. I want to end this chapter with a plea to those who are in bondage to religious systems that require priestly mediators to take them into the presence of God, to offer daily sacrifices on an altar, to interpret Scripture for them, and to absolve confessed sin. Maybe you, dear reader, are having doubts that what you have been taught is truth you are willing to rest your eternity security upon. God has appointed a great High Priest. He is the Jesus of the Bible, and He says the work of salvation is finished. Confess your sin to *Him*. Turn from your sin, from all that dishonors God, believe on Him, and enter boldly the throne room of God.

16
The Three-Faceted Jewel of Salvation

"Say to my soul, 'I am your salvation.'" In times of trouble, sorrow, suffering, doubt, fear, and even arrogance when I tend to puff myself up, I need to meditate on those words. I cannot save myself. I dare not look to any man or religion to save me. Christ alone is my salvation. Salvation is **all** of God.

The world looks at the cross of Christ as foolishness. **For the word of the cross is foolishness to those who are perishing, but to us who are being saved it is the power of God. For it is written, 'I WILL DESTROY THE WISDOM OF THE WISE, AND THE CLEVERNESS OF THE CLEVER I WILL SET ASIDE.' Where is the wise man? Where is the scribe? Where is the debater of this age? Has not God made foolish the wisdom of the world? For since in the wisdom of God the world through its wisdom did not come to know God, God was well-pleased through the foolishness of the message preached to save those who believe.** (1 Corinthians 1:18-21) *Foolishness* is **moria**. It means silly, absurd—from where we get the word *moron*. 1 Corinthians 2:14 says that a natural man does not accept the things of the Spirit of God, for they are foolishness to him, and he cannot understand them for they are spiritually appraised.

The stubborn, hard-hearted, unbelieving Israelites had witnessed the miraculous deliverance of God on their behalf. Yet, Moses said to them: **"You have seen all that the LORD did before your eyes in the land of Egypt to Pharaoh and all his servants and all his land; the great trials which your eyes have seen, those great signs and wonders. Yet to this day the LORD has not given you a heart to know, nor eyes to see, nor ears to hear."** (Deuteronomy 29:2-4) They *could not believe* because the Lord had not given them a heart to know, eyes to see, nor ears to hear.

It is important not only to know salvation is yours, but to also understand how that salvation occurs. We were dead—but God—made us alive together with Christ. **By grace** we have been saved through faith. And that faith was *not of ourselves but a gift of God*, not as a result of any works we may have done, so that none of us can boast. Because my salvation was in the heart of God before the foundation of the world, how could I ever think I had anything to do with it? Scripture is clear, yet this is a great stumbling block of offense for many.

The **way** of salvation *should* humble me to my knees causing me to cry out, "Why me, Lord?" That is what I did cry out when my eyes were opened to the glorious doctrine of God's sovereignty in election. **Blessed be the God and Father of our Lord Jesus Christ, who has blessed us with every spiritual blessing in the heavenly places in Christ, just as He chose us in Him before the foundation of the world, that we would be holy and blameless before Him. He predestined us to adoption as sons through Jesus Christ to Himself, according to the kind intention of His will.** (Ephesians 1:3-5) My Father set His love on me in eternity past and betrothed me to His Son, in order that He would be glorified. The 'us' He chose are His elect. So the chosen, or the elect, are true believers. Once you have eyes to see this doctrine of the sovereignty of God in salvation, I promise you will see it everywhere in Scripture. From that moment on, reading Scripture with a 'me' focus will be impossible. Knowing I am His betrothed, and the extent to which He has gone to save me, will I live like the rest of the world, or will my every thought and action be intent on honoring Him?

In these next two chapters, I want to look at a beloved portion of Scripture throughout all ages. In this chapter, I want to keep our focus upon Romans 8:28-30. **And we know that God causes all things to work together for good to those who love God, to those who are called according to His purpose. For those whom He foreknew, He also predestined to become conformed to the image of His Son, so that He would be the firstborn among many brethren; and these whom He predestined, He also called; and these whom He called, He also justified; and these whom He justified, He also glorified.**

In John 16:33, Jesus told His disciples: **"In the world you have tribulation but take courage; I have overcome the world."** Everyone knows that all things in life are not good. But believers know something that helps them live in this world. **Believers know** God is causing all things to work together for good in their lives. We do not have to wonder, and there is no cause for doubt. He is not just working *some* things together for our good, but *all* things—

even those things that are evil or are meant for evil against us. The **good** is that we will be conformed to the image of His Son. How do we know this? *He* foreknew, *He* predestined, *He* called, and *He* justified. What He began will end in glorification. What does it mean that He *foreknew* us, *predestined* us, and then *called* us? We will see that the chain of our salvation in this passage runs from eternity past to eternity future. God's foreknowledge and predestination took place in eternity past. In time, He called us and justified us. In eternity future, He will glorify us.

The word *foreknew* is often misunderstood to mean that God looked down the corridor of time and saw that I would choose Christ. So then, based upon my decision, He chose me. That makes God's choosing me based upon *what I would do* in time. Once the ball starts rolling in that direction, it makes a lot of what God does based upon what man does first. That interpretation dethrones God and makes man ruler over his own destiny. Foreknowledge has nothing to do with foresight. It **does not** mean that because God foreknew the future, He chose me. Most churches I had attended in the past taught this. Having been exposed to teaching that stressed God's sovereignty in election as well, I was in a state of perpetual confusion until God opened my eyes and cemented these truths firmly in my heart shortly after Melissa's death. At once, things became clearer, and so much of what never made sense now did.

That God foreknew me means the Father chose to set His love upon me in eternity past. He chose to have an intimate, loving relationship with me for all eternity. Lest I get puffed up by that fact, God chose to set His love upon me **not** because of anything good in me, but despite my depravity. He chose me according to His purpose and plan. The Lord called Jeremiah in 1:5 saying, "Before I formed you in the womb, I knew you; and before you were born, I consecrated you."

God's salvation begins with His foreknowledge. Everything falls into place with a right view of that doctrine. Foreknowledge is **not,** *they will believe, so He chose them.* Instead, He chose them, so they will believe. This word *know* in *foreknowledge* is a word for loving intimacy often used in Scripture to speak of intimate relations in marriage. Foreknowledge is all about a predetermined relationship wherein God chose to set His electing love upon a certain people. Setting His love upon them long before time began, God chose to intimately know them and work in their lives. We saw earlier that we love Him *because* He first loved us.

Those He foreknew, He also predestined. He set His love upon His elect and predetermined their destination—to be conformed to the image of His Son. God's *predestination* (predetermining or marking out a destination) is based upon His foreknowledge according to His sovereign will and purposes alone. Paul, in Romans 9, speaking of Jacob, who was chosen, and Esau, who was not, said: **...for though the twins were not yet born and had not done anything good or bad, so that God's purpose according to His choice would stand, not because of works but because of Him who calls...**(Romans 9:11) **For He says to Moses, "I WILL HAVE MERCY ON WHOM I HAVE MERCY, AND I WILL HAVE COMPASSION ON WHOM I HAVE COMPASSION." So then, it does not depend on the man who wills or the man who runs, but on God who has mercy.** (Romans 9:15-16) **But you do not believe because you are not of My sheep.** (John 10:26) The reason men don't believe has to do with God's purpose according to His choice. If you have never been taught this, your flesh has just gone into attack mode. But focus on what Scripture says and not on your emotions.

On some (the elect), God sets His mercy by not giving them what they deserve (His eternal wrath); He allows others to remain in their sinful state of rebellion. It has been said that there will be none on Judgment Day who will say to God, "I wanted to believe, but You wouldn't save me!" God didn't have to set His electing love on *any.* But He did choose *some.* Since we have no way of knowing who is elect and who is not, we are to call everyone to repentance.

For many are called, but few are chosen. (Matthew 22:14) Many are *invited.* There is an external call that is a *general call* to the many (everyone), and that call is *effectual* to those who are chosen (the elect). Many will hear the external call to repentance and faith in the gospel, but they will not respond. The external call goes out from God to the sinner inviting him to faith, but it only reaches the ear. Those who reject this call, do so willingly. Left to themselves, without God doing a work in their hearts, they have no desire to repent and turn to Him. *Most* will not believe. For some who hear the general or external call, that call is effectual.

The effectual call is God's sovereign drawing of a sinner to salvation. Because the effectual call is internal and reaches the heart, it produces the 'effect' or purpose for which it is given. It is irresistible because it happens when, at the same time, God is doing a work internally in the heart of the one who hears. God draws the elect, opens the heart to receive the message, and gives him the power, will, and desire to believe.

God *draws* the elect to Himself by irresistible grace. In the context of the New Covenant first spoken about in the Old Testament, God through Jeremiah, says: **"I have loved you with an everlasting love; therefore, I have drawn you with lovingkindness."** (Jeremiah 31:3) *Lovingkindness* is a covenant word. The word phrase *have drawn* comes from a word that means to draw, drag, or seize. Jesus, speaking to His disciples about His upcoming death, said in John 12:32, **"And I, if I am lifted up from the earth, will draw all men to Myself."** *Draw* means to draw, drag off, to draw by inward power, lead, or impel. When God draws the elect to Himself, the call is so powerful that it literally captures or apprehends the soul. If He didn't draw us, we would never come on our own. Drawing us, we would never **not** come.

Some will believe; but most will not, regardless of how things appear. One thief on the cross next to Jesus believed and was saved, the other did not believe. Judas walked with Christ as one of His disciples; but in the end, it was manifest that he was not of the elect. In John 6, the crowds were following Jesus *because* He was supplying their most basic need for food. He gave these diners an indictment they were not following Him *because* He was God who could give them eternal life, but because He was meeting their felt needs. It was all about them, not Him. It was all about living for the 'here and now' with no thoughts of eternity. They wanted food, but they did not want God.

Like all who *only profess* to follow Him and know Him, they were only focused on what He could do for them materialistically and physically in this life. He wanted them to focus on eternal life. He wanted their hearts. **Jesus said to them, "I am the bread of life; he who comes to Me will not hunger, and he who believes in Me will never thirst. But I said to you that you have seen Me, and yet do not believe."** (John 6:35-36) **"All that the Father** gives Me will come to Me, and the one who comes to Me I will certainly not cast out." (John 6:37) "This is the will of Him who sent Me, that of all that He has given Me I will lose nothing but raise it up on the last day." (John 6:39) "No one can come to Me unless the Father who sent me draws him; and I will raise him up on the last day." (John 6:44) As a result of these hard truths Jesus spoke regarding salvation, many withdrew and were not walking with Him anymore. Jesus asked the twelve if they wanted to go away also. I love Peter's response: "Lord, to whom shall we go? You have words of eternal life. We have believed and have come to know that You are the Holy One of God." (John 6:68-69)

The effectual call by God is like the call of Jesus to Lazarus in John 11 when He raised him from the dead. It has the power within it to produce the desired effect. The effectual call is individual in that He calls us by name. Just like when He called creation into existence, when Jesus commanded, "Lazarus, come forth," the call quickened new life in Lazarus who responded. The effectual call wakes us from spiritual death giving us new life and new hearts to believe spiritual truth. Every true believer has heard and has responded to the effectual call by God's grace.

God chose to set His love upon me in Christ before the foundation of the world. In time, I was born in sin, a daughter of Adam. My life revolved around me. Later in time, God began drawing me to Himself, calling me to repentance through His Word. When He called me, He also did a work of regeneration in my heart so that I not only would respond, but that I would willingly *desire* to respond. Replacing my heart of stone—rebellious and indifferent to the things of God—with a heart of flesh—soft and able to be molded and sculpted into the image of His Son—I was born again of His Spirit. **He saved us, not on the basis of deeds which we have done in righteousness, but according to His mercy, by the washing of regeneration and renewing by the Holy Spirit, whom He poured out upon us richly through Jesus Christ our Savior, so that being justified by His grace we would be made heirs according to the hope of eternal life.** (Titus 3:5-7) **Jesus answered and said to him, "Truly, truly, I say to you, unless one is born again, he cannot see the kingdom of God." Nicodemus said to Him, "How can a man be born when he is old? He cannot enter a second time** into his mother's womb and be born, can he?" Jesus answered, "Truly, truly, I say to you, unless one is born of water and the Spirit he cannot enter into the kingdom of God. That which is born of the flesh is flesh, and that which is born of the Spirit is spirit. Do not be amazed that I said to you, 'You must be born again.' The wind blows where it wishes, and you hear the sound of it, but do not know where it comes from and where it is going; so is everyone who is born of the Spirit." (John 3:3-8) When God gave me life and a new heart to respond to the effectual call, He led me to repent of my sins and put my faith in Christ. At that point in time, He *justified* me (Romans 8:33). Justification is a one-time event. Salvation became real in my soul the moment I was justified.

Justification is a legal term which means that God declares the sinner righteous before Him. God sees me *just-as-if-I'd* never sinned and have lived the righteous life of Christ. At the cross, Jesus took upon Himself my filthy rags and robed me with His own righteousness. Because Christ's perfect life was credited to my account, my *position* before God, in a moment, became 'righteous as He is righteous'. The debt I owed but could never pay was marked 'Paid in Full'. I don't stand righteous or justified on my own merit but only upon the basis of faith in the finished work of Jesus Christ on my behalf.

I like to think of salvation as a three-faceted jewel sparkling from every side. We are awed by its brilliance as we turn it this way and that gazing on it as if into the very glory of the face of God. Salvation involves **justification, sanctification,** and **glorification**. Looking at this golden thread or chain of salvation in Romans 8:28-30, do you wonder why Paul didn't include sanctification in this list in Romans 8? He certainly did not hesitate to emphasize the doctrine of sanctification in other places. Why doesn't Paul include sanctification here? God foreknew us, predestined us, called us, justified us, and will glorify us. There is no cooperation by us (we are completely passive) in any aspect of this great work God does in us. The context of the passage we are looking at in Romans 8 is of the believer's victory in Christ. We will overwhelmingly conquer because of what God alone has done in our lives.

In our sanctification, though it is still God's work in us, we actively cooperate with His grace in the process of being made holy.

We could say that sanctification is a gracious gift of God that requires our active cooperation. In Philippians 2, we see God's work in us and man's coinciding responsibility. **So then, my beloved, just as you have always obeyed, not as in my presence only, but now much more in my absence, work out your salvation with fear and trembling; for it is God who is at work in you, both to will and to work for His good pleasure.** (Philippians 2:12-13)

Both **justification** and **regeneration,** or the new birth, take place at the same moment. Each of these is a one-time event. **Sanctification** also *begins* at that moment. In this aspect of sanctification, I am set apart from sin unto God for holiness (also a one-time event). *Sanctify, sanctification, saint, holy, set apart*—all have the same root in the Greek. When the writers of Scripture address their audiences, they often call them 'saints'. One who is sanctified, or set apart for God, is a saint. That is his position or standing. The newest believer, whose life may look dramatically different than the most mature one, both share the same standing in that they are both saints who have been justified and sanctified. The temple and the things used for worship in the temple were sanctified. They were set apart or consecrated for God's use. Items that were sanctified were chosen by God and were not to be used for less than the holy tasks for which they were ordained.

The moment you were saved, your *position* or standing before God changed radically. Your position went from enemy of God to beloved of God, from child of Satan to child of God. You went from spiritually dead to spiritually alive. *Practically,* your life began to line up with your position as you started learning what is pleasing to the Lord walking step by step in this new standing. You started to grow up into your position or status.

The first part of sanctification has to do with the believer's standing—in being set apart *by God for God.* The second aspect of sanctification has to do with the believer's walk. This aspect of sanctification is progressive in that it is the process of being made into the image of Christlikeness. It takes a lifetime of walking with Christ to grow in holiness. Sanctification begins at new birth and continues throughout my life. It is my growing up or maturing into Christlikeness. According to 1 Thessalonians 4:3, it is God's will that we be sanctified.

True believers are *separated* and called to be *separate*. Just like the world persecuted Jesus, it will persecute those who belong to Him. In Jesus' high priestly prayer to the Father before He died, He asked God to sanctify all those who belonged to Him. **I have given them Your word; and the world has hated them, because they are not of the world, even as I am not of the world. I do not ask You to take them out of the world, but to keep them from the evil one. They are not of the world, even as I am not of the world. Sanctify them in the truth; Your word is truth.** (John 17:14-17) Peter called us strangers and aliens in this world. Not only will we have conflict with the world and the enemy, but there will be a war raging inside each one of us because of our flesh. **Beloved, I urge you as aliens and strangers to abstain from fleshly lusts which wage war against the soul.** (1 Peter 2:11)

For years I believed I was saved in 1979. I now question whether the supernatural birth took place at that time or about twelve years later. I had read the Scriptures, at times with great hunger—even though I had learned to read them with a view to spiritualizing the text so that I could make it say anything I wanted it to say. I had been drawn to bad, even utterly false, teaching. I know now that true life results in a transformed life, that a believer's life is a pursuit of holiness focused on walking in obedience separated unto God. Looking back, I'm not sure I understood the message of the true gospel.

Later, I would come to *know* that true conversion had taken place. I still sinned, but my desires changed dramatically. My heart was now bent toward God and the things of God. I wanted to glorify His name to the world. I had a new desire to love believers. In 1991, I started reading, studying, meditating on, and living out His Word as if my life depended upon it. I was drawn to sound teaching like a thirsty man is drawn to pure mountain spring water. And that sound teaching refreshed my soul like nothing else had ever been able to do.

Whatever the exact time, God saved me. And since God began the work of salvation in me, I know He will continue that work in me to glory. That always gives me hope when I have blown it or am going through some deep, dark trial. **For I am confident of this very thing, that He who began a good work in you will perfect it until the day of Christ Jesus.** (Philippians 1:6)

The practical aspect of sanctification (the process of growing in holiness) is the evidence that is seen when salvation has occurred. We can see that our desires have changed. We know that we have radically different allegiances to God instead of ourselves. We are set apart for God's use, and we can see that struggle between our flesh and our spirit as we set ourselves apart in this world. Some say that sounds like bondage, "Hey, I have to be free to do what I feel I have the right to do, what I want to do." A sanctified believer would say that being set apart for God's use is the ultimate freedom to which he could be called. **For you were called to freedom, brethren; only do not turn your freedom into an opportunity for the flesh, but through love serve one another.** (Galatians 5:13)

As my pastor, John MacArthur, has said on numerous occasions in his recent sermons on Galatians: "A believer is a human being who is incarcerated in unredeemed flesh." In other words, I still have the capacity to sin, and I still feel the temptation to sin in my flesh. The daily battle for the believer is to war against his flesh by choosing to walk in obedience to God by the power of the Holy Spirit working in his life. The desire of my heart walking in the Spirit is to pursue God's holy standards, not to be free from them.

Today, people like to use the term *addiction* for what is really sin. Understanding addiction helps us better understand the destructive nature of sin. In the Christian, the addiction is broken but there is still an attraction in me to the sin drug. The flesh is attracted to sin and still able to be tempted by it. The flesh is weak, and it is from that base of operations that Satan attacks me. Crucifying the flesh is a daily battle that can only be won as we walk in the Spirit.

For the mind set on the flesh is death, but the mind set on the Spirit is life and peace, because the mind set on the flesh is hostile toward God; for it does not subject itself to the law of God, for it is not even able to do so, and those who are in the flesh cannot please God. (Romans 8:6-8) We *were* slaves to sin, but now we are free to walk in righteousness. This is our desire to walk in obedience as He sanctifies us step by step. Growth in the life of a believer is not a sprint any more than that of the life of a child from infancy to adulthood. It's a lifelong walk putting one spiritual step in front of the other learning to walk as Jesus did.

Paul said, **Therefore I, the prisoner of the Lord, implore you to walk in a manner worthy of the calling with which you have been called, with all humility and gentleness, with patience, showing tolerance for one another in love, being diligent to preserve the unity of the Spirit in the bond of peace.** (Ephesians 4:1-3) *Prisoner of the Lord* lights up like a neon sign to me now. Living for his Lord was costly for Paul. In so many treacherous circumstances, Paul put forth the call of the gospel. He counted the cost, and he did not hesitate to pay the price. What did that? Love and gratitude. All the ways he, as the Lord's prisoner, called us to live, he exemplified in his own life. He was not a prisoner of the guards or any ruler. He was a bondslave of Jesus Christ, set apart for God's use in whatever circumstance in which he found himself.

A life that is being sanctified is being continually filled with the Spirit. In Ephesians 5:18, Paul said: **Be filled with the Spirit.** Colossians 3:16-17 is a parallel verse giving further clarification to what it means to be filled with the Spirit. **Let the word of Christ richly dwell within you, with all wisdom teaching and admonishing one another with psalms and hymns and spiritual songs, singing with thankfulness in your hearts to God. Whatever you do in word or deed, do all in the name of the Lord Jesus, giving thanks through Him to God the Father.** Galatians 5:16 says: **But I say, walk by the Spirit, and you will not carry out the desire of the flesh.** In His high priestly prayer, Jesus asked the Father to sanctify us in the truth. Then He said, "Your word is truth." John 1 says Jesus is the living Word. Peter said we are to long for the pure milk of the Word like newborn babies so that we can grow in respect to salvation. *Walking in the Spirit* means to be filled by the Spirit. John 16:13 says He is the Spirit of truth. Walking in the Spirit or being filled with the Spirit is to let the Word of Christ dwell in you richly. Being saturated with the Word, we are to walk as Christ walked in obedience to the Father.

The Spirit of God comes to indwell all believers at the time of their salvation. Paul tells us in 1 Corinthians 2:16 that believers have the mind of Christ. Romans 12:1-2 says: **Therefore, I urge you, brethren, by the mercies of God, to present your bodies a living and holy sacrifice, acceptable to God, which is your spiritual service of worship. And do not be conformed to this world, but**

be transformed by the renewing of your mind, so that you may prove what the will of God is, that which is good and acceptable and perfect. We are to present our bodies a living and holy sacrifice and to renew our minds. Paul starts this passage with the word, *therefore*. The first eleven chapters of Romans are doctrinal and lay out for us the gospel of God's righteousness that is ours when we put our faith in Christ. The last five chapters are practical. Because of what we now know and believe has been done for us and given to us, it is *reasonable* to expect that we would live a certain way in service and loving gratitude.

Christians are given divine help to fight against their flesh in the gift of the Holy Spirit who takes up residence in them when they are born again. Through the Spirit's illumination, they can know the very thoughts of God as revealed in Scripture. When we study it, meditate on it, and embrace it as truth, our minds are transformed. Before Christ, we were conditioned to think like the world around us, the world which is controlled by Satan; but the Word of God, illuminated by the Spirit of God, transforms us by renewing our minds. We must replace the error of the world's way of thinking with God's way of thinking. We repent of what we used to believe which led to how we used to live. Repentance is a change of mind resulting in a change of action. Our minds are the key to the Christian life because as we think, so we live.

There is an intense conflict that rages in God's children still living in bodies of flesh. The flesh sets its desires against the Spirit and the Spirit against the flesh. Through yielding to the Spirit by obeying the truth of the Word, we crucify our flesh or put to death the desires that conformed us to this world. When we say, "Not my will, but Thine be done," we are denying our flesh and being transformed into Christlikeness. Deliberately setting ourselves apart in this way for God's perfect will is practically working out the sanctified position we were given at new birth.

The Holy Spirit in us restrains us from doing those things we want to do in our flesh by empowering us to live in godliness. So, it does not mean that we never sin, but it means that we don't *always only* sin. Everything we did before we were saved was sin because it did not honor God as God. This included not only our actions, but our attitudes and our motives. Now, we are free to walk in godliness; before, we were not.

The Law, which is good, can never make us holy. The Law says, "You will be holy *if you keep* these external behaviors." The Law keeps us in custody, imprisoned, held in bondage—so that we can't sin freely without judgment. The response to the call in Romans 12:1-2 is a response to grace, not the Law. This is important to understand.

This is my sour cream/cream cheese story. I had been out of prison for a year when I moved to California where my boys had lived since college. There, they had grown to love Mexican food. Now, there is what I *thought* was Mexican food, and then there is *'real'* Mexican food. It was soon evident that I was going to have to learn to cook *'real'* Mexican food because serious lovers of Mexican food apparently need it at least once or twice a week! I learned to enjoy it as well, but my version of Mexican food always includes sour cream which I find myself forcing upon the boys who do not want to ruin their authentic Mexican food with anything that even resembles sour cream. Exasperated, they ask, "Mom, why do you find it necessary to have sour cream? We don't want it!" Then, it hit me. We were rarely able to have sour cream in prison. Cream cheese was even more rare.

Working on the salad bar, we quickly learned the menus which ran on a repeating five-week cycle. Occasionally, there would be something added to the menu that was unexpected. For example, on special occasions we would get one small container (about the size of a loaf pan) of sour cream to feed the whole compound when we had *their* version of Mexican food (which is *nobody* else's version of Mexican food anywhere on the planet). Using a small cookie scoop to serve with, everyone got a small, equal portion. More women than usual came down the hill for what were considered the 'good' meals. The girls who pulled food from the warehouse the night before always knew when we were having something special beforehand, and that information made its way up the hill giving us ample time to plan our 'runs'. Though it seems ridiculous to me now, you never saw a comedy show that was any funnier. Imagine, if you can, between 500-800 ladies 'power walking' (whatever could be considered just a little less than running) in stampede fashion down the hill to get a space in line for a teaspoon of sour cream.

We had this little guard who was always intent on catching inmates in the act of breaking prison rules. She was the Barney Fife of Alderson. She had a 'stake out' in our cube one evening. I liked her; my bunkie did not. My bunkie didn't want me talking to her for the reproach it could bring on our cube. This is the same guard who, rumor had it, dressed all in black one night and climbed a tree and fell out and broke a bone in the process of nabbing a 'criminal' in the act. So while all these woman were speed walking down the hill for that teaspoon of sour cream, you never knew when you would round a corner only to be caught in the cross-hairs of this guard who was sitting in her truck just waiting to put you at the back of the line. It was always worth it, though!

Like on a strict diet, when someone says, "You can't have… or else," what is the thing you can't stop craving for and thinking about? The Law is oppressive to our flesh. The law entices the flesh by stirring it up. The Law cannot save you, and it cannot sanctify you because legalism doesn't restrain the flesh but unleashes the flesh to sin more. The reader will be happy to know I no longer run for dairy! (Well, I might pick up my pace for ice cream…)

We've looked at the purpose of the Law. The unbelieving heart needs the Law to expose its need for salvation. Believers need the Law as a standard of righteousness. Without understanding the Law, multitudes profess to follow Christ who believe they can live any way they want. The Law says, "You must do this, or you must not do that, or else." Grace says, "I've done *for you* what you could not do." Christians no longer under the Law but under grace **desire** to obey the Law. (See Romans 6:14.) Positionally, we are righteous before God. Practically, however, we struggle with our unredeemed flesh. While the struggle is real, the absurd idea that it is okay for a believer to live like the world, with no desire to pursue holiness, belies all claims that true salvation has taken place.

When my kids were old enough to do yard work, we would spend Saturdays in the summer working outside. The sun was hot, and it was humid in Pennsylvania, so there was a lot of sweat and dirt involved. By the end of the day, we were ripe. It felt so good to discard those disgusting old work clothes and step into a shower. Once thoroughly cleansed, we would put on better clean clothes and usually go to dinner somewhere. How absurd would it have been for me to step back into those disgusting clothes? Spiritually speaking, I once lived comfortably in those disgusting clothes, but when God saved me, He outfitted me with the royal, priestly robes of Christ's righteousness. I should walk accordingly.

In a recent sermon, John MacArthur said that Lazarus coming out of the grave in his grave clothes is a great picture of our spiritual condition. Still wrapped in our stinking grave clothes (our flesh), we can't be unwrapped as quickly as Lazarus because our flesh is not literal clothing. With this body of death attached to us, we are to put off the desires of the flesh and put on Christ. Positionally, we already wear the robes of Christ's righteousness. Practically, we are taking off these stinking grave clothes, little by little, and replacing them with the righteousness of Christ.

Paul ties being clothed or robed with His righteousness with the baptism of the Holy Spirit at the time of our conversion. **For all of you who were baptized into Christ have clothed yourselves with Christ.** (Galatians 3:27) There is the past tense positional part of our sanctification. We were baptized into Christ when we were united with Him. By faith we put on Christ, and we stand in His robes of righteousness before God. But we are also practically to keep putting on Christ in the present. **But put on the Lord, Jesus Christ, and make no provision for the flesh in regard to its lusts.** (Romans 13:14) Basically, this is what you already are, so live like it.

With my history in the charismatic movement and my experiences in prison with many charismatics there, I can see how this is where what we believe comes down to a great divide. Walking in the Spirit, or being filled with the Spirit, is not a mystical thing. Obedience to the will of God found in Scripture is what sanctification is all about. Nowhere does the Word even hint at what is being attributed to the filling of the Holy Spirit today. Being filled with the Spirit is not something I **feel,** but it is something I *know* when I desire to be obedient to the will of God as the Spirit reveals truth to me in His Word. It is thinking and then living biblically.

Before Jesus ascended into heaven, He said to His disciples: **But you will receive power when the Holy Spirit has come upon you; and you shall be My witnesses both in Jerusalem, and in all Judea and Samaria, and even to the remotest part of the earth.** (Acts 1:8) The flesh is powerful. The battle is real. The power of the Holy Spirit is the only power that can crucify our flesh. He has the power to save and to sanctify. Jesus said we would receive power *to be His witnesses.* To what do we witness? We testify that Jesus Christ is God when we walk in a manner worthy of our calling because without His work in us, we could *never* be like Him.

We don't need His power to speak in unknown languages that are no languages at all (ecstatic gibberish), to roll on the floor, to bark like dogs, or to manifest any number of other bizarre behaviors. What many falsely call private prayer languages have been manifested in diverse cults throughout the ages which have no affiliation with the Spirit of God whatsoever. A *witness testifies to what he knows* so that others will believe it is true. John MacArthur has said: "Knocking people down does not interest the Holy Spirit." When did you ever see Jesus do anything like that? The churches that promote these types of things dishonor the very Spirit they proclaim to worship because they are doing things supposedly in His name that are not in keeping with His Word or His example.

You tell me the Holy Spirit is working in your life? First, you wouldn't need to tell me if He really is because I could see it in the sweet fruit of the Spirit manifested in your godly life (Galatians 5:22). Second, your focus would be on living like Jesus while repenting of sin and crucifying the flesh and its deeds. In short, you would resemble Jesus Christ who lived to do the Father's will. That is what those who are in Him live for as well.

In prison, I witnessed a lot of bizarre behavior in the name of 'Christianity', but I never heard the true gospel proclaimed. The guard over the chapel told us a girl got so 'worked up in the Spirit' during a 'revival' meeting one year she fell and broke her collarbone. I'm not sure how anyone believes wild, frenzied, out-of-control behavior glorifies God when one aspect of the fruit of the Spirit is self-control. I saw two women 'helping' another woman 'birth the Spirit', through a process of bizarre labor—wailing and all! That was *very* disconcerting and sad. To believe that you are honoring the Spirit of God when, in fact, you are dishonoring and grieving Him by doing these things in His name is to be gravely deceived.

One day I was sitting in a room with 20 or 30 other workers in the chapel. The woman sitting next to me who professed to be a Christian was having a discussion with a known cult member assuring her that the religion she practiced was Christian! When I told the 'Christian' quite blatantly that this was not true, she responded somewhat aghast and apologetically, "I had no idea." But put your finger on their unbiblical *practices* (their *experiences)* and they were ready for a fight. It was hard to convince them their experiences and feelings were not the evidence of the Spirit's work. One relatively new 'believer' said to me, "Do you speak in tongues?" I said very pointedly, "No." She said, "Well, do you want to?" I said, "Not at all." Refusing to take 'no' for an answer, she persisted, "I don't understand; why not? I can help you. It's the best feeling in the world. You may not think you want it now, but you will. Believe me." I was able to show her what Scripture said about the issue and why I was confident I would never have a desire to speak in "tongues". But it didn't change her mind. Incidentally, this was the same girl in Chapter 9 who later gave all her things away because the Lord had purportedly 'told her' He was going to release her on a specific date—and who was devastated when it did not happen.

So when you are looking at the lives of people who profess to follow Christ, at churches who profess to teach the gospel, do you see this doctrine of sanctification being taught, stressed, and lived out? **Sanctification** is the mark of every true believer. It's not what happened to you years back, it's not an outward show of ecstatic gibberish and religious gyrations, but what is going on today as you live your life in your pursuit of holiness.

I learned this saying awhile back: At justification you *were saved* from the **penalty** of sin. In your sanctification you *are being saved* from the **power** of sin, and in glorification you *will be saved* from the **presence** of sin. The last facet of salvation is glorification.

Glorification is the ultimate perfection of believers. It is when our practice will finally align with our position. It was God who foreknew us, predestined us, called us, and justified us; and it is He who will also glorify us. Our glorification in eternity future is put in the past tense by Paul because it is as much a done deal as the rest that God has already accomplished. In control of my salvation from start to finish, He will not stop sanctifying me until I am one day glorified as well. **But we should always give thanks to God for you, brethren beloved by the Lord, because God has chosen you from the beginning for salvation through**

sanctification by the Spirit and faith in the truth. It was for this He called you through our gospel, that you may gain the glory of our Lord Jesus Christ. (2 Thessalonians 2:13-14)

When my daughter died, there was one verse that came to my mind almost immediately. At that time of intense grief, I could only think of one thing: Fix my eyes on Jesus, the *author* and *perfecter* of my faith. **Therefore, since we have so great a cloud of witnesses surrounding us, let us also lay aside every encumbrance and the sin which so easily entangles us, and let us run with endurance the race that is set before us, fixing our eyes on Jesus, the author and perfecter of faith, who for the joy set before Him endured the cross, despising the shame, and has sat down at the right hand of the throne of God.** (Hebrews 12:1-2) The word here for *witnesses* is where we get our word *martyr*. It is the same word for *witnesses* in Acts 1:8. Witnesses can have a judicial tone to it as a witness in court. It can also mean: Those who, after His example, have proved the strength and genuineness of their faith in Christ by undergoing a violent death. Christianity is a walk to death of self daily crucifying the flesh to walk in righteousness. Every true believer has a deep longing to be a good witness for Christ.

Many Scriptures that have to do with our future glory are housed in the context of our suffering here and now. Why? Because understanding what our glorification means offers hope in a way that nothing else can. **...and if children, heirs also, heirs of God and fellow heirs with Christ, if indeed we suffer with Him so that we may also be glorified with Him. For I consider that the sufferings of this present time are not worthy to be compared with the glory that is to be revealed to us.** (Romans 8:17-18) We are first hit in this passage by the majestic idea of being children of God who are also heirs of God and fellow heirs with Christ. As we revel in that thought, we proceed to the next words—*if indeed we suffer with Him*. A new believer may say, "Wait, back up the truck! What just happened here?" As we look to what is to come, keeping it in view *always*, we can't possibly forget where we are right now, living in a fallen world full of heartache and suffering.

When a trial hits our life, our flesh naturally wants to cry out, *"Why? Why are You allowing me to suffer so, Lord?"* If we could keep our eyes on Jesus, that question would fall flat as soon as it comes out of our mouths, and we would repent in humble sorrow. If Jesus, God's own beloved Son, suffered for my sake before entering glory; why *not* me? He learned obedience from the things He suffered (Hebrews 5:8); how can we think we should have an easier path to follow? The fact that Christ suffered and overcame death, that greatest enemy of all—the fact that His Spirit indwells every believer—these truths are the Christian's greatest hope. For Jesus, suffering is the pathway to victory. Colossians 1:27 says that Christ in the believer is the hope of glory. **For momentary, light affliction is producing for us an eternal weight of glory far beyond all comparison...**(2 Corinthians 4:17) **After you have suffered for a little while, the God of all grace, who called you to His eternal glory in Christ, will Himself perfect, confirm, strengthen, and establish you.** (1 Peter 5:10) **For it was fitting for Him, for whom are all things, and through whom are all things, in bringing many sons to glory, to perfect the author of their salvation through sufferings. For both He who sanctifies and those who are sanctified are all from one Father; for which reason He is not ashamed to call them brethren...**(Hebrews 2:10-11)

If we believe these words, why are we so surprised by fiery trials and suffering when they suddenly come into our lives? I hope by now we all know the answer to that question. Our flesh is that which recoils at suffering as if we do not deserve it, hating to be subjected to anything it cannot control. When suffering comes, we must know exactly what we believe and why we believe it so that we are able to crucify the flesh and submit to the Lord's will for our lives as He uses all things He calls us to endure for our good sanctification and His glory.

Trials teach us to trust as they drive us to depend on God. They purify us as we keep our eyes fixed on Jesus and the glory that awaits us. As Romans 5:3 says, they produce perseverance, proven character, and hope. All things *do* work together for our good and God's glory. How do we know? Because we were prepared *for* glory from the foundation of the world. **And He did so to make known the riches of His glory upon vessels of mercy, which He prepared beforehand for glory...** (Romans 9:23) And glory was prepared for us. 1 Corinthians 2:9 says we cannot even imagine what God has prepared for those who love Him.

"...to those who by perseverance in doing good seek for glory and honor and immortality, eternal life..." (Romans 2:7) As we keep our eyes focused on Christ through His Word, relying on His Spirit to change us, each step in the sanctification process molds us and shapes us little by little into the perfection of Christ's own glory. **But we all, with unveiled face, beholding as in a mirror the glory of the Lord, are being transformed into the same image from glory to glory, just as from the Lord, the Spirit.** (2 Corinthians 3:18) Even our bodies will be newly fitted for eternity when we enter His glory. **...who will transform the body of our humble state into conformity with the body of His glory...** (Philippians 3:21)

In every way imaginable, living in glory will mean complete freedom to live the life we were created to live before the Fall. Our position in Christ guarantees our salvation with no condemnation from God. The Almighty Judge who reigns over all has declared to each believer, "There is now no condemnation for you!" (Romans 8:1) Every believer is free from the **penalty of sin**. (Romans 8:2-4) Jesus, the believer's Substitute, defeated sin on the cross by bearing the condemnation of all the elect.

Believers are free from the power of sin. While the Law could detect sin, it could not defeat sin. While living in a body of flesh, Jesus perfectly fulfilled the righteous Law of God; therefore, the power of sin in the believer has been broken. Obedience to the Spirit is the mark of every believer (Romans 8:5-8). And the believer is free to walk in righteousness.

Where do you set your mind? That simple question will reveal whether you walk by the flesh or the Spirit. We must never forget that our minds are the battleground where the flesh and the Spirit war against each other. The flesh does not want to be crucified and surrender to the lordship of Christ, so it fights hard against the Spirit. It is only through the Spirit's power that we are enabled to subdue the flesh. (Romans 8:9-15)

God's children are led by God's Spirit. The test of sonship is determined by whether this leading of God's Spirit is evident in one's life. The Spirit leads the sons of God to repentance, to holiness, to truth, to love, to service, etc. These are the new desires of our hearts because we have a great Father whom we love *because* He first loved us. God's children know who they are because the

Spirit bears witness to this fact. As His children, we are called to share in His suffering. We will also share in His inheritance and His glory. In fact, sharing in His suffering is a condition for sharing in His glory. We do not get the crown without the cross. (Romans 8:16-18)

The glory that is to come far outweighs the suffering of this life, which is short and fleeting, compared to eternity. It's all about perspective. The excruciating pains of childbirth are nothing compared to what lies at the end of that birth. All creation was subject to the curse of the Fall. All trees, flowers, plants, insects, and animals can fall prey to disease, and all eventually die. God's purpose in creation was that it would last forever with no death, no sickness, and no suffering. For now, all creation eagerly awaits the day when all things will be made new, and God's purposes in creation will be fulfilled. (Romans 8:19-22)

The first fruit of the season that appears on the tree gives the farmer hope that there is more to come. While we groan knowing the sin that remains in us, we can endure the suffering of this world by faith with perseverance because of the first fruits of the Spirit. With His Spirit dwelling inside us, we can anticipate, with complete certainty, the day when we will be like Christ. (Romans 8:23-25)

Christ lives to make intercession for the saints. Likewise, we are told the Spirit intercedes for us when we do not know how to pray. Undoubtedly, one of the hardest disciplines in the Christian life is prayer. This is a verse that should give us great hope. How often do we come to the throne of grace to pray and become painfully aware of our failure to know God's will and how to petition Him specifically with assurance for any given request? But the Holy Spirit knows God's will and can perfectly express those petitions accordingly. How often have you prayed for something and, in retrospect, have been grateful He *didn't* answer the prayer the way you wanted at the time? (Romans 8:26-27)

God sacrificed His own dearly beloved Son—for me. Oh, there can be no doubt! After God has given us His greatest gift, His most valuable treasure, why would He not give us all things of lesser value? He will finish what He started when He set His love upon me. He will bring me all the way home to glory!

Suffering, Separation, and Sanctification

I had a great uncle 'Bug' who had a brother named 'Boog'. Bug's real name was Virgil. Uncle Bug lived alone up in the mountains of Pennsylvania in a one-room cabin his whole life. With no running water or electricity, an outhouse was his 'lavatory' come the heat of summer or the sub-zero temperatures of winter.

A weekend retreat, my grandparents' cabin was about a half mile from Uncle Bug's cabin. Inching along the narrow, heavily-rutted, weed-covered road, we would start yelling, "Yoo-hoo!" to signal we were getting close to them. We knew we were very close when we heard, "Yoo-hoo!" echoing back at us.

I questioned Uncle Bug's sanity for choosing to live the way he did. My grandmother told me he was a 'hermit'. Visiting my grandparents in the summer, I would swing in the hammock, look up at the sky, and ponder why anyone would want to live as a hermit. This secluded haven in the mountains *was* peaceful and refreshing, but I was always ready to go home. It was just too separated from the rest of the world. Naturally, I considered the dangers of having no neighbors, no phone to call anyone, and no protection but a shotgun. Yet, my parents let us roam freely down to the creek or deep into the woods without fear of any real danger.

We usually spent extended stays on the mountain in our camper. But on one rare occasion, we slept in my grandparents' cabin. In the mountains, when the lantern went out, it was so dark one could not even see her finger in front of her face. Except for night sounds of katydids, crickets, and the intermittent 'hoo hoo hooooooo' of the lonely hoot owl, it was eerily quiet. It took me a long time to go to sleep, even with my parents in the bed next to me. One day, someone burned down my grandparents' cabin and several others a mile or so away down the road. Uncle Bug could see the fires from his place, but he could do nothing. I was devastated by the loss.

I knew I would never want to live alone, but I didn't know at the time that God never intended anyone to live like that—a man on his island. What type of person chooses a life sentence in voluntary, solitary confinement? I was intrigued by Uncle Bug;

nevertheless, I kept my distance from him because he was so different. Some people enjoy being by themselves. I get that. I saw that same tendency in my grandmother and my mother. Sometimes, there's a little 'Bug' in me, too.

To get away occasionally from the hustle and bustle of life is necessary. I can still smell the crisp, fresh mountain air, the smoke from my grandfather's pipe, and even the outhouse. I can imagine lying on the dusty, old burlap hammock swinging back and forth, using the old carnival cane wedged up against a root in the ground to push myself as I stare at the towering trees overhead. The voice of 'The Gunner', (Bob Prince), the announcer for the Pittsburgh Pirates' game mingles with static on the old transistor radio in the background fading in and out. The mountain teaberries are sweet to the taste and free for the picking. When I remember the ice-cold waters of the creek where we played, the smell of moss on the trees flanking its banks floods my nostrils. In my mind's eye, I see the old tire swing hung from the towering oak tree swaying by the plank board shed—seemingly remembering the delight it provided to carefree children. Sometimes, getting away *is* refreshing.

Obviously, prison was a shock to my system for many reasons. Lonely and separated from the ones I love most, I was surrounded with people 24/7. With no peace, no quiet, and no privacy—ever—I could understand the need to live a 'Bug's' life. And yet, even among 800-1,200 women, I *did* sometimes feel as though I was living like a woman on an island. Then, there was the vital, desperate need to find that 'alone' time with the Lord amidst all the pandemonium of prison life—time that did not belong to me. But those times of intimate fellowship with Jesus were some of the sweetest I have ever known. I was alone with Him while living in very close proximity to hundreds of other women.

When my friend first asked me to speak in the 'Separation and Divorce' class that she facilitated, I could only relate the word *separation* to the beginning-of-the-end of a marriage relationship. I balked at her request, but she persisted by asking me to pray about it. Later, in my cube with pen and paper I prayed, "Lord, please show me what I could possibly share with these women about separation that would glorify You." And I started writing. It did not take long to see that I could relate the gospel to these women through this idea of separation. In the instances of separation in my own life, I began to relate those times to feelings and emotions of great pain, loneliness, and mental anguish. Death, rejection, failed relationships, prison, and even timeouts as a child—all of these involve some sort of separation *in our relationships*.

My earliest recollections of separation were timeouts. We had a tiny wicker chair my mom put in the corner. When we got in trouble, we were told to go sit in the corner facing the wall. It was torture! Later, there was separation in what I perceived as 'rejection' by various friends throughout my life. Death, prison, and even good things like my son going off to college far away from home, were occasions when separation caused me pain and suffering. (We play separation anxiety music for my puppy when we leave him alone!)

Why did we experience more pain in some situations than others? We were created to love, fellowship, and know oneness with God and with others as eternal beings who long for lasting relationships. As we grow in intimacy with one another, our hearts begin to beat as one. Thus, the greater the love, the greater the pain felt when those two hearts experience separation.

Separation sometimes results from experiencing punishment such as timeouts as children—and certainly prison. But what about a different type of punishment? Have you ever received the cold shoulder or the silent treatment from someone? This separation is meant to punish and often to manipulate. Sometimes a wife in a disagreement with her husband will not only withdraw her *words* but *herself,* physically withholding affection and intimacy. This form of punishment is hurtful because it is received as conditional rejection. "If I please you, then you want to commune with me. If I don't please you, then you withdraw your love." Mature adults in a relationship *communicate* to get back to loving *communion*!

When my middle son went away to college across the country, the separation was painful. Just like all children who eventually leave home, that separation is normal and can be used by God for radical growth in the lives of all loved ones involved. Separation teaches us to lean on God, to trust Him for the lives of those we love, and to be our Comforter and Sustainer in suffering. Suffering separation from those we love is also a good reminder that God is our all in all, and that He will always be our constant source of satisfaction and joy. No human being can or should ever fill the place in our hearts that He alone can fill.

The pain of separation became a reality when sin entered the world. Immediately after Adam and Eve sinned, *they* hid themselves from God. (Genesis 3:8-10). Later, God removed them from the Garden—from that paradise He had created where they could live and enjoy His presence. Isolating them from the tree of life, He did not want them to live forever in their fallen condition. The tree of life would have sustained Adam's life in a physical sense—and in his sinful state—for all eternity. In God's mercy, He kept Adam and Eve away from the tree of life shortening the lifespan of man.

The way the world views death, it is a shock when encountered up close and personally. The fight for longevity in this life can be seen literally everywhere. For some, it is ***the focus*** of all life. Believers, however, should never look at death the same way the world does. Death, for the believer, is release from this cursed world. A precious, sacred moment between us, I shared some mutually encouraging truth I had read with my mother just before she died. It was something stated along these lines: Physical death for the believer is an easier transition than spiritual death to spiritual life when that one is born again. When a believer dies, she just wakes up in God's presence to continue living the eternal life she began living when she was saved. At that time, she will be free from sin and all its evil consequences. When the doctors walked into the room to tell my family there was nothing more they could do for her, my mother looked at me and said, "I get to see Jesus first!"

Adam and Eve sinned and hid themselves from holy God. They had known freedom from sin and, thus, understood how much they had lost. Suddenly, they must have known a sick feeling, as their thoughts became dark. We, on the other hand, are born into sin. When we are saved, Christ's righteousness is imputed to us and our *position* is right as He is righteous. *Practically,* we are a mess; and God begins the work of sanctification in our hearts. We only know how far short we have fallen the holier we become. The longer we are Christians, the more wretched we become in our own eyes, because the longer we are Christians, the longer our eyes have been focused on Christ. As He sanctifies us, that picture continues to get clearer and clearer. The reality of being instantly made like Him one day in glory should fill us with jubilation, awe, and wonder. **Beloved, now we are children of God, and it has not appeared as yet what we will be. We know that when He appears, we will be like Him, because we will see Him just as He is. And everyone who has this hope fixed on Him purifies himself, just as He is pure.** (1 John 3:2-3)

It is hard to fathom losing what Adam and Eve had before the Fall. Positionally, believers are holy and will never know separation from God. Waking up in prison in the middle of the night wondering for a dazed moment if I was in hell, eternally separated from the love of God—was a sick feeling akin to the moment I realized my beloved daughter was gone. I can only explain it as feelings of utter despair and dark waves crashing over my soul.

When God drove Adam and Eve out of the Garden—a merciful act—it was discipline for their own good. Think about the separation of Cain who offered false worship to God, obviously having no love for God nor regard for His holiness. God offered Him the grace of forgiveness should he choose to repent of those actions coming from his wicked heart. Cain chose sin, stubbornly resisting God's grace and refusing His love. God told Cain that he would then live as a vagrant and a wanderer on the earth. He replied: **"My punishment is too great to bear! Behold, You have driven me this day from the face of the ground; and from Your face I will be hidden, and I will be a vagrant and a wanderer on the earth, and whoever finds me will kill me."** (Genesis 4:13-14)

Had Cain's heart been repentant, the object of his first statement would have been God, not himself. It would have been a *plea to* God, rather than an *accusation against* God. It would have been Cain seeking God's mercy to forgive him for offending His holiness. But self—who loves self more than any other—is only thinking about self-protection and self-preservation, not self-denial. Cain does not want God but only what blessings God can offer him. Cain blames God when he says that it is God who has driven him from the face of the ground. Without God's protection, Cain is afraid for his own self. Cain *still* believes he is entitled to his best life now, lived his own way.

Eight years old, I witnessed the pain and agony my mother and grandparents experienced when my aunt died. I didn't understand death, but I understood what separation looked like. Aunt Gloria left behind a husband and three young boys. Two years later, my Aunt Deloris (Sis) had a baby girl who died at birth. When I was twelve, Uncle Jack, a police officer, who had also lost that baby girl, was killed in a high-speed police chase leaving my aunt and another three young boys behind. When I was 18, my first love, Pat Podlucky, was killed in a tractor trailer accident. Two of my first cousins died young. Death has taken from me cousins, uncles, aunts, grandparents, my beloved daughter, my father-in-law, and my mother. Acquainted with death from a young age, it has been a reality ever since. Death brings with it an awareness that there is something more than this life and that relationships were meant to last.

In the next six months after Pat died, I would supposedly 'get saved' and engaged to his brother, Greg. Within the next year, I was married and living six hours from the only home I had ever known, a very lonely newlywed expecting her first child. In his second year of college, Greg was often traveling on the weekends with the football team. With no friends or family, I stayed home reading my Bible. We lived in a modest one-bedroom apartment with one other room that was everything else.

Our first Christmas together, I was towards the end of my first pregnancy, so we had thought it unwise to travel the six plus hours to go home for the holidays. We could not afford a tree, but one day after the other students had left for the holidays, we looked outside; and to our great delight, we saw lying in the dumpster a Christmas tree that someone had already used and discarded. We brought it in, put candy canes tied up with little red pieces of yarn all over it, and my husband ingeniously made a tree topper star out of a toilet paper holder and aluminum foil. Baking cookies the night before Christmas Eve, however, we knew something was not right. The next morning, we put the cookies in the car and drove straight home. To everyone's great surprise, we walked in the door to sit down for Christmas Eve dinner at Greg's grandpap's house with all his immediate and extended family. There was joy all around the table, and we were home with people who loved us.

Divorce was something I was not familiar with until I was a little older. The thoughts of divorce, from my perspective as a child, gave me a sinking pit in my stomach like that of death. Similarly, I knew of only one person from our community who went to prison. I did *not* love hearing the details of his circumstances because it made me sad for his family. People everywhere today are intrigued by incarceration as evidenced by many popular television shows documenting prison life.

Webster's Dictionary defines the word *separation* 'to set or keep apart, to make a distinction between, to set aside for a special purpose, to dedicate, to sever contractual relations with, to isolate from a mixture, or to divide'. Some form of the word is represented in the Old and New Testaments by many different words.

In several places in the book of Numbers, the word *separation* is used in making some reference to a Nazarite. The word **nezer** is defined as consecration, crown as a sign of consecration, woman's hair, or dedicated, among other things. One verse reveals the use of two different Hebrew words with a similar meaning. **All the days of his separation he is holy to the LORD.** (Numbers 6:8) Here, *separation* is **nezer** and *holy* is **qadowsh** which means sacred or holy, Holy One, saint, or set apart. *Consecrate* in Numbers 6:11 means to sanctify, prepare, dedicate, be hallowed, be holy, be sanctified, or be separate. The Nazarite was under a 'Law of Separation'. (Numbers 6:21) The Nazarite was an individual who voluntarily took a vow dedicating or yielding himself completely to God—always involving sacrifice. We see this word used is in Isaiah 59:2—**But your iniquities have made a separation between you and your God, and your sins have hidden His face from you so that He does not hear**. In this verse, *separation* means to divide, sever, set apart, to make a distinction, difference, to separate oneself from, to withdraw from, or to be excluded. We can see that this word can be used in a negative or positive sense depending upon the context of the verse.

Separation is used in the creation account in Genesis when God separated light from darkness. In Numbers, God wanted the Levites to be distinct from the Israelites. It is used several places in the book of Ezekiel when it speaks about the separate areas in the temple—separate areas for distinct purposes and distinct people. Matthew 19:6, speaking of marriage, says: **So, they are no longer two, but one flesh. What therefore God has joined together, let no man separate.** No man is to separate what God has joined because they are now one flesh. Genesis 2:24—**For this reason, a man shall leave his father and his mother, and be joined to his wife; and they shall become one flesh.** A different version uses *hold fast* to his wife or *cleave* to his wife. It essentially means 'glued' to his spouse—'*super* (naturally) *glued*' together as one entity. Notice it is God who has joined the two in matrimony. God takes marriage very seriously. Deuteronomy 13:4 uses the same phrase for our relationship with Him but uses the word *cling:* **You shall follow the LORD your God and fear Him; and you shall keep His commandments, listen to His voice, serve Him, and cling to Him.**

A similar definition for *separation* is associated with the word *sanctify* used in some verses: **Sanctify them in the truth; Your word is truth.** (John 17:17) **Therefore, Jesus also, that He might sanctify the people through His own blood, suffered outside the gate.** (Hebrews 13:12) *Sanctify* is **hagiazo,** which is to cleanse, to purify, or to make holy. It means to separate from profane things and dedicate to God.

I have always believed God *allows* His children to go through times of suffering as seen in the life of Job. We obviously know what good came from Jesus' suffering on the cross—His death was clearly ordained by God. Was prison ordained for me? What I *know* is that God is not the author of evil. He permits agents of evil to work, while sovereignly ruling over that evil and using it for His holy purposes. He works all the evil formed against His children together for their good. It has been said: God **causes some things;** God **allows other things**; and, God **controls all things**. I'll leave it at that. Sitting with paper and pen in my cube, the little Greek I have learned over the years began to flash like a neon sign across my mind. I knew the word *sanctify (sanctification)* had a similar meaning to the word for *separated*. Could it be God was using my suffering separation in prison to sanctify me? The only question I had in my mind before prison was: As a Christian, when should I separate myself from people or situations?

As a child naturally grows up to maturity, so should a babe in Christ become more like Him as she grows. Is a child's maturity gained by her parents shrouding her from all danger that may come from her own choices or circumstances? Is it from failing to test and prove her? A good parent allows her child to suffer and learn from her mistakes and to work out difficult circumstances to further her maturity. And a good parent knows that all a child has learned will undoubtedly need to be tested at some point.

I once wrongly equated head knowledge with sanctification. I was learning, ergo I was growing. We **must** learn in order to grow. However, Christian maturity can't be measured by how much we know. Knowledge must be tested and proved. I didn't enjoy taking tests in school, but tests prove what we *know* in the academic world. In the spiritual world, tests prove what we really *believe*. They also reveal to us areas where we are weak and need to grow.

Did you ever really consider why Jesus needed to suffer to save you? We ask God, sometimes directly or indirectly, why **we** must suffer. But do we all too easily accept as fact that Jesus had to suffer to save us from our sin and its effects? Are we quick to offer, "Well, that was just part of God's plan," and not really think about the depth of suffering He willingly submitted to for us? Do we really understand why He had to suffer?

How do we respond to someone else's suffering? Do we give pat answers acknowledging that all will suffer because sin entered the world? While that is true, that is the negative side of suffering. But, could there be a positive reason for my suffering? How, specifically, does God use my suffering for my good?

For it was fitting for Him, for whom are all things, and through whom are all things, in bringing many sons to glory, to perfect the author of their salvation through sufferings. (Hebrews 2:10) **Although He was a Son, He learned obedience from the things which He suffered. And having been made perfect, He became to all those who obey Him the source of eternal salvation, being designated by God as a high priest according to the order of Melchizedek.** (Hebrews 5:8-10) "And having been made perfect…" *Perfect* is **teleioo** which means to make complete, mature, to bring to the end proposed goal. If our perfect Lord learned obedience from the things which He suffered, surely, we need not question how God could allow us to endure suffering. Understanding our own depravity and our need to grow up, even times of testing make sense. Suffering is vital to our sanctification. It is not right that we should remain children in our thinking or our behavior.

Jesus didn't need to grow up in that sense; He was perfect. Jesus knew suffering—persecution, rejection, separation, pain, and more. He suffered more loss than we will ever know. We can't begin to comprehend what He willingly gave up when He came to earth to accomplish redemption for those whom the Father had elected to salvation. Suffering persecution at the hands of His own creation, He knew some of them would one day be given eyes to see Him as their Redeemer—those same ones the Father had set His love upon long before they were born. There were those who would hate Him and, led by the devil, try to hinder His work of redemption. He knew all the nuances of separation that we will ever know in this life.

Why do we seek out people who have gone through what we're going through in a trial? It's because there's that mutual fellowship of suffering we believe few others know or understand. When I think of comforts I might lack today, I remember that Jesus often didn't have a place to lay His head. The pain of walking through this sin-cursed world as perfect holiness knowing that it was not at all how He created it to be, would be devastating. Looking at my own children, knowing their lives don't look anything like what their father and I had dreamed for them, through no fault of their own, it hurts. That's when I must rest in the Father's good plan for them and consider Jesus, a man of sorrows, acquainted with grief.

Oh, what He suffered at the cross! All the types of suffering of any who would ever suffer were laid upon Him there. The sin of His children—the weight of it all—He bore on His shoulders as the Father poured out His wrath upon Him for that sin—none of it His own. The apex of all agonies, however, was when His Father, with whom He had known intimate, eternal fellowship, turned His face away from Him for the first and last time. As our great High Priest, there is nothing—no pain ever known to man—He does not know and understand experientially. I daily reminded myself in prison of what Jesus endured in this world. It helped me tremendously to know that He knew, understood, and had *experienced* whatever I was going through. When I was lonely, when unjustly accused and convicted, when friends and family did not believe in me, I knew He had experienced the same types of circumstances, and I rested in that realization.

Shortly after my husband was indicted, and the wrecking ball of that great trial started swinging towards us, I was praying one night when the thought that I needed to learn to be more compassionate popped into my mind. I loved the women God had put in my path as I prayed for them and taught them. But in that moment, I knew I needed to learn how to feel the pain of those who were hurting more fully, and I needed to learn to offer myself to them in my own vulnerability. Ministry was never meant to be glamorous. It is often messy and humbling. I needed to learn how to minister to those who were face down in the sin-infected cesspool of this world, humiliated, ashamed, and broken—those who could not feel or display anything but raw, real emotions. What *cannot* be learned by reading a book is: "I've been there." **Blessed be the God and Father of our Lord Jesus Christ, the Father of mercies and God of all comfort, who comforts us in all our affliction so that we will be able to comfort those who are in any affliction with the comfort with which we ourselves are comforted by God.** (2 Corinthians 1:3-4)

The way of the cross is grueling, agonizing, bloody, and anything but glamorous. Yet, some modern-day 'churches' wrongly teach that you can have your best life now. That *is true* if you are destined for hell! They also say that God doesn't want you to be poor, sick, or suffering. The smoke and mirrors they display portray Christianity as a regal walk to the crown, not a walk to the cross of death following in the footsteps of our dear Lord.

As an impressionable, 'new believer' in Christ, I went with a group of members from the church to which I belonged to visit another member in the hospital. The poor man on the bed was in agony with excruciating back pain (a pain I know well today). The members accused him of hidden sin they were certain 'must be' contributing to his suffering, coaxing him to repent and be delivered from the demon that was causing his turmoil. I experienced an eerily similar situation in prison while suffering horrendous back spasms. A side bunkie showed up in my cube wanting to rebuke a 'demon in me' and help me 'let go of the burden of sin' she was convinced I was carrying. (Just the simple fact that she showed up beside me after 'lights out' because she smelled the back rub I had applied before going to bed was creepy enough.) This is *not* biblical Christianity!

Jesus was the suffering servant of Isaiah 53. He knew experientially any suffering those He came to serve would endure. We look to Him as the model of perfect obedience in His suffering. In His journey to the cross, He kept His focus on the Father knowing He could deliver Him from it if He chose to do so. We must remember this as well. If God chooses **not** to deliver us in the way we think He should, God is still God, and His purpose is greater in sustaining us *through* the suffering than delivering us *from* it.

When the Bible speaks of Christ learning obedience, R.C. Sproul says John Owen's comments on the passage in Hebrews 5 are helpful. Owens says it is talking about *experiencing* obedience. According to Owen: "One special kind of obedience is intended here, namely a submission to great, hard, and terrible things, accompanied by patience and quiet endurance, and faith for deliverance from them. This, Christ could not have experience of, except by suffering the things he had to pass through, exercising God's grace in them all." Dr. Sproul says that, essentially, Owens meant that though the Son, prior to the Incarnation, knew what obedience would involve theoretically, He gained full experiential knowledge of obedience only when He endured the Cross.[1]

When Jesse was 10 years old, he was extremely disappointed when he made the AA hockey team instead of the AAA team. Let's just say he didn't handle very gracefully what he viewed as a major defeat. (I think there may have been some hyperventilating and throwing up in the parking lot.) He didn't want to hear that God had a plan. Shortly thereafter, I had my mother embroider a blanket for him with this Scripture: **And not only this, but we also exult in our tribulations, knowing that tribulation brings about perseverance; and perseverance, proven character; and proven character, hope; and hope does not disappoint, because the love of God has been poured out within our hearts through the Holy Spirit who was given to us.** (Romans 5:3-5) Jesse grew as a hockey player on that AA team and went on in later years to be an All-Star player, one who played amateur travel hockey. The Lord exulted him in His time, but he had to learn to suffer loss. Later, when he played on his college hockey team, he missed several practices due to his sister's death so that he could be there for his family for different events, one major event being a move to another home. For this choice, he was benched indefinitely. It was heartbreaking to watch him go through this trial, but he handled it with grace and strength. The Scripture on his hockey blanket was, indeed, truth known experientially.

Paul knew of the walk to the cross. In Philippians 3, he says he had counted all things as loss in view of the surpassing value of knowing Christ for whom he had suffered the loss of all things. James says, **Consider it all joy, my brethren, when you encounter various trials, knowing that the testing of your faith produces endurance. And let endurance have its perfect result, so that you may be perfect and complete, lacking in nothing.** (James 1:2-4) Interestingly, the word for *perfect* used for the Christian whose faith is proved through trials, is the same Greek word used for perfecting Jesus in Hebrews 2:10. No doubt, suffering is one of the primary ways God sanctifies His children. And suffering loss usually involves some sort of separation.

We were created for union, unity, oneness, fellowship, and community. The Lord's body, the Church, is a called out people He is putting together for Himself. We see unity in marriages, families as units of people related by blood, or who are bound together by law. And we see unity in the church between brothers and sisters in Christ. We even see it in unhealthy relationships like gangs. People want to belong; they want to fit in somewhere.

Most women in prison professed to believe in some sort of 'higher power' or were involved with some sort of spiritual enterprise. In some religions, their adherents exclusively participated in their own ceremonies. But under the label of 'Christianity', the spectrum of participants was broad. This wildly diverse group of women marched into chapel almost every time the doors were open singing something akin to the song, "We Are Family". As they dispersed after services, even before they were out the door, the cursing, sexual escapades, and all sorts of lewd behavior would resurface. These *same* women read their Bibles and even quoted Scripture. I had many invitations to join in with them. And some just couldn't understand why I had no desire to participate.

One woman I was discipling begged me to go to a service with her. Exasperated, she finally said, "At least go with me and tell me what is wrong with it!" It was an old Baptist preacher, so I agreed.

How bad could it be? On our way out of the building, she was ready to burst. "Well, what did you think of it?" I simply said, "I won't be going back." She was frustrated. The preaching was your average feel-good message with one missing component glaring back at me from the podium. The true gospel. Not the, "Jesus has a wonderful plan for your life", false gospel. That was there in full regalia amid all the "Amen, Brother! Preach it!" outbursts of affirmation. The next day I handed her several pages of notes on why what we heard was not sound teaching.

We had a couple extra hours of quite time on Sunday mornings. Most girls slept in until count. Gloriously quiet, I woke up early to spend that precious time in prayer and the Word. My dear friend from the previous story (who lived in another range), wanted me to listen to the same sermons and church services she was listening to on her radio. There is very little accessibility for Christian fellowship in prison—fellowship for which she was starving. Wanting to be able to talk about what she was learning, she needed to know I was listening to the same sermons. When I told her I had not listened that week because I had desperately needed my quiet time with the Lord, she was disappointed.

We worked together in the chapel for awhile, eagerly searching the Scriptures together and talking for hours on end. She would bring people to me even when I was working out in the gym to have me tell them about Jesus. My friend went to the head guard over the chapel and begged her to let us have a Bible study on the compound; the request was denied, even though inmates taught many other religious studies. It was clear there was no room for authentic Christianity.

One day my friend ran into work excited about a new book she had received entitled *Strange Fire,* by John MacArthur.[2] Exceedingly relevant to the spiritual atmosphere of our prison, we devoured this book as we discussed it together. We each got several copies and passed them around the compound. It was a sad day for both of us when she got transferred to a new job dramatically cutting our time together. However, there is a bond between us that's eternal because we are sisters in Christ.

She left several months before I did. My Christian friends on the 'outside' found a church for her to attend once she got home.

After I was released, I found out, unbeknownst to me at the time, the pastor of the church had been my Facebook 'friend' for years. He was a graduate of the seminary affiliated with John MacArthur. She had been attending for only a short while when she told me, "I get it!" She later gave her testimony and was baptized in her new church. I love this dear lady and know that we were put in each other's lives providentially by the Lord. Her sweet presence in my life in prison was one way He affirmed His presence to me.

We know that Christian unity is based upon shared life in Christ. But we cannot join in spiritual enterprises with everyone who calls themselves a Christian. Mutual alignment with the true Gospel must be the determining factor for joining in ministry with anyone who professes to follow Christ. Vital to a true profession of faith is that one is justified by grace through faith in Christ alone apart from works. Defining or clarifying the true gospel is a major theme in every one of Paul's letters. In 2 Corinthians, the apostle presents a clear picture of how an understanding of the true gospel will naturally affect our relationships. The fact that the gospel is so radically opposed to human thinking *should* naturally cause divisions in the realm of our spiritual enterprises.

Do not be bound together with unbelievers; for what partnership have righteousness and lawlessness, or what fellowship has light with darkness? Or what harmony has Christ with Belial, or what has a believer in common with an unbeliever? Or what agreement has the temple of God with idols? For we are the temple of the living God; just as God said, "I WILL DWELL IN THEM AND WALK AMONG THEM; AND I WILL BE THEIR GOD, AND THEY SHALL BE MY PEOPLE." "Therefore, COME OUT FROM THEIR MIDST AND BE SEPARATE," says the Lord. "AND DO NOT TOUCH WHAT IS UNCLEAN; and I will welcome you. And I will be a father to you, and you shall be sons and daughters to Me," says the Lord Almighty. (2 Corinthians 6:14-18) In Revelation 18:4, God calls His people out of the false religious system of the end days. In the end, we see what appears to be a one world church. God's people have always been called to separate from false teachers and false religious systems. There is no place there to negotiate, for the distinction between truth and error (especially regarding the gospel), is sharply divided.

Called to be separate, believers are not to be unequally bound with unbelievers. What this means needs to be understood. The word *bound* is **heterozygeo** which means to come under an unequal or different yoke, to have fellowship with one who is not an equal. The definition of this Greek word specifically references this passage saying: "speaking in 2 Corinthians 6:14 where the apostle is forbidding Christians to have intercourse with idolaters." *Say what?*

Many passages of Scripture use terminology relating to what is known as spiritual adultery. *Adultery* is used by the Lord as a metaphor for sin committed by His children when they love other gods more than Him. This sin especially grieves His heart. It is basically being spiritually unfaithful to God. A main theme in the book of Hosea, we see the same metaphor all throughout the Old Testament. Israel is God's wife; the church is the bride of Christ. **"Surely, as a woman treacherously departs from her lover, so you have dealt treacherously with Me, O house of Israel," declares the Lord.** (Jeremiah 3:20)

As His bride, when the church dabbles in spiritual idolatry, she betrays her Belove just like a wife who commits the sin of adultery against her husband in marriage. All these scriptures are talking about joining together for purposes relating to spiritual enterprises, or joining together for ministry purposes. My kids grew up in a world of hockey. My sons would never intentionally pass the puck to one who is wide open on the opposite team. That would not be logical. They are only going to intentionally pass to another team member who is working for a common goal!

You remember the illustration of two fellows in the same ship? While we are to have relationships with unbelievers, we can have no partnership in a spiritual endeavor. It would be like two sailors in that same ship (boat) both with oars. One sailor is a believer and one is not. Spiritually speaking, both men are rowing in opposite directions. Their working together is futile, unproductive, and dangerous. More than that, it is sin in God's eyes.

Spiritual discernment literally means 'cutting it straight'. It is the *separation* of thoughts into two categories—truth and error. Today's lack of discernment is seen in 'ecumenism'. Ecumenism is "the principle or aim of promoting unity among the world's Christian churches" according to Oxford Dictionary. Ecumenism is a compromise with error where there needs to be separation. Ecumenism is intentionally blurring all the dividing lines for the purpose of fellowship and some sort of unity. But true unity can never be realized when the entities are working against each other. For spiritual unity to be realized, two parties must embrace the one true gospel of Jesus Christ. Otherwise, you have two radically different kingdoms working against each other. **You adulteresses, do you not know that friendship with the world is hostility toward God? Therefore, whoever wishes to be a friend of the world makes himself an enemy of God.** (James 4:4)

The Bible says the whole world lies in the power of the evil one. The Church in every age is tempted to love and be conformed to the *image of the world*. Our flesh is tempted to lean towards the world, but the indwelling Spirit pulls us toward the heavenlies where Christ is seated at the right hand of the Father. Enticing us with lies, deceitfully shrouded in sparkling delights, all the world offers us is intended to woo us away from our Lord. But just as cubic zirconia glistens and shows like a diamond to the undiscerning eye, it is not what it appears to be. All the world offers us is worthless compared to the glories of eternity promised to those in Christ. When we embrace the world's standards and impulses, we are forsaking the one who gave His life to save us from that very system. Believers are given a command in 1 John 2:15 that we are not to love the world or the things of the world. God has established a difference and distinction between saved and unsaved, and that difference should be obvious. The Bible tells us how to avoid spiritual adultery. Colossians 3:2 says we are to set our **minds** on the things above, not on the things that are on earth.

To what extent does the believer go in maintaining or pursuing this separation from the world? Some who profess Christ go to the extreme of not drawing any lines of distinction at all. They live among the world and look like the world, yet they profess to be a follower of Christ. Likewise, there are many who profess Christ and go to an extreme in their understanding of what it means to live separated lives—they separate themselves to the extent that they have no influence over anyone who doesn't know Christ. We are called to be separated, but not isolated.

If scripture *was* calling us to cloister ourselves away in isolation from unbelievers, the irony of being tossed into prison would be a very bitter pill for me to swallow, especially in light of viewing my circumstances as God's providence for my good and His glory. Biblical separation cannot mean that we are to live like the world *or* in a Christian bubble. Jesus was a friend to sinners. He ate with them and walked among them. It was the self-righteous Pharisees who condemned Jesus for befriending those they deemed to be the outcasts and the socially unacceptable.

There was a member of the church in Corinth in 1 Corinthians 5 who was living in grave sin. Paul exhorted *the congregation* to repent of *their* sin of not dealing with this man. They had tolerated his sin by looking the other way. Paul was upset with *them*! He said they should have removed him from their midst practicing church discipline. If he was unrepentant, church discipline would have led to putting him outside the church where he would not have been protected spiritually. Paul had judged him and delivered him over to Satan for the destruction of his flesh. **I wrote you in my letter not to associate with immoral people; I did not at all mean with the immoral people of this world, or with the covetous and swindlers, or with idolaters, for then you would have to go out of the world. But actually, I wrote to you not to associate with any so-called brother if he is an immoral person, or covetous, or an idolater, or a reviler, or a drunkard, or a swindler—not even to eat with such a one. For what have I to do with judging outsiders? Do you not judge those who are within the church? But those who are outside, God judges. REMOVE THE WICKED MAN FROM AMONG YOURSELVES.** (1 Corinthians 5:9-13) This should have been a Matthew 18 situation. We are not to associate (share in spiritual enterprises, ministering together, worshiping together, fellowshipping together) with people who profess to follow Christ but who live like they follow Satan. The congregation knew of the man's sinful lifestyle. When Paul says we are not to associate with an immoral person, the covetous, etc., he is talking about people who practice sin as a lifestyle but still profess to follow Christ. When confronted, these are those who remain unrepentant.

This disassociation is a distinct process. Matthew 18 situations call for church discipline which is a process that does not happen overnight. Church discipline is the responsibility of the church for the sake of the purity of the Lord's bride because bad company corrupts good morals. *Always*, one of the main purposes for church discipline—in calling the one living in a sinful lifestyle to repentance, and calling for separation until repentance takes place—is the restoration of fellowship with God and the body. The church is to act in love with gentleness and kindness. We shouldn't go into attack mode because someone doesn't have a complete understanding of something. Viewing the social media pages of some Christians, you would think they have never heard of the verses in 2 Timothy 2:24-26: **The Lord's bondservant must not be quarrelsome, but be kind to all, able to teach, patient when wronged, with gentleness correcting those who are in opposition, if perhaps God may grant them repentance leading to the knowledge of the truth, and they may come to their senses and escape from the snare of the devil, having been held captive by him to do his will.**

Not being unequally yoked applies to Christians in marriage as well. A believer is not to marry an unbeliever because the goal and purpose of Christians is to honor and glorify Christ in all things. Marriage is a spiritual enterprise because it is a ministry. A believer and an unbeliever cannot work together for the same goal of glorifying God through their marriage.

What do we do about the gray areas of life where we live day to day? We are to live in the world while not letting the world influence us, so we must be on guard and have our minds renewed with truth continually. We are to shine the light of the gospel into all the world as an influence for His Kingdom. We are to live pursuing holiness in all things. There will be things we cannot do and places we cannot go. We will make those choices based on whether it will glorify Christ and help us grow or lead us away from Him. As in prison for me, sometimes the separation happens quite naturally.

Romans 8:1 says: **Therefore there is now no condemnation for those who are in Christ Jesus.** I have stood a condemned convict before men. But God is working even that together for my good. All things are *not* working together for good for everyone—only for those who are *in Christ*. God is for His children. **What then shall we say to these things? If God is for us, who is against us?** (Romans 8:31) '*These things*' are all He has done to secure our being joined together with Him in Christ. Men can and do betray us. They may put together complicated, diabolical schemes to come against us. But look at the great lengths to which God has gone to make us part of His own beloved family. Because God Almighty is for us, what does it really matter who is against us? God is for me now and forever. **He who did not spare His own Son, but delivered Him over for us all, how will He not also with Him freely give us all things? Who will bring a charge against God's elect? God is the one who justifies; who is the one who condemns? Christ Jesus is He who died, yes, rather who was raised, who is at the right hand of God, who also intercedes for us.** (Romans 8:32-34)

Who will separate us from the love of Christ? Will tribulation, or distress, or persecution, or famine, or nakedness, or peril, or sword? Just as it is written, "FOR YOUR SAKE WE ARE BEING PUT TO DEATH ALL DAY LONG; WE WERE CONSIDERED AS SHEEP TO BE SLAUGHTERED." But in all these things we overwhelmingly conquer through Him who loved us. For I am convinced that neither death, nor life, nor angels, nor principalities, nor things present, nor things to come, nor powers, nor height, nor depth, nor any other created thing, will be able to separate us from the love of God, which is in Christ Jesus our Lord. (Romans 8:35-39) There is absolutely nothing that can separate the believer from the love of God which is in Christ Jesus our Lord. Here, we see a picture of covenant. The word *separate* or **chorizo** is used two times in these verses. The definition uses another word we used to hear more often in wedding ceremonies. This word for *separation* means to put *asunder*, to separate one's self from, to depart, to leave a husband or wife, divorce, to depart, to go away. What God has joined together, let no man put asunder. Basically, God has joined Himself to every believer, and nothing can ever separate us from Him.

He saved us while we were sinners (enemies of God), knowing that we would continue to sin. Unlike human relationships, we can trust He will not reject us when we behave in ways that are not pleasing to Him. Our loving Father may discipline us as His children, but He will never love us less. Nothing inside us or outside us can separate us from His love, because it is not our love for Him that secures us but His love for us.

When tragedy or trials come suddenly—when it feels as though the earth is shifting and you are being shaken to your very core—when you can't imagine how you will be able to go on living in your present state—when life changes dramatically causing you fear and doubts—you need to have something to hold onto. Romans 8 is one passage that will anchor your soul securely. What you will realize is that there is One who holds *you* so you will not stumble so as to fall. We will win in Christ in the end. We win now, too. Trials are win-win situations for the believer. Our faith and love for Him grow as we see how He brings us through each trial; then, we look back and see the blessings we gained in the process of having gone through the trial. In eternity, we will see how our suffering glorified Him. We overwhelmingly conquer in Christ!

Whatever the trial, by faith, *not by feelings*, we must always come back to standing firmly on the foundation of God's love for us. If you know that Christ died for you, then you can also know that God loves you, and *nothing* can separate you from that love. He has made me one with Him. For Christ to separate Himself from me would mean that the Father made a mistake when He chose me. Dare I even go so far as to say that it would be like the Father separating Himself from the Son.

People will often separate themselves from us. We sometimes need to separate ourselves from people in certain situations. We are a separated people *by* God and *for* God—set apart for His holy purposes. While we will undoubtedly know pain of separation in this life, we can also know for certain that a day is coming when there will be no more separation. We will only know life as it was intended to be: **Then I saw a new heaven and a new earth; for the first heaven and the first earth passed away, and there is no longer any sea. And I saw the holy city, new Jerusalem, coming down out of heaven from God, made ready as a bride adorned for her husband. And I heard a loud voice from the throne, saying, "Behold, the tabernacle of God is among men, and He will dwell among them, and they shall be His people, and God Himself will be among them, and He will wipe away every tear from their eyes; and there will no longer be any death; there will no longer be any mourning, or crying, or pain; the first things have passed away."** (Revelation 21:1-4)

Beyond the Veil

In the Middle Ages, kings and lords hung massive tapestries in their cold stone castles to help keep heat contained in smaller rooms. Because these exquisite tapestries also told a story, they were decorative, as well as functional. For centuries, Christian authors have been correlating the idea of tapestries to God's providence over our suffering. Some have stressed the Weaver's need for the dark threads, representing trials and tribulations, as much or *more* than the threads of gold and silver.

Years ago, my mother told me Christians grow more in valleys than on mountaintops. Growing up in a valley, that still did not make sense to me; but she was right, as usual. Geography and I do not go together. I had a telephone conversation with my father while incarcerated in Alderson, West Virginia, that illustrates my point. At Alderson FPC, mountains surrounded us, but we were also up on a hill. I told my father one evening how beautiful it was being on top of the mountain. He said, "Uh, Honey, you are not on a mountain; you are in the valley. Wait until you see the hills you have to climb when you leave there." Well, that was nothing short of prophetic!

> "Providence is like a curious piece of tapestry made of a thousand shreds, which, single, appear useless, but put together, they represent a beautiful history to the eye." – John Flavel, *Keeping the Heart: How to Maintain Your Love for God.*[1]

We sometimes say, "My life is in tatters," literally, torn to shreds. In this magnificent quote, John Flavel says the pieces of our broken lives *appear* useless. We may look at our current situation as life begins to unravel and be tempted to believe there is no hope. The fact that we can't see things as they really are threatens to undo us.

When my oldest son was two years old, I crocheted a king-size afghan. Climbing up beside me every evening while I worked, Jesse couldn't wait for 'the rainbow blanket' to be finished. One night, as I worked fastidiously on the last stripe, Jesse asked me once again,

"When will the blanket be done, Momma?" I told him it would be done in time for his Daddy's birthday, and that I was excited to see it on our bed. I barely noticed his countenance falling, but he didn't say another word before falling asleep. I worked long into the night.

The next evening as I began to work on the blanket, I shrieked, "Oh, no! What happened to my blanket?" A large cut ran up the finished end of the blanket. Jesse wouldn't look into my eyes, but only down at his feet. I asked, "Jesse, did you cut this blanket?" He replied in a timid yet matter-of-fact way, "Yes, I did." "But why, Jesse?" I begged. As he lifted his head with tears in his eyes, he said, "I thought you were making the blanket for *me*, Momma!"

I never did figure out how to salvage the blanket. To my eyes, it was hopeless. Beloved, our lives will never be like that blanket. Unfastened, loose threads threaten to fray and unravel the whole design *I may be working on*. But even when our circumstances appear hopeless, the loose threads of our lives are all secure and purposeful in the hands of the Master Weaver.

We don't see the whole picture now. Consequently, we *must* learn to walk by faith and not by sight. What we can see with our physical eyes is the underneath side of the tapestry with all its wildly-frazzled threads splayed out in all manner of disarray. But the Master Weaver is the God who sees all. He is intimately aware of the suffering of His chosen ones, none of it taking Him by surprise. He is Sovereign Lord over my life orchestrating every strand of thread for my good and His glory.

Our salvation is all His work in us. If we could grasp the value of our salvation in glorifying Him, we would never question the suffering He calls us to endure in this world. Eager to prove our love for Christ, we would surely "count it all joy when we encounter various trials" knowing that, as we abide in Him under the pressures of such trials, the testing of our faith produces maturity. That maturity brings deeper communion with Him and a more accurate reflection of Him to a watching world.

Instead, when trials come, our first response often betrays what we say we believe when we fall into temptation and respond like the world. Some who profess to follow Christ go through life believing trials should be foreign to them. This lie caters to our flesh and helps line the pockets of every prosperity gospel preacher on the television circuit. We are not saved to skip merrily through this world all the way to heaven. The journey, at times, is grueling. It was the same for Christ, the early Church, and all true believers down through the ages. We are never alone in our walk to glory.

My first earthquake in California was only an aftershock, but it was enough to shake me up. Those who have been through bigger earthquakes have told me that it shakes them up every time. Just like earthquakes, major trials shock us and are unsettling because they take us completely by surprise and are utterly out of our control. When trouble first hits, the ground feels as though it is being ripped out from underneath us.

When my daughter died, I found myself mentally working through my whole belief system. The death of a child will shake you to your very core. As I brought my sorrow, with all its questions, up against my theology at the time, I went deeper into the Scriptures to fine-tune and sharpen the edges of what I truly believed. One doctrine led to another and then to the next. All the while, there was a battle going on between my mind (in what I knew to be truth), and my flesh. It wasn't a battle that most people could see, but it was intense, and it was real.

When I was walking in the Spirit, my focus was fixed on Christ, and my hope was sure—holding me as secure as any anchor of any ship in the deepest ocean. But when my flesh fought for control, I started to sink fast. Then, all the *why me, woe is me,* and *what if I had done this or not done that* questions would assault me as fast and furiously as arrows released from the most experienced archer stalking his prey. Like Peter walking on the water, the only thing that will keep us in a trial is keeping our eyes fixed on Christ. When we begin to focus on ourselves, we're going down!

Sometimes, as His beloved children, we start to believe we have 'arrived' in this life. Suffering comes, and we are confused because *we* can't see a purpose for it. We may be able to point to things we believe caused our circumstances, but the bottom line is our suffering, as God's children, is always for His good purposes relating to our salvation in some way. The truth is that we still have more sin in us than we would ever want revealed. And the effects and consequences of sin in the world will wax worse until the Lord returns. The fact that we are called to endure trials and tribulations emphatically points to the fact that God is in the business of molding and shaping us—sanctifying us. We have **not** arrived! We have boarded the ship, but we have not yet reached our destination. We can be certain that choppy waters and storm clouds are still on the horizon of our life which we have yet to endure. Our salvation is certain, but we are still *working out our salvation* as God works in and through us because we're still on earth in bodies of flesh. And it pleases God to see Christ formed in us.

We're looking at the three facets of our salvation—justification, sanctification, and glorification. Glorification is the final stage of our salvation, that state wherein we will live eternally in perfect fellowship with Him. There will be no more sin, no more sorrow, and no more suffering. For now, suffering reminds us how weak and dependent we are. Also, it reveals the sin onto which our stubborn, selfish flesh still clings. Therefore, suffering is a vehicle that moves us ever closer to glory. The grandest stage upon which the Lord gives the Christian opportunity to shine the brightest is the most uncomfortable one because it is a stage set against the backdrop of humility. Humility is produced in us when we suffer in a way that honors and glorifies God. John Flavel also wrote this:

> "It may support thy heart, to consider that in these troubles God is performing that work in which thy soul would rejoice, if thou didst see the design of it. We are clouded with much ignorance, and are not able to discern how particular providences tend to the fulfilment of God's designs; and therefore, like Israel in the wilderness, are often murmuring, because Providence leads us about in a howling desert, where we are exposed to difficulties; though then he led them, and is now leading us, by the right way to a city of habitations. If you could but see how God in his secret counsel has exactly laid the whole plan of your salvation, even to the smallest means and circumstances; could you but discern the admirable harmony of divine dispensations, their mutual relations, together with the general respect they all have to the last end; had you liberty

> to make your own choice you would, of all conditions
> in the world, choose that in which you now are."[2]

If I could see what God sees, I would have chosen each trial in my life just as it has, in God's providence, played out on the stage of my life. I would have chosen each dark thread to accentuate the glorious finished design. But full of pride, my flesh hates to suffer. Suffering reminds me that I am not in control. There is another to whom I must bow my knee in humble submission. My flesh, like a veil over my eyes, clouds my view and my perspective to be able to clearly see things as they are. If I could see the glory to come, I would not kick so against the goads.

I am neither able to see with full eternal perspective, nor can I see myself as I really am. Just as our skin is a covering over our internal organs, our flesh is the veil that masks to those around us, and even to ourselves, what is in our own heart. But, our Maker, our Father, sees our hearts and knows exactly what is needed to expose it—to others who are His ministers to us and to ourselves. He will continue to mold it and shape it into a heart that rightly reflects the glory of Christ. Our great Physician will use every necessary means to pull back that veil and perform radical heart surgery so that we might live a life free from the disease called sin.

When life is good—when placid waters soothe our souls like a lullaby—we often lose our focus and let down our guard. Trials surface, and we frantically seek to root out and rid ourselves of the causes of our distress. We entertain the thought that we must have done something wrong to deserve these circumstances (forgetting what we *deserve* is eternity in hell.) Instead of rightly searching our hearts before Him for that which will bring Him glory, we bargain with God. We reason that if only we learn this lesson, if only we repent of this or that sin, surely our Father will rescue us from our trial delivering us from every painful blow. We vow to 'do' better. Once we have vetted and exhausted every 'reason' for our trial we can think of, only to find our circumstances have not changed, we go to His Word taking another look at His promises.

Does He not promise to deliver us from every trouble? How can we understand His promises, believing He is faithful to keep them, when what we see and are experiencing do not line up? I must ask the right questions. Why don't I ask the right questions? My flesh wants everything *right now* and lives in a right now world. My flesh doesn't want to hear God's answers. I don't want to see how my deliverance looks in *His* eyes. It might be deliverance in death or deliverance from the sin I am holding onto in the circumstances of my trial. Deliverance might come in the realization that He is more than enough, and that circumstances have little bearing on the abundant life He promised we will find only in Him.

While He is fully able to deliver us from any circumstance or trial He has allowed and ultimately appointed for us in this life, we would do better to search our hearts to root out any trace of sinful disease that keeps us from wholly loving God and others as we ought—whether He removes the trial in our time frame, or even in our lifetime. We would do better to focus on submitting to the Master Weaver's plan with the tug of each thread. If we understood what is at stake in response to trials—these gifts given to sanctify us and glorify Him—we would bow before Him and worship.

After Missy died, my mind repeatedly wanted to go to the *what if's* which gave me back imaginary control over her life. Psalm 139 was a warm embrace that soothed the eyes of my anxious heart as I slowly began to focus on the eternal picture. All her days were pre-ordained long before she was ever conceived or born. She was a gift I had been given for a short time, almost 17 precious years, but she did not belong to me. That understanding freed me to praise God for her life and to thank Him for His lavish gift to me. It also enabled me to cut one more chord that keeps me tethered to this earth giving me a greater longing for eternity.

This psalm encourages and comforts my heart as it reminds me how intimately God knows me, loves me, and is aware of every facet of my life—controlling it all. If that wasn't enough, He is not a distant God who just *knows about the details of* what I'm going through. Whether I am like Daniel in the hottest of fiery trials, or like Paul in the darkest of dungeons—even when I *feel* alone—I can **know** He is right there with me. With each trial, I not only come to know more *about* Him, I come to know Him experientially.

A lightbulb came on in my understanding one day as Psalm 139:13-16 came to mind. I usually read from the NASB version which reads: **For You formed my inward parts; You wove me** in my mother's womb. **I will give thanks to You, for I am fearfully and wonderfully made; wonderful are Your works, and my soul knows it very well. My frame was not hidden from You, when I was made in secret, and skillfully wrought in the depths of the earth; Your eyes have seen my unformed substance; and in Your book were all written the days that were ordained for me, when as yet there was not one of them.** I am also familiar with the NIV version which translates the word *wove* to *knit*. Some commentators say the word *cover* is the best translation for this passage. Any of these words paint a vivid picture in our mind's eye.

The cross references took me to a passage in the book of Job. **Your hands fashioned and made me altogether, and would You destroy me? Remember now, that You have made me as clay; and would You turn me into dust again? Did You not pour me out like milk and curdle me like cheese; clothe me with skin and flesh, and knit me together with bones and sinews? You have granted me life and lovingkindness; and Your care has preserved my spirit.** (Job 10:8-12) In verse 11 we see this word *knit* again, and it is the same word used in Psalm 139. John Gill comments on this verse:

> Gussetius seems inclined, could he have found an instance of the word being used for making a tent, which it has the signification of, to have rendered the words, "with bones and sinews, thou hast given ate (sic) the form of a tabernacle; or, thou hast made me to be a tent; so the human body is called a tabernacle, 2 Corinthians 5:1; the skin and flesh being like veils or curtains, which cover; the bones are in the room of stakes, and the nerves instead of cords, the breast and belly a cavity: in a spiritual sense, a believer's strength lies in the grace of Christ, in the Lord, and in the power of his might; his defense is the whole armor of God provided for him, particularly the helmet of salvation, the shield of faith, and the breastplate of righteousness, with which he is fenced and protected from every spiritual enemy; and will God suffer such an one to be destroyed, whom he hath taken such care of, both in a natural and spiritual manner?[3]

I wonder in awe as I consider this loving God who speaks creation into existence, molds and shapes Adam from the dust, and takes one of Adam's ribs to make Eve. Then, with the same loving hands that would one day be nailed to a tree by those whom He had fashioned, He intimately knits us together inside our mothers' wombs. He could have put each of us on this earth as He did Adam. Instead, His design was to weave together relationships beginning with families. This familial relationship reflects the bonds of love intended to be realized between ourselves and our God. Lovingly, uniquely, He created each of His children for His good pleasure and glory. Albert Barnes comments on Psalm 139 using the KJV:

> **Thou hast covered me in my mother's womb.** The word here rendered *cover* means properly to interweave; to weave; to knit together, and the literal translation would be, "Thou hast "woven" me in my mother's womb, meaning that God had put his parts together, as one who weaves cloth, or who makes a basket. The original word has, however, also the idea of protecting, as in a booth or hut, woven or knit together—to wit, of boughs and branches. The former signification best suits the connection; and then the sense would be, that as God had made him—as he had formed his members, and united them in a bodily frame and form before he was born—he must be able to understand all his thoughts and feelings.[4]

> **And curiously wrought.** Literally, "embroidered." The Hebrew word—**râqam**—means to deck with color, to variegate. Hence, it means to variegate a garment; to weave with threads of various colors. With us the idea of embroidering is that of working various colors on a cloth by a needle. The Hebrew word, however, properly refers to the act of "weaving in" various threads—as now in weaving carpets. The reference here is to the various and complicated tissues of the human frame—the tendons, nerves, veins, arteries, muscles, "as if" they had been woven,

or as they appear to be curiously interwoven. No work of tapestry can be compared with this; no art of man could "weave" together such a variety of most tender and delicate fibers and tissues as those which go to make up the human frame, even if they were made ready to his hand: and who but God could "make" them? The comparison is a most beautiful one; and it will be admired the more, the more man understands the structure of his own frame.[5]

Consider it all joy, my brethren, when you encounter various trials, knowing that the testing of your faith produces endurance. And let endurance have its perfect result, so that you may be perfect and complete, lacking in nothing. (James 1:2-4) James uses the word *various* to describe trials we encounter in life. Peter uses the same word in 1 Peter. This word means multicolored or variegated. Just like the hues displayed in a tapestry are woven together to create a beautiful design, so too the multicolored trials in our lives are being used by the Master Designer to display the uniquely foreordained design that will most glorify Him. Trials, blessings, and intimacy all have a common thread weaving them together throughout Scripture. That thread is God's glory. **In this you greatly rejoice, even though now for a little while, if necessary, you have been distressed by various trials, so that the proof of your faith, being more precious than gold which is perishable, even though tested by fire, may be found to result in praise and glory and honor at the revelation of Jesus Christ; and though you have not seen Him, you love Him, and though you do not see Him now, but believe in Him, you greatly rejoice with joy inexpressible and full of glory, obtaining as the outcome of your faith the salvation of your souls.** (1 Peter 1:6-9) The believer has been given sure and certain promises to stand upon or rest her faith upon. The blessings that have been secured for us who believe, by the work of Jesus Christ through His life, death, and resurrection, will be fully realized on that day when Christ is revealed in all glory and honor. These blessings are anchors of hope that hold us steadfast in trials while our faith is being proved or tested. Though we have not seen Him, we love Him.

That love looks like a life of obedience and faithfulness to Him as we submit to His will for our lives, even and especially in trials.

In the aftermath of Melissa's death, well-meaning people tried to encourage me with words commending my faith in that trial. I remember saying again and again, "I just want to pass the test." At the time, I didn't fully understand why that was my one driving thought. Further, I didn't realize that He would not let me fail but would produce endurance in me that would strengthen my faith and draw me closer to Him. I was clinging to Him for dear life not fully realizing how tightly He held me in the palm of His hand.

Ephesians 1 says God, the Father, chose me in Christ before the foundation of the world. I had not even begun to understand the weight of that truth in my 2001 heartache, but I longed to be faithful to my Lord and Savior Jesus Christ—my Betrothed. With weak and shaky faith, I knew I was prone to wander, prone to leave the One I love, as the hymn says. How would my wedding gown stay unsoiled? The Father designed my bridal gown before time began. Purchased for me by my Beloved, it cost Him His very life. God will never let me go to my own undoing.

My wedding gown will fit perfectly because it was designed for me by the One who wove me together in my mother's womb. **Positionally,** even now, I stand fully clothed in the righteous robe of Christ, a robe no physical eye can see. **Practically,** in what can be seen, I fall far short of God's standard of Christ's perfection. Ephesians 5:27 says that He will present to Himself the church in all her glory, having no spot or wrinkle or any such thing, and that she will be holy and blameless. One day soon, all the elect will be revealed in Him in all His glorious splendor. When I think of that day, I cannot help but think of the marvelous details of His revelation.

The Book of Revelation is literally the *revelation* of Jesus Christ. The word *revelation* is from the Greek word **apokalupsis,** which means an uncovering, an unveiling, or lifting the veil. Christ's full glory will be unveiled at the culmination of all history. That glory includes all who are in Him. Some beheld glimpses of His glory the first time He came; but for the most part, His glory was not recognized clothed behind the veil of His flesh. But no one will be able to miss His full glory the second time He appears. Every eye will see our Beloved coming on clouds of Shekinah glory. In 1 Thessalonians 1:10, Paul tells us that our Bridegroom is coming to be glorified in His saints—His bride. On that day, all who have believed in Him will marvel at Him.

One of the most life-changing topical studies I have ever done was the study I did on our covenant-keeping God back in the 90's when my marriage was far from what God intends godly marriages to be. My marriage didn't change overnight; in fact, it still has a long way to go (just like me). However, the conviction to remain faithful to the Lover of my soul through keeping the bonds of my earthly marriage covenant grew deep roots that would sustain me in treacherous storms to come. Because God is a covenant-keeping God, I know He is coming back for His bride. This world has never been my home. My forever home is with Him.

Another enlightening study takes a closer look at ancient, Jewish marriage customs giving us a better understanding of the covenant Christ made with His bride. The Church in the world is a bride being made ready for her glorious wedding day. A modern-day bride, after months or years of preparation, on that special day, takes a slow walk down the aisle with all eyes upon her, especially the eyes of her beloved. Upon reaching her bridegroom, he lifts the veil that covers her face so they may look fully into one another's eyes—eyes that reflect the glories of the intimate love they have for each other. In the marriage ceremony, lifting the veil symbolizes intimacy. After they have been joined in holy matrimony, there will be nothing to separate them from total intimacy.

The traditional lifting of the veil has symbolism relating to what occurs when a believer is saved. The veil is lifted from our eyes as we see the glorious face of Christ in the pages of Scripture and believe by faith His love for us in the work He accomplished on our behalf. When the veil of our flesh is finally removed in our glorification, we will see Him as He is, more fully than we ever have before. Never will the words "I am my Beloved's, and He is mine," have more meaning to us. With our the veil removed, we will fully reflect His glory. **Beloved, now we are children of God, and it has not appeared as yet what we will be. We know that when He appears, we will be like Him, because we will see Him just as He is.** (1 John 3:2)

On that glorious day with that one look of love in His eyes, all the heartaches we experienced on earth will fade away and all will have been worth it. As the song says, "…and the things of this earth will grow strangely dim, in the light of His glory and grace."

In the context of a suffering people, the prophets of old pointed God's people to that glorious day when all would see His glory and they would be glorified in Him. **I will rejoice greatly in the Lord, my soul will exult in my God, for He has clothed me with garments of salvation, He has wrapped me with a robe of righteousness, as a bridegroom decks himself with a garland, and as a bride adorns herself with her jewels.** (Isaiah 61:10) **And I saw the holy city, new Jerusalem, coming down out of heaven from God, made ready as a bride adorned for her husband.** (Revelation 21:2) When He saved me, He clothed me with His robes of righteousness. The glory reflecting Christ being formed in me is veiled to the world. Living in this world in a body of flesh, I am sometimes tempted to put off that glorious robe and climb back into my stinking, sweaty, soiled, work clothes after having been washed by the waters of regeneration. When that happens, I must gaze at the glory in the face of Jesus in the pages of His Word. Why? Because everyone who has this hope *fixed* on Him purifies himself, just as He is pure. (1 John 3:3) The hope is knowing that we will one day be like Him.

There are many veils mentioned in Scripture. There is the veil in the temple, the veil of Christ's flesh, and the veil over the heart, to name a few.

A *veil* is a covering or curtain that hides something from being seen. A veil separates or prevents access from one place to another. We looked at the veil in the temple earlier. The veil that separated the Holy of Holies from the rest of the temple pointed to at least two things we must consider.

First, the veil in the temple indicated that there was something separating the people from God's presence. We know, and Isaiah 59:2 tells us, that it is our sin that separates us from God. The veil represented that separation to the people of Israel.

The second thing we observe about the veil in the temple is what happened when it was ripped from top to bottom by God. The old sacrificial system was done away with by a new and living sacrifice. The Old Covenant, with all its bloody sacrifices, was done away with once for all when the only perfect sacrifice that could ever *take away* sin laid down His own life as a substitute for all who would believe in Him. This was the establishment of the New Covenant in His blood. Luke 22 depicts for us what happened when on the last Passover, Christ, the Passover Lamb, instituted the New Covenant eating the first Communion meal with His disciples in anticipation of the cross.

At the moment of Christ's death, as a picture of what was taking place spiritually, the veil was split from top to bottom. **And Jesus cried out again with a loud voice and yielded up His spirit. And behold, the veil of the temple was torn in two from top to bottom; and the earth shook, and the rocks were split. The tombs were opened, and many bodies of the saints who had fallen asleep were raised; and coming out of the tombs after His resurrection they entered the holy city and appeared to many. Now the centurion, and those who were with him keeping guard over Jesus, when they saw the earthquake and the things that were happening, became very frightened and said, "Truly this was the Son of God!"** (Matthew 27:50-54)

I learned something very interesting while reading Greg Harris' book, *The Face and the Glory*.[6] What signified the beginning of Jesus' ministry was His baptism by John the Baptist. Mark 1:9-13 describes for us what took place at that event. Specifically, it says when Jesus came up out of the water, **He saw the heavens opening, and the Spirit like a dove descended upon Him; and a voice came out of the heavens: "You are My beloved Son, in You I am well-pleased."** We must not miss what is in those passages with which we are most familiar. The language is straightforward. Mr. Harris pointed out that we may not observe at first glance a simple word that demands a word study. It's the Greek word for *open* referring to the heavens opening. Both Matthew's and Luke's accounts use the normal Greek word for *open*, but Mark uses a different word. He uses a word for *open* that means 'to tear or to rip'. Mark and Matthew both use this word later when referring to the veil in the temple being torn open. This word is a strong action word, so Mark's emphasis at Jesus' baptism is not on the heavens opening, but on the fact that they were **torn open** or *ripped open*. Mr. Harris says, "This violent ripping of heaven was

God's opening challenge to Satan and all who were hostile to God's Son, in total contrast to the gentleness of the Holy Spirit descending in the form of a dove, and was a mighty call to battle to the highly intensified spiritual warfare that was at hand." We know immediately following His baptism, Jesus was led into the wilderness by the Holy Spirit to be insidiously tempted by Satan.

I think it is interesting that both times this word is used there is testimony given to Christ being God's Son. At the beginning of Jesus' ministry, the Father ripped open the heavens and proclaimed, "You are My beloved Son, in You I am well-pleased." At the end of Christ's earthly ministry, after He had completed the work He was sent to do, the Father ripped the veil in the temple, made the earth quake, and released the bodies of saints from their tombs, but it is the guards who witnessed all these events who exclaimed, "Truly this was the Son of God." (By the way, make sure you allot a great amount of time for savoring one of Mr. Harris' books because, if you are like me, you will need to stop and worship often!)

The veil in the Temple forcibly came down opening the way into the Holy of Holies for all who would walk through the rent veil of Christ's flesh. Access to God comes through believing in and appropriating the death of Christ for oneself. All who enter through the torn veil of His flesh will have intimate communion with the Father for all eternity. The veil came down, and the Father opened His arms to receive us in the Son as if to say, "Children, come home!" And we ran through that ripped veil welcomed by our Father to live beyond the veil with Him forever. **Therefore, brethren, since we have confidence to enter the holy place by the blood of Jesus, by a new and living way which He inaugurated for us through the veil, that is, His flesh...** (Hebrews 10:19-20)

Jesus answered them, "Destroy this temple, and in three days I will raise it up." The Jews then said, "It took forty-six years to build this temple, and will You raise it up in three days?" But He was speaking of the temple of His body. (John 2:19-21) **And the Word became flesh, and dwelt among us, and we saw His glory, glory as of the only begotten from the Father, full of grace and truth.** (John 1:14) *Dwelt* in this passage can also mean 'tabernacled'. Jesus, God in flesh, dwelt among or 'tabernacled' among man. To understand the richness of this is to know what was lost. Because Adam was created righteous, without sin, he walked and talked with God as a man talks with his friend. Life in the Garden of Eden was perfect, and man was fulfilling that for which he had been created.

Man was created to glorify God. We don't know it until our eyes are opened, but our greatest need is to glorify God. To that end, the lost are found and truly set free. We glorify God when we know Him and have intimate communion with Him. The more we come to comprehend His greatness, the more we exalt Him and give Him glory. In our fallen state, we have no capacity to know Him or to glorify Him; we may know *of* Him, but we cannot ever know an intimate relationship with Him. Sin in us is the barrier that keeps us from that perfect fellowship.

In order to gain back (or redeem) what was lost at the Fall, the barrier of sin that separated us from God had to be done away with once for all. Only the removal of this barrier would allow us direct and free access to our heavenly Father. Because only He lived a perfect life *in His flesh* when He came to earth, only He could be the perfect Lamb who could take away the sins of the world. Our Father gave His Son to die in our place. The Son willingly laid down His life for us. There was no other way.

Before we ever realized it, we desperately needed a way back to God. We were restless, searching for something to fill the void we had inside, not knowing what that void was. Augustine said, "Thou hast made us for Thyself, O Lord, and our hearts are restless until they rest in Thee,"[7] and, Blaise Pascal who said, "There is a God-shaped vacuum in the heart of every man which cannot be filled by any created thing, but only by God, the Creator, made known through Jesus."[8]

The mother of a wayward son or daughter desperately longs for that child to return home to her, to an intimate relationship with her. To what lengths would she go to bring that child back to a restored relationship? Whatever it takes. Even more important than that relationship is the need of every child of God to be restored back to the heart of the Father.

Isaiah 53 is a vivid chapter detailing what took place at the cross for you and for me. Read the whole chapter, then carefully meditate on these two verses: **All of us like sheep have gone astray,**

each of us has turned to his own way; but the Lord has caused the iniquity of us all to fall on Him. (Isaiah 53:6) **But the Lord was pleased to crush Him, putting Him to grief.** (Isaiah 53:10)

To what lengths did the Father go? The Father was *pleased to* crush His only begotten, beloved Son to redeem all those whom He had predestined to be in Christ. The crucifixion of Jesus was the orchestration of God from start to finish. It was the Father's good will to sacrifice His Son for us; why is it so hard to believe He would do whatever it takes to make us like His Son (which is our ultimate good)? It wasn't evil men who killed the Son of God. With all the power and authority they believed was theirs, they could not have raised one finger against Jesus unless the Father allowed it, unless it had been ordained by Him, part of His perfect plan. Every single moment of your suffering and mine has been ordained by God. In our suffering, God loves us perfectly! Unless you can come face to face with that truth—unless you can throw your arms around that truth—you will not be able to suffer in a way that fully honors God. You, Beloved, must bow the knee to that truth just as Christ bowed in humble submission to the perfect will of His loving Father in His crucifixion.

Bear with me as I try to describe this in less than sophisticated, theological terms, because I struggle to convey what I know to be true. God is all about His glory. He has *got* to be all about His glory—*because He's God!* There is no greater object of glory than God. God is true to Himself when He is all about His glory. You and I are *not* all about His glory but our own. This is the gravest of all sin. While we are saved, we still occupy a body of flesh with its old remaining sin nature that must be crucified daily. We are not yet glorified. We do not yet have the capacity to fully give God glory. That's a problem which demands regular repentance.

Every sinner dishonors God by not loving Him with all his heart, soul, mind, and strength one hundred percent of the time. His holiness, His greatness, demands that level of worship. We simply cannot give God the glory that is due Him; and He had to deal with that. Between the arms of Christ, nailed to the cross was the reconciliation of all the tension of God's love for His glory and His love for sinners. Christ opened His arms wide to embrace the Father's will so the veil of His flesh could be pierced.

Fully propitiated by the Son's sacrifice, God the Father dramatically *opened* the way *for us* to come into His presence by ripping the veil in the temple from top to bottom. It was as if when Christ said, "It is finished," the Father was echoing the same from heaven. In ancient days, mourners displaying their intense grief, as a public and powerful expression of a broken heart, tore their clothes. Was God's heart broken in restoring our hearts to His? Did those in the temple that day make the connection?

Access to the heart of God was made available by the Father when He crucified His own Son on our behalf. This was the **only** way to welcome the children back to the heart of their Father. The only way for us to go to the Father is through the cross of Christ. As we suffer rightly, our flesh is being ripped away little by little in the process of our sanctification. We are a bride being made ready for the most intimate love we could *never* imagine. God controls our suffering because in His perfect plan and purpose for each of us, He alone can make us like Christ, a choice bride perfectly fit for her Bridegroom. He will bring us into full communion and fellowship with Himself. Counting all things loss in order to gain Christ, we willingly submit to the fellowship of His sufferings conforming us to His death, so that we might know Him more intimately. Every time we embrace suffering from His hand with this attitude, we are moved one step closer to glory.

And we can now come within the veil. We can come often, and we can come boldly to our Father. **This hope we have as an anchor of the soul, a hope both sure and steadfast and one which enters within the veil, where Jesus has entered as a forerunner for us, having become a high priest forever according to the order of Melchizedek.** (Hebrews 6:19-20)

One thing I focused on in the dark trial of prison was going home. I no longer had a physical home to speak of, but home was where my family was. When looking at our present circumstances of suffering through temporal eyes, things are not always as they seem. Christians, with eyes of faith, must keep their focus on the eternal. Like Paul, we must press on toward the goal for the prize of the upward call of God in Christ Jesus. Like every runner who desires to win the race, we must fix our gaze on the goal ahead of us, not on the ground beneath us or the circumstances around us;

the prize is too great to lose the race. The prize is Christ, and we are going home!

Staying my mind on one specific portion of Scripture after my daughter died, I wanted to pass the test, to win the race, to suffer well—to suffer in a way that honored and glorified Christ. I did not want to stumble, fall, or lose focus in my grief. I had started to become lukewarm towards Christ before her death. This verse— when I thought I didn't remember Scripture at all—literally popped into my head, and I held onto it for dear life. Five years later, when my husband was first indicted, a pastor friend came to our home and had a Bible study with me, my husband, and the Bible study girls. Guess what Scripture he taught from? And I knew the Lord was with us in our new trial from the start. **Therefore, since we have so great a cloud of witnesses surrounding us, let us also lay aside every encumbrance and the sin which so easily entangles us, and let us run with endurance the race that is set before us, fixing our eyes on Jesus, the author and perfecter of faith, who for the joy set before Him endured the cross, despising the shame, and has sat down at the right hand of the throne of God. For consider Him who has endured such hostility by sinners against Himself, so that you will not grow weary and lose heart.** (Hebrews 12:1-3)

We are to *fix our eyes on* Jesus and to *consider* Jesus. That, Beloved, is what will keep us in times of suffering. To *fix our eyes* is to turn our eyes away from other things and to fix them on something else. It is to turn our minds from whatever our flesh is focused on that is tempting us to sin and set our minds on Jesus. To *consider* Jesus is to think over, to ponder, to give a right estimate of something, to consider by weighing or comparing.

We tell people to 'focus' when they are distracted, and we want to get their attention onto something important. Turn your eyes from the storm raging around you, and fix your eyes on Jesus. Look deeply into His loving face as you see Him revealed in the pages of Scripture. He's not twiddling His thumbs in heaven waiting for us to be together one day. He's fixed on you, His bride. We need to be fixed on Him, the Lover of our soul, as we walk through this world. We will not be moved when we know our God is the One who holds us safe and secure.

We must trust the Master Weaver to bring to completion the exquisite tapestry of our lives, designed before the foundation of the world to tell the story of His work in and through us. Though the shreds and threads *we* see appear disheveled and a tangled mess of confusion, we do not have the full capacity to gaze on the vision reflected in the eyes of the Master.

When Paul was speaking within the context of spiritual gifts in 1 Corinthians 13, he talks about the extent of our vision here on earth. I don't want to get too carried away with the verse, as we aren't talking, specifically, about spiritual gifts. However, I believe there's a biblical principle here that ties in with what we're talking about. **When I was a child, I used to speak like a child, think like a child, reason like a child; when I became a man, I did away with childish things. For now, we see in a mirror dimly, but then face to face; now I know in part, but then I will know fully just as I also have been fully known.** (1 Corinthians 13:11-12) David Guzik quotes Charles Spurgeon regarding this passage:

> We couldn't handle this greater knowledge on this side of eternity. If we knew more of our own sinfulness, we might be driven to despair; if we knew more of God's glory, we might die of terror; if we had more understanding, unless we had equivalent capacity to employ it, we might be filled with conceit and tormented with ambition. But up there we shall have our minds and our systems strengthened to receive more, without the damage that would come to us here from over leaping the boundaries of order, supremely appointed and divinely regulated. (Spurgeon)[9]

There are things that pertain to childhood that become obsolete once maturity is reached. No matter how long we live on this earth, we will never see with the eyes of full spiritual maturity. In this life we will never be able to attain to the perfection of wisdom, as Calvin says regarding this passage. He also said, "The measure of knowledge, that we now have, is suitable to imperfection and childhood, as it were; for we do not as yet see clearly the mysteries of the heavenly kingdom, and we do not as yet enjoy a distinct view of them."[10] For now, we see in a mirror dimly. The mirrors of Paul's day were made from polished metal. One's *reflection* would be unclear and somewhat distorted. In other words, we see, but our vision is obscured. What obscures our full vision of Christ's glory is our flesh. The 'mirror' Paul is referring to in this passage is the Word. (See also James 1:23-25.) God has given us His Word to 'see' Him. He has revealed Himself to us in His Word clearly and perfectly. Paul also said in 2 Corinthians 3:18: **But we all, with unveiled face, beholding as in a mirror the glory of the Lord, are being transformed into the same image from glory to glory, just as from the Lord, the Spirit.** The more we focus on Christ in His Word, the more fully we come to know Him and to reflect His glory. Being transformed into the image of Christ from glory to glory is the process of sanctification.

God knows us. The more we come to know Him, the answers to all our questions in our suffering no longer matter because our goal is only Christ in all things. Like Moses, in Exodus 34, we want to see God's glory, not our own. We long for Him to be glorified, and we long to share His gospel with others so that their lives will glorify Him. That was the sole desire of Paul's heart. Yet, Paul, certainly no stranger to all manner of suffering, was persecuted—from outside the church and even from within the church—for the truth He shared. We will be, too.

In 2 Corinthians, Paul contrasted the Old Covenant with the New Covenant, much as the writer of the book of Hebrews did. The stubborn adherents to the Old Covenant were outraged by Paul's message and tried to subvert his teaching. This precious church God's apostle loved, whose foundation had been built on the truth of the Gospel of Jesus Christ, had been infiltrated by false apostles sowing lies about Paul and casting aspersions on the veracity of his apostleship. These demonic lies of the false apostles appealed to the fleshly desires of the Corinthian believers. How this must have cut Paul's heart to the quick. He had labored over these beloved saints as a father would to grow up his own children.

Paul speaks of his suffering alongside the glory which is to come. He speaks of the letter of the Law contrasted to life in the Spirit. The purpose of the Law was twofold: to reveal to us the holy glory of Almighty God and to expose our utter need for salvation, driving us to Christ for mercy in granting us salvation. Jesus is *the* way, *the* of truth, and *the* life. No man comes to the Father but by Him. **And even if our gospel is veiled, it is veiled to those who are perishing, in whose case the god of this world has blinded the minds of the unbelieving so that they might not see the light of the gospel of the glory of Christ, who is the image of God.** (2 Corinthians 4:3-4) **But their minds were hardened; for until this very day at the reading of the old covenant the same veil remains unlifted, because it is removed in Christ. But to this day whenever Moses is read, a veil lies over their heart; but whenever a person turns to the Lord, the veil is taken away.** (2 Corinthians 3:14-16) A spiritual veil lies over the heart of every man in Adam until it is removed in Christ. What that means is that a person cannot and will not believe until that veil is removed. We need the mind of Christ to be able to understand the truth of the gospel that leads to salvation.

The veil over Paul's heart was radically removed on the road to Damascus. Once part of the religious elite—impeccably clothed in self-made robes of righteousness, having strictly adhered to all Old Covenant rituals and regulations—Paul came face to face with his own unworthiness in the face of the glorious treasure of Christ. Sought-after self-righteousness, supposedly gained through the keeping of ceremonies and rituals, soothes the flesh. Once the flesh is arrested by the truth of the gospel, crucified by the sword of the Spirit and the veil removed, the regenerated one only seeks to soothe his spirit by resting in the knowledge that he has peace with God as he glories in the light of Christ's righteousness.

There are only two kinds of people—only two options: One either has a veil over his heart, or he has walked through the veil of Christ's flesh into the presence of God. One is proud, and one is humble. One is in bondage and does not know it, walking through life as a dead man. One has found true freedom by walking the way of death to life. **Now the Lord is the Spirit, and where the Spirit of the Lord is, there is liberty. But we all, with unveiled face, beholding as in a mirror the glory of the Lord, are being transformed into the same image from glory to glory, just as from the Lord, the Spirit.** (2 Corinthians 3:17-18)

Just like looking into my intensely magnified make-up mirror getting up close and personal to scrutinize every detail of my face—we, with unveiled face, behold the glory of the Lord as we look into the mirror of His Word considering every detail of His revelation to us. The living Word reflects, reveals, and magnifies Him to us, and we see ourselves in His light. **For the word of God is living and active and sharper than any two-edged sword, and piercing as far as the division of soul and spirit, of both joints and marrow, and able to judge the thoughts and intentions of the heart.** (Hebrews 4:12) As we gaze at His glory, our minds are renewed, and we are transformed into the same image from glory to glory.

Like sailors who search for the sun to break through the dark clouds when tempestuous waves rage all around, how much more urgently and deeply do we search for His face when storm clouds darken the horizon of our lives? Beloved, in times of affliction, persecution, and suffering, we must remember that we are children of the Light. The Light shows us the way through the darkness. When we *feel* as though we can see no light at the end of the tunnel, we must turn towards the light of His Word. **For we do not preach ourselves but Christ Jesus as Lord, and ourselves as your bondservants for Jesus' sake. For God, who said, "Light shall shine out of darkness," is the One who has shone in our hearts to give the Light of the knowledge of the glory of God in the face of Christ.** (2 Corinthians 4:5-6)

In all our trials, we must turn to Jesus, the radiance of God's glory. This is the one who has overcome the world and who has given us His Holy Spirit to comfort and strengthen us with power to endure and to overcome—giving strong testimony to our faith. Our refuge, our strength, our shield, and our strong tower, He will never leave us or forsake us. The weakest servant is granted immediate access to His presence. Seek His face on the pages of Scripture until you are bathed in peace and power from on high.

There is only one way to walk through a storm. I would explain it to a friend like this: *Get your focus right. Run to the Word. Stay there gazing on the glory of Jesus' face until your soul is quieted and strengthened. Do it often as those waves of anxiety and despair crash over your head. Get above your circumstances, and get His perspective from His viewpoint. Remember Colossians 3:1-4 which says:*

Therefore, if you have been raised up with Christ, keep seeking the things above, where Christ is, seated at the right hand of God. Set your mind on the things above, not on the things that are on earth. For you have died and your life is hidden with Christ in God. When Christ, who is our life, is revealed, then you also will be revealed with Him in glory. This world, this life, is not my home. My life, who I really am, is in Christ. Eternity began for me on the day He saved me from myself.

In the Book of Revelation, we see what will take place in the imminent future. Revelation is the *'unveiling'* of Jesus Christ in all His glory. **BEHOLD HE IS COMING WITH THE CLOUDS, and every eye will see Him, even those who pierced Him; and all the tribes of the earth will mourn over Him. So it is to be. Amen.** (Revelation 1:7) John had a vision of what we will all one day see. He saw the glory of the Lord. Caught up to the third heaven, Paul, likewise, saw and heard things he was not permitted to reveal at that time. Although he suffered greatly in this life, he could see more clearly than we can the bigger picture. Suffering beyond what he could humanly endure, he encouraged us to not lose heart.

Attempting to comfort someone who is going through great difficulties, people will often say, "Remember, God will not give you more than you can handle." That's not true! He often gives us way more than we can handle in our frail human flesh and strength. Our difficulties may even result in our physical death. It would be better to say God will keep us or sustain us in whatever He gives us. Most important to believers—our greatest blessings—are all things spiritual—our faith, our salvation, our relationship with Him. We may lose **everything** in this world! He promises we will never lose our greatest treasure, and that is Him. True faith endures.

Many women told me they knew they could never have handled the death of their child like I did. Meant as an encouragement or testament to my faith, that is an absurd statement. Trust me when I say *I did not handle* Melissa's death. I'm a clay pot; and her death shattered and crushed me into a million pieces. My response to them was from an experiential knowledge—God will give us the grace to handle whatever He calls us to endure.

Gardeners know the fragile nature of clay pots. They are hard to get from the store to our home without a crack or chip. Who, in their right mind, would put a treasure—a prized possession—in a clay pot? God did! Why? Let's say I just went down to the local garden center. I have bought the most gorgeous flowers you've ever seen and planted them in my large, very ordinary clay pot. At the peak of their blooms, do you suppose my friends will look at that arrangement and exclaim, "Oh, what an exquisite clay pot!" Never! The clay pot is so plain and so common that it could never detract from the breathtaking beauty inside. **But we have this treasure in earthen vessels, so that the surpassing greatness of the power will be of God and not from ourselves; we are afflicted in every way, but not crushed; perplexed, but not despairing; persecuted, but not forsaken; struck down, but not destroyed; always carrying about in the body the dying of Jesus, so that the life of Jesus also may be manifested in our body. For we who live are constantly being delivered over to death for Jesus' sake, so that the life of Jesus also may be manifested in our mortal flesh. So, death works in us, but life in you.** (2 Corinthians 4:7-12)

We are weak vessels—weak and fragile as clay pots. Remember my broken lantern illustration in an earlier chapter? The treasure is the gospel message. It is the light of the gospel displaying the glory of Christ that shines through us when we are crushed and broken. The gospel message is the glorious truth of Jesus Christ who alone has the power to save sinners. The fragile clay pot has no value apart from being a vessel to hold the treasure, fulfilling its purpose in putting the treasure on display. Paul was, no doubt, mindful of the clay pots that were used in his day for human waste and garbage disposal. Those clay pots had one purpose they were designed for, and in as much as they fulfilled that purpose, they were useful.

What Paul knew when he encouraged believers to not lose heart was that God won't allow anything in the life of a true believer that will cause her to lose true faith. He *will* give us more than we can handle in our own strength in order to break us and fill us with Himself so that He might sanctify us. A true believer can't lose her salvation. This is called 'the perseverance of the saints'. Every true believer will continue in faith until the end. In prison, my family and I signed off our correspondence, 'Faith endures, and love lasts forever.' Believers are *in Christ,* raised up and seated with Him in the heavenly places. True believers will never fall away from Christ. They will persevere to the end.

The Lord is pleased to crush me in my trials that I might be sanctified, just as the Father was pleased to crush His own Son for me. *Gethsemane* in Hebrew means 'olive press', which has that same idea of crushing olives to produce oil used for anointing priests. In Revelation 2, a message is given to the church at Smyrna. *Smyrna* means myrrh or bitter. One of the gifts the Magi brought to Jesus at His birth was myrrh. Myrrh was also used as an anointing oil by priests in the temple. When crushed, it gave a fragrant aroma.

Smyrna is often called the suffering church because it was being persecuted. Smyrna, in its day, was an exceptionally beautiful city, known as the 'crown of Asia,' or 'the glory of Asia'. The Lord said to them: **Do not fear what you are about to suffer. Behold, the devil is about to cast some of you into prison, so that you will be tested, and you will have tribulation for ten days. Be faithful until death, and I will give you the crown of life.** (Revelation 2:10) They would be given the **crown of life** *after* they have been found faithful until death. Suffering will not last forever in this life. But our Lord does not sugarcoat the heartache in this world. He does not tell us to wish upon a star and all our fairytale hopes and dreams of living happily ever after *in this world* will come true. **Blessed is a man who perseveres under trial; for once he has been approved, he will receive the crown of life which the Lord has promised to those who love Him.** (James 1:12) James says we must persevere under trial. Here we see mentioned another **crown of life** reference. 1 Peter speaking to the elders of the suffering church in his day talks about the **unfading crown of glory.** In 1 Corinthians 9, Paul speaks about the **imperishable wreath** we are running the race to receive. It's the victor's crown, the crown of the overcomer. All these verses have **suffering** and **glory** in common.

Submitting to suffering under the controlled hand of sovereign love is a fragrant offering that is pleasing to God. **But thanks be to God, who always leads us in triumph in Christ, and manifests through us the sweet aroma of the knowledge of Him in every place. For we are a fragrance of Christ to God among those who are being saved and among those who are perishing; to the one an aroma from death to death, to the other an aroma from life**

to life. And who is adequate for these things? (2 Corinthians 2:14-16) **Therefore, be imitators of God, as beloved children; and walk in love, just as Christ also loved you and gave Himself up for us, an offering and a sacrifice to God as a fragrant aroma.** (Ephesians 5:1-2) All true believers will receive the crown of eternal life, and they will share in His glory. All true believers will persevere to the end in His strength alone and will worship Him alone forever.

Several months after Melissa died, my mother said she had somewhere she wanted to take me. Rather curious, I was eager to find out why she was being so secretive. We ended up in a local art gallery where she led me to a painting. At first glance, I was captivated by the colors of the painting, because they were *my* colors. I knew immediately I wanted this painting that depicted a little ship being tossed about on a rolling sea. The sky overhead was dark and threatening, but this little ship was headed toward the small ray of light forcing its way through the storm clouds. The light was reflected on the masts above as if it was guiding the ship to itself. The painting was entitled, "Perseverance". The manager of the store, a distant cousin who had also lost a young daughter years earlier, approached us with tears in her eyes. "Of course you are looking at this one," she said. "I get it."

When we go through trials in a way that the life of Jesus is manifested in and through us, people will be drawn to *Him*, not us. And He is glorified. **Therefore, we do not lose heart, but though our outer man is decaying, yet our inner man is being renewed day by day. For momentary, light affliction is producing for us an eternal weight of glory far beyond all comparison, while we look not at the things which are seen, but at the things which are not seen; for the things which are seen are temporal, but the things which are not seen are eternal.** (2 Corinthians 4:16-18)

All is not as it seems in the light of our frail, human sight. When it feels as though I have been given more than I can handle, when I'm at the end of myself, if I turn to Him in complete surrender for His help, He will whisper to me: **My grace is sufficient for you, for power is perfected in weakness.** (2 Corinthians 12:9) When I am beaten down and broken by life's circumstances, when I am emptied of myself and turn to Him, then He fills me up with Himself, and through my life, shows the world who He is.

The Lord had revealed unimaginable things to Paul, yet he was not permitted to speak about them. Therefore, he was given a thorn in the flesh to keep him from bragging and exalting himself. **Most gladly, therefore, I will rather boast about my weaknesses, so that the power of Christ may dwell in me. Therefore, I am well content with weaknesses, with insults, with distresses, with persecutions, with difficulties, for Christ's sake; for when I am weak, then I am strong.** (2 Corinthians 12:9-10) In essence, Paul says, "Lord, if Your power—Your glory—is put on display when I am suffering, then I will most gladly boast about my weaknesses."

We must learn this lesson on suffering well *before* storms break out upon our heads. *This* is Christianity 101. Suffering in a way that honors Christ is a mark of a true believer. When all hell breaks loose and fierce winds threaten to knock us off our feet, we must know how to stand firm, not just for our own sake, but for the sake of Christ's glory. Instead of kicking, fighting, and focusing all our endeavors on trying to escape the trial, we must learn to trust and submit. Standing firm involves stretching our arms out wide to embrace all suffering—trials, tribulations, sorrows, afflictions, and all He has ordained for us from His sovereign, loving hands. That speaks more volumes about our belief system than just words that come out of our mouths alone. We must learn to sing resolutely in our hearts with the hymnist: *When darkness veils His lovely face, I rest on His unchanging grace. In every high and stormy gale my anchor holds within the veil.*

In American Christianity, especially, we have picked up this preoccupation with blessings relating to *this* life. Even if we do not say it out loud, we truly believe we deserve all the richest physical and material blessings of Christ *in this lifetime*. How can we read our Bibles and allow ourselves to believe this way? Because our hearts are desperately wicked. When these types of lies slither into our minds through doubt holes, we must be equipped with truth to slay them quickly.

The whole creation is groaning under the curse of sin, anxiously longing for and awaiting eagerly the revealing of the sons of God. On that day, when we are glorified in Him, all of creation will be released from all effects of the curse. **The Spirit Himself testifies with our spirit that we are children of God, and if children,**

heirs also, heirs of God and fellow heirs with Christ, if indeed we suffer with Him so that we may also be glorified with Him. For I consider that the sufferings of this present time are not worthy to be compared with the glory that is to be revealed to us. (Romans 8:16-18)

Paul has thought through his beliefs about Christian suffering, and he wants us to do the same. To *consider* is to reason, calculate, reckon, compute, deliberate, or weigh something. It is a process of careful study or reasoning which results in arriving at a conclusion. When trials come into our lives, we must process our emotions through the grid of biblical truth. For example, *I feel as though God has forsaken me. But I know He said He will never leave me nor forsake me.* If we do not do that, we will be swept under a powerful current with waves of fleshly emotion that can devastate us. In trials, we are especially vulnerable to Satan's attacks. He prowls around seeking to devour us. But Peter says we must resist him by standing firm in our faith. How? By having a biblical perspective on trials and suffering, by standing upon truth.

We can't begin to understand the weight of God's glory. Nothing we know in this life can compare. Paul has had visions we have not seen with our physical eyes and has suffered more than most of us. Yet, he assures us our present sufferings are not worthy to be compared to the glory to come. We mothers can understand this to a small degree in every childbirth. Most people don't stop having children after one child because of the pain experienced in having given birth. In every trial, we must keep our eyes on the future glory He has promised. Hope in future glory helps us persevere in trials. When you stand by the bed of a dying loved one reading Revelation 21:3-4, the glimpses of future glory become a hard stare as you long for that hope you can clearly see with the eyes of faith. **And I heard a loud voice from the throne, saying, "Behold, the tabernacle of God is among men, and He will dwell among them, and they shall be His people, and God Himself will be among them, and He will wipe away every tear from their eyes; and there will no longer be any death; there will no longer be any mourning, or crying, or pain; the first things have passed away."**

All those blessings and riches my flesh craves—and I think I deserve here on earth—if I could have them all right now would never compare to the glories that are mine in Christ Jesus. Put beside God's glory, they would be as decaying garbage. All my earthly dreams could never compare to those blessings that are mine to come in the One who created the whole universe.

In this world we will have trials. Peter says we need not be surprised by fiery trials (1 Peter 4:12). The word for *fiery* means drawn from a refiner's fire, calamities, or trials that test the character. The Lord has *called* us to suffer in a way that glorifies Him. You may not understand—things may look chaotic and spinning out of control—but nothing has happened to you by chance. As the Master weaves every dark strand of pain and suffering through the tapestry of your life, each thread is held securely by those same loving hands that wove you together in your mother's womb. Each stitch reflects the designer's plans unique for you alone. Every painful blow of affliction is a dark backdrop for the glorious masterpiece which was fixed in the mind of God before the foundation of the world.

Therefore, prepare your minds for action, keep sober in spirit, fix your hope completely on the grace to be brought to you at the revelation of Jesus Christ. As obedient children, do not be conformed to the former lusts which were yours in your ignorance, but like the Holy One who called you, be holy yourselves also in all your behavior; because it is written, "YOU SHALL BE HOLY, FOR I AM HOLY." (1 Peter 1:13-16)

Verse 3 of the hymn, "The Perfect Wisdom of our God"[11]:

O grant me wisdom from above, to pray for peace and cling to love,

And teach me humbly to receive the sun and rain of Your sovereignty.

Each strand of sorrow has a place within this tapestry of grace;

So, through the trials I choose to say, "Your perfect will in Your perfect way." ~

NOTES

Chapter 2

1. https://www.challies.com/articles/gods-tapestry/
2. https://hymnary.org/person/Tullar_Grant
3. Ten Boom, Corrie, *The Hiding Place*, Chosen Books; 35th Anniversary edition (January 1, 2006) Print.
4. Ten Boom, Corrie, *Reflections of God's Glory*, Grand Rapids: Zondervan Publishing House, 1999. Print.
5. Wuest, Kenneth: https://drive.google.com/file/d/0B6smVijz2aFdMXBFcDZxN19SR00/view online commentary on Hebrews. https://www.preceptaustin.org/hebrews_10_resources
6. https://jerusalemchannel.tv/2014/05/31/will-temple-veil-soon-restored-jerusalem/

Chapter 3

1. "The Reichenbach Fall." Season 2, Episode 3. *Sherlock*, BBC One HD & PBS. Aired May 20, 2012. Television.
2. Challies, Tim, Defining Discernment blog, February 8, 2007, https://www.challies.com/articles/defining-discernment/
3. Sproul, R.C., Ligonier Ministries website, "The Five Solas of the Reformation", October 31, 2017, https://www.ligonier.org/blog/five-solas-reformation/
4. Owens, John: https://www.preceptaustin.org/hebrews_1030-31
5. Max McLean CD reading "Sinners in the Hands of an Angry God", a sermon by Jonathan Edwards.

Chapter 5

1. "Hawaii Bound." Season 4, Episode 1. *The Brady Bunch*, ABC. WTAE, Pittsburgh. Aired September 22, 1972. Television.
2. https://www.biblestudytools.com/dictionary/curse/
3. MacArthur, John, Jr., *The MacArthur Study Bible*, New American Standard Bible Updated Edition, Thomas Nelson, 2006. (Study Bible Note on Galatians 1:6).
4. Council of Trent on Justification XXIV, Session VI, http://www.thecounciloftrent.com/index.htm
5. https://www.blueletterbible.org/faq/don_stewart/don_stewart_166.cfm
6. Chilly Billy Cardille, Pittsburgh Personality, https://en.wikipedia.org/wiki/Bill_Cardille
7. *Dark Shadows*, American Television Series, Aired from June 27, 1966 through April 2, 1971.
8. *The Twilight Zone*, American Television Series, Aired from October 2, 1959 through June 19, 1964.
9. "Little Girl Lost." Season 3, Episode 2. *The Twilight Zone*, CBS. KDKA, Pittsburgh. Aired March 16, 1962.

Chapter 7

1. Harris, Thomas Anthony, *I'm Okay, You're Okay*, Harper & Row, 1967. Print.
2. https://www.biblestudytools.com/commentaries/treasury-of-david/psalms-140-3.html

Chapter 8

1. The Charles Spurgeon Sermon Collection, "The Disowned". https://www.thekingdomcollective.com/spurgeon/sermon/2808/

Chapter 9

1. Veruca Salt is a character in the movie, *Willie Wonka & the Chocolate Factory*. Release date June 30, 1971. *Willy Wonka & the Chocolate Factory* is a 1971 American musical fantasy family film directed by Mel Stuart and starring Gene Wilder as Willy Wonka. It is an adaptation of the 1964 novel *Charlie and the Chocolate Factory* by Roald Dahl.
2. Puritan Stephen Charnock quote: https://www.preceptaustin.org/delight_yourself_in_the_lord

Chapter 10

1. MacArthur, John, Jr., *MacArthur New Testament Commentary Series (Book 25) 2 Timothy*, Chicago: Moody Publishers; New Edition (August 1, 1995) Print.

Chapter 11

1. Sproul, RC, *Vol. 4: Before the Face of God: Book Four,* Grand Rapids: Baker Book House; Ligonier Ministries
2. Lewis, C.S., *Mere Christianity*, Geoffrey Bles (UK), Macmillan Publishers, HarperCollins Publishers (US), 1952. Print.

Chapter 12

1. MacArthur, John, Jr., *The Gospel According to the Apostles: The Role of Works in the Life of Faith,* Thomas Nelson, March 6, 2005. Print.

Chapter 13

1. https://www.pewresearch.org/fact-tank/2019/06/11/only-2-of-federal-criminal-defendants-go-to-trial-and-most-who-do-are-found-guilty/
2. R.C. Sproul YouTube Video Clip dated October 29, 2016, https://www.youtube.com/watch?v=iP4A3C3E4Cs

Chapter 14

1. *The Bad Seed*. Directed by Mervyn LeRoy. Performances by Nancy Kelly, Patty McCormack, and Henry Jones. Warner Bros., 1956. https://www.imdb.com/title/tt0048977/ Movie. Novel by William March.
2. Bonar, Horatius, *Earth's Morning or Thoughts on Genesis,* New York: Robert Carter and Brothers, 1875. Print.
3. Hodge, Charles, *The Way of Life*, Minneapolis: Curiosmith, 2016. Print. Previously published by The American Sunday School Union, 1841.
4. Robert Murray McCheyne quote: https://www.goodreads.com/quotes/538636-the-seed-of-every-sin-known-to-man-is-in
5. Gerstner, John, *The Problem of Pleasure*, Soli Deo Gloria, 2002, p. 15.

Chapter 17

1. R.C. Sproul quoting John Owens, https://www.ligonier.org/learn/devotionals/suffering-and-obedience/
2. MacArthur, John, Jr., *Strange Fire: The Danger of Offending the Holy Spirit with Counterfeit Worship*, Nashville: Thomas Nelson; 1st Edition, November 19, 2013. Print.

Chapter 18

1. Flavel, John, *Keeping the Heart: How to Maintain Your Love for God*, Christian Heritage, revised edition July 20, 2012, Print.
2. Ibid.
3. John Gill on Job 10 https://www.studylight.org/commentaries/geb/job-10.html9?print=yes
4. Albert Barnes on Psalm 139:13 https://www.studylight.org/commentaries/bnb/psalms-139.html
5. Albert Barnes on Psalm 139:15 https://www.studylight.org/commentary/psalms/139-15.html
6. Harris, Gregory H., *The Face and the Glory: Lessons on the Invisible and Visible God and His Glory*, The Woodlands: Kress Biblical Resources, 2019
7. Augustine quote: https://www.goodreads.com/author/quotes/6819578.Augustine_of_Hippo
8. Blaise Pascal quote: https://www.goodreads.com/quotes/801132-there-is-a-god-shaped-vacuum-in-the-heart-of-each
9. David Guzik quoting Charles Spurgeon on 1 Corinthians 13 https://enduringword.com/bible-commentary/1-corinthians-13/
10. John Calvin quote on 1 Corinthians 13 https://www.studylight.org/commentaries/cal/1-corinthians-13.html
11. Copyright 2010 Getty Music Publishing/BMG (ADM. By MUSICSERVICES.ORG) & THANKYOU MUSIC/ADM. By WORSHIPTOGETHER.COM SONGS EXCL. UK & EUROPE, ADM. BY KINGSWAY MUSIC https://www.gettymusic.com/the-perfect-wisdom-of-our-god